A Plague of the Imagination:

Cruentation, the Night Visitor, and the Names of the Vampires

Richard Swiderski

Oil and Blood

In tombs of gold and lapis lazuli
Bodies of holy men and women exude
Miraculous oil, odour of violet.

But under heavy loads of trampled clay
Lie bodies of vampires full of blood;
Their shrouds are bloody and their lips are wet.

William Butler Yeats

Table of Contents

Introduction

Snoopy is alert atop his dog house and Woodstock the bird lies asleep beside him. In the next frame both are sitting upright. Woodstock then perches on the belly of the sleeping Snoopy. In the final frame the thought bubble appears over Snoopy: "One of us always stays awake in case of vampires."

Whether consciously or not, Charles Schultz alluded to a historic fact in this May 6, 1970 Peanuts cartoon. In the early 18th century officials reported that people took shifts staying awake and sleeping in Serbian villages where vampires were thought to prowl (Medveđa, Serbia, February, 1732). At that time Serbian villages were on territory contested between the Austro-Hungarian and Ottoman empires. Wakefulness was not exclusively a deterrent against vampires.

On May 4, 1970 National Guard troops fired on, wounded and killed protesting students at Kent State University in Kent, Ohio. I do not know if that event had any influence on the making of the cartoon. I do recall a sense of apprehension and a wish to take action and not to be a passive victim, which the cartoon might have touched if I had seen it.

This is a book about fictions of blood, one of which is vampires. A strategy of these fictions is to situate them in the past emergent into the present. Despite defying what is known to be true they must have satisfied moral, emotional and political needs. They are fictions of blood because that is the most intimate and personal fluid shared among all of us whether we like it or not. Blood's appearances outside the body, being released, flowing, congealing, spreading, being taken back in, are fraught with meanings and proposed systems. Was the release voluntary? What is directing the flow?

A number of interconnected histories of and in blood are traced over common time. In general blood has become less visible in itself and more visible as a fiction and as the representation of a fiction. From the congealed bleeding epitomized by the Roman concepts of *cruor* and *sanguis* to the structured bleeding of bloodletting and cruentation to the primitive transfusion of vampirism, and the technology of storage and transfusion, blood has become increasingly confined over time. Mechanized warfare and mass consumption firearms have both expanded and distanced the bloodbath of conflict. With chemical, genetic and forensic analysis blood has become increasingly formalized into codes and measures.

The scattered exsanguination wrought by swords and daggers has turned to the internal bleeding caused by gunfire, without blades being completely abandoned. The vampire goes from a corpse bathed in blood to the surgical penetration of the victim by needled teeth. The bleeding by swords, daggers and guns still happens; the bleeding by and from vampires never happened but it remains a constantly updated fiction.

There was no one word for blood in Roman discourse: a dense, congealing fluid called *cruor* was present in the body together with and apart from the light, racing *sanguis*. They described the conditions of the exit of blood from the body. The poet Lucretius compared them to flames leaping through the roof of a burning house or water rush forcing the logs lining a channel in irregular array back to the source. The *sanguis* appeared that way as it broke and thrust through the encrusting *cruor,* which also moved in response to the force of flow. From cruentation to vampirism is the loss of the experience of bleeding.

Roman imagery of the body's vital fluids in accident, warfare and poetry called up this dynamism. In a passage of Ovid's *Metamorphoses* the god Apollo memorialized a youthful companion felled by a blow during a game with a stream of flowers from his *cruor*. The eternal mythic past was realized in a present state of the blood always observable but seldom observed. The heavy solidifying and swiftly flowing properties combined to form blood of many measured components.

Deliberate, therapeutic release of blood from the body, bloodletting or phlebotomy, was widely practiced before the Romans. This most accessible and voluminous fluid in the body was more likely than other fluids to cause illness or malaise in its excesses. Opening blood vessels to allow it to flow freely could be planned according to a *cruor* and *sanguis* conception of its material, or as a single vital fluid, the blood, *sang*, and *krov* of European languages. The fiction of bloodletting was the force of flow and volume of blood's presence in the body, permitting such great quantities to be spent. This imagery was fixed in representations and written accounts of successful procedures despite a strong tradition of cautionary criticism.

Spontaneous bleeding of the dead in the presence of the suspected murderer was utilized to induce a confession, when he was forced into the vicinity of the corpse surrounded by witnesses. Cruentation was a legalistic fiction evincing the supposed judgment of God. It was known as a general principle with its own name only from historic instances in which the blood did happen to flow from a corpse. Cruentation always was in the past, and even in the past of the past, isolated from empirical testing that sometimes was proposed. It served as a dramatic device in epics looking back to the violent roots of later polities.

The bleeding corpse of the victim dead from a blow or a shot was used to explain an outbreak of a wasting illness attributed to the loss of life force in the form of breath or blood. The corpse was connected to a revenant, a shadowy presence that visited relatives and neighbors of the dead man with lethal results like passage of plague. The visits were ended and the plague curtailed by the unearthing, staking, decapitation and burning of the offending corpse. These widespread beliefs mingled in border areas of Central Europe where Germanic, Slavic and Turkish populations, Protestant, Catholic, Eastern Orthodox and Muslim in religion, lived in close proximity to one another..

The Slavic word "vampire" and variant forms such as *"upir"* or *"upior,"* originally signified the spirit of a dead person invited to a final funeral feast, and then dismissed. It was coupled with Greek Orthodox beliefs promoted by the clergy about the corpse of a sinner stressed with a surfeit of blood.

The name given to these unusual corpses, some form of "vampire," was brought into German Protestant discourse by the reports of imperial officials called upon to witness the unearthing of the corpses of specific individuals confirmed to be vampires by their postmortem bleeding. This small number of cases, in Croatian and Serbian villages passing between Turkish and Austro-Hungarian rule, were "vampires or blood-suckers," as most of the dissertations and books published in Leipzig and other German cities were titled.

These writings treated vampirism as a mass delusion, a deceit of Satan and a plague of the imagination, while providing a complex of orientations toward the reports, religious, philosophical, medical, satirical, that shaped the image of the vampire. The image was disseminated by French and English Protestant writers, and by Roman Catholic writers in Poland, Italy, Austria, and France, each of whom contributed to the dismissal and continual revivification of the living dead.

The original cases of named individuals identified as vampires centered on the cruentation of the corpse of a well-known local, always in the increasingly remote past and greater distance of a small village. As new cases did not materialize, and the authorities penalized unearthing and mutilation of suspected corpses in the areas where they might, a cultural wish to manifest vampires in the present led to the creation of fictional vampires.

The great difference between the original vampires, the preserved and bleeding corpses, and the new fictional vampires was in the blood. The original vampires were called blood-suckers but never were detected in the act of taking blood or breath from their victims. The new fictional vampires traveled far and wide. They were adult males who finely channeled the blood and life essence from young female victims. Their activity was less like bloodletting and more like transfusion. Craven aristocrats or rapacious businessmen, they might pass completely into metaphor and be hungry for the figurative life's blood, the property, of the less advantaged.

The furtive, nocturnal male vampire and the alluring, triumphant female vampire shift in their prominence, Dracula and Theda Bara, Angel and Shiela, bottled blood and raw, bleeding flesh. The dictatorial vampires who extracted the blood of their people to sell the plasma to moneyed foreign buyers were all males.

However distanced fictional vampires might become from the basic story of a living corpse that hunts victims by night, figments of the past always remain, as in the Peanuts cartoon. It may seem bloodless, but the threat of blood outside the body always is present. Cruor and sanguis, bloodletting, and cruentation put in their appearances. Vampirism is a plague of the imagination that has spread lively beyond the grave wherever life is taken.

1. *Cruor* and *Sanguis*

Blood displays what causes it to appear.

Outside the body blood is a changing red coloration with the appearance of being a material that has reached where it is through the application of force. It spatters, streaks, smears or flows in accordance with the action that sent it. Its appearance allows its source and history to be read. Ritual purpose, accidents or criminal acts are among the interpretations given to the blood figure.

The discovery of the circulation of blood in the body, and the analysis of its composition and varieties have not altered these primordial protocols of representation, which apply to Paleolithic burials as to present-day crime scene photographs.

The representation of blood extends to the measurement and cinematography of its movement within and outside the body, depicted in still forms from ancient times onward, and captured by instruments, film and video more recently. None of this has confused the recognizable still picture of blood.

Blood has two visible states: the stream within the veins and arteries, and the congealed solid that most of the representations evoke, standing for both states. When it represents itself blood is not entirely itself, while what is not blood can stand for blood.

This would be just a disjuncture of representation: pictures of the sun seen by sunlight are not the sun, and rain drawn on paper is not rain. Images are not what they display. Books do not open on other worlds emerging from their diagrams.

Stilled blood seen outside the body is a question. It initiates a longing to identify the source of the blood and the manner of its arrival. It must be returned to the moving fluid it once was, to the life it once supplied. A representation of blood is a picture echoing the motion of life at the point of its loss. It is the life force going without life.

The English collocation "blood and gore" imprints that stillness after violence, but does little to recover the lost motion of the blood itself. It covers up the life and motion lost. The Latin words *sanguis* and *cruor*, sometimes used contrastively but not together like "blood and gore," help recover the warmth and motion of the blood from its representations. By searching for the physical meaning of the two words we search for what has been lost in the release and drying of blood.

The Roman poet Lucretius (99-55 BCE) compared *sanguis* with *cruor* in book 2, lines 194-95 of his philosophical poem *de rerum natura (on the nature of things)*.

quod genus e nostro cum missus corpore sanguis
emicat exultans acte spargitque cruore

in like manner when sanguis is sent from our body
spurts out rising and in the act spreads as cruor

Lucretius observes that this outpouring, like other natural events, is not impelled by an inherent
motion of the blood, but is the result of a force being applied, like the flames that rise up from
the roof of a burning house, or the wooden logs of earthworks rearing when forced back into a
water source. Bleeding is not seepage but ejection of *sanguis* followed by fallback of *cruor*. Forceful
motion of fluid is followed by inertia and solidification, all imprinted in the marks.
Translations of this passage into European languages do not distinguish between *sanguis* and *cruor*

"our blood shoots forth, and sprinkles all around" Creech, 1715
"comme quand nous voyons le sang tiré de nos veines rejaillir avec impetuosité, et
se repandre de tous cotez" Parrouin des Coutures, 1695
("when we see the blood briskly drawn from our veins, and spread to all sides")

or they find a vivid term not present in the original to differentiate the two.

"when blood, sent forth from the body, spurts out, springing up on high,
and sprinkling abroad a purple stream" John Selby Watson, 1851
"ainsi ton sang fougueux, repoussé de ton coeur, en jet de pourpre, au loin,
s'élance de ton veine" Le Blanc le Guillet, 1788
("so your fiery blood, pushed by your heart, leaps far from your vein in a purple jet")

There is a precedent in *de rerum natura* and other Latin writings for seeing *cruor* as purple in color,[1]
which the modern European translators used to accentuate the emergent blood, but they do not
differentiate *cruor* from *sanguis* in motion and change of state.
　　Lucretius' examples of force moments-spurting wounds, burning houses, collapsing
structures, meteors-suggest the turbulence of his age. The two words for bleeding epitomized the
violence affecting the body. A hundred years later an epic poem, Lucan's *Pharsalia* (61-65 CE), set
during the civil war between Julius Caesar and the forces of the Senate (48 BCE) made
considerable use of the contrasting terms. From Book 1, lines 618-20, a *vates* named Arruns
divines the coming battle by reading the organs of a sacrificed bull.

terruit ipse color vatem: nam pallida tetris
viscera tincta notis, gelidoque infecta cruore
plurimus asperso variabit sanguine livor

the very color alarmed the priest: for the pale viscera
were tinted with foul marks, and chill infected *cruor*
much bruising streaked with dispersed *sanguis*

Both states of blood, discernible from their color, texture, and temperature, are present in the organs of the sacrifice victim. The priest, well aware what these signs foretell, is terrified to see the upheaval of battle fought and lost in the flowing *sanguis* and cold dead *cruor* at the same time. Like Lucretius' leaping flames or flooding waters.

When the beast was being prepared for sacrifice it resisted the offering, and when its throat was cut (lines 614-15)

nec cruor emicuit solitus; sed vulnere largo
diffusum rutilo nigrum pro sanguine virus

nor did cruor emerge as usual, but from the wide wound
a diffuse black venom in place of red sanguis

From the beginning the order of the fluids is replaced by the black venom that flowed like red *sanguis* instead of the expected *cruor*. This anticipates the disorder inside the animal, where *cruor* and *sanguis* coexist. All is death and decay. The condition of the internal organs, the shape of the liver and the heart, only confirm this prediction.

Cruor and *sanguis* were words in the Roman world of swords, knives, exposed skin and many everyday acts of violence. They were words for the moment when the vital fluid forcibly emerged from the body and changed, in color, state of matter, temperature and impetus, bracketing a moment of body cosmology.

Lucretius' lines reflected the understanding that this emergence was a natural event like many others under the influence of external forces. By dramatizing a scene in which the usual order of *cruor* and *sanguis* was disrupted Lucan highlighted the usual order. The interior of the inauspicious sacrifice reflects a chaotic exterior when the two are present simultaneously inside the body rather than one exiting to become the other, and the exit of *cruor* is replaced by decay flowing like *sanguis*.

Many other instances of the use of the two words can be found in classical Latin literature. Studying them deepens and complexifies the imagery of the life force they expressed.

The Romans brought into language play two words which floated freely and independently of each other in Indo-European language traditions. Latin was the only language with this doublet. In Classical Greek *kreas* (κρεας) signified raw, bleeding flesh and spilling, coagulating blood.[2] This led to the use of derivations as the general word for blood in all the Slavic languages: Russian *kruv* (кровь) and Polish *krew*.

The Romans paired this word with *sanguis* for the inside/outside flow dichotomy, and *sanguis* (French *sang*, Rumanian *sango*) became the exclusive word for blood in all the Romance languages, without the accompaniment of *cruor*. Forms of *cruor* (crude, *crue*) carried the primordial sense of "uncooked" in the Romance and other Indo-European languages without emphasis on external bloodiness as opposed to internal blood. Instead, the meaning extended to all unfinished, rudimentary things, ideas, and people. As the root of "cruel" in English and other languages, it does retain bloody margins.

The *cruor/sanguis* pairing persisted in the medieval Latin writings of theologians and natural philosophers. Citing Isidore of Seville, the Dominican encyclopedist Vincent of Beauvais (c.1190-1264) derives the word *sanguis* from a Greek original meaning "sweet" (*suavis*).[3] "It dominates, it is the dominant humor, in pleasant and amiable men. As long as it is in the body. Verily, pouring out it is called *cruor* because it flows out and in flowing becomes corrupt." Using Scholastic logic, Vincent derives this meaning from an association of word forms with meaning: *vero cruor dicitur eo quod decurrat, vel ab eo quod currendo corruat. Cruor de<u>currat</u>* (flows out) <u>*currendo*</u> <u>*corruat*</u>, in flowing becomes corrupt. The *curr/corr* syllable corresponds both to the form and meaning of *cruor*.

Vincent uses the same logic to derive *cruor* from *crudelitas* (cruelty) and associates it with *crudus* (crude). *Cruor* appears much less frequently than *sanguis* in his volumes of natural history. When dragons are overwhelmed by elephants in battle and are left bleeding from all sides, the *cruor* falls upon the earth and forms what apothecaries call *tynarim* (dragon's blood).[4] *Tynarim* resembles congealed blood. Despite stating the distinction between *cruor* and *sanguis*, Vincent uses *sanguis* for all the occasions of blood except this one, where the product is specifically identified with the dried form.

Vincent's collapsing the dichotomy between *cruor* and *sanguis* is consistent with usage in late medieval Latin texts.[5] In liturgy referring to the blood of Christ, for instance, the response, *Salve, sanguis Christi* (Save, blood of Christ) is followed by the versicle, *Ave, cruor salutaris* (Hail, blood of the savior).[6] The 12th century poet/composer Hildegard von Bingen embodied the convergent but not fully merged proximity of the blood-kinds in her antiphon, *O cruor sanguinis,* which is almost perfectly untranslatable into modern European languages.[7]

In language in general the words "blood, *sang, kruv"* in their respective languages came to occupy the semantic territory that *cruor* and *sanguis* did in classical Latin. Latin prayers translated into Anglo-Saxon substituted "blod" for both words in the Latin originals. As Mark Antony rouses the citizens of Rome against the conspirators in his funeral oration, Act 3, Scene 2 (1721-25) of Shakespeare's *Julius Caesar* he uses the word "blood" projecting the underlying sense of *cruor*.

Through this the well-beloved Brutus stabbed;
And as he pluck'd his cursed steel away,
Mark how the blood of Caesar followed it,
As rushing out of doors, to be resolved
If Brutus so unkindly knock'd, or no;

Caesar's wounds, elsewhere in the Antony's speech, also are like mouths issuing blood. Brutus in his justifying oration that preceded Antony's referred to the bloodshed as a cleansing operation; Antony reverses that and ascribes the corrupt blood that should be cleansed to the assassins. There is no *sanguis* in the blood released, only *cruor* as parting and diseased blood. Antony juggles these meanings to the detriment of Brutus and the others. He also speaks of Caesar's noble "blood," his Roman heritage, which takes the place of *sanguis* blood.

A poet-dramatist could take advantage of the residual meanings of blood in the same word (Antony after all was speaking Latin in Elizabethan English). Other examples could be cited from the literatures of all European languages from during the late Middle Ages. Another common ground was the preservation of the *cruor/sanguis* distinction in the language of medicine, which was Latin gradually replaced by national languages during the 19th century.

Experimental confirmation of the circulation of blood in the 17th century did not immediately lead to a shift in the vocabulary. For William Harvey the moving blood was *sanguis*, as it was for Galen, and *cruor* was its breakdown-dispirited product.[8]

> As old wine is not wine (having lost all its spirit), but flat wine, or vinegar;
> no more *sanguis* without spirit is *sanguis,* but in the same way *cruor*.

In his later work on the generation of animals Harvey asserts contrary to Aristotle (whom he quotes at length) that *sanguis* inherently possesses spirit and heat, without which it no longer is *sanguis* but is called *cruor*.[9] He uses words besides *cruor* for voided *sanguis*: *grumus* (clot) and *sanies* (spilled blood), which cannot perform its functions, and uses a term, *crassamentum,* for the dense component of *sanguis* that contains its spirit and humor.[10]

Harvey dismissed the identification of *cruor* as the state of *sanguis* emergent from the body and instead made it a component of *sanguis* that manifested when spirit and warmth are lost, only released under those circumstances, otherwise inseparable. For those who viewed *sanguis* as a vital circulating fluid impelled by the muscle of the heart *sanguis*/*cruor* no longer was an exclusive dichotomy but an inclusive one with *cruor* the subordinate term. In medical Latin *sanguis* was made up of components, and it remained a subject of inquiry just what they were and how they corresponded to existing names.

Those correspondences bridged by Latin terminology allowed writers on the blood such as Harvey to continue to link the life of the blood to other fluids with spirit and heat, such as air, water, and wine using the same words. Latin was the universal language of inquiry in the 17th century. First or early editions of Harvey's *Exercitationes* were printed in Frankfurt, Rotterdam and Amsterdam, with translations into European languages to follow. The vital role of *spiritus* in circulation was conveyed by precisely that word to speakers of various languages who also were readers of Latin.

The first English translation of *de cordis et sanguinis motu (Anatomical exercises concerning the motion of the heart and blood in living creatures)*, published in London in 1653, twenty-five years after the Frankfurt Latin original, used "blood" for "*sanguis*" and "goar" (gore) for "*cruor*." This did not become established as the standard for scientific writing in English. Gore was an Anglo-Saxon word that stood for "dirt," the mess of blood outside the body, and had a visual impact that interfered with the componential makeup of blood that Harvey and his followers examined. As scientific writing was decreasingly in Latin alone, with translation into national languages, Latin terminology was retained for greater precision than the equivalent terms in the national language could provide. The long game was to keep up with definitions of *cruor* as a blood component as blood was ever more exactingly analyzed.

Blood also was consolidated into a physical fluid that obeyed physical laws. It was visually represented as a stain or discoloration where it was represented at all. Artemisia Gentileschi's 1620 painting Judith Slaying Holofernes has the blood spurting in an arc from the sword-cut neck of the warrior as Artemisia's correspondent Galileo would have predicted.[11]

The pharmacologist Jonathan Pereira (1804-53) differentially defined *cruor* and *sanguis* in his anthology of Latin prescriptions serving as models for physicians.[12]

> *Cruor* differs from *sanguis* in never denoting blood confined and circulating
> through the veins, but such as is shed and no longer subservient to the
> support of "animal life"-in other words, *gore*. The same fluid which, in
> coming from the vein is called *sanguis* (blood), is afterwards denominated
> *cruor* (*gore*).

Pereira repeats Harvey's language distinguishing *sanguis* from *cruor* in terms of circulation and the support of animal life. This is the dynamic dichotomy of the two terms, now distinguished from each other by the presence and absence of motion and vital essence. Circulation is the sole motion, that of *sanguis* and the life it maintains. *Cruor* no longer has its motion of escape from the wound.

The systematization of chemistry that followed the work of Lavoisier in the late 18th century inspired encyclopedic attempts to define known substances in terms of their chemical composition. Blood was one of these substances. The analysis did not start from the *sanguis/cruor* dichotomy, but instead attempted to place *cruor* among the components of blood. The ninth volume, on natural substances, of Antoine-François Fourcroy's *Système des connaissances chimiques* (1800) contains a chapter on *cruor* in the section on the makeup of *sang*.[13]

> When the blood, after several hours of coagulation, has rendered all the
> serum that can flow away and be expressed spontaneously, the coagulated
> material, half-solid and drawn in upon itself, which swims in the middle, is
> known under the name of *caillot, placenta, insula*. This mass was named *cruor*
> before there was the means to separate the two different materials that
> constitute it.

There follows several pages on the relative weighting of the serum and *cruor* elements in the blood, chemistry being the science of composition. *Cruor* now is a visible product of a chemical process, coagulation, which can be induced experimentally to measure the results under different conditions. It is an old-fashioned term based on visual observation alone, yet Fourcroy still used it to name the solid part of the coagulant, for which there were several other terms.

The 1804 English translation of Fourcroy's substitutes *coagulum* for the French word *caillot* while maintaining *cruor* as the section title.[14] Other words added to the list of names for the visible matter in coagulating blood under the general heading of *cruor* included clot and *crassamentum*.[15]

A tradition of reporting the experimental analysis of blood did without the *cruor* label and concept. William Hewson examined samples of coagulating blood as they expressed *crassamentum* and serum.[16] He concluded that the proportion of *crassamentum* to serum varied according to the constitution of the person: the stronger the constitution the more *crassamentum* in proportion to serum. This in turn suggested a principle of treatment for disease. "Bleeding, diluting licquors and a low diet" for patients with a lesser proportion of serum. Hewson also investigated the action of neutral salts in inhibiting coagulation, which had therapeutic significance and enabled him to study blood as a fluid outside the body. At no point does he use the word *cruor*.

The appearance of the word *cruor* in English medical and technical texts related to medicine spiked between 1835 and 1845.[17] From the contexts of its appearance this seems to be the result of attempts to include it among the elements of blood being distinguished experimentally. Andral and Gavarret, who in 1840 published in a chemistry and physics journal the proportions of various components of blood observed in specific diseases listed "fibrin, solid materials of serum and water" (*fibrine, materiaux solides de serum, eau*) in the title of their paper, made no mention of *cruor*.[18]

Yet Salvator Renzi, who applied Andral and Gavarret's proportional analysis method to the blood of typhoid patients at the hospital of Loreto in 1841, did resort to the ancient term in his report.[19] A veterinary text on the health of sheep ascertained from the chemical profile of their blood did not neglect to include *cruor*.[20]

Though science banished the absolute change of state that once made *sanguis/cruor* an exclusive dichotomy, the expanding general category of blood (*sang, kruv*) craved a place for *cruor*.

In part the retention of the word was historical, with a look back toward Roman times when blood could be equated with other natural fluids on the basis of parallels. The author of the chemistry section of a popular encyclopedia published in 1839 related *cruor* to the consistency of curds precipitated from milk.[21] "The older physicians," he continues, "distinguished the ingredients into which blood voluntarily separated by terms which denoted what took place in milk, that is, curds and whey." The use of the word "voluntarily" for the action of blood also harks back to the time when *cruor* had independent status.

Chemistry placed *cruor* was placed among the visually recognizable components of blood subject to further definition, or elimination. It was assigned and reassigned by stages of discovery and analysis to blood fractions where it might physically be located and isolated for inspection. Red and white blood cells were seen by microscopists from the late 17th century onward but were treated as blood solids subject to chemical analysis, not as structured bodies.

Water, fibrin and albumin were the fractions into which blood could be uniformly separated according to the physiological chemist Prosper Denis. The coloring matter he chose to name *cruorine* using the nomenclature set by Berzelius.[22] *Cruorine* was the chemical compound of which *cruor* was formed, as fibrin was the fiber chemical and albumin was the chemical origin of *albumen*, the eggwhite and similar materials. The task of chemistry was to analyze visible substances in their underlying chemical forms to be further broken down into other chemicals by analysis. That began with naming the chemical basis of the substance, often its common name in Greek, Latin or a modern language affixed with the –in(e) suffix.

A substance known from texture and color like *cruor* became *cruorine* by way of a chemical process the chemist attached to the name. It might be a process of extraction, rendering the substance from a mixture, or of synthesis, building it up from constituents. Urea, the first organic compound to be synthesized from inorganic ingredients, was recognized when Friedrich Wohler smelled its characteristic aroma when he experimentally treated silver cyanate with ammonium chloride.

Keeping careful track of the minimum amounts of each ingredient required to complete the reaction enabled chemists to determine the proportions of each element in a specific compound and to write an empirical formula for the compound.

The year after Denis named *cruorine*, Louis-René Le Canu localized iron in the red pigment of the blood, which he named *hemostatine*, from the Greek *haimatos*, "of *haima*," the Greek word for blood closest to *sanguis* in meaning.[23] He suggested two other names for the pigment, both using the *haima* root: *zoohematine* and *hemochroïne*.

Having defined *hemostatine* chemically with five different preparation techniques, Le Canu pronounced it a compound of albumen plus another coloring material with stated properties, which he termed *globuline*. It is an index of the lack of communication (or cooperation) among even French-speaking researchers in the field of physiological medicine that Le Canu didn't bring up Denis' *cruorine* or *hematin*, introduced by a Dutch follower of Berzelius, for a material that may have been the same. Le Canu made no reference at all to *cruor*.

There then followed a complex dance lasting many years between *haima*-based words and *cruor*-based words naming the coloring matter of blood.

Jöns Jacob Berzelius, the Swedish chemist who set methods and standards for chemical research in the early 19th century, also analyzed the components of blood and arrived at a roster of ingredients. He examined *cruor* and found that it consisted of fibrin, albumen and coloring matter. The pigment of blood consisted of what he called globulin, likely the source of Le Canu's term, plus iron oxide. The Dutch physician and organic chemist, Gerardus Johannes Mulder, who applied Berzelius' word "protein" to albuminous substances, determined the empirical formula for the iron-containing blood protein he named *hematine*. This word was sometimes used in place of Le Canu's *hematosine*, sometimes taken to be a separate chemical entity.

Le Canu's 1837 doctoral thesis on chemical studies of human blood listed eight different names for the red coloring matter, including his own *hematosine, zoohematine, hemochroïne, globuline* and Berzelius-Mulder's *hematine*.[24] "The *cruorine* of M. Denis" he placed in a category of its own. The degree of differentiation of the names depended upon the author's degree of analytic focus, the name's attachment to a method of extraction (and the researcher) and standards of interaction with other compounds. The production of red color remained the tangible standard.

A forester examining the effects of iron-containing compounds on plants could define the coloring principle of blood as *cruorine* or *hematosine* with no further comment.[25] The author of a histology text apportioned *hematosine* and *hematine* to Berzelius, *cruorine* to Denis and *globuline* to Le Canu.[26] Nomenclature according to separate researchers' methods of extraction/preparation led to a proliferation of names each designating what may or may not have been the same substance. Most of the names derived from *cruor* or *haima*.

Focus on the red blood cells as the envelope for the substance returned to the elements but then was drawn gravitationally into the whirlpool of names. By the late 1860's red blood cells were described as "composed of a colorless, structureless and transparent envelope, enclosing a peculiar matter named cruor, or, as may be termed, cruoro-globulin."[27]

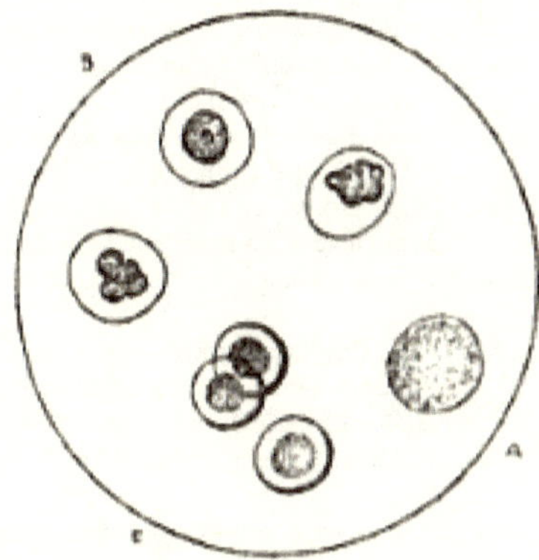

A white blood cells, B white blood cells treated with acetic acid,C red blood cells
Kirkes (1869: 86)

A new technique of investigation, absorption spectroscopy, introduced the possibility of greater technical precision of identification. The physiologist Felix Hoppe-Seyler separated the pigment by crystallization, and replaced the German name *blutfarbstoff* for the substance with his own coinage, *haemoglobin*.[28] He used the recently developed method of sunlight spectrographic analysis to determine the characteristic absorption spectra of haemoglobin when oxygen was bound and not bound to it, and found that oxygen could readily be replaced by carbon monoxide and nitric oxide.

George Gabriel Stokes, a British physicist, independently determined the absorption spectra of the red pigment of blood when oxygenated and deoxygenated, and associated a distinct color with each state.[29] Aware of Hoppe-Seyler's papers, but somehow having missed his name for the pigment chemical, Stokes suggested the terms scarlet and purple *cruorine* for the two oxidation states of the pigment. He reformulated the colored blood solid *cruor* as an iron compound with spectra that correspond to its interactions and color changes, and unknowingly repeated Denis' word for the same substance adding the spectroscopic parameter. He compared cruorine to the first synthesized dyestuff indigo, which also exhibited color variation with change in oxidation states.

The greater specification of physical qualities did not put to rest the *cruor*/*haima* dialogic. At first Stokes' physically refined measurements gave his *cruorine* priority in usage, but in the long run hemoglobin has prevailed as the name for the compound.[30]

A medical chemist of German origin working in England, John Thudicum, added to the list of blood coloring compounds one that he named *cruentine*.[31] Thudicum's report on the chemical identification of diseases gave instructions for preparing this "new derivative of *hematocrystalline* and *hematine*" by boiling *hematocrystalline (hemoglobin)* with sulphuric acid and washing the insoluble "brownish red grumous matter [that] remains suspended in the fluid in an insoluble state." This iron-free compound was taken to be the true coloring matter of blood. The uniqueness of *cruentine* was confirmed by adding sulphuric acid after washing and rendering it soluble again.

Cruor alone was not a part of this mixture, or a name for the whole. Thudicum had brought into medical currency another ancient word by attaching it to a specific chemical identity. *Cruentus* was a present participle form in Latin, meaning "flowing *cruor*," and was more common in usage than the corresponding *sanguis* derivative, *sanguineus*.[32] "*Cruenta victoria*" was a "blood-stained victory"; "*Cruentus Mars*" was the god of war after battle. Cicero used the tension between the words for a rhetorical flourish in his fourth Philippic (2.4): "*Antonius…sanguine cruentus civium Romanorum,*" "Antony… smeared with the blood of Roman citizens," a more vivid denunciation than if he had used either word alone. Thudicum used *cruentine* to emphasize that it was the true source of blood color.

The term did gain currency among experimenters, who classically trained or not, found it a useful designation for the sulphuric acid preparation of hemoglobin. It was identified with the same as the blood-derived chemical Hoppe-Seyler named *"haemato-porphyrin,"* or just *"porphyrin,"* which became the accepted label and eventually the title of a structurally similar class of organic compounds.

Thudicum continued to insist on the distinctiveness of *cruentine* and the appropriateness of the name for several decades.[33] He elaborated the spectrographic signatures of its variants.

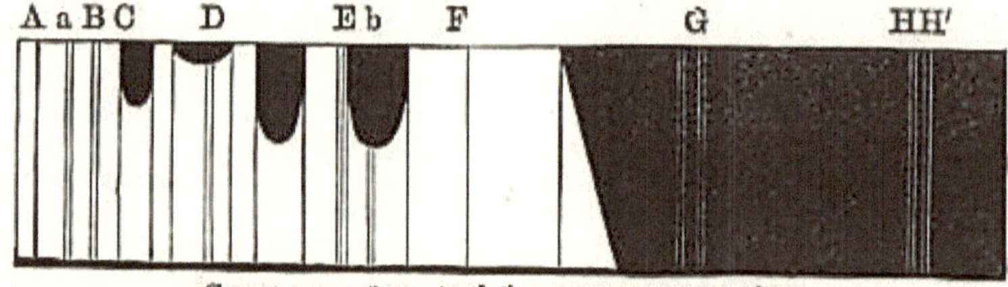

Spectrum of neutral fluorescent cruentine.

Thudicum (1882: 109)

In the early 20th century it no longer was a term of discourse. Another use of *cruor* has persisted to the present day.

This was not like *cruentine* a revived ancient version of the word deemed singularly applicable to a new discovery; it was an 18th century application of the *cruor/sanguis* distinction to internal blood flow. P.A. Michelotti, a Venetian physician and mathematician who was a member of both Italian and English science academies, prefaced his 1721 treatise on the separation of fluids in the body with dedications in Italian, but the treatise itself was in Latin. He viewed blood flow in terms of Newtonian physics, as a measurable dynamics within the body, and the difference between *cruor* and *sanguis* as the difference between halt and motion in the fluid.[34]

> *Sanguis* in a living animal is everywhere fluid and with all the properties
> attributed to other fluids…but *cruor* surrenders the power of flowing and
> all agitation immediately, as its drive of motion ceases.

In a later work on the pathology of blood vessels Michelotti applied this *cruor* as stilled blood definition to a mass carried by the flowing *sanguis* into the pulmonary vessels.[35]

There were two forms of internal *cruor/sanguis*: a thickening and halt of the fluid and the formation of a clot, a solid blockage. Internally *cruor* could be used to label and characterize a range of conditions of the blood. It could be the blood "that was pre-existent in the arteries."[36] It could be the thick, stalling blood of the aged and the inactive.[37] Named *cruor,* these were textural conditions of the blood connected to illness and disease which warranted treatments such as blood-thinning medicines and blood-letting.

As a solid mass that formed in the flowing, circulating *sanguis, cruor* became a material in the formation of the thrombus and the embolism once those terms were articulated for types of circulatory blockage. *Cruor* was sometimes identified with thrombus.[38] Red, white, black shades of *cruor* were described in the formation of internal clots and other agglomerations. This terminology, red cruor especially, survived into the twentieth century and is sometimes used in the present day as a name for the physical makeup of blood clots.[39] Here it is the full stop of the flowing *sanguis.*

The repeated appearance of forms of the word *cruor* in the discourse of blood and its composition corresponds to a sense that there is a living fluid in the body composed of a part that is thicker and slower to move, but not entirely unalive. This is one material basis for the life force in the body after death and immediately discernible in the corpse. *Cruor* may not be named, but it is there

---

[1] Armstrong (1917: 24-25)

[2] Ernout (1922: 25-26). The Greek *'aima* stood for blood in general.

[3] Vincent of Beauvais (1591: 343) *de sanguine, Book 28, Chapter 27 of his Speculum naturale*

[4] Vincent of Beauvais (1591: 239) *Book 11, Chapter 41*
…cum biberint sanguinem, dum ruant belvae, dracones obruantur. Sic utrimque fusus cruor terram imbuit, sitqe: pigmentum quicquid soli tinxerint,quod tynarim vocant.

[5] Bynum (2007: 17-18)

[6] Nichols (2014: 123)

[7] Hildegard von Bingen (1998: 102) Antiphon for the Redeemer
O cruor sanguinis/qui in alto sonuisti,/cum omnia elementa/se implicuerunt/in lamentabilum vocem/cum tremore/quia sanguis Creatoris sui/illa tetigit,/ungue nos/de langoribus nostris.
O hardening blood that bled into a cry!/The elements/felt its touch and trembled,/heaven heard their woe./O life-blood of the maker,/scarlet music/salve our wounds.

[8] Harvey (1648: 70)

[9] Harvey (1651: 244). Harvey refers to the Latin translation of Aristotle's Greek text, on which the *cruor-sanguis* distinction was forced.

[10] Harvey (1648: 39)
[11] Gamwell (2016: 58-59)
[12] Pereira (1847: 7§)
[13] Fourcroy (1800: 147-50)
[14] Fourcroy (1804: 201)
[15] Duglison (1832: 46)
[16] Hewson (1771:
[17] Google N-gram search
[18] Andral and Gavarret (1840)
[19] de Renzi (1842)
[20] Spooner (1844: 182)
[21] Curtis, ed. (1839: 520)
[22] Denis (1829: 209)
[23] Le Canu (1830). *Ichor*, the other Greek word for blood, was recruited for more general use in European languages.
[24] Le Canu (1837: 12)
[25] Burgers (1842: 634)
[26] Burggraeve (1845: 474)
[27] Kirkes (1869: 80)
[28] Hoppe Seyler (1862)
[29] Stokes (1864)
[30] Holmes (1995: 234)
[31] Thudicum (1867: 227)
[32] *Cruentus* was "normal in prose." Goldberg (2012: 164n21)
[33] Thudicum (1882: 108-11); Thudicum (1896: 18-19) "I shall continue to use…"
[34] Michelotti (1721:83)
[35] Michelotti (1731: 418) cited by Leibowitz (1970: 418). Originally reported by Littré.
[36] Greene (1727: 406)
[37] Manget (1695: 693)
[38] Ypey (1785: 29)
[39] Blumer (1908: 519); Malone and Agutter (2008: 307)

2. Bloodletting

Cruor was the thickness of the blood (sanguis), its sometimes robust sometimes fatal thickening, its essential body and substance of many names and components. It was a way of conceiving the blood and operating upon it to preserve the life force dramatically. It was a way of achieving or restoring a balance between life and death, between the movement and drag of the body.

The Edinburgh physician Andrew Fyfe summed it up in his 1801 treatise:[1]

> Health, therefore, cannot subsist without a dense and red blood; and, if its
> quantity be too much diminished, a stagnation of the juices takes place,
> whence the whole body becomes pale, cold, and weak. Nor can life or
> health subsist without a sufficiency of thinner juices intermixed with red
> blood; since the cruor, deprived of its watery part, congeals and obstructs
> the smallest passages of the vessels, and causes too great a heat.

This passage treats cruor as a constant component of the blood that can congeal internally to the detriment of health. It is halfway between humor and chemical, before the language of thrombosis and embolism became predominant. The observable density of cruor outside the body had encouraged this sense of its role in general body health by unobservable obstructive thickening within the body. The halt of blood flow was accompanied by a buildup of heat in the cruor-blocked vessel, with resultant fever and other complications.

One solution to this excessive thickening was to restore the balance between thin juices and red blood by reducing the proportion of cruor with the long controversial therapy of bloodletting, accompanied by pharmaceutical measures.

That the density of blood could be controlled through cruor reduction was a theory applied to bloodletting practice only later in its history, and not by all its practitioners. At first bloodletting was evacuation of blood grown too great in volume, by venesection, scarification, cupping, and/or leeches. These techniques displayed the quantity of blood released in the fountain of the cut vein, the welling of blood on the cut skin, and the distension of the leech. The ancient Egyptians, Mesopotamian cultures, Aztecs, Mayans, ancient Chinese and many other peoples all used bloodletting for ritual and therapy.

The strongest advocate of bloodletting in antiquity, Galen (129-c.216), a Greek physician practicing in Rome, considered blood one of the four humors contained by the body and determining the state of health in the balances and imbalances. Too much blood, a plenitude or plethora, required reduction. Bloodletting by venesection, a practiced cutting into a vein at a key location, was one of the methods for the control of blood quantities. Galen distinguished venous blood from arterial blood, and two separate systems for their distribution in the body: venous blood from the liver and arterial blood from the heart. Though he taught that one type of blood was transformed into the other, he did not anticipate the discovery of pulmonary circulation.

Galen observed that blood (haima), "the best of the humors, the most proper and personal,"[2] varies in color and texture, from person to person, at different times, in different places and in accordance with temperament. It also changes within the body, infused with *pneuma* as is passes from one side of the cardiac septum to the other, through imaginary pores. The Latin translators

23

from Galen's Greek texts nowhere use the term cruor for any state of the blood, though it was a commonplace term in the Latin of the time. The blood's many variations for Galen always were *haima* or sanguis with a descriptor.[3]

The history of bloodletting and its various techniques is the fluctuating acceptance and rejection of the technique by schools and practitioners and their articulation of rationales for their practice. Blood's role in the widely accepted humoral system helped define the likely effects of bloodletting on body and mind, but did not give blood a fixed physical quality and composition, which is what cruor qualified. At the same time an understanding of blood's physical nature suggested techniques of bloodletting. When cruor did enter the therapeutic picture it was an uncertain component or form of sanguis that must be accounted for in the treatment process.

The School of Salerno, formed at the confluence of Mediterranean medical influences in a university town of southern Italy, trained physicians and translated texts from the 11th to the 13th centuries and beyond. It was a likely place for the syncretism of Hippocratic and Galenic medicine with Jewish and Arab traditions. Constantine the African, who began lecturing in Salerno in 1077, rendered into Latin the Arabic curing manual *al-maliki haly abbas,* whose author had in turn been an exponent of the humoral system. In discoursing on blood (sanguis) Constantine made no reference to cruor.[4] Which was consistent with both his Galenic and Arabic forbears.

Yet a handbook of treatments attributed to the School, the Latin *Regimen sanitatis Salernitanum*, circulating in copied texts and printed from the late 15th century onward, used the term in a couplet referring to bloodletting:

Fac plagam largam, mediocriter
Ut cite fumus, exeat uberius, liberiusque cruor

The wound make meane, for meanely done:
The fumes may passe, & blood may runne.[5]

The translation following the Latin, from an English phlebotomy method book of 1592, folded cruor into the English word "blood." Initially it appears that the *Regimen*'s advice specific to cruor has been rendered useless by being generalized to blood in English translation. This section of the phlebotomy manual elaborates on the bleeding strategy to include the sense of cruor without using the word.

The size of the incision ("wound") matters, the author declares, and a large wound is best. If it is small only the "thin blood" flows out, keeping the humors inside the body. When the blood is gross and thick and the humors abundant, in a hot country or season, a large wound accomplishes the therapeutic release of "subtile and thinne blood." When it is cold, and the blood flows as a mass, or the body is weak, it is best to keep the wound small to prevent the vital spirits from escaping.

The Galenic variability in the substance of the blood with atmospheric and climatic conditions suggests a strategy around the thick component which must be retained or released to a degree determined by a range of factors. Blood as humor under external influences has overtaken cruor as a component of the blood. Those external influences determine the thickness of the blood as a whole which in turn contribute to blood volume.

If the blood as a humor is influenced by the environment, and its composition is the source of personality and health, then controlling that composition can affect mood and well-being. Releasing fractions of the blood to cause it to thicken or thin is one possible method for treating the entire person through the blood. Other methods such as medication or hydrotherapy are less direct, less provident of diagnostic information than bloodletting. Practitioners of such methods do emphasize that there are alternatives to bloodletting.

Bloodletting had a history of acceptance and rejection by practitioners and members of the public. The drama of its assertion, by forceful individuals and in the case of conditions calling for extreme measures such as epidemics, made its presence all the more erratic. Further injury caused by its vigorous application could be written off as the result of heroic measures that did not work in that one case. Conceiving of blood as having a thick portion, whether or not it was called cruor, enabled a physical technique like bloodletting, and offered a convincing pretext for refinements that preferentially drew off or retained the thick part of the fluid.

Paracelsus defined cruor (cruror) as a form of tartar, a sediment like the solids of wine, with both interior and exterior aspects. Cruor was a distinct substance carried about the body. "When nature wishes to purge itself, it purges itself through cruor, that is, sweat."[6] The fluid was a "power residue," a product of digestion, which spontaneously parted from the body. It could not be separated by phlebotomy, which was incapable of purging the body.[7] Paracelsus treated cruor as the product of internal processes analogous to other processes in nature. He minimized the utility of bloodletting for general body health, and confined it to certain specific conditions, and there in a limited way.

Cruor was too much a part of the whole body system, and its presence in blood was not subject to deliberate separation, in the Paracelsan account. Phlebotomy would not be effective in the management of cruor, which increased and decreased in the body as a whole in response to environmental influences. Cruor deposition was affected by diet, atmosphere, and medical treatment but could not be directly acted upon to influence health and fortune.

Johann Baptista van Helmont (1580-1644), like Paracelsus a chemist and physician, defined cruor apart from sanguis in terms of the dynamics of substances in the body's vessels. Venous cruor is transformed into arterial sanguis by ferment passing from the right to the left chamber of the heart.[8] Residual venous cruor becomes a volatile salt by contact with the air in the lungs and is expelled as a gas. van Helmont maintained Galen's distinction between the two species, and the cardiac pores of transition. There was no single unified entity, "the blood," by either name though it became the habit to translate sanguis with the words that stood for the blood whole in European languages, which can cause confusion in translation.

"When sanguis loss proceeds with such vigor," van Helmont wrote, "it is not possible to inhibit the released cruor, not even for those who draw acid inside that they may deposit it."[9] The cruor released from the vein pours out uncontrollably, coagulates and is released as a volatile salt, even for those people whose ability to draw in acid would neutralize the alkaline salts formed.

The chemical nature of cruor and its transformations in the body makes it very difficult to control the proportions of what is released from a ruptured blood vessel. Cruor is an independent chemical substance with a character that varies from one organ to another, in the living body and the corpse, and under changing external conditions. van Helmont uses the word in his works as often as sanguis. It is an independent chemical substance with a character that varies from one organ to another, in the living body and the corpse, and under changing conditions.

The distinction between the two is not only chemical and textural. Cruor is sanguis without the vital spirit; sanguis is cruor without the weight and force. "God disdains cruor to be offered him, even in burnt offerings, and man to be nourished with cruor, because cruor (in which there is a sensate soul) emerges from eating the apple."[10] van Helmont equates cruor with the weighty materiality that drew humanity down to sin and death. It is a primary ingredient of bone, tissue and organs. Its fundamental role in the matter and spirit of the body, in its downcast state, makes it difficult to manage through such techniques as bloodletting. This was a spiritual reflection of its physical properties, and the other way around.

The iatrochemical definition of cruor and sanguis minimized the value of bloodletting, which was nonetheless upheld by humoral considerations, taking blood as a whole which could have body-wide effects due to the quantity and therefore the quality of its presence. Practitioners and writers took varying stands on the value of bloodletting, and often implicated cruor and sanguis in their theories and prescriptions. The chemical characterization of the substances by Paracelsus, van Helmont and their followers, despite their opposition to bloodletting as a primary technique, often figured positively and negatively into the quarrels about the procedure. Cruor was the weightiness that could not be the whole of blood; it had to be a part of blood and the reason blood falls.

Could bloodletting selectively alter the thickness of the fluids in the body by taking away cruor, or did it release cruor and sanguis indiscriminately? Would it be possible to use one technique or another in one part of the body or another and achieve a successful treatment of a specific disease, a disease specified humorally? Treatment assumptions arose and were opposed based upon the nature of the materials.

The "sanguinary way of curing diseases in all Ages" and "prodigal emission of blood" to the destruction of mankind can only have been first suggested by the Devil himself, wrote the medical doctor George Thomson in his *Chymical Trial of the Galenists*.[11] An avowed disciple of van Helmont and opponent of the phlebotomist, purgative Galenists, Thomson did not use the chemical language of acids, salts and gases of the Dutch iatrochemist.

Cruor "consists of partly excrementitious matter, and partly wholesom juyce, disposed, and in a fair way to be made *Sanguis* by long Circulation…" By opening a vein and bleeding a patient the Galenists let out "without any election," both the "laudable" and the "depraved" parts of the cruor as well as its "inseparable companion" the sanguis. The quantity of both released "produces more *hurt* than *profit* any way," aiming at a result that might have been achieved with medicines that respect the quality of the blood.

Thomson maintained the transformation of cruor into sanguis in circulation, though without the specifics of cardiac diaphoresis and induction of spirit that van Helmont elaborated. The blood as a whole was composed of cruor enclosing a vile portion carrying away excrement and a wholesome portion poised to become sanguis, and the sanguis that resulted from the process.

Phlebotomy interrupted this constant circuit of transformation and elimination by removing the entire body of the blood. Thomson did not see cruor pervading the body in stages of composition and decomposition outside the circulating fluid as Paracelsus and van Helmont did. His critique of bloodletting, specifically of venesection, was addressed to the catastrophic impoverishment of the body whole in the release of blood. He compared the profligate Galenists to a madman who cleans a house throwing out both trash and furniture.

The most favorable position on bloodletting was represented by the surgeon and anatomist Leonardo Botallo (1515/19-1587/88) who acquired much battlefield treatment experience during wars of religion and dynastic struggles in the service of the French monarchy. Botallo recommended venesection for every physical affliction, disease and injury. He began his therapeutic treatise *de curatione per sanguinis missionem (on healing by release of sanguis,* 1582) announcing that venesection benefits both children and the aged, and is of great help to pregnant women, exceeding even the claims of his declared master Galen.[12]

One of the etchings on the frontispiece of the book illustrates the technique in action, the lancets in a wall rack behind the bleeding patient attended by a surgeon's assistant as the sanguis from a vein opened in his left forearm spurts and arches into a bowl held by a boy crouching at his lap. This depiction of active bleeding was an iconography of the practice that supported claims of sanguis plethora, an overabundance of the humor in the body powering a continual fountain that would in fact last no more than a second. Illustrations of the preliminaries were more common.[13]

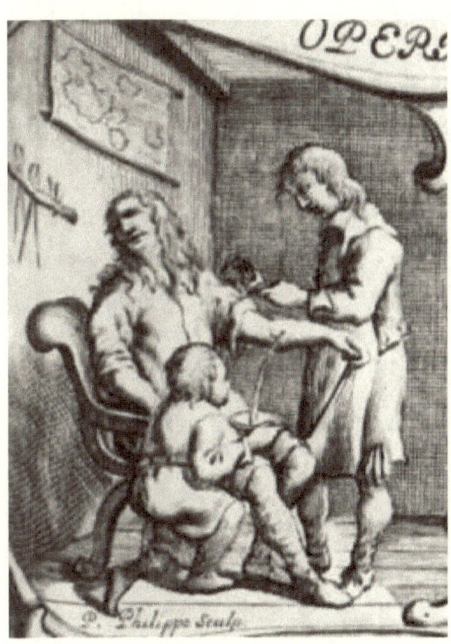

After numerous chapters on applications to specific diseases, conditions and injuries Botallo makes claims based on Avicenna and other authors of the quantity of blood contained in any body (25 *librae*, of which 17 can be evacuated with no harm) and the capacity to generate more.[14] The large volumes removed, pouring out in a fountain, need not alarm the patient, who will rapidly recover by replacing the bad blood with good blood. The bleeding was treatment and would require no recovery.

By present-day measures that is a gross overestimate of blood weight. 25 *librae* at 328.9 grams per *libra* is 8.2 kilograms of blood, which is 1.7 times the weight of blood in the body of a person weighing 70 kilograms (154 pounds). 7% of body weight is blood: 0.07x70=4.9 kg. The 17 librae (5.6 kg) harmlessly evacuated would exceed the actual blood weight of an adult. Botallo's followers operated under even more expansive estimates of individual blood contents.

Botallo's rhetoric of persuasion is illustrated in the recollections of Estienne Pasquier (1529-1615), a royal councilor and advocate before parlement. Pasquier wrote in a letter to a fellow councilor that during his youth doctors were very sparing in bleeding patients.[15] One doctor he respected punned that he was a *petit seigneur*, an amusingly self-deprecating phrase meaning a pretentious, overbearing man, but which can be heard as *petit saigneur*, a "small bleeder."

Then Botallo came to France to serve as physician to King Henri III, and applied bleeding in all cases, even in gout, repeating it four-five times for a patient. Pasquier, as the king's advocate, remonstrated with Botallo that instead of healing this would exacerbate the illness. Botallo replied that to the contrary it was like taking foul water from a well, allowing good water to replace it; it was like a wet nurse's supply of milk increasing after feeding a child. The belief that bleeding removed noxious matter from the body to be replaced salubrious was one of the most persistent arguments for its practice.

The Paris faculty of medicine took exception to Botallo's procedures and published a book cautioning restraint. After the death of Botallo the technique took on new life among French doctors, who hardly spared bleeding anyone-outside patients, their own children and wives-and reported "a very happy success."

Nowhere does Botallo use the word "cruor" in any capacity; sanguis alone is being released and replaced in bloodletting. Botallo does give an account of sanguis generation from the process of digestion but without associating chyle with a distinct component of the resulting fluid. Demonstrating the ready renewability of the sanguis was his main aim. His treatment emphasized sanguis as a whole fluctuating in volume and quality like that eternally renewed well water. His system had no place for the gross subtleties of cruor.

From the early 16th century onward the literature on bloodletting, often focusing on venesection, became voluminous and polemical. It was possible to tell a writer's stand on the subject immediately from the title of a work. While medical treatises were in Latin, there was a choice between the cruor/sanguis pairing or just sanguis, but when French, English, Spanish, Italian, German and Dutch became the predominant languages of discourse and dissension, there existed a cover-all sang/blood term that might project cruor into a specialized definition or leave it aside entirely. Botallo writing his technical works in Latin resorted exclusively to sanguis; Pasquier commenting on his practice in French need refer only to *sang*. van Helmont in Latin contrasted cruor with sanguis; George Thomson in English wrote of cruor, sanguis and blood.

The Paduan physician Dominico La Scala confined himself to sanguis, but with an import the opposite of Botallo's, in his *Phlebotomia damnata* (1696). He prefaces his diatribe against phlebotomy with pages of Biblical and patrological citations affirming that the "sensitive soul" resides in the sanguis, which must not be diminished by extraction.[16] For the same reason that Botallo found the sanguis a reservoir of body character, subject to alteration through its extraction, La Scala agrees with van Helmont and forbids its removal.

> Phlebotomy chief of all medical procedures, name derived from the phlebotome (vulgarly, the lanceola), commonly, and most in usage, is called venesection, or emission of sanguis made by a vein opened or incised with a scalpel. Not to exclude artificial release of cruor from whatever part of the body by whatever instrument, means or manner, phlebotomy in a stricter sense, appropriately and accurately applied: arteriotomy, leech, and scarification, to that further are adjoined and extended.[17]

This definition of phlebotomy introduces a book entitled, as in the first line, "Phlebotomy, chief of all medical practices": clearly a strong endorsement by the author, a Paduan physician writing twenty years after La Scala.

This phlebotomy has as a primary objective the release of sanguis by penetrating a vein with a sharp instrument, the phlebotome or lanceola (lancet). Cruor also is an objective of this treatment, not from the same point of release but from anywhere in the body and by any means. This cruor is the decaying matter that accompanies injury wherever it may occur, and is removed using any number of instruments and methods. The sanguis released from a vein is distinct from the cruor that might appear anywhere, which passes through arteries, enters the bodies of leeches applied to the skin and wells up from small scars.

Cruor in precisely this state was recognized adhering to surgical instruments. The 5th century Christian poet Aurelius Prudentius Clemens asks if you recoil from the surgeon as from the executioner, "when the living flesh is cut and new cruor stains the scalpel as the decayed part is withdrawn."[18]

The bloodletting of this definition distinguishes between sanguis and cruor and the techniques that release them. They were distinct substances attacked with techniques peculiar to their nature. This approach was an attempt to integrate long-existing techniques into the general practice of medicine as the craft became professionalized.

For instance leeches, the mainstay of some doctors from antiquity onward, were thought to take up cruor preferentially from wounds and from the skin after scarification. The Roman poet Horace, in his epistle on the poetic art, compared a poet attaching himself to an audience to a leech "full of cruor" in persistent sticking power.[19] Horace expected that his own audience would have a visceral grasp of the metaphor, having seen leeches distended during bloodletting treatment.

Any attempt to articulate a neat grouping of bloodletting techniques by the fluid released meets with confusion. A Latin word for "leech" alternative to *hirudo* is *sanguisuga,* sanguis plus *sugere,* to suck, the parent word of the French word for leech, *sangsue.* This transition neatly summarizes the ambiguity of cruor/sanguis, separate entities or separate words for the same entity in different stages. The many words associated with cruor and the body matters it named (clot, placenta, crassamentum, and so on) and the many techniques under the general heading of bloodletting were in free association. The advocacy and denunciation of bloodletting alternated accordingly, between unified "blood" and separation of terms, each offering an explanation why bloodletting was healthy or detrimental to health.

Advocacy and opposition to bloodletting were arrayed along a line of variation that included cruor and sanguis in their appearances and meanings. The sanguis spouting from the sectioned vein might carry cruor along with it, might flow with no reference to cruor or might be confined to blood vessels while cruor is removed from the body. The technique, and the body substance it extracts, was preferred for certain conditions, for instance pneumonia and other "inflammatory" disorders. Advocacy and opposition were joined in texts that allowed for bloodletting, favoring certain techniques and advancing cautions for their use.

The Neapolitan anatomist and surgeon Marco Aurelio Severino (b. 1580) practiced an "iron and fire" approach to his trade, overcoming with bold strokes the timidity that had been inherited from the approach to extractions inherited from the recently routed Arabs. He railed against the "seilo phlebotomy" that focused on the salvatella vein between the ring finger and the little finger of the hand. Cruor was not prominent in his estimations, but he did not believe that the modest technique could remove enough of the dense cruor to achieve the weight prescribed by Galen.[20] Specialization of phlebotomy drew the cruor/sanguis contrast into discussions of the use and abuse of techniques aimed at specific anatomical sites.

Around the same time Severino's critique was published three English advocates of bloodletting, including a doctor-astrologer and a "doctor of physic," composed instructional treatises on "bloodletting and the diseases to be cured thereby" and on cupping and scarification.[21] They made no reference at all to cruor or sanguis, but relied entirely on controlling the plenitude of blood that arose at certain times and in certain parts of the body.

The veins are indexed according to the conditions that can be addressed by bleeding them, and the conditions are listed alphabetically in entries that include the veins best bled for their relief with some attention to seasonal and astrological factors.[22] Sections of aphorisms drawn from the works of famous physicians Hippocrates, Galen, Celsus, Arnold of Villanova, Avicenna, and others give practical advice to the bloodletter: he should be young, energetic and not drunk, says one.

The texture, coloring, component fractions, smell and taste of blood are all made clear to the reader who must show expertise in the signs of what he has released from the patient's body. None of these estimable physicians is quoted in the Latin of their original or translated works. This is a fully English manual for the bloodletter, including the barber surgeon.

There are some cautions for whom and when bloodletting should be undertaken: limited for children and the elderly, little specific to women, though "abortion" is the first "disease" for which there is vein advice. The last paragraph of the first treatise addressed recovery, not with advice for bandaging the wound, which would only develop if the bloodletting is mishandled, but a warning to avoid "bad Air, eat white Bread, wel baked Veal, Hens, Chickens, Lamb, rear Eggs and that which breeds good humors and blood, drink cleer Wine pure and thin, abstain from Cheese, Milk, Herbs, Fish, Ale and Meath, Anaer, Sadness and Copulation."

Around a hundred years after this endorsement of bloodletting another English physician in a "compendium of the modern practice of physic" made the compendious statement:...by the evacuation of the cruor or crassamentum, the thickest and most consummate part of our humors, many of the effects produced by blood-letting are to be accounted for..."[23]

Hugh Smith's essay on the circulation of the blood and bloodletting that prefaced his published lectures originally was printed in a Latin version for his students in 1761. The English translation, which went through several editions up to 1804, retained Latin words such as cruor and crassamentum, and espoused a Harveyan conceptualization of the role of cruor. Its varying concentration in the blood explains rapidity or sluggishness of the blood's circulation, which in turn corresponds to the state of health. As is apparent in the quotation above, he retained the humoral quality of the blood, and with it the explanatory role of plethora, quantity of blood, which was mass due to cruor.

Yet in the other lectures of his compendium, which encompass the topics of a medical education in body systems, disorders and treatments, Smith several times calls for the use of bloodletting but never recurs to cruor and its humoral physics of circulation. As preventive and remedy for sea scurvy, for example, he recommends dry air and summer fruit with acid content because scurvy is a cold, moist disease, but offers no explanation how changes in the thickness of blood are behind the disorder. In cases of inflammation caused by injury or penetration by a foreign body bloodletting is the chief means of reducing the increased oscillatory contractions of the blood vessels, presumably by removing the mass of blood from the system.

The humoral system of disease and treatment emphasizing interconnections between the body microcosm and the macrocosm, heat and cold, dryness and moisture in balance and imbalance preexisted the engagement with cruor and sanguis and could involve them in any one diagnostic and therapeutic formulation. Into this humoral arrangement came the circulatory mechanics which could be explained by the variable weighting of the blood. Smith, Andrew Fyfe and a number of other practitioner/writers arrived at this theoretical linkage between cruor/sanguis blood composition, humoral diagnosis and bloodletting therapy but allowed it to remain an implicit condition in their accounts of practice.

One important strand in this linkage was the relationship between environment, weather and climatic conditions, the weighted composition of the blood and evacuations, involuntary as in vomiting and bleeding, and intentional as in bloodletting. Observations of the relationship between diseases, diet and the climate in different settings related cruor to symptoms and bloodletting success.

"…Englishmen, from the nature of their food and drink, had their veins filled with a watery, crude and feeble fluid, which therefore could ill bear to be impoverished by large evacuations; but the natives of southern Europe, the Spanish and Portuguese, derive from their flesh meat, which is much more *spiritous* and *nutritious* than ours, and from their *wines*, an abundance of thick, juicy, and compact cruor, which must, of absolute necessity, be freely evacuated in fever, in order to preserve the life of the persons affected."[24] The superintendent of a fever hospital established during the 1818-19 epidemic in Edinburgh connected the ability to withstand bloodletting to the composition of the blood, the proportion of rich cruor, with the diet and national origin of the patient.

Benjamin Welsh justified the use of bloodletting as a primary treatment by the release of heat that accompanied the thick blood of the fever. He prefaced his report on the epidemic with meteorological tables with temperature readings, and included a survey of the diet of the patients together with recipes. Most of his tabular evidence was to support his conviction that the healing directly corresponded to the frequency and care of bloodletting of different categories of patient, complicated by the relapsing nature of the fever. He also compiled a history of the use of bloodletting in fevers from antiquity to his present, surveying the principles set down for its operation and why it was believed to work so well. Yet the passage above was the only instance he cited the substance of cruor in the blood. The measurable proof of bloodletting was of greater importance than the role of the ancient humoral ingredients of blood.

Another doctor writing in the same period, who gave a similar account of the presence of cruor in the blood and made a historical review of bloodletting, gave the opposite advice for the treatment of tetanus. Jean-Louis Faucher believed that draining blood removed equal amounts of cruor and serum (*serosité*), but by an effect called *spoliation* more of the red part remained afterward. Less blood should be evacuated from people in warm climates than from those living in temperate climates because of their greater proportion of the hot, red component in the first place.[25]

The "unrestrained vampirism" advocated by the prolific bloodletter Leonardo Botallo was explained by "the habituatedly inflammatory constitution" of the northern Italians, who were the who were the regular patients of the Piemontese Botallo.[26] The continual inflammation denoted the presence of large concentrations of rich, red blood, which Welsh attributed to diet and climate.

Away from Italy, Botallo treated soldiers, men of robust constitution who also could withstand, and needed his exactions. The history of bloodletting was examined by later advocates to explain past excesses in terms of present usages.

An Edinburgh doctor who had studied in Vienna and opposed the use of "heroic remedies, especially bloodletting" in inflammation, particularly pneumonia was told by his colleagues that however pneumonia might comport itself in Vienna, "it certainly required bloodletting in Edinburgh."[27] Eleven years later, he wrote in his historical sketch of "hematophobia," fear of bloodletting, venesection was no more practiced in Edinburgh than in Vienna. What seemed to be a regional-climatic-dietetic rationale for differences between the two cities given way to a reformation of medical practice common to both of them.

Parallel to this change in orientation was the distance between Marshall Hall's statement in 1836 "It sometimes requires no little boldness to abstain from the use of the lancet"[28] and Fordyce Barker's inability in 1870 to find a lancet for purchase when, not having brought his own instruments, he required one for a bloodletting operation.[29]

Early in the 19th century there were a variety of lancets for use in venesection. Alfred Velpeau's multi-volume surgical elements illustrates three shapes of the blade for that use in particular-grain of barley, grain of oats and pyramidal, or serpent's tongue-and both pictures and describes the exact motions of cutting the vein, a combination of inward and upward strokes so rapid they are indistinguishable, followed by the familiar arc of the blood flow into a bowl held by an assistant.[30]

"a sensation like no other"
Velpeau (1839: 297,fig.150)

Velpeau's volumes are accompanied by an atlas of colored plates of surgical instruments and specific operations. Phlebotomy and the lancets used are not included in those plates but confined to a section in the text on simple operations. None of the illustrations depict, and the text does not mention anywhere, blood or cruor. These are entirely mechanical, bloodless procedures. Even bloodletting is.

Barker's 1870 quest for a phlebotomy lancet, which existed in such variety thirty years earlier, would not have been fulfilled by going to the store of a large urban surgical supply company, the likes of which did not exist earlier in the century. The stock of such companies as George Tiemann and Company (New York), Chas. Truax and Company (Chicago) or Noyes Brothers and Cutlery (St. Paul, Minnesota) included lancets, but for specialized uses such as vaccination and throat surgery.[31]

Where "phlebotomy" (never "bloodletting") was listed as a separate category of surgical instruments, it designated spring lancets, which mechanized the deft venesection Velpeau described, scarificators, cupping vessels and "artificial leeches." Folding lancets with points like the one held in the illustration above were not in stock.

The withdrawal of blood, cruor and bloodletting from the pictures and practice of surgery was not complete. The fluid released by bloodletting no longer contained cruor, which was seen as a characteristic component of what emerged from the stomachs of people suffering from yellow fever or malaria. One analysis of the pathology of yellow fever revived the old idea of the formation of blood from the process of digestion only in reverse: blood and chyle in the stomach yielded a black vomit-cruor.[32]

33

At the end of the century, when a physiologist used the word cruor for coagulated blood he added, that "it hardly is a happy name."[33] John Abel asserted in 1915 that, after decades of not being practiced, bloodletting was back in use, and was not being misused.[34]

[1] Fyfe (1801: 242)

[2] *Humorum optimus et maxime proprius ac domesticus sanguis est. De temperamentis, Liber II.* Kuhn (1823: 603)

[3] There is no entry for *cruor* in the Latin index of Galen's complete works compiled by Kuhn (1833). There are entries for *cruenta (enaimaton)*, all referring to *vulnus cruenta*, bleeding wound, and applications to stanch the bleeding. In contrast, *sanguis* occupies five pages of the index (539-44)

[4] Ronca (1994: 275n23).

[5] N.G. (1592: 196)

[6] Paracelsus (1563: 17) *de tartaro*

[7] Paracelsus (1603: 5, 116)

[8] van Helmont (1707: 188) *spiritus vitae*

[9] van Helmont (1707: 380) *pleura furens*

[10] van Helmont (1707: 634) *thesis demonstratur*

[11] Thomson (1665: 49)

[12] Botallo (1660: 95-344)

[13] Zigrosser (1970: plates 35 and 36) illustrates venesection with a 16th century woodcut and a 17th century etching, both of preparation for venesection, not the act itself. Sudhoff (1907: 27-48)

[14] Botallo (1660: 271)

[15] Pasquier (1619: 548-49)

[16] La Scala (1696: 1-7) *"rationibus quoque constat animam sensitivam in sanguine esse"*

[17] Verna (1716: 1)

[18] Aurelius (1845: 264, 499-500)

[19] *Epistles Book II, de arte poetic:* 476 *"no missura cutem nisi plena cruoris hirudo"*

[20] Severino (1654: 141, 363)

[21] Culpeper, Ruland and Cole (1663)

[22] This is in the tradition of vein maps of the body described and illustrated from the 15th century. Sudhoff (1907: 27-48)

[23] Smith (1781: xxvi)

[24] Welsh (1819: 100-01)

[25] Faucher (1810: 15-16; 329)

[26] Haeser (1853: 439); "Vampirism" was a critique leveled against unrestrained bloodletters during the early 19th century when the word was coming into common use. Risse (1979: 4)

[27] Balfour (1859: 214)

[28] Hall (1836: 251)

[29] Barker (1871: 28)
[30] Velpeau (1839: 293-97)
[31] From a survey of the catalogues of these companies printed 1888-90.
[32] Oswald (1879: 383)
[33] Landois (1893: 49)
[34] Abel (1915: 135)

3. Men into flowers

In the 10th book of Ovid's *Metamorphoses* there are two instances of men becoming flowers, or, more specifically, of cruor emerging from men who have died being transformed into a flower that by its shape, coloring and markings memorializes the death.

Orpheus sings of Hyacinthus, a youth, the son of the king of Amyclae near Sparta, who became the companion of the god Apollo in love and sport. Hyacinthus dashed to retrieve a metal hoop that had been tossed high into the air in a game of quoits, and was struck at the head when the hoop rebounded from the ground. Apollo applied his herbal remedies to no avail; the young man died in his arms. In his grief Apollo spoke (Book 10.209-13):

Ecce cruor, qui fusus signaverat herbam,
Desenit esse cruor: Tyrioque nitentior ostro
Flos oritur; formam capit quam lilia: si non
Purpueus color huic; argenteus esset in illis.

Behold the cruor, which marked the grass
Ceases to be cruor: brighter than the Tyrian dye
A flower is born, takes the shape of a lily. This one
Purple in color; silvery the others.

Apollo inscribed his lament, "AI" on the petals of the plant. Ovid, or Orpheus, added that the honor bestowed on Hyacinthus was perpetuated in an annual festival, the Hyacinthia, celebrated by the Spartans.

The flowering of *Hyacinthus orientalis*, the ornamental bulb sold in pots at Eastertime, projects an image of the cruor welling up from the wounded Hyacinthus. The leaves tightly sheath the stalk bearing many small flowers radiating on uniform stems from a central spike, which break through the separation of the leaves like innards pouring from a split body. While this is the most suggestive connection of Hyacinthus with a flower known by that name today, other candidates have been suggested[1]

Gerard (1633: 194)

The young man's sinking shoulders and bowing head as his life ebbs in Ovid's verses call up a withering plant. Frazer classes him with the gods of "vegetation which blooms in spring and withers under the scorching heat of the summer sun."[2] He falls to earth when the discus falls and rebounds releasing his cruor onto the earth where it rises up again as a flower carrying his image.

The process is repeated annually in the spring recovery of plant life and in the corresponding festival.

The long tradition of illustrating the fables of the *Metamorphoses* with a sequence of woodcuts or etchings established a standard iconography for the death of Hyacinthus by the mid-16th century. The etching by Antonio Tempesta below contains the typical image of the series: Apollo cradling the slumped form of Hyacinthus in a forest setting. Though both cruor and the flower are named in the caption, neither is visible in the etching. This seems to be an accidental hunting death rather than a sports accident. Apollo's lyre and bow rest on the ground as he grasps the head of the arrow protruding from Hyacinthus' side.

Tempesta, *Metamorphoseon…Ovidianarum* 95 (1585). Cruor of Hyacinthus into the flower of his name.

The large number of illustrated sets of the *Metamorphoses* printed between the mid-16th century and the present, and the individual paintings by Rubens, Tiepolo and others, all contain this scene of god attending the dying man.[3] The circumstances vary. Many followed Tempesta's hunting scenario. Others associated the death with a group game, showing a scene of men tossing a discus in the background, and a solid discus lying inert by the side of the fallen player. Only a few of the prints showed it to be a quoit. In one of them a figure is approaching the pair with a hoop around his neck. Ovid refers to the object of play as *discus*, and only a quoit could have rebounded in the solar manner that injured Hyacinthus.

Micyllus, *Pub. Ovidii Nasonis Metamorphoseon* 1582: 400

The illustration in this edition preserves features of the hunting mode: Apollo's quiver, the two dogs but no arrow, only the excited hoop bearer. Jacobus Micyllus was the adopted name of the German humanist and Latin scholar Jacob Moltzer (1503-58) who edited and published with notes a number of Roman texts. His 1543 Ovid's *Metamorphoses* was a revision of an earlier edition by Raphael Regius. Here Ovid's original text is surrounded by prose remarks labeled for each of the editors, including the brief remarks by the first Christian writer to comment on the *Metamorphoses,* the Church father Lactantius.[4] The 1582 edition was in turn edited by Gregor Bersman with etchings by an unnamed artist well after Micyllus' death.

It was an edition of Ovid's text, each separate fable preceded by the illustration and an *argumentum,* a summary in Latin, which in the Regius-Micyllus-Bersman text puts the transformation plainly:[5]

Hyacinthus igitur sic moriente, cruor emanans ab eodem, Apolline in florem eiusdem est conversus.

Hyacinthus thus dying, cruor spreading from him, the same was converted into a flower by Apollo.

In the 1582 edition the dense text surround of its 1543 predecessor was reduced to margin notes. The appearance of the actual cause of Hyacinthus' death in the illustration was in strict fidelity to Ovid's original text.

The Latin summary had been borrowed from yet another illustrated edition of the *Metamorphoses*, this published in 1563 by the Augsburg *Meistersinger* Johann Spreng, with etchings by Virgil Solis. Spreng's verse text does not include Ovid's original words, but is made up of the summary directly below the illustration, an *enarratio*, a retelling of the fable in Spreng's own Latin verses, and an *allegoria*, which renders the fable into moral instruction. The transformation in Spreng's re-versification of the fable is put in language different from Ovid's.[6]

Sanguis at in florem rutilus mutatur olentem
Ne prorsus iuennis concidat omnis honor

Ruddy sanguis changed into a fragrant flower
That the youth not concede all honor entirely

The cruor of the summary has become sanguis in the retelling to Spreng's own purpose. In this fable Spreng finds an allegory of combat between a younger and older man, modelled on a wrestling match in Vergil's Aeneid, which he also translated.[7] Cruor and flowers are not part of it. Solis' illustration is the hunting scene with the fatal arrow lying beside the recumbent youth and no sign of play. Following a hint in Lactantius, Spreng made the accidental death into the outcome of a competition *(certamen)* between the two men, and the flower arising from Hyacinthus' sanguis a scant preservation of his honor rather than a memorial.

The classical life force of the cruor has been lost in the bleeding of the sanguis.

The 1582 edition of Micyllus, which uses Spreng's Latin summary and reprints Ovid's text with Micyllus' notes, uses no word other than cruor and visually holds to Ovid's discus-quoit play. It seems to be a reproach against Spreng, whose version was reprinted toward the end of the 16th century, for violating the classical wording. The love between the two men was eclipsed by the competition. Yet Spreng's disjuncture between the two words proved persuasive to other editors and illustrators of the *Metamorphoses*.

The renowned engraver Crispin de Passe, drawing upon an earlier incomplete series by his Dutch countryman Hendrik Goltzius and that by Antonio Tempesta, issued a *Metamorphoseon Ovidianarum* in 1602-04, each print accompanied by four lines of Latin verse. The Apollo-Hyacinthus fable is illustrated by the death in a hunting scene with arrow and no suggestion of a game.[8]

Victus Amyclaeus iuvenis cetamine disci
Victoris Phoebi funus, amorque fuit
Purpureus sanguis florem succrevit in illum
Quique Hiacinthus erat, flos Hiacinthus erit.

Defeated the young Amyclaean in the discus contest
Was the lament and the love of the victor Phoebus
Purple sanguis developed into that flower
Where Hiacinthus was, the Hiacinth flower will be.

Ovid's text isn't present in word or image. The fable has become the Spreng-Solis tale of rivalry and defeat ending in death and a floral grace note.

Two oak tree trunks one crossing the other parallel the bending haloed Apollo and the fallen Hyacinthus in the etching representing that fable in Johann Wilhelm Baur's 1641 collection.[9] Apollo has dropped his bow and still carries his quiver as he attends his companion. A large disc with a hollow center lies on the ground nearby. In the background is a recapitulation of the game that led to the tragedy. Apollo, identifiable from his Christian saint-like halo, watches as a man, apparently Hyacinthus, stands on the ground gazing up at a tossed disc about to fall back to earth while a group of men look on. The hunting and the game-playing modes of the illustrations have been merged.

The cursive script below the picture frame is a four line poem.

Occidit infelix Hiacinthus vulnere disci,
Quem tulit in miseri fortior aura capit,
Phoebus amans florem pueri de sanguine nasci,
Perpetuo et tristes iusset habere notas.

Died unhappy Hiacinthus by a wound of the discus,
Carried to the hapless one more powerful than an aura of the head,
Phoebus loving the flower born of the boy's sanguis,
Endlessly also decreed to bear sad notes.

Baur, *Metamorphoseon* 1641: 95

The verse reflects the almost comic strip abruptness of poor Hyacinthus' demise made plain in the etching. Ovid's text with its mechanism of death by recoiling quoit and its cruor become flowers is not present, not even in a Latin summary. Instead a German verse account of "Hyacinthus changed into a flower" follows the illustration page in tight *Fraktur* paragraph lines separated by slashes. Here the discus doesn't reach the ground; it lands right on Hyacinthus' head, causing him to fall dead. Apollo transforms the "rich blood" (*gestoffene Blut)* into a red lily and inscribes upon the leaves the letters of the lament he raises in memory of his companion.

Baur's Germanized edition was reprinted several times during the 17th and early 18th centuries. It was paralleled by the appearance of illustrated translations into European languages borrowing, adapting illustrations and poetic captions, or inventing new ones. In all of them the transition to sanguis and the comparable word in the modern language (*sang, sangre, Blut, blood)* was sustained. Editions of Ovid's original text remained thick with commentary gathered, combined and revised by one editor after another.

Peter Burmann's 1727 multi-volume edition of the *Metamorphoses* continued the Latin notes from Micyllus onward, and the brief Latin summary of the text had cruor running from Hyacinthus' wounds.[10] Burmann's edition was incorporated in turn into an annotated complete edition of Ovid's works published in London in 1821. Some changes and emendations were made in the notes of the original from the previous century. The most striking for the present fable is that in the Latin summary on discovering the recumbent Hyacinthus Apollo exclaims, *"Ecce sanguis…"* in reflection of the *"Ecce cruor…"* in Ovid's original.[11] The sanguinization had reached back to the text itself, which remained eternally the same.

At the end of Book 10.708-39 Orpheus sings the death of Adonis, who against the advice of Venus speared a wild boar and was in turn gored by the enraged animal after it ejected his spear. She found him lying in a pool of his own sanguis, tore her hair and clothes in grief, exclaimed that he could not be returned to life, and declared that his cruor would be changed into a flower. Sprinkling a fragrant nectar onto the cruor caused a flower the color of sanguis to rise "like bubbles from the yellow mud." It was named "anemone" after the wind that stirs it.

Bernard Salomon's illustration of this episode shows Venus, her swan chariot parked in the background, bending over the fallen man. His French verse makes no reference to *sang* until the line where the fallen Adonis is changed into *"une fleur sanguine"* ("a blood-red flower" or "a blood flower"). The illustrations of Adonis' transformation over the next centuries keep to the tableau of the disconsolate Venus over the boy's body.

Salomon set the standard and anticipated the construction of cruor into sanguis in the summaries and re-versifications in Latin and vernacular languages of the Adonis fable that followed. The flower Venus conjures from the cruor is sanguis-colored, and in some editions cruor is given priority as the source and sanguis is absent. This is visible in Spreng's 1563 reworking of the Ovid text. In the *argumentum* cruor is converted "into a purple flower" rather than a sanguis-red one. The *enarratio* has Venus noticing the cruor of his members as she approaches, and the sanguis soaking the soil. She does not make the flower from the cruor; she does not make a flower at all. "Lest the youth entirely lack a monument/there now is a flower red as sanguis." The *allegoria* lacks cruor or flowers.

The phrase cruor "into a purple flower" replaced the sanguis coloration of Ovid's original lines in all Latin prose and verse versions of Ovid's death of Adonis fable from the mid-16th to the early 19th century.[12] Purple, often given as the color of blood, was exclusive to emperors, and had a commemorative function. Adjoined to Crispin de Passe's etching, the four line epigraph concludes with Venus' declaration:[13]

Moestáque purpureum iusset de sanguine florem
Surgere, perpetuus quo tuus esset honor.

And sadly she commands a purple flower
To rise up from the sanguis, by which be thy perpetual honor.

Cruor is replaced by sanguis which is replaced by purple. Sanguis is no longer just the color of the flower, but its source.

This pattern of changing Latin words reflects the consolidation of the cruor-sanguis pairing into sanguis and its color. The change was consistent wherever the two words were used in contrast with each other, for different aspects of the fluid released from the body.

At the beginning of Book XIII of the *Metamorphoses* the heroes of the Trojan War negotiate with each other for the armor of the fallen Achilles. When the decision grants the prize to the eloquent Ulysses, the enraged and resentful Ajax runs himself through with his own sword. No hand can remove it.

Expulit ipse cruor; rubefactaque sanguine tellus
Purpureum viridi genuit de cospite florem
Qui prius Oebalio fuerat de vulnere natus. (Book XIII: 294-96)

The cruor itself expelled it; and from the ruddy sanguis the ground
Bore a purple flower out of the green turf
That first had been born from the Oebalian wound.

The Oebalian, or Spartan, was Hyacinthus. Commentators and translators usually add a line not in Ovid's original text explaining that the first two letters of the name of Ajax (AIAS), identical with Apollo's lament, were imprinted on the leaves of the plant.

Ajax did not require the intervention of a god to make his sanguis/cruor into a flower. Neither Hyacinthus nor Adonis was a warrior like Ajax, who possessively thrust his sword into his chest so forcefully that only the explosive outrush of his own cruor could push it out. The contact of the fluid with the earth was enough to repeat the form of the Hyacinthus flower with markings that corresponded to the hero's name.

Most of the writers providing summaries in Latin and translations of this metamorphosis do not make a distinction between the cruor released and the sanguis transformed on the ground. Cruor and sanguis are combined into cruor which becomes the "purple" flower. Spreng's 1863 summary is repeated in Micyllus 1582, Lactantius 1591, Burmann 1727 and Burmann 1821:

…ex cuius cruore deinceps flos purpureus, similis Hyacintho, natus est.

…from which cruor spontaneously is born a purple flower, as with Hyacinthus.

Spreng does treat the expulsion of the sword by cruor and the rise of the flower from the dispersed sanguis as distinct events in the *enarratio* section of his section on Ajax's suicide, but his exclusively cruor summary was widely copied.

The illustrations that accompany some of these texts picture the words with a corresponding succinctness. The following is a gallery of four instances.

Salomon (1557)

Spreng (1563: 152)

Micyllus (1582: 510)

Lactantius (1591: 309)

Salomon's figure jabbing himself with the sword point and releasing a cascade of cruor that springs back as a flower in the forward plane of a landscape set with churches and Roman ruins is the model for the other etchings. Ajax's breastplate, which would have inhibited his suicide jab, is cast off at the bottom of the scene. Salomon's French verses offer no outcome to Ajax's rage-propelled thrust other than his release from misery. Blood and flower are not present. The accompanying picture visualizes Ovid's words.

Besides stylistic variations and differences in the type of architecture in the background, the four etchings differ from each other in the hand Ajax uses to hold the sword, the angle of attack and the consistency of the cruor stream. Salomon's Ajax grips the sword in his left hand and drives it upward into the ribbons of cruor emerging from his wound. Spreng's Ajax does the same holding it with his right hand. Micyllus and Lactantius have the warrior stabbing himself horizontally into the chest, left then right hand.

The cruor gushes out in a divided stream, arches out high in strands of spray or pours down in a column. In all of the illustrations it is powered by energy that might have forced the lodged sword out of the body, though Ajax is still holding it. Stages of the event are simultaneously present. The cruor stream resembles visualizations of bloodletting during the 17th-18th centuries in the force, volume and coherence of the flow.

The flower standing at the fall point of the cascade is in the same simultaneous time frame as Ajax's sword. It appears to be a lily in some of the frames, a larkspur in others. In all of them the bloom is at the end of a long stalk originating in basal leaves like a fountain erupting from the earth. The force of the expelled cruor gives the shape of rising fluid to the plant. Cruor conveys the characteristics of sanguis to the memorial flower.

Another personal transmission of sanguis markings to a memorial plant by way of cruor culminates Ovid's telling of the fable of Pyramus and Thisbe (Book 4). The two Babylonian youths, in love with each other but facing parental disapproval, agree to meet outside the city by a fountain and flee together.

Thisbe arrives first, but hides from a lioness who comes to drink at the fountain. Pyramus finds her torn and cruor-covered veil the lioness savaged, and assumes Thisbe has been taken by the beast. In despair he runs himself through with his sword, to wet Thisbe's veil with his own cruor. "Spurting out like water from a breach in a lead pipe," Pyramus' cruor stains the fruit of a mulberry tree growing nearby, and enters the roots of the tree darkening the fruit blackish red.

Seeing the tree with strange-colored fruit, Thisbe discovers Pyramus' dying body, her tears mingling with his cruor, and declaring that the tree will forever bear witness to their love, she falls on his sword. The gods grant her wish, and the mulberry tree's fruit is the color of their mingled cruor.

The tree did not grow out of the cruor of fallen humans, but received its own peculiar coloring from their spilled vital fluid. The mulberry invades water sources with its thick horizontal mat of crisscrossing roots, yellow to red in color beneath their dark sheath. They might well drink up the spreading cruor from the wounds of Pyramus, and carry the fluid to the fruit, also stained by Pyramus' spurting cut. Mulberry fruit, a composite berry, is white then ripens to red and black. The dark cruor carried the sanguis to the berry where they both were manifest. The entire tree, its roots resting one on the other, bears the memory of the wounded pair.

The 16th century summaries of Ovid's vegetative metaphors captured only part of the mulberry's conversion. Spreng's 1563 words were repeated verbatim by several others.

Quorum cruore morus arbor aspersa albos suos fructus in sanguinem cruorem convertit

By whose cruor stained the white mulberry fruits converted into sanguis cruor

Cruor carries sanguis and imparts both black and red/purple to the mulberry.

The Ovid illustrations of the Pyramus and Thisbe tragedy are divided into two: Thisbe leaving the vicinity of the spring when the lioness appears and Thisbe taking her own life with Pyramus' sword. She may be driving the point into her own breast with a visible burst of cruor, or bending over her fallen intended, the sword connecting her to him. In both variants the mulberry tree, known from the shape of its leaves, rises over them, without fruits visible. The inability to represent color in the print excludes cruor except by allusion to common knowledge of mulberry trees.

Ovidian cruor is a medium for the body that releases it with force and in quantity into the world, where it takes a form in plants recalling the events of its release. It is mingled with sanguis, with a color that continues the lives that ended. Its resemblance to contemporary dramatic blood grows more apparent with another fable from Ovid, Hercules slaying of Nessus and his own death (Book 9.89-158)

Hercules is unable to ford a raging river carrying his wife Deineira, and entrusts her passage to the centaur Nessus. On the other bank he hears Deineira cry out that Nessus is threatening to violate her. Hercules commands the centaur to stop and, when he evidently does not, shoots him with an arrow its head dipped in the venom (cruor) of the Lernaean hydra he had slain. Sanguis springs out of the entrance and exit wounds. The dying centaur tells Deineira that if Hercules should ever be drawn to another woman she should give him a garment dipped in his cruor to bind Hercules to her. In time she comes to believe her husband is straying and offers him the garment, which clings agonizingly to the demi-god's skin. The tormented Hercules orders his own funeral pyre.

According to Ovid, Nessus bleeds out sanguis that becomes sticky, poisonous cruor because it has mingled with the venom of the hydra that makes his arrows instantly deadly. Nessus gets his revenge on Hercules by delivering the cruor-venom back to him in the ironic guise of a love potion. He has implanted in the mind of Deianeira that notion that Hercules will leave her, and has given her a means to regain his adherence.

Ovid did not include a version of the second labor of Hercules, the joint defeat of the Lernaean hydra by the hero and his nephew, in the *Metamorphoses*. While Hercules is visiting Achilles and his tutor, the centaur Chiron, (Book 5 of Ovid's *Fasti*), Chiron accidentally drops one of Hercules's arrows on his foot

…sanguine centauri Lerneae sanguis echidnae mixtus ad auxilium tempora nulla dabat

…the sanguis of the Lernean hydra mixed with the blood of the centaur gave no occasion for help

The hydra-centaur sanguis there proved an inescapably lethal combination. Another much less benign centaur, Nessus, died passing the same mixture on through his venomous cruor.

That is the explanation appearing in Spreng's Latin summary, and copied in subsequent adaptations and editions of the *Metamorphoses*.

…mox ab Hercule Nessus telo confixus est, qui cum expiraret, uestem suam sanguine aspersam dedit Deianairae, indicans hanc fore remedium, aduersus desertum amorem coniugis, quam primum ea indureretus: Cruor autem iste in uenenum mutabatur

immediately Nessus was transfixed by an arrow from Hercules, and as he died gave to Deianeira his garment soaked with sanguis, saying that this would be a remedy for the lost love of her husband, when first hardened against her: this cruor however is changed into poison.

The cruor that conveys the lethal mixture of centaur's sanguis with the hydra's sanguis in Ovid's original words is simply transformed into a poison in the Latin summary without the hydra's sanguinary input.

The illustrations that accompany the summaries and adaptations of the Nessus episode in the *Metamorphoses* of Spreng and his successors only show Hercules shooting the centaur, Hercules on his funeral pyre and being carried off to the sky to be placed among the stars. The hydra, the sanguis and cruor of Nessus and the unremovable, burning garment are nowhere to be seen. A hidden passage of cruor bore the venom of the past to Hercules' skin, originally from the hydra by way of his own arrow.

Ovidian cruor emerges from the body to bear the body's traits into the world in another form. It can even bear the color and the marks of sanguis, transmit its origin's poisonous properties if it pours out of a hydra or a centaur. The adapters and illustrators of the *Metamorphoses* held to Ovid's verbiage in his original language, condensed cruor and sanguis into sang or blood in translation, and generally evaded displaying the substance itself pictorially. They used the visual rhetoric of bloodletting when they showed its flow out of the body. Its presence outside the body was men becoming flowers, not bleeding men, or the bloodstained surroundings. Yet the force of cruor, and its resonant shapetaking properties, demanded resolution in the pictorial space outside the body.

From The Death of Hyacinthus, Italian school, 17th century

---

[1] Giesecke (2014: 48-51). "a little purple iris with letters of lamentation" Frazer (1919: 313)
[2] Frazer (1919: 313) cites a number of authorities for this interpretation.
[3] Over forty sets of the illustrated 16th to 18th century *Metamorphoses* can be accessed through *Ovid Illustrated:The Renaissance Reception of Ovid in Image and Text* http://ovid.lib.virginia.edu/ovidillust.html
[4] Lactantius *Narrationes* quoted by Micyllus (1543: 232)
[5] Micyllus (1582: 399)
[6] Spreng (1563: 123)
[7] Allegoria
Qui certare cupit,pugnasq: subire feroces
Athletas ista querat in arte pares:
Nam qui maiores iuuvenili pectore flagrant
Despicit, is capiti nil nisi damna struit.
Praecipiti feruore Dares animoqq; superbus
Corruit, Entellus praemia nictor habet.
[8] de Passe (1602: 95)
[9] Baur (1641: 95)
[10] Burmann, et al. (1727: 699)
[11] Burmann, et al. (1821: 1424)
[12] Besides Spreng (1563: 131-32), also Micyllus (1582: 426-27); Lactantius (1591: 266); Burmann (1727: 739); Burmann (1821: 1457) among others. Baur (1641: 97) leaves out cruor and sanguis entirely.
[13] de Passe (1602: 97)

4. Cruentation

The sculptor and printmaker Pierre Roche (1855-1922) chronicled the First World War in bronze medallions.[1] They were Symbolist evocations of the effects of the war and profile portraits of important figures. One of the 1918 medallions is occupied by the figure of a seated woman, her legs crossed at the ankles, her left arm reaching to the ground, her right crossing to her left breast where the fingers separate a copious flow from within her. Her mouth is open in a moan. On her head rests the royal crown of the French crown jewels long since sold to forestall any return of the monarchy. The general disposition of her body matches the contours of France, and the outflow is the area of the Western Front of the war, then reaching its sanguinary culmination. The legend in large capitals about the rim reads, in Latin: *Cruentam Cruor Cruciat,* Cruor torments the bloodied [female=France]. The wound does not cease pouring out the nation's life cruor.

This is a new strain of war art, not the celebration of victory or the determination to fight on in the face of the enemy's onslaught. It is an art of witness of the agonized present. The Symbolist aloofness is overcome by the present wound which bleeds a past cruor into the future. The cruor is seen by many, who attest to its emergence.

France seen bleeding cruor is a national ordeal envisioned in a single body. It was a model of the cruenation that was long seen to be a visible response of a corpse to the environment and persons of its death.

Thomas of Cantiloupe, Bishop of Hereford in England, died in Orvieto, Italy on August 25, 1282 awaiting the verdict of a papal court on his petition to have rescinded his excommunication by the Franciscan John Peckham, Archbishop of Canterbury. Thomas, an administrator, teacher and scholar, had held civil and academic office in England during the turbulent years of the mid-13th century. He became embroiled with Peckham over theological issues and matters of episcopal jurisdiction.

The absence of a verdict restoring Thomas to communion allowed Peckham to refuse burial in sanctified ground to Thomas' bones which had been separated from his fleshly remains and transported back to England. "Strange fancies came to the birth in after years that, as the bearers passed through the diocese of Canterbury with their precious freight, the blood poured from the dry bones..."[2] These fancies were first set down in writing years later as evidence for Thomas' sainthood.[3] The implication, or the purpose for which the story was told, was that the Archbishop's enmity was the primary cause of Thomas' death. Only secondarily was he the victim of physical ills, including the malaria he caught in Italy.

Thomas' remains were enshrined in Hereford and became the focus of pilgrimages. The miraculous revival of a hanged man who had called upon Thomas to save him was one of several miracles that impelled the drive for his canonization.[4] A papal court of inquiry in 1307 determined that Thomas was not in a state of excommunication at his death, and after more miracles he was canonized a saint in 1320.

Scholars attribute the first colloquy on the blooded corpse in European religiojural history to the incident of Thomas' bleeding bones. Six months after the death of the prelate, Roger Marston, a Franciscan teacher at Oxford University and disciple of John Peckham, took up a quodlibetic question on whether the wounds of a corpse would bleed in the presence of the murderer.[5] The quodlibets were Latin question and answer statements that formed the chief method of exchange and argument among scholastics during the late Middle Ages. Many medieval philosophers left manuscript collections of quodlibets, which subsequent authors compiled in manuscripts and later published in printed editions organized by book and indexed by subject.

Roger made no mention of the Peckham-Cantaloupe incident, and denied on general principles that dry bones boiled free of flesh could bleed at all. He believed, however, that corpse bleeding had precedent in the works of Aristotle and thus had to be explained. The physical act of vision was greater than mere seeing to Aristotelians. It could move the spirit to a physical reaction.

The gaze of the wolf eclipses the power of speech by occluding human spirit with animal spirit. When a murderer looks upon the corpse he made, his thirst for blood draws upon that essence both spirit and fluid and the blood comes forth. Roger allowed for cruentation as a further affirmation of the bleeding wounds of Christ and their reanimation in the lives of the saints, in particular Saint Francis, when envisioned by the believer.

Between the year of Thomas' death and oblique resurrection in the questions put to Roger Marston, and his canonization, at least four other scholastics took up the question without making reference to Thomas or to each other. [6]

In 1290 the Augustinian B. Aegidius Columna (Giles of Rome) submitted to examination by the Faculty of Theology of the University of Paris on a number of questions, including the question of a corpse becoming blooded and bleeding when the murderer approaches. Giles was a political philosopher of both ecclesiastical and secular power, a logician and a commentator on the Bible and on Aristotle.

It is asked concerning violent murder; whether in the presence of the murderer the wounds emit blood (*sanguis*). And it is argued, no: because, as it is said, when someone is dead, there is no soul (*anima*) there. But this does not seem to give the reason for such a quantity of sanguis. To the contrary, as it is said, since experience is so, as also public report (*fama publica*) alleges.[7]

In the statement, argument, contradiction process of scholastic reasoning Giles lays out the disparity that Roger only skirts: the sanguis shouldn't pour out because the soul has left the body, yet rumor has it that bodies bleed in the presence of the murderer. All of his reasoning depends upon what is said. Like Roger he offers no circumstantial accounts of a corpse pouring out sanguis in the presence of the murderer. He just evaluates how some believe it happens.

The presence of the murderer may raise a tumult in the body of the victim, yet without stirring the voice and causing a movement of the limbs. The clothing or the knife of the murderer might retain traces of the victim's sanguis and, like attracting like, would draw the sanguis out of the body in his presence. That clearly can't be so.

Avicenna defines three stable states of nature, heat, emptiness and mixture, which are formed from dissimilar components coming together. If one of these states is attained it does not continue to draw in the components that made it. The perfect object draws upon the imperfect one, as the magnet draws iron. Then the sanguis on the clothing or knife, being outside the body and therefore imperfect, should be drawn to the corpse, and not the other way around.

The exchange of vapors through the eyes of murderer and victim raising a tumult that causes the sanguis to rise is not observed in nature and can be discounted as an explanation of the bleeding. The providence of God to make certain that the crime does not go unpunished; the deceptions of demons attempting to mislead the faithful by causing the appearance of guilt; or accident (*ex contingentia casuali*), as you might be struck by lightning while out walking: all are possible explanations. If these causes apply it may well be that sanguis can be stirred in a body without the presence of the soul (by God, demons or accident).

Given the marvelous nature of the happenings, one experience will generate rumors that it always is so, that a body will bleed in the presence of the murderer. Whatever theories are put forward, refutable or not, belief based on a reputed event will broaden into expectation that it happens that way. Giles did not reject the doctrine of remote causes; he saw no way to apply it to the corpse in the presence of the murderer. If it did ever happen to bleed then rumor would turn the experience into a principle. A plague of the imagination.

Both Roger and Giles separate the vision of the bleeding corpse from reasoning about why it bleeds. Giles makes the public the carriers of the image. They both subscribe to a concept of influence passing between corpse and viewer-murderer through the eyes as the result of the immaterial composition of a substance, blood. Neither denies that bleeding can happen, and neither finds that it is the result of the operation of any one effect. This indeterminacy, and appeal to the eyes as recipients and emitters, places it in the flow of visual impact while dispersing the causes.

At no point in these discussions is the fluid that emerges from the body referred to as cruor; it is always sanguis still imbued with life. Other writers on the subject of cruentation, contemporary and subsequent, did not bring cruor into the discussion. Cruentation was persistently discussed over the following centuries because it was a matter of life and death, in medicine, law and poetry, and a source of imagery after the original meaning of the word was forgotten. Proof of the circulation of the blood did not end the assumption. The movement of sanguis according to sympathy was too compelling to be put to rest by observation.

A doctor of medicine, Andreas Libavius (1550-1616), was for a time professor of history and poetry at the University of Jena, and always an engaged controversialist.[8] He laid out lists of argumentative theses in a dual tractatus on two separate beliefs: that anointing the weapon that caused a wound with unguent would heal the wound, which he dismissed as at best a way to build the victim's confidence; and that a corpse would bleed in the presence of the *percussor*, the person who administered the fatal blow. This he accepted as truth.

Libavius admits that many people do not have faith in corpse bleeding and observable instances are rare.[9] Through the 314 theses that comprise his argument, followed by pages of citations and comment, he deduces cruentation from the sensitivity of the blood imbued with spirit that imparts its motion. The agitation of the murderer in the presence of the corpse of his victim raises his temperature and puts his spirits and humors into turmoil. This disturbance influences the blood of the victim and sets it into motion, much as a fearsome rumor can radiate panic and disease.

Linking phenomena by force of contact and resemblance leads Libavius to propose experiments. If cruentation happens among humans then it also should happen when a dog nears the body of a dog he has killed. Libavius does not know of any attempts to test this, and he doubts that a beast's sanguis is as receptive to influence from another beast as a human's sanguis is to another human's.

Human perturbation in the presence of a victim would not be confined to the murderer. A relative or close friend might also project agitation into the corpse and cause the sanguis to come forth. Only those suspected of striking the blow should be allowed first into the perimeter of the dead person, for an accurate observation. If renewed sanguis flow does not spur a confession from the guilty party, it may be extracted by torture.

The appearance of magic functions emotionally to help the victim summon up the spirit of healing when he sees the weapon that wounded him anointed. Cruentation does actually take place and can be explained humorally. It is not magical though its effect on the spirit of the murderer can be the same. Much of Libavius' inquiry is sorting out what can be attributed to forces of nature and what can be assigned to credulity. He had the means to test weapon anointment, and dismissed it, but never having encountered circumstances for the application of cruentation he was left asserting its validity. He disallows magic as unexplained connection between events but does not dismiss its psychology. And he makes allowances for the work of demons.

Sanguis is the nourishment of the body, the vehicle of spirits and of heat, but it is not itself alive and is not sentient. "It is not the instrument of humans as man is…"[10] It is not directed by will or intention; it responds to the spirits it contains as a physical fluid. This sense of sanguis as matter responsive to the sensations and sentiments of the person it flows through and to others in the vicinity when it is free to do so placed it just within the empirical, and just outside the magical.

Being nearly empirical gave cruentation many names, and allowed it to persist into the chemical analysis of blood, and pass on to become a design for bloodletting. It was named for its appearance, for role as an ordeal and as a form of jurisprudence. Belief in the bleeding of the victim in the presence of the attacker was promoted by legal, medical and religious authorities for its ability to induce confessions, as the step before torture. *Effusio* or *eiaculatio sanguinis, ius feretri, Bahrprobe,* and bier test were among the expressions for the physical event of sanguis emission by the corpse, and for its legal environment.

The pioneering scholar of medical forensics Paolo Zacchia (1584-1659) addressed the validity of "sanguis flowing from the murdered in the presence of the murderer" to support the presumption of guilt, with numerous citations from classical, medieval and contemporary writers.[11] Zacchia assumed, as did Libavius, whom he quotes extensively, that cruentation did take place. He was not as occupied as Libavius was with the reasons for the phenomenon or the nature of sanguis that prompted it to happen. He analyzed the variables of the death in relation to the exhibit of the corpse: how long after death the corpse would still bleed, how copiously and from which apertures, what was the relationship with the person who activated the bleeding, how much different causes of death-stabbing with a blade, strangulation, poisoning-activated the bleeding.

Zacchia sought a schematic that would allow the known fact of cruentation to be most effectively applied, to give the method a scientific rigor more likely to impress the guilty party with its infallibility. Zacchia did not personally witness any cases of its application.

All writers who recurred to cruentation assumed that it did take place, and cited reported instances without having witnessed one themselves. They sought empirical explanations rather than relying on the assumption that the blood itself was alive or under the influence of invisible beings. Yet maintaining the belief that it constituted one strong evidence of guilt, that it could identify the murderer by proximity alone and induce a confession, perpetuated a mystique that surrounded cruentation with its own peculiar science of the life force, similar to what later surrounded vampires, who were taken by some to exhibit cruentation.

Two examples of cruentation follow, one of them induced and witnessed by officials, the other a fictional play with cruentation belief.

---

[1] Roche (1922) contains photographs of all 92 medallions, also on view at http://data.bnf.fr/12384723/pierre_roche/

[2] Capes (1807: 52)

[3] Boureau (1999: 251)

[4] Bartlett (2013:25)

[5] Vincensini (2005: 840) quoting Titulo II, Quaestio XXIV of Roger's *Quodlibeta* (Etzkorn and Brady, eds. 1968: 281)

[6] *Revue Thomiste* 100 (2000): 657

[7] B. Aegidius Columna (1646: 339-40), *Quodlibeta*, Quodlibet Quintum, Quaestio II Quodlibeti XXV

[8] Thorndike (1941: 238)

[9] Libavius (1594: 100) Theses 6 and 7.

[10] Libavius (1594: 190)

[11] Zacchia (1726: 387-91) *De sangue manante ab Occiso coram Occisore, de ejus veritate, ac de praesumptione inde deducta contra homicidii reum*/On sanguis flowing from the Murdered in the presence of the Murderer, on its veracity, and on the presumption deduced therefrom on the guilt of homicide

Discovery of the murderous deed done by Hans Spiess at Ettiswill. Luzerner Schilling fol. 215b.Hand A: 28. Zemp (1897: 113)

In this illustration, a line drawing based on an illumination in Diebold Schilling's 1513 Lucerne chronicle, the neighbors have arrived in the rustic bedroom of Margret Spiess to find her lying dead beneath the covers on her rope mattress bedstead. The gestures and positioning of the two women at bedside reflect the figures in the Crucifixion scene visible hanging on the wall to the left of the bed. Another women looks out the open shutter toward the wood pile suggesting that it was found open. Two men in doublets, one of them barefoot, enter at a fast pace, expressions of astonishment on their faces. Beneath the bed is a wooden chamber pot with handle; at the bed's foot a four-legged coffer.

Schilling's written entry does not dwell on this scene in as much detail as the illumination. His account and language resemble an unillustrated earlier account, the 1507 Basel chronicle of Petermann Etterlin, which was composed four years after the 1503 events.[1]

They both tell of Margret's husband, Hans Spiess (Hans "Pike"), a mercenary in foreign wars, who returned to the Willisau district in the canton of Lucerne and without visiting his wife went on a spree of drinking, eating and gambling in the town, all charged to her account, leaving her impoverished. He told her he would come by night to her house and reimburse her for the expenses. She lived in the Ettiswill settlement among neighbors known for their generosity. After consuming the meal Margret prepared, the couple went to bed. As she lay in bed he suffocated her by holding a pillow over her mouth, and tried to make the death look like an accident. He left the house and returned to the town where he acted as if nothing had happened.

Neighbors came to Margret's house planning to share warmed wine and food, but when the day passed and she did not appear they entered her room where they found her dead with no sign of wounds. Her remains were soon brought to the church and buried. Murmurs spread from Ettiswill to Lucerne of the debts Hans owed his wife and that he was visiting her on the night of her death. The authorities apprehended him and brought him to the tower in Willisau where, beaten nearly to death, "the will was strong in him that he would not renounce his claim."

Therefore, "a strong device was made against him," and "according to the recognized ordeal," the woman was disinterred and laid out on a bier. Shaved and naked, held by a rope fastened by the hangman to his leg like a pig, he was driven ahead to the churchyard where the corpse lay. The procedure set down in writing was for him to place his right hand on the corpse and swear by God and the saints he was innocent of the crime.

As Hans Spiess approached, the woman began to foam at the mouth, increasing the closer he came. He kneeled at the side of the body; blood poured from her in such a quantity that it overran the sides of the bier. He quickly confessed that he had suffocated her with a pillow, and begged for mercy. Honest people who had been called to witness confirmed that this had happened. The confessed murderer was broken on the wheel (fastened to a large wheel and beaten), dying with great remorse, and the woman was returned to her grave. The almighty and compassionate God, the chronicle concludes, does not allow good to go unrewarded and crime to go unpunished. The "right word" for this is, "No murder long remains concealed."

How Hans Spiess of Ettiswill was subjected to the bier-proof.
Schilling (1862: 164)

This print based on another of the miniatures in Schilling's illuminated chronicle fills the frame with the buildings of the town as shorn, naked and tethered Hans Spiess faces the bleeding corpse of his wife in the churchyard. Witnesses stand in awe of the divinely caused signs of his guilt. Another illumination paired with this one has his broken body deposited on the ground below the wheel of his punishment.

Valerius Anshelm's 1527 Bern chronicle repeats the same report (*Von einem wunderbaren Mort-Handel*, On a wondrous death investigation) in similar language but without many of the details of Hans Spiess' treatment.[2] At the end Anshelm cites the crying out of the blood of the slain Abel in the Biblical Book of Genesis, a primal demonstration of God's not allowing a murderer to conceal his crime. The sign reveals the consistency of divine justice through time.

Anshelm succinctly identifies Hans Spiess at the beginning of his entry as a warrior, fornicator, gambler and glutton (*Krieger, Hurer, Splier, Prasser*), which juxtaposes several of the deadly sins with his profession, using words that Etterlin and Schilling also use, except fornicator (*Hurer*). For the first two chroniclers he is just a mercenary (*Kriegs Knächt*) returned from campaigns (*Reise*), who throws himself into gambling and overconsumption in the town at his neglected wife's expense. He isn't labeled with the vices from the start.

For the Swiss, mercenaries did not have the negative connotations they acquired for other peoples. Men from the Swiss cantons, some of which formed a Confederacy (*Eidgenossenschaft*), had for centuries served as fighters for hire in the wars of neighboring states. They perfected a tactic of advancing on an enemy in formation using a long-shafted pike (*Spiess*) which made them very effective skirmishers much in demand.[3] Participation in warfare for hire required bravery, reliability and a nation-based esprit de corps, coupled with a degree of independence. The captain was usually the chief official in the town the band of mercenaries came from; he often occupied that position because of his prowess as a soldier.

They accepted pay as a group, and scorned anyone tempted to take money to betray the name of their employer. The war from which Hans Spiess returned to Lucerne was likely the struggle of Ludovico Sforza to secure the Duchy of Milan against forces supporting the claims of Louis XII of France (the Second Italian War, 1499-1504). Ludovico hired Swiss pikesmen, but so did his opponents, and when the Swiss recognized that they would be fighting each other they agreed not to fight at all.[4] A Swiss fighter who betrayed Ludovico attempting to flee in disguise was tried, convicted and executed by the Swiss governing body in 1503, the same year Hans Spiess was brought to justice. Sometime later the Swiss armies joined to take control of the process of installing the Duke.

This joint refusal to fight may explain why Hans Spiess did not have pay or booty to bring to his wife, and instead of attending to her as a returning soldier was expected, went on a binge for which she was accountable. The mercenaries maintained their position in the community and therefore their identity as soldiers through respect for sacralized kinship and marriage bonds despite their long absences. The image of the roistering veteran back from the wars is of limited applicability.

Hans Spiess violated those bonds by neglecting his wife, repeatedly named a "good woman" (*guot frouw*), and exploiting the trust she had built among merchants and inn-keepers. He compounded his violation by entering her house on the pretext of making restitution for his debts, consuming a meal she had prepared and smothering her in the conjugal bed. His final act of disdain for civil society was to try to evade punishment by concealing his crime.

The neighbors in the small and mutually supportive settlement of Ettiswill where she lived quickly linked the prodigal husband to the demise of the wife, and were not deceived by the lack of signs of violence on her body. The woman looking out the window in Schilling's illumination is the visual representation of this communal vigilance.

Hans Spiess' intransigence even under judicial torture caused those who apprehended and imprisoned him to resort to an ordeal (*urteil*). Secular authorities, represented by sword-bearing men, were in charge of the investigation, though the burial and the bier were on church grounds. The hangman, clearly not a cleric, both is named and is shown in the illustration holding the rope that restrains Hans Spiess like an animal being brought to market. He is shorn and naked without accoutrements to define and protect him.

The reaction of the corpse as he approaches, spewing at the mouth and bleeding copiously though not wounded, after twenty days of interment, is God's sign Hans Spiess is guilty, which then precipitates his confession and execution. The breath and the blood, the two tangible forces of life, bear witness against Hans Spiess. To execute him without a confession, guilt proven or not, would condemn him for all eternity with no hope of redemption. A Roman Catholic priest is present in the miniature of his execution, to hear his confession and administer last rites.

The ordeal, one of several judicial techniques to place the accused in a condition that would induce a confession, was conducted as "written" (*geschriben*), that is, as set down in the records of the community and not just spoken custom. Etterlin and Schilling refer to it as an urteil only, a word that Anshelm does not use. In the 19th century transcription of Schilling's chronicle the miniature of the approach to the bier (see illustration above) is captioned with the word *Bahrprobe*, bier-test. That was a classification of the ordeal described in the chronicle according to a history of law developed centuries afterward.

The first two chronicles, ending in 1507 and 1513 respectively, focused on events in Lucerne, while Anshelm's later chronicle concerns Berne, from its founding to 1536. After an early life as a soldier, Petermann Etterlin was appointed town scribe and then town chronicler of Lucerne. Diebold Schilling, the Younger was the nephew of a man of the same name who served as a town official and scribe, and produced illuminated chronicles for Berne, Spiez and Zurich in the 1480's.

The town authorities of Lucerne imprisoned the younger Schilling, an ordained priest, for behavior not unlike that he ascribed to Hans Spiess, and after his release required him to say a mass each year for the soul of a man he killed. He took his account of the Spiess affair from Etterlin but added some details in the miniatures he painted for the book.

The great difference between the authors of the first two chronicles and Valerius Anshelm is that Anshelm was a Protestant sympathizer as the Reformation spread to Switzerland. He returned to Berne after the city became Protestant in 1528 and in addition to composing the city chronicle served as city physician. He took his information about Hans Spiess from the chronicles of Lucerne, which remained Catholic and loyal to the Pope.[5] Anshelm cast his considerably reduced account of the ordeal as a manifestation of divine intervention in human affairs without the communal paraphernalia of the Catholic city.

The decayed corpse of Margreta Spiess-the chroniclers make it clear there was no remarkable preservation-reacted to the approach of Hans Spiess not out of revenge or recognition of his presence but as a sign from God, to whom Hans had sworn his innocence. The spit and blood, which would not normally emerge from a twenty day-old corpse, were not controlled by the spirit of the dead woman. They were memorable effects God commanded and humans witnessed.

The proverb Etterlin quotes at the end, the German equivalent of Chaucer's "Modre wol out, that see we day by day," is given a Protestant Old Testament turn by Anshelm's citation of Abel's crying blood. Anshelm advances a vengeance interpretation of the bleeding which the earlier chroniclers do not explicitly support. The corpse's response is a sign (*zeichen*) from God which the ordeal is intended to place the accused in a position to call forth (as only he can).

One of the earliest historical accounts of this ordeal, a narrative rather than a formula, is in the second volume of Aegidius Tschudi's *Chronicon Helveticum,* which covers the period from 1415 to 1460. On November 29, 1417 the provost of Lucerne was murdered. In December the unburied corpse was placed on a bier under the open sky.[6] "And the murderer was tried (*verurteilt*) on the wheel. The corpse began to bleed and was as red and as full (*schön*) as if he were alive. 300 people stood by the corpse and saw all of this. The murderer was set upon the wheel and the corpse of the provost was buried."

This entry has several elements in common with the Hans Spiess case: the exposed corpse bleeding in the presence of the murderer; the witnesses; the wheel punishment. The murderer is already known and the bleeding is not used to ascertain his identity. Inducing his repentance is not mentioned but likely assumed. The several days old corpse now filling with blood is a wonder which can only be viewed under the circumstances as verified by the witnesses.

Tschudi wrote his chronicle, in effect the first general history of the Swiss states, in the mid-15th century looking back to events the latest of which Tschudi could not have witnessed or recorded from witnesses. He was later discovered to be an unreliable and manipulative source with the aim of aggrandizing his own family. Yet the resolution of the murder of the provost of Lucerne, not reported elsewhere, resonates with the truth of sacred history which is further transacted by later chroniclers who repeat this story, among others, in the chronicle of humans before God.

The late 19th century historian Jakob Baechtold studying the application of the bahrprobe in Switzerland, in addition to the instances above, found one in the handwritten notes of the Lucerne schoolmaster Hans Golder for the year 1528.[7] The very brief account ends with "no sign" appearing on the corpse when the accused approached. In 1534 the Lucerne chronicler, dramatist and mercenary Hans Salat recounted the ordeal of Toni Späni accused of murdering his wife: "*schwur er, aber kam kein zeichen*," "he swore the oath, but no sign came." Another murder ordeal by oath before the corpse Salat witnessed that same year had the same outcome.

Baechtold believed that the bahrprobe was a formula applied to circumstances yielding a consistent outcome in cases from across Switzerland and in German speaking world. He cited a common Germanic tradition visible in the *Nibelungenlied* and local law codes as early as the 14th century. It was a mechanism for bringing forth an astonishing act of God leading to confession and redemption based on a pagan precedent.

 The earliest examples were of the probe yielding blood and the admission of the murderer. They were evidence of a communal tradition centering on historic events in which the murderer was forced to confess by swearing his innocence before the bier of his presumed victim. Those positive results then laid the basis for ordeals in which the charged party was exonerated by the lack of bleeding. The image of the blooded corpse was so compelling that the absence of the sign was a sign of the absence, of guilt.

Some Swiss towns, Lucerne included, wrote the ordeal into their legal code. The *Landrecht von Schwyz* included an urteil of the corpse in 1342. The *Formelbuch* compiled by Batt Rippel in 1542 for Lucerne spells out the procedure: the bier under the open sky and the naked accused on his knees, the prayers to be said in making the oath and the words to be uttered as the accused places his hand on the corpse.[8] In 1554 it was noted that though the procedure was written down and known by many it was no longer applied to specific cases.[9] It still was not designated by a unique name.

Baechtold concluded that it ceased to be practiced by the end of the 16th century due to opposition from the churches, both Protestant and Roman Catholic. It seemed less a miracle of God and more a form of magic conducted outside the precincts of faith and state. The accused went naked to prevent him from concealing magic in his hair that would befuddle the witnesses or hold back the sign. How could those conducting the ordeal believe this if it was a sign from God they were seeking? This ordeal, like others, moved into the province of folklore, beliefs of an earlier age retained by ignorant rural people. It was found at first in the countryside and only later in the chronicles and laws of the cities.[10]

The ordeal was a strategy for extracting a public confession by playing upon the credulity of the guilty party when there was insufficient evidence to convict him. The confession he was tricked into making would preserve his immortal soul from damnation. Three levels of engagement were present in the ordeal: the observable blood and breath of the corpse; the susceptibility of the guilty party to belief ascribing their movement to a signifying divine intervention; and the framework of judgment and punishment surrounding the whole.

Hans Spiess was the returning husband who partook of his wife's bounty, her credit in town, the meal she provided and sexual relations, following which he murderously suffocated her. Despite his intransigence on being accused as the obvious perpetrator, he was forced into a confession when the corpse began to foam at the mouth and bleed copiously on his approach. Hans Spiess took the livelihood and life of his wife, and on the most basic level of observation was accused by signs of blood and breath visible to all.

The ordeal was recorded by chroniclers as a series of events that actually occurred. The aim was to pry a confession from the suspect, whose immortal soul was at stake if he continued to deny his deed. It was most important that Hans Spiess accept in public that the motility of blood from a victim who was not wounded was in response to his guilty presence. Cynically or not, officials used the belief to achieve the formal end of a confession. Later uses of the ordeal exonerated the accused because the blood did not flow. The framing story was a means of social control that used a belief about blood to restore order disturbed by a death.

The enactment of a belief about bleeding after death leading to condemnation of an individual under the supervision of civic officials is a pattern that will recur.

---

[1] Schilling (1862: 163-65); Etterlin (1764: 264-67)

[2] Anshelm (1527: 254)

[3] McCormack (1993: 13-14)

[4] Groebner (2002: 99)

[5] So loyal that from 1548 until the present most of the captains of the Papal Guard have been from Lucerne.
McCormack (1993: 204)

[6] Tschudi (1736: 90).

[7] Baechtold (1889: 224)

[8] Segesser (1854: 2, 702 n.1) quotes the 1568 version; Baechtold (1889: 223-24) quotes the 1542 version

[9] Hoffman-Krayer (1974: 1049-50)

[10] Löwenstimm (1897) marvels that a number of the barbarous peasant customs he describes were worked into early legal codes.

6. The accusing corpse

Yvain pursues the wounded Esclados to his castle, and is trapped at the entrance when a portcullis drops down before him and another behind him, cleaving his horse in half. He would have been doomed to capture were it not for the maid Lunete, who gives him a ring that renders him invisible and enables him to escape to the interior of the castle. Undetected, Yvain watches the funeral procession of Esclados, who has died of his wounds.

Esclados' wife Laudine, walking in the procession, enraptures the concealed Yvain. The corpse begins to bleed anew, which to the castle attendants can only mean that the master's killer is among them undetected. They begin a frantic search without finding the unseen knight. With the help of Lunete, Yvain makes himself known to Laudine in her chamber, and quickly convinces her to marry him, making him the master of the castle. He then leaves for more adventures.

Several themes in this passage from the Arthurian verse romance, *Yvain, le Chevalier au Lion* (*Yvain, the Knight of the Lion*) would not strike contemporary (1170's) listeners as unusual. The hunt for a killer; the mediacy of a clever servant; one knight assuming a defeated adversary's property and wife; the fascinating draw of a woman. The author of the romance, Chrétien de Troyes, might expect his audience to marvel at his brisk interweaving of marvels into dramatic plot support.

The ring of invisibility (a clever servant might have independent uses for such a device) enables Yvain to be charmed by his fallen adversary's consort, and in turn allows him to set off the bleeding without facing the consequences. In the text (lines 1179-1185)[1]

And the procession passed,
but in the room amassed
around the bier a great assembly
who saw warm blood, clear and vermillion,
rise from the corpse around the wound;
and this was true proof
that then was near, without doubt,
the one who had made battle,
killed and conquered him.

Wendelin Foerster headed this page of his edition of the text of *Yvain, Die Blutprobe,* The Bloodproof, equating the event with the judicial ordeal not being applied here. Chrétien uses a plural noun and adjectives (*sans, chauz, clers, vermauz*) to capture the vital multiplicity of the blood(s), which wells out of the wound as from someone alive, though Esclados is pale in death. *Clers* and *vermauz* form a collocution used in other romances by Chrétien to evoke a resplendent sight.[2] Here the dramatic fluid is rising from the body of a dead man. Only the image in the Biblical Book of Genesis of Abel's blood crying out from the earth after his murder by his brother Cain is more pronounced.

Chrétien combines Yvain's invisibility with Esclados' bleeding to unique dramatic effect, precipitating the almost comic confusion as the retainers begin searching for the killer they know is there but cannot see. When Yvain does appear he is the spouse of the dead knight's wife.

65

Laudine appears to the concealed Yvain. She is watched without seeing her watcher, allowing her qualities to enter his eye without bestirring her. She is like many a courtly woman seen by a knight from afar, in a picture, engaged in pious and genteel pastimes.

This contrasts with the bleeding corpse, a *provance*, a proof that acts to disclose the murderer present. Only in this instance he is not captured. The sight of blood momentarily transcends the solemnity of the procession and the mournful beauty of the woman. It is antecedent to the other sights, an engine of action about to be, and an intrusion of divine justice into human affairs, which passes away into the machinations of Yvain's errantry.

The earliest illustrated text of *Yvain*, an illuminated manuscript in the *Bibliotheque Nationale de France*[3], dates from the first half of the fourteenth century, a hundred and fifty years after the composition of the poem. One set of panels (folio 69v) illustrates the battle between Yvain and Esclados, the flight into the palace (including the cleaved horse) leaving Yvain to gaze upon the procession, the meeting with Lunete as Yvain holds a lion skin (from a lion he has slain) close to himself, and the bier of Esclados with Laudine and attendants as the "invisible" Yvain peeks over their shoulders. Esclados lies pale and shrouded. There is no representation of the bleeding wounds. The shroud is firm and uniform about his body.

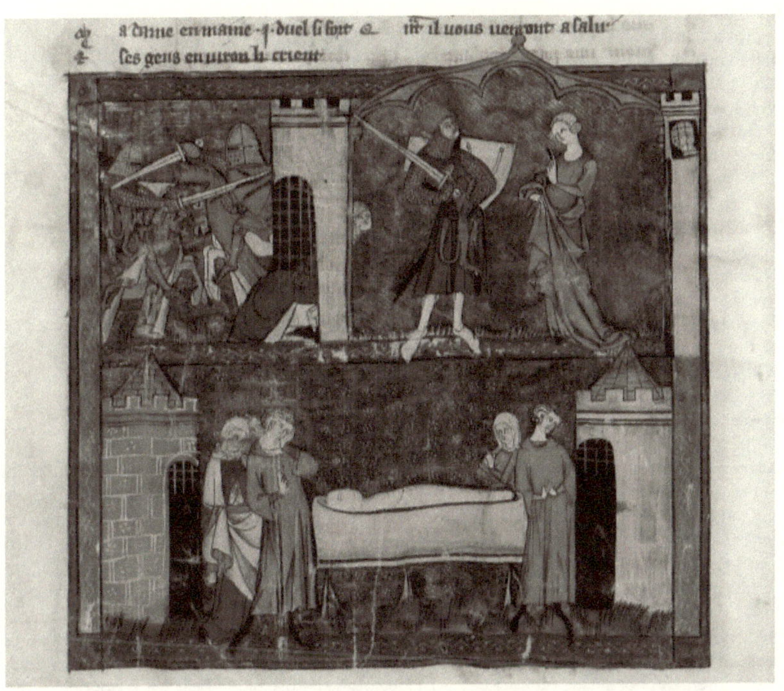

Yvain battles Esclados; is aided by Lunete; Esclados' corpse in state. Folio 69v Bnf fr. 1344.

The text that the illustrations accompany is abridged, and does not include the lines encompassing the ring of invisibility and the search for the lurking killer. This is not the only part of Chrétien's *Yvain* set aside in the illuminated manuscript. Sandra Hindman attributed deferring the marriage of Yvain and Laudine, celebrated before he leaves on his knightly escapades, to an enforcement of the proper order of events in a knight's relations with a lady.[4] In this version only after he has fulfilled his pledge of love with valorous deeds can he return to win her acceptance and join her in bed. One hundred and fifty years after the poem was written, Yvain's perfidy entered an ellipsis.

The first complete rewrite of *Yvain*, by the Lyon courtier and medievalist Pierre Sala, was presented to King François I in 1522 under the title *Le chevalier au lion*, making Chrétien's subtitle the main title, in the form of a manuscript with illustrations. Sala didn't have the text printed but intentionally preserved the hand lettered form with this as with his other antiquarian remakings of 13th century Arthurian romances. The French king found himself addressed in the new title as the Lion Knight, guardian of Sala's native city of Lyon.

Sala remade Chrétien's *Yvain* to satisfy both the nostalgia for knightly virtues and the preference for narrative coherence fostered by print culture. He fashioned a 12th century vision of the 9th century for a 16th century audience. *Le chevalier au lion* is a verse novel based upon *Yvain* with some filling in rather than abridgement. After placing his focus on the funeral procession and the beauty of the disconsolate Laudine, Sala sharpened the scene where the invisible Yvain causes the corpse of Esclados to bleed anew.[5]

For, when the corpse was at the place
Where mylord Yvain is,
Each one saw clearly and at once
That in the head the scalp was opened
And a great amount of blood came from the wound
From which was well known
That the knight was there
Who had slain and conquered him.
As soon as they recognized that
Speaking, they all began to move.

A scene of confusion follows with Sala comparing the attendants to blind men flailing about trying to find the unseen killer. Sala fully accepts that his own audience, like Chrétien's, would consider any sudden bleeding of a corpse to mark the presence of its murderer. He glosses the original text "*provance,*" "proof," with the verb "*coneust,*" "recognized." Archaic beliefs validate current beliefs. Sala does not retain the language emphasizing the brilliance and color of the blood, only its quantity, and he specifies the location of the wound. The emphasis has shifted to recognition of what the blood flow means, to the reaction of the crowd and to Laudine.

Subsequent translations of *Yvain* into modern French, German, English and other languages retained Sala's *Le chevalier au lion* retitling. Reworkings and romanticizations, especially those made for children, did not always repeat Sala's tolerance of the corpse blood belief. It is not one of the marvels associated with the fictive world of knights and ladies, however much bloodshed is otherwise represented.[6]

The Middle High German adaptation of *Yvain*, entitled *Iwein, der Löwenritter* (around 1200), was the last of four Arthurian narrative poems by the knight-retainer and Crusader, Hartmann von Aue. Hartmann's German reflects the same 9th century Celtic court and adventuring life in 12th century vernacular as does Chrétien's French, augmented with new lines containing the author's comments and emendations. Arthur's court and Iwein's relations with other knights and with ladies is as fraught with backbiting and betrayal as Yvain's, with an added emphasis on sin and redemption. Hartmann's elaboration of the funeral of Askalon (his name for Esclados) does not envision the wounds themselves. He specifies a belief that was only implied by the reaction of the retainers to the sight of the bleeding in *Yvain.*[7]

Now among us is the saying
Many take for the truth,

Who has slain another,
And is brought to him,
However long before he was wounded,
He begins to bleed anew.
Now is seen, also begin
His wounds to bleed.
So was sought in the palace
Who was among them, who killed him.

Ludine (Laudine) exclaims that the killer has clouded their senses and is among them still. Hartmann enunciates as a common saying the belief that is implicit in the crowd's reaction to the new bleeding. The corpse bears witness to the one who caused the bleeding in the first place. It ceases to be just a visual spectacle and becomes an oral tradition. The absence of a visible stranger who must be the cause of the bleeding is explained by magic. This magic originated within the household, provided to Iwein by the servant Lunete whom Iwein had previously helped out of a compromising situation at King Arthur's court. It not only saves Iwein but allows him to insinuate himself beside Ludine, whom he could never approach in his visible form.

Hartmann's poem has not been the basis of as many translations into modern languages as *Yvain*.[8] Another Middle High German work of the 13th century that harks back to the 9th century also contains a scene of murderer-induced corpse bleeding in a context different from *Yvain/Iwein*.

The *Nibelungenlied* is an epic poem by an unidentified author, gathered from a number of manuscripts and homogenized into several modern German translations, which in turn have been translated into other languages. Its status as the national epic of German speakers made it especially attractive to cultural and political nationalists from the early 19th century onward.

For the first time in any literary work a protagonist calls for those present to pass before the bier of the slain hero and prove their innocence of his ambush murder, by subjecting themselves to the ordeal.[9]

They denied it, resistant; Kriemhild began to speak:
"Who knows himself to be innocent, show it here and now;
He will go to the bier, before all the people here,
So thereby the truth, his speech can reveal.

That is a great wonder, that often takes place,
If the death-sullied murderer stands by the corpse
So the wounds will bleed, as they did before.
Whereupon the guilt of death was seen on Hagen.

The wounds flowed as heavily as they did before.
Those who mourned earlier, now they mourned much more.
Thus spoke King Gunther, now I say to you:
"Robbers killed him, Hagen didn't do it."

"Oh, yes, the robbers are well known to me," said she.
"Now let God avenge it, through his friends' hand!
Gunther and Hagen, they did it."
So for Siegfried's retainers, now the battle will begin.

Kriemhild has challenged Hagen to prove his innocence, She and Siegfried's followers know
Hagen is the assassin. He speared Siegfried from behind while he bent to drink from a spring.
The thrust of the spear, according to the poem (stanza 981 "), caused Siegfried's heart's blood to
spring out upon Hagen's clothing.

As the lord Siegfried, from the river drank
Hagen shot him through the cross, so that from the wound sprang
The blood from his heart, up onto Hagen's clothes
So great a crime, did no hero any time.

The test of bleeding is again not given a name, and instead of being cited as a principle of
the ordeal it is stated as a fact of history. A wonder, and a fact: the corpse recalls the moment of
the wounding in the presence of the killer. King Gunther denies that Hagen is responsible for
Siegfried's death. He is complicit in Siegfried's murder himself, as is Kriemhild unknowingly, and
wants to forestall the reckoning which will mean bloodshed in the palace.

Andreas Heusler, a commentator on the *Nibelungenlied* texts, contended that the trial before
Siegfried's corpse was imported by the author of the text that contains it from *Iwein*.[10] The
Hundeshagen Handschrift (1436-40), the only continuously illustrated version of the *Nibelungenlied,*
does not contain a verbal or pictorial reference to it.[11] One of the woodblock prints
accompanying the text shows Kriemhild aghast when, as a bloodied Hagen and Gunther watch,
she discovers the corpse of Siegfried laid at her door. Another shows her seated as Hagen kneels
before the dead Siegfried who bleeds from the spear wound and at the neck.[12]

Kriemhild seated, gazing at the blood-marked Hagen kneeling at Siegfried's bleeding corpse.
Hundeshagen Handschrift. Staatsbibliothek zu Berlin

The manuscript now designated *Handschrift C* (1230), the earliest of the three complete texts from
the period soon after the poem's composition (1190-1200), does contain this episode and formed
the basis for Bartsch's 1867 modern German translation. All told there are 38 manuscripts of the

Nibelungelied known (not all extant), 11 of which are complete, which can be divided into two major groupings ultimately based on widespread oral traditions.[13]

There has not been a survey of the occurrence of the corpse bleeding episode in these manuscripts. Its presence or absence in the many later iterations of the epic is due both to the sources available, the biases and preferences of the authors/composers/artists. Some believed that its presence made their presentation more "authentic," others didn't. Since it was in Bartsch's translation and Zarncke's transcription, both of which went through numerous editions from the mid-19th century onward, some of them school texts, it is likely that many people at least were aware of it and fixed it as a component of the *Nibelungenlied.*

By the middle of the 17th century printers were turning out chapbooks titled with some variant of the "history of the horned Siegfried," based on a song that followed the hero's adventures. Siegfried was "*gehörnte*" by the dragon's blood that gave him invulnerability over most of his body by turning his skin thick and horny. The woodcuts sometimes interspersed through the chapbook texts identify him wearing a helmet with two horns.[14]

The song and the chapbooks end with Siegfried's death, run through with a rapier by an unnamed antagonist or by Hagen. The aftermath is the rapid demise of chivalry and the sickness and death of the king and Siegfried's beloved, Florigunda.

A two part "folk novel" *Der gehörnte Siegfried* was the last work (1783) of the theologian and collector of student lore Christian Wilhelm Kindleben. His Siegfried goes through an extended version of the horned hero's adventures: he is a king at the time of his immemorial spring-side backstabbing. At the very end Kindleben adds a sentence on the downfall of Siegfried's assassin in the war that follows: "he died in the most miserable way, for he had to die a slow death from the wounds he received without doctor or aid."[15] A faint echo of Siegfried's lingering and repeated bleed-out.

Old Norse and Icelandic sagas containing Nibelung tales were transcriptions of these manuscripts and emergent scholarly studies of "Teutonic mythology" attempted to position the German epic as Homeric, as well as a reflection of an underlying *Volk* spirit.[16] This was the environment in which Richard Wagner outlined the drama (*Siegfrieds Tod*) that was to become *Die Gotterdammerung,* the fourth opera of the *Ring den Nibelungen* cycle and the only one based on the *Nibelungenlied.*[17]

Wagner concentrated on the ring fashioned from the gold hoard of the Nibelungs, the unifying theme of the four operas of the "Ring" cycle, culminating in the death of Siegfried and Hagen's confessed guilt without reference to Siegfried's wounds. The hand of the corpse rises when Hagen reaches to remove the ring he has long sought. The Rhine maidens rise on the flood to reclaim the ring and submerge Hagen, and the flames of Siegfried's pyre rise to the hall of the gods.

A three-part dramatization, *Die Nibelungen* (1862) by Friedrich Hebbel, preceded both Bartsch's translation and the premiere of Wagner's Ring cycle in 1876. Near the end of the second part (Siegfried's Tod) Hagen approaches the bier of Siegfried (Act 5, Scene 9: lines 1090-96) and the Chaplain speaks, commenting on what others have registered but no one has named.[18]

Chaplain
It is the finger of God
That quietly bathes in these holy wells
For He must write a sign of Cain.

Hagen (leans over the coffin)
The red blood! I didn't believe it!
Now I see it with my own eyes.

Kriemhild
And you don't cringe?
(leaps toward him)
Now off with you, you devil!
Who knows if each drop doesn't pain him?
The drops your murderous nearness releases.

Hebbel has drawn out the few Christian allusions in the manuscripts of the epic and introduced the character of the Chaplain, who gives a figurative and Biblical rendition of what Hagen plainly states without acknowledging the crime the Chaplain implies. The enraged and confrontational Kriemhild attempts to drive Hagen off. For her the blood is not just a sign of the killer's proximity; it marks the suffering of Siegfried as long as Hagen remains nearby. The crowd of witnesses and the evocation of a widespread belief are absent; Hagen himself doesn't believe that the corpse is bleeding until he approaches the coffin.

Die Nibelungen was the last of Hebbel's dramas and is the most frequently performed. It gave the national epic a form that could be designed and enacted on the stage, parallel to and in competition with Wagner's Ring operas.

From the time of the manuscripts onward scenes in the *Nibelungenlied* were taken as the subject of drawings, prints, paintings and sculptures. Artists chose specific events-the spearing of Siegfried was popular[19]-or fashioned sequences, often as illustrations for the many translations of the poem.

The Swiss-English artist Henry Fuseli exhibited in the 1820 Royal Academy show the last of his *Nibelungenlied* evocations:[20]

291 Chriemhild, the widow of Siegfrid the Swift, exposes his body, assisted by Sigmond his father, King of Belgium, in the minster at Worms, and swearing to his assassination, challenges Hagen Lord of Trony, and Gunther King of Burgandy, her brother, to approach the corpse, and on the wounds beginning to flow, charges them with his murder.—Lied der Nibelunge, Aventure XVII. 4085. &c.   H. Fuseli, R. A.

I have not found the location of the original or any reproductions of this painting. Visitors to the exhibition mention it.[21] This description is repeated in the list of paintings in Fuseli's biography but it is not included in present-day catalogues of Fuseli's works. Between 1805 and 1820 Fuseli made several other works from *Nibelungenlied* episodes, most of them centered on Kriemhild. In one painting she has thrown herself onto the body of the slain Siegfried almost fusing with him; in another she stands towering above the kneeling Siegfried engulfing him as she holds his head in her hands. Kriemhild Dreams of the Dead Siegfried with a hint of his blood on her clothing as she reclines in Fuseli's gray-wash night space. Her dead husband is shown in a distant circle. An athletic male nude approaches stage left.

The most comprehensive *Nibelungenlied* illustration project ever undertaken were the *Nibelungensäle* of the Munich *Residenz*. Julius Schnorr von Carolsfeld labored on this sequence of frescos for forty years (1827-67), during the reigns of three kings of Bavaria: Ludwig I, who commissioned the frescos in 1827 and though forced to abdicate in 1848, lived to see them completed during the reign of his grandson, Ludwig II, a patron of Wagner. Each stage of the epic was given its own room. The Saal des Verraths (Room of Treason) was decorated with the planning, execution and aftermath of Hagen's plot against Siegfried.

Carolsfeld's interpretation of Hagen's advent at Siegfried's bier fills a portion of the fourth wall of this room. The cartoons (base drawings) for the frescos were reproduced as illustrations for a *Nibelungenlied* translation published in 1840, the centennial of the epic's rediscovery.[22] A haughty Hagen stands forward of the scene, his left hand grasping the hilt of his sheathed sword. He looks back at Kriemhild leveling her right hand at him as her left reaches down toward the unseen left side of the clad Siegfried supine upon a stone table. Gunther bends to examine Siegfried's side away from the viewer. An acolyte swings a censor as he climbs the stairway toward a landing where monks sing the requiem mass and a bell ringer tolls the chapel bell. The architecture and the garb of the figures place the scene in Renaissance Florence, where the Roman Catholic ritual favored by the Catholic monarchs of Bavaria would be in place.

The same style and setting pervades all the paintings and cartoons of the *Nibelungensäle*. The text remains the same, but the intrigues and rivalries among the Nibelungs, Burgundians and Huns have acquired an Italian courtly veneer in the visualizing. Siegfried visually bleeds in the presence of Hagen only by connection to the text. The illustration is less diffuse than the original fresco, which does not call attention to Siegfried's wounds at all. No one is looking at them, hidden as they are. In the presence of the text some attention had to be directed to the subject.

195
Da sprach der König Gunther:
„Ich will's Euch zeigen an,
Ihn erschlagen Schächer,
Hagen hat es nicht gethan." —

„Wir sind die Schächer,"
Sprach er, „wohl bekannt:
Nun lasse Gott es rächen
Noch seiner Freunde Hand:
Gunther und Hagen,
Ja! habt Ihr das gethan!"
Da kam die Sigfrids Degen
Starke Lust zu streiten an.

Compare Carolsfeld's rendition of the scene with that of F.W. Gubitz for an 1840 translation.[23]

Gubitz was a printmaker and man of letters. As editor of the literary journal *Gesellschaft* he published (with judicious censorship) the first poems of Heinrich Heine. Heinrich Beta's "Bedeutschung" (Germanization), titled *Das Nibelungenlied als Volksbuch (The Nibelungenlied as Folk Composition)*, was a rendition of the original poem in contemporary German imbued with the metre and syllabification of the old heroic songs.[24] The woodcuts carry the drumming rhythm of the verse.

Siegfried is laid out on a bed chest carved with vaguely visible "Teutonic" ornament. The left side of his bare torso is exposed to reveal a dark stream downward from the point of the exit

76

wound. His pale body is framed by the arch of Kriemhild's arm and pointing finger, and the dark figure of Hagen in a belted tunic bearing the gryphon device of Burgundy repeated at the peak of his helmet. His facial features are obscured, his arms flared in a gesture of denial, but a dagger is showing at his hip. Gunther in crown and royal robes raises an arm to halt the agitation, but the attention of the crowd is on Kriemhild-Hagen.

This series to which this print belongs introduces the gothic mode of *Nibelungenlied* representation from the ponderous beat of the poetry to the heavy furnishings of the space where the characters act. If the scene takes place in a church the superstructure is not evident, and the attempt of the secular authority to restrain vengeance is evanescent. The wound is not hidden.

Heine had written of the *Nibelungenlied* seven years before this translation was published:[25]

"It is a speech of stone and the verses are similarly rhymed quatrains. Here and there, from the columns, flow red flowers like drops of blood, or drop down long trains of ivy like green tears. Of the grand passions moving in this poem you form a small enough notion like tiny people."

Carolsfeld's Renaissance setting of Siegfried's funeral conceals the hero's blood by making it Catholic and monumental. Folk Gothic had already been established as the style and mood of the song for an emergent, progressively unifying Germany.

This in turn was subject to revision as the epic became enshrined in a permanent state of present past. A 1907 production of Hebbel's *Die Nibelungen* featured costume and set design by Otto Carl von Czeschka, who also provided illustrations for Franz Keim's 1909 children's book based on the *Nibelungenlied* ("retold to the German people").

Thea von Harbou, who had played Kriemhild in a childhood school production of the *Die Nibelungen*, in 1923 published *Das Nibelungenbuch*. The first edition of the book was printed in Fraktur, and dedicated "to you and Germany," the "you" (*Dir*, familiar) being her husband at the time, the film director Fritz Lang. The book was illustrated with 24 stills from the Decla-Ufa film *Die Nibelungen: Siegfrieds Tod* not yet released. The text showed the influence of Keim, and the costuming of the actors and sets in the stills recalled von Czeschka's designs for the 1907 production and Keim's book. The stills, reflecting the book's dialogue-heavy narrative, depict Siegfried run through with a spear, lying before an altar with a grieving Kriemhild kneeling at his head and Kriemhild discovering the blood spots in the snow where the slain Siegfried fell.

Kriemhild recollects Hagen's arrival in her chamber as she knelt over the body:[26]

Two-fold death this was, for Siegfried and for me. Since the deed was done,
I think only these thoughts.
Blood from wounds began to flow. Hagen Tronje entered my chamber.
Murderer, I cried, and pointed my hand to Hagen.

The following year *Das Nibelungenbuch* was republished by the same press to coincide with the release of the film *Die Nibelungen* in two parts, each over two hours long: *Siegfrieds Tod (Siegfried's Death)* and *Kriemhilds Rache (Kriemhild's Revenge)*. The first showing of the film was accompanied by a 60-musician orchestra playing a score summoning up the music of Wagner's Ring operas in their instrumentation and use of leitmotivs. Jurgen Fehling's 6-hour production of Hebbel's play was on the Berlin stage.[27] Lang, newly a German citizen, and von Harbou, demonstrated their solidarity with the national spirit in its unified political form by placing a wreath on the tomb of Frederick the Great. The *Nibelungenlied* cultural moment took place as Germany reasserted itself in the aftermath of the First World War.

At two hours and thirteen minutes into *Siegfrieds Tod*, Kriemhild is in her chamber kneeling on the floor at the head of the fallen hero, as King Gunther and her brothers stand in attendance. The camera shifts to the open doorway where the shadow of wings cast on the wall precedes the arrival of Hagen in his winged helmet, his black mass filling the doorway. Kriemhild gazes down at Siegfried's bare chest and the exit wound of the spear point Hagen cast into his back. A drop of blood rises and runs down the curve of Siegfried's ribcage.

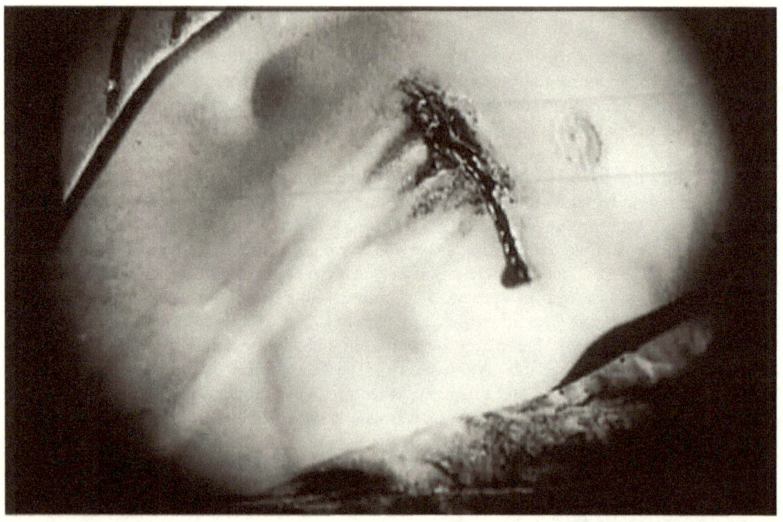

Siegfried's wound bleeds at Hagen's approach. *Die Nibelungen: Siegfried's Tod* (1924)

The tremulous Kriemhild rises and points an accusing finger at Hagen, who remains at the doorway and does not move closer to the corpse. There are no intertitles.

Kriemhild points an accusing finger at the newly arrived Hagen, far left. Gunther stares down.
Die Nibelungen: Siegfrieds Tod

Kriemhild addresses her brother Gunther, pleading with him to punish Hagen, but Gunther positions himself before Hagen, and her brothers join him, forming a defensive barrier. She will work the vengeful destruction of Hagen, her family and herself in the next film.

Das Nibelungenbuch sold 70,000 copies by the mid-1920's, one of the most popular book-movie tie-ins of the time.[28] The film *Die Nibulengen* (especially *Siegfrieds Tod)* was shown often in Europe and America, becoming a factor, for instance, in the return of Wagner's operas to the American stage after the World War I period ban.[29] Hebbel's play continued and continues to be staged in new productions. The Christian orientation of Hebbel's work has at times proven an inconvenience, though not insurmountable. At a Hebbel festival at Bochum during the Nazi era censors required that the reference to Christ at the end of the third part of *Die Nibelungen* be removed.[30]

Editions of the original texts and their translations, often bearing old illustrations or new ones, have continued to be published. A 1982 new translation published simultaneously in East and West German editions was accompanied by 33 illustrations by Ernst Barlach.[31] They have been joined by films, videos, television programs, graphic novels, video games, installations and at least one museum entirely devoted to the *Nibelungenlied,* in Worms, Germany.[32]

The *Yvain, Iwein* and *Nibelungenlied* versions of the corpse bleeding moment are all part of 12th-13th century imaginings of 4th century chivalry preserved as literary works and recreated by later writers as national heritage, politico-familial gamesmanship and adventure stories. The elements of critique of knightly behavior and courtly callousness in Chrétien's and Hartmann's poems have been suppressed as the nobility of the characters in all of them has been heightened to conform to the assumed ethos of the earlier age. The authors of these works looked back to form a critique of their contemporaries while entertaining them. That critique has been remade in the many parodies of Arthurian and Wagnerian heroics in the media today. But corpse bleeding has not been parodied.

None of the authors, medieval or modern, questioned that their predecessors believed that a corpse would bleed in the presence of the assassin. A clear division is visible between the backward-looking authors of the original works, who employ bleeding as a dramatic device, and their 19th-20th century editors, who have a name for the belief to define and explain it, or simply present it as part of the fabric.

Bypassing these later frameworks, which will reassemble as this book progresses, and looking directly at the anachronizing language of the three works, it is possible to distinguish the image when it first explicitly appears in works before print. Chrétien sees (that his predecessors saw) a brilliant fountain of accusatory blood. Hartmann, the *Nibelungenlied* poet and their successors see the resonance of past miracles retained in folk memory as law. The single droplet of dark fluid that issues from Siegfried's wound in the film finalizes this tradition, now part of the décor.

All three verbalize the extraordinary tension in palace life when a death by violence has occurred and a funeral is taking place which might be attended by the killer. The possibility of a revenge cycle circumscribes every action. All three also center on the woman who was married to the dead hero, and who mourns his passing. Yvain is first taken with Laudine when he sees her tearing at her clothing as she stands before the slain Esclados.

The bleeding is shown as reminder of the woman's certainty of the murderer's presence yet helplessness to avenge her husband at the moment. Yvain is invisible and Hagen is untouchable. Eventually this tension is resolved by Laudine marrying Yvain and his engagement in a series of knightly adventures before being reunited with her. Kriemhild marries the King of the Huns, whose soldiers slaughter her feckless Burgundian relatives.

This condition of human relations was familiar to the original authors and their contemporary audience. The status of warrior hero is held in balance throughout. Despite the sign neither Yvain nor Hagen is immediately punished. Both are remarkably free of guilt or shame. Men who fight and kill each other in open combat or by guile enter into relations with those around the dead man. The external appearance of blood at the funeral, which is lost and recovered in this stream of fiction, is the new life they will lead. The murderer's relations with the kin and close friends of the murdered in the remote past meant new blood was injected into the social group in the form of the murderer himself. Revenge was less important than recruitment and continuation of the line. Yvain's marriage to the widow and Hagen's being defended against her by her own (and his own) family are both signs of this.

The re-creations of the stories look backward to fictive times but no longer show even an antiquarian interest in corpse bleeding. It only survives as one more way to show blood outside the body, to motivate an all too comprehensible revenge. Blood had its occasions in the *Nibelunglied* representations but now it has become universalized. There was an alternative version of *Siegfrieds Tod* in which the corpse does not bleed. Michael Manning's 2010 graphic novel *The*

Nibelungen was issued in two versions, one in black and white and the other in a *Blood* version, with the inclusion of red in each scene.

At no point in the long saga of the hero's accusing corpse was there an inquiry into why the corpse bled in the presence of the killer. It was taken as a given and finally as an image of what would have happened under the circumstances. The corpse bleeding and the belief about corpse bleeding were enclosed in a story repeatedly deferred backward to a time when people were thought to believe such things. Putting it in the form of an immemorial story at the roots of nationhood or in the form of judicial procedure linking the historical operations of divine justice with human institutions both place the sanguineous corpse in an eternal present.

Von Harbou 1923

Alternate version. Chest not exposed

---

[1] My English translation from Foerster (1887: 41 and 289-90 notes on toauz and chauz)

Et la processions passa,
Mes anmi la sale amassa
Antor la biere uns granz toauz:
Que li sans chauz, clers et vermauz
Rissi au mort, parmi la plaie,
Et ce fu provance veraie
Qu'ancor estoit leanz sanz faille,
Cil qui feite avoit la bataille
Et qui l'avoit mort et conquis.

Recent English translation: Raffel, trans. (1987: 37)
[2] Gallais (1987: 3, 1838) *Cligès* 2720 to evoke a woman's beauty and *Perceval* 646 an alighting eagle.

82

Vermauz signifies not just a color but the color's resplendence, much as the Russian *krasnyi* means both
"red" and "beautiful."
[3] BnF Français 1433 Le Chevalier au Lion, virtual copy:
http://expositions.bnf.fr/arthur/livres/yvain/index.htm
[4] Hindman (1994: 52)
[5] My English translation from Sala (1966: 28a)

Car, quant le corps fut a l'endroit
De la ou est messire Yvein,
Chescun veit a cler et soudein
Que du test s'entreovrit la taye,
Et sourtit grant sang de la playe.
Pour quoy ont [l. on] coneust a cella
Que le chevallier estoit la
Qui l'avoit navré et conquis.
Adoncq de rechef ilz l'ont quis;
Par leans ont tout remué,

[6] For instance *The Knight with the Lion: The Story of Yvain* "retold and illustrated by John Howe" (1996) does not allude to the bleeding episode in the text or the illustrations.
[7] My English translation from Benecke and Lachmann (1827: 49-50) lines 1355-1364

Nû is dinc geseit
Vil dicke vür die wârheit,
Swer den andern habe erslagen,
Unt wurder zuo ime getragen,
Swie langer dâ vor waere wunt.
Er begunde bluten anderstunt.
Nû seht, alsô begunden
Im bluoten sîne wunden,
Dô man in in das palaz truoc:
Wan er was bî im, der in sluoc.

[8] Hartmann (1979) is the first translation of the text into English.
[9] My translation into English from stanzas 1043-1046 of Bartsch's modern German translation. Bartsch (1867: 158). Zarncke (1875: 158) provides the original text from a manuscript source. Stanza 1043 is slightly different in Bartsch, whose translation used different manuscripts.

‘Dir ist von mînen liuten   leides niht geschehen:’   3
-sprach der künec Günther-   ‘des wil ich dir verjehn.’
‘die wellen sîn unschuldec,   die heizet nâher gên’
-sprach si- ‘zuo der bâre,   daz wir die wârheit verstên.’

Daz ist ein michel wunder,   vil dicke ez noch geschiht: 4
swâ man den mortmeilen   bî dem tôten siht,
sô bluotent im die wunden,   als ouch dâ geschach;
dâ von man die sculde   dâ ze Hagene gesach.

Die wunden vluzzen sêre,   alsô si tâten ê: 5
die ê dâ sêre klageten,   des wart nu michel mê.
dô sprach der künec Gunther   ‘ich wilz iuch wizzen lân:
in sluogen schâchære,   Hagene hât es niht getân.’

[10] Heusler (1969: 132). There is no ring of invisibility in the *Nibelungenlied*, a ring of power being put to other uses there. There is a cap of invisibility, which Siegfried uses in a way similar to Yvain/Iwein's ring.
[11] The Hundeshagen Handschrift illustrations were reproduced as an accompaniment of Simrock's translation.
Simrock, trans. (1924)
[12] Simrock, trans. (1924)
[13] Heinzle (1998)
[14] *Die wunderschöne historie von dem gehörnten Siegfried* (1750) is one example. Golther, ed. (1889) contains
transcriptions of the song and the prose tale but only notes where the woodcut appeared.
[15] Kindleben (1783: 2,338)
[16] Making a national myth from the "ill-suited cloth" of the *Nibelungenlied*. Creating Germany's National Myth:
The Nibelungenlied and its Homerian Context.
http://www.brbl.archive.library.yale.edu/exhibitions/nibelungenlied
[17] Haymes (2010: 1-39)
[18] Hebbel (1862: 4, 173-337) Die Nibelungen, Zweiter Teil: Siegfrieds Tod
www.nibelungenrezeption.de/literatur/quellen/Hebbel-Nibelungen.pdf
KAPLAN
Es ist der Finger Gottes
Der still in diesen heilgen Brunnen taucht,
Weil er ein Kainszeichen schreiben muß.

HAGEN *neigt sich über den Sarg.*
Das rote Blut! Ich hätt es nie geglaubt!
Nun seh ich es mit meinen eignen Augen.
KRIEMHILD.
Und fällst nicht um?
Sie springt auf ihn zu.
Jetzt fort mit dir, du Teufel.
Wer weiß, ob ihn nicht jeder Tropfen schmerzt,
Den deine Mörder-Nähe ihm entzapft!

[19] Zeune (1814), one of the earliest 19th century translations, is illustrated with a sole copperplate, of the spearing.

[20] *The Exhibition of the Royal Academy, 1820-The Fifty Second.* London: McMillan, 1820: 10.

[21] An anonymous article in *London Magazine* (1: 635+, 1820) purported to explain the unfamiliar context of Fuseli's painting to interested exhibition-goers.

[22] Pfizer, trans. (1843: 195)

[23] Beta, trans. (1840: 148)

[24] "…these authentic German heroic stanzas are given the aspect here they had in many songs of
our singing books in diverse versions…" The philologist Heinrich von den Hagen, who had published one of the early critical editions of the text, in the Forward to Beta's translation.

[25] Heine (1833: 152)

[26] My English translation from von Harbou (1923: 110)

      „Doppelmord war dies, an Siegfried und an mir: Seit
die Tat geschehen, denk ich nur diesen Gedanken.

      „Das Blut aus Siegfrieds Wunde begann zu strömen.
Hagen Tronje war in mein Gemach getreten.

      „Mörder!" schrie ich und reckte auf Hagen die Hand.

[27] Kaes (2009: 133-34)

[28] Lange (2010: 132-33)

[29] Mueller (2010)

[30] Stobl (2007: 176-77)

[31] Kramer, trans. (1982). No bleeding Siegfried but several bloody decapitations.

[32] Olivier Auber, et al. The Nibelungen Museum: A Virtual Museum for a Myth. http://km2.net/aplush/nibelungenmuseum

7 .The sanguineous corpse

Cruentation and the bier proof was one occasion exposed corpses emitted cruor or sanguis after death. There were others.

Uncovered again after burial, still in a time when that was possible if not entirely allowable, corpses also might remarkably still contain cruor or sanguis which they emitted after being struck. But why strike a corpse? The set of beliefs and expectations which had led to the uncovering also led to the striking.

The Augustinian monk and chronicler of medieval England, William of Newburgh (1136-98) took time from the marriages and battles of the reign of Richard I to recount "various prodigies" occurring in 1196 for their edifying qualities.[1] There were many tales of this sort, he wrote, but to try to tell them all would be laborious.

The first concerned a profligate priest who served as the chaplain of a lady. He was so fond of hunting he was known as the "dog priest." On his death he was buried within the precincts of the Cistercian abbey Melrose (Mailros), but unquiet in his sins, he issued forth at night. The virtue of the monks prevented him from troubling them, and he took to haunting the bedchamber of his patroness with howls and murmurs.

She pleaded with the monks to redouble their prayers on her behalf. One of them decided that standing guard over the graveyard would prevent the deceased priest from making an appearance, and joined by another monk and two young men, stood watch until midnight with no sign of the revenant.

Left alone when the others went away to warm themselves, the monk was noisily set upon by the dead priest, the devil in him. The monk wounded him with an axe and pursued him back to his tomb, which opened then closed after receiving him. Together the members of the party opened the tomb and unearthed the corpse.

Quod cum egesta humo nudassent, ingens in eo vulnus quod acceperat, et cruoris plurimum qui ex vulnere fluxerat, in sepulcro invenerunt.

When he was denuded of the accumulated earth, they found deep in him the wound he received, and a great quantity of cruor which flowed from the wound in the sepulchre.

The team quickly removed the corpse from the grave, burned it and scattered the ashes. That was the remedy. William heard this told by religious men.

The second prodigy he had to tell came from a certain aged and well respected monk. A man of dubious repute fled his misdeeds and found shelter in the service of the lord of Alnwick Castle (Anantis). Led to suspect his wife of infidelity, he pretended to go on a long journey and secretly arranged to be hidden in the rafters of her bedchamber. His rage at seeing his wife in the embrace of a young man of the area caused him to lose his handhold and fall down where the couple lay. The young man ran off, and the wife took advantage of his daze to dismiss the sight he claimed to see as a "sickness."

The man's condition worsened, and the monk who told William of these events was going to administer the Eucharist to him when he died. His Christian burial did not prevent him from rising from the grave at night and passing among the houses followed by a pack of dogs. He beat anyone who was outside and spread a pestilential miasma with his foul presence. Many people abandoned the township rather than risk death by remaining.

During a Palm Sunday banquet hosted by the monk for the remaining townspeople two brothers who had lost their father to this plague determined to end it, and slipped away on their mission. With a blunt spade they dug in the grave and quickly came to a body swollen to an enormous size and covered in the remains of a chewed-up shroud.

Nec territi juvenes quos ira stimulabat, vulnus examini intulerunt ex quo tantus continuo sanguis effluxit et intelligeretur sanguisuga fuisse multorum.

And not frightened, the young men anger drove pierced a wound on the corpse from which so much sanguis continually flowed that it seemed to be a leech ("sanguis-sucker") of many victims.

The pair then dragged the corpse out of the town and laid it on a funeral pyre, one of them tearing out its heart through a wound in the side. The burning, witnessed by many who arrived, lifted the pestilence from the town.

William does not give a specific name to either of these animated corpses. The description in each case strongly associates the corpse with the miasma of pestilence, sickness that was understood to infest a locale and spread by contact from one afflicted person to another. Both corpses travel by night and are noisy: that is the main source of the grief caused by the Melrose Abbey haunter.They are not insubstantial ghosts. The evidence of their substance is in the wound inflicted on the apparition then discovered in the unearthed corpse, and in the fluid flow they both emit from the body breach. Burning halts their visits and decontaminates the region.

These living corpses have fundamental characteristics: they are identifiable individuals who have died and are buried in a known location, who travel by night bringing a pestilence that they convey to one person after another, they bleed cruor or sanguis as the result of a strike, and their plague is halted by the staking, dismantling and possibly the burning of the uncovered corpse, which shows signs of life. These characteristics were set in written chronicles by the end of the 11th century in Europe and mutated from alleged fact to outright fiction in the centuries that followed. The rousing blow, the sounding of the dead, the accompaniment of dogs, the hunger of the dead including masticating the death shroud also appear.

William of Newburgh's two stories were situated in well-known buildings, Melrose Abbey and Alnwick Castle, both of which still exist today, and the stories were conveyed by reliable informants, extending their authority to William himself and his written text. They are instances of the sinful occupation with body pleasures which invites possession by demons only to be undone with the complete destruction of the body vehicle. The human agents determined to protect their community from the intrusions of the dead are themselves imperfect, the defenders seeking warmth and shelter when their task becomes trying, the remaining monk preferring not to confront the all too material revenant if he can avoid it.

When the monk in the Melrose Abbey story does defend himself against the dead priest he succeeds in wounding him severely. The wounded body found in the grave emits cruor, usually translated into English as "gore." By contrast the body of the fallen profligate in the Alnwick Castle story the daring brothers find in the grave is bloated with sanguis, and its resemblance to "a leech of many victims" suggests that it has been absorbing the sanguis of the people it has attacked who like the victims of leeches are not aware of the attacker.

Cruor flows from a wound, but sanguis flows within and from a living body, a perversely life-like dead body. William does not contrast the two stories, yet his chapter of various prodigies does parallel other contrastive pairings of cruor and sanguis in the animated dead in and from the grave.

Both stories are instances of Christianity framing and providing a means to control the incursions of the recent and remembered dead into the lives of their own community members. The wayward priest and the jealous husband cause havoc among the living because their bodies are taken over by demons, providing a Christian explanation for the activities of spirits, nonmaterial intelligences, that preceded organized religion.

There were many accounts of this happening, some of them casual reports inserted into chronicles like William's, others literary in nature.[2] The degree and means of possession was debated by scholars and clergy. The means of putting the corpse out of commission was as material as the corpse itself: decapitation and burning. The demon-motivated return to life was a profane resurrection that could be terminated once and for all. The resurrection of the body promised to humanity at the return of Christ was denied the sinner, who would remain in Hell.

The cruor and sanguis of the corpses are also signs of their materiality, of two types that might be separate or united in the same gross body. The combative and wounded corpse spilling cruor is the template of the zombis of popular culture centuries later; the sanguis-bloated corpse with the suggestion it acquired the sanguis from living victims is the harbinger of the vampires sooner to come.

That word "vampire" applied anachronistically obscures more than it reveals, as "blood" of the vernacular languages obscures both cruor and sanguis of the Latin. In England and Scandanavia the returned dead comprise two distinct types of interaction of animated dead bodies with the living. In one the animated dead can be physically resisted while outside the grave; in the other the only evidence of contact with the living is in the dead body itself. Looking directly at the Latin where it is the language of use shows the cruor and sanguis of those bodies.

Asmund, who had been by his oath buried alive with his slain companion Aswid, reemerges from the tumulus in a bucket the Swedes who hoped for grave wealth had lowered with one of their number. King Eric tries to call back the soldiers who fled at the sight of this man covered with the corruption of the grave.[3]

Quem videns Ericus praecipue cruentati oris eius imaginem mirabatur: in vultu siquidem profluus emicabat sanguis.

Seeing whom Eric suddenly marveled at the image of his cruenting mouth: in spurts as well as flowing, the sanguis was emerging.

The colorless Asmund speaks in verse and at length about how he acquired his horrific aspect. At night in the grave the spirit of Aswid rose from hell and devoured his horse and dog also buried there. He then set upon Asmund, tearing off his left ear and scratching his face. Asmund fought back, decapitating the corpse and pinning it down with a stake. Asmund's lacerated face is hideous. Sanguis spurts from the ugly wound.

This episode from one of the "mythological books" of the first Latin history of the Danes places the living dead man Asmund in direct opposition to the demonized corpse of his former companion he was buried alive to join with his dog and horse in the afterworld of the grave. The ravenous Aswid attacks Asmund with a warrior's fury. Asmund is the bleeding dead man, emitting both cruor and sanguis in response to the cannibal's slashes. William of Newburgh's two revenants are enclosed within the same tumulus, and one of them takes on the role of the living person who destroys the rampaging corpse.

Saxo Grammaticus (c. 1130-1220), a contemporary of William of Newburgh, was the secretary of the bishop who forcibly Christianized the Danes, and he placed indigenous beliefs in the context of the new religion. Though it is unlikely that the two writers were aware of each other's work, they both responded to the living dead traditions in terms of the cruor and sanguis of the body between life and death.

In the second book of the *Gesta Danorum* Saxo evokes the movement of bodies drained in the slaughter of battle:

Danicus undescit sanguis, stagnatque cruenta latius eluvies, et corpora sparsa revolvit elisus venis vapidum spumantibus amnis.

Danish sanguis moistens, and stagnates the cruenting spread wide, and the river convulsed by collapsed veins turns the scattered corpses.

Like the wounds on Asmund's scratched face the sanguis cruents. It becomes solid enough to cause the bodies to turn as their veins release contents that wet the area as they dry. This is presented as a physical reality of slaughter witnessed by anyone actively sensate in its midst.

These post-mortem flows of the contents of veins are cruentation, powered by the force of sanguis becoming cruor. In the confines of the grave these flows charge the body's wanderings outside the grave or its actions within the grave. On the battlefield they roil bodies as they change from one state to another. In *de bello civile*, the poetic history of the Roman civil war by Lucan, the sorceress Erichtho has the art of warming the cruor in the veins of corpses back to sanguis, causing the wounds to close and reanimating the bodies.[4]

The remains of Thomas Becket, Archibishop of Canterbury, lay on the tiled floor of the cathedral where he was slaughtered (1170) by four knights at the implicit command of King Henry II. Benedict of Peterborough (d. 1194) was one of several contemporaries who wrote a Latin *Vita* of the martyr. He paid close attention to the disposition of Becket's flesh and garments.[5]

Et cum cruor adinstar diadematis, forsitan in signum sanctitatis, capiti circumfusus jacuisset, facies tamen a cruore prorsus immunis apparuit, excepto tractu quodam gracili, qui a dextra frontis parte in faciem sinestram per transversum nasi descenderat...Jacente adhuc autem in pavimento sanguine alii oculos suos liniebat...Pars autem cruoris quam ecclesiae dimiserant in vas mundissimum mundissime collecta, in ecclesia reponitur conservanda.

And when the cruor like a crown, be it as a sign of sanctity, lay about the head, the face appeared entirely free of cruor, except for a light tract, which descended from the right part of the front into the left side across the nose...Still, lying nonetheless on the floor, others anointed their eyes with his sanguis…Part of the cruor which they left in the church was collected in the most commonplace of containers and put away in the church for safekeeping.

The marks of the cruor lying about Thomas' head took on a symbolic significance; the people arriving after the knights had left applied the sanguis from Thomas' body to their eyes, drank some and placed it in vessels, and dipped pieces of cloth in it. The cruor that was left was gathered up in the humblest vessel and kept apart in the church.

The words are not used interchangeably: cruor is the thick deposit spread about and streaked over the face (for the most part remarkably free of cruor) and sanguis is the fluid taken directly from the corpse, applied to the eyes and drunk. Both are placed in containers for future use.

Powdery relics of saints could be mixed with water to form a healing liquid, but Thomas Becket's sanguis, unique among saints, was diluted with water, stored in sealed metal ampoules, drunk and poured on afflicted areas of body, and given as gifts. Another of Thomas' contemporary hagiographers, Herbert of Bosham, repeatedly referred to him as the *fons sanguinis*, the fount of sanguis, and made no mention of cruor.[6]

There were other characterizations of Thomas' sanguis: it was compared to lotuses and roses upon the floor (a man's sanguis into flowers); it was said to glow with the color purple, royal and sacred to Jesus. According to Herbert of Bosham, Thomas underwent "transubstantiation," the mystical transformation of bread and wine into the body and blood of Christ during the Mass.

On January 4, 1171, seven days after the assassination, "a poor little woman" (*paupercula*) named Brithiva was healed of blindness in Canterbury, according to Benedict, when a "ruddy kerchief" stained with "liquid cruor" from Becket was placed over her eyes.

The following day William, a London priest "of simple innocence and innocent simplicity," who had recently been struck with a paralysis that rendered him unable to speak, and who had not responded to treatment with theriacs, learned that another priest had a vision of a stately man who advised William to go to Canterbury and receive a drop of blessed cruor on his tongue to recover his speech. After spending a night vigil in prayer at the tomb of the martyr, William received a drop of sanguis to which an equal drop of holy water was added, "no doubt initiated by divine will and continued up until the present day." As soon as the priest tasted the cruor of the martyr he recovered his speech and despite the attempts of those "like the Jews" (*Judaizantium*) who tried to suppress the fame of Thomas Becket, sang forth his praises.

Before the outcome of William's taking the cruor/sanguis is revealed, Benedict of Peterborough inserts a homily on the priest's imitation of Thomas Becket, who imitated Christ.[7]

Sicut beatum Thomam in vita et passione perfectissimum sui fecit imitatorem, ita ei et post mortem sui simulitudinem admiranda perfectione concedere voluit, ut quemadmodum Christi sanguis cum aqua transit ad vegetationem animarum, ita et servi sui sanguis cum aqua bibitus transeat in sanitatem corporum. Nec credimus aliquem hactenus extitisse, cui Dei hanc similitudinis praerogativam concesserit; solius enim Agni Bethleemitici sanguis et cruor Cantuariensis in universo mundo hauriri legitur.

Such a perfect imitator [of Christ] did Thomas make in his life and passion, and so it comes to concede to him after death his resemblance with admiring perfection, that in the same manner the sanguis of Christ with water reaches to the nourishment of souls, so the sanguis of his servant drunk with water might reach to the health of bodies. We do not believe anyone has existed to whom God would concede this prerogative of resemblance; therefore the sanguis of the lamb of Bethlehem and the cruor of the lamb of Canterbury alone in the entire world are chosen to be taken.

The priest was advised by the vision to take cruor, was given sanguis and water, and was said to have tasted cruor. Both Christ and Thomas Becket bestow sanguis, of a spiritual and of a medicinal grade, and in the end Christ gives sanguis and Thomas gives cruor. If they are two names for the same thing, why does Benedict make the distinction?

Benedict charters a practice of distributing Thomas' cruor and sanguis for healing. William's paralysis was the first condition treated by sanguis offered with blessed water, the combination known as "water of Thomas Becket" or "Canterbury water" and offered in treatment of blindness, deafness, paralysis and other conditions. The water was taken internally, sometimes in tandem with cruor applied to the afflicted organ. The miniscule amounts used in acts of treatment lent credence to the authenticity of the limited supply, which was extended by the addition of blessed water to the sanguis. Benedict added further miracles accomplished by the water used where its fluidity was of advantage, and in tandem with the cruor applied directly.

For instance a woman afflicted with deafness and pain in the head was treated with "water mixed with sanguis."[8] Amid much clamor it seemed that an abscess broke inside and abundant *sanies* (pus) flowed from her ears, followed by sanguis, and thanks to the saint's sanguis hearing was restored.

"Young Edmund" was troubled by a disorder of his left eye.[9]

Instillatur eius oculo sacratissimi stilla cruoris; sanguis et aquae commistione potatur.

A drop of the most blessed cruor is infused in his eye; a mixture of sanguis and water is drunk.

And a complete cure was effected.

The curative sanguis is always in water solution. Sanies is a sickly fluid driven out by sanguis. Cruor is a thick liquid in one droplet applied directly to the afflicted area, accompanied by the sanguis water taken internally. While Becket lay dead in the cathedral people smeared their eyes with his fresh sanguis but some time later all that remains of that is cruor and the sanguis reconstituted in water. For the treatments the difference between the two is a matter of state, dark liquid (cruor) or water (sanguis).

A monk who arrived in Canterbury after Benedict was placed in charge of Thomas' tomb (1171) undertook an extensive catalogue of the miracles attributed to the martyr, at the sacred sites and elsewhere in England, at sea and abroad. Some were the result of the martyr's (then saint's, 1173) direct intervention in a crisis, but many were brought about by the chief reliquary instrument of the saint, by the sufferer receiving his cruor and sanguis. William of Canterbury's *Miracularum gloriosi martyris Thomae* is longer than Benedict's, containing brief entries for hundreds of miracles, but unlike Benedict's it makes scant reference to cruor or sanguis. *Aqua sancti Thomae,* the water of Saint Thomas, has taken their place.

In the town of Wedeford the young daughter of the miller having wandered into the water and drowned, as the parents and townspeople stood about the girl's corpse a "boy of refined face" approached bearing "an ampoule of the Saint Thomas".[10] Seeing this as a sign, the father asked, "Is this the water of the man of God?" "It is," the youth answered. "Son, we ask that a little be imparted." He poured some in the mouth of the deceased and after a brief interval the girl's spirit returned. The youth took up the ampoule and disappeared.

A boy named Henry in the village of Hythe was from birth paralyzed from the navel downward, and his leg from ankle to buttock did not hold together.[11] An old woman suggested plunging him in a trough of hot water to loosen his joints, which it did so violently that his legs sprang open and tore his knees, pouring out cruor. Around this time a priest named Robert from Canterbury brought to the local monastery a sackcloth soaked with the sanguis of the martyr Thomas. Henry's mother engaged to have her degenerating son carried the distance to the monastery where he was received and given the water of St. Thomas to drink for five days. He convalesced, and by the end of the time was able to walk between supports or a staff.

Several people are raised from the dead in Benedict's and William's accounts by receiving the water of St. Thomas, not uncommonly after having died by water (drowning in rivers and ponds, shipwreck, etc.). The boy who spontaneously appears bearing the water that all at once restores the girl seems angelic. The water he brings is life-giving rather than life-taking: it contains the vital element, the life force of St. Thomas that is not named.

The cruor that appears in these miracles pours out of the bodies of the injured, sick or dead (in one miracle it is from a lamb restored to life by St. Thomas' water). Cruor and sanguis in Thomas' remains and the first miracles lead to sanguis and water and finally just water with a background of sanguis. In a liturgy of St. Thomas the water itself changes, first to milk and then to four kinds of cruor.[12]

Besides the need to develop an efficient supply and distribution of Thomas' sanguis, the turn toward water resulted from "doctrinal complications". The transubstantiation of bread and wine into the carnis and sanguis of Jesus to be consumed by the faithful in Communion was and is a central mystery of Christianity. Thomas' cruor and sanguis could not be reproduced in this way; they could only be extended by dilution. Water dissolved and concealed the sanguis and eclipsed the cruor.

The ampoules that distributed the water of Thomas Becket far and wide and were the main representation of the works of his sanguis did not refer to sanguis.[13] Contemporary biographers other than Benedict of Peterborough and William of Canterbury, even Edward Grim, who lost an arm defending Thomas against the knights, wrote of miracles but did not detail the cruor and sanguis of his remains or the sanguis in the miraculous water. Henry VIII's November 16, 1538 proclamation denying Thomas Becket's sainthood and ordering the destruction of his shrines and images led to the suppression of Becket's cult.[14] Some ampoules survived.

While Latin prevailed as the medium of discourse verbal evidence of a significant differentiation between cruor and sanguis in dead and living bodies continued to present itself. The theologian and Bishop of Lincoln Robert Grosseteste wrote a treatise on the reliquary container of Christ's blood sent to King Henry III by the Patriarch of Jerusalem in 1247 and ceremoniously lodged in Westminster Abbey on a day of several other ceremonies. The king's own piety, and the wish to build support for a crusade, motivated the enshrinement.[15] The organizers of this and other proposed blood cults may have been looking to Thomas Becket, his extendable remains and miraculous cures and rescues.

Grosseteste recognized that there were doubts about the authenticity of the relic, and set about to provide a scriptural basis for its powers. Drawing upon the apocryphal Gospel of

Nicodemus and Acts of Pilage, he recounted the story of Joseph of Arimathea attending to Christ's body after its deposition from the cross. He settled upon four species of emission collected: "the rubicund water (*aqua rubicunda*) from washing Christ's body that was distributed by friends to the infirm for medicinal purposes; the sanguis from the puncture wounds to the head and forehead and from the breaches of the flail with sweat, the two liquids distinguished from many mixed together; sanguis from the wounds of the hands and feet which was pure and unmixed; the mighty precordial cruor of most terrible and reverent memory from Christ's heart itself, which flowed from at least one side. In addition to these four fluids, the water with sanguis we know emanated from the side."[16]

The fluids of Christ deposited on earth prior to his Resurrection were forms of water, sweat, sanguis and cruor. Theologians debated whether Christ left any material traces of his presence. Relics were both profitable and useful politically, hence claims were made and gained fame both by association with powerful patrons and by dispute. They were authenticated by their display, the pomp and honor accorded them, the vessels that held them. Thomas Becket's water was known by its ampoule containers. Christ's sanguis might still exist as water; his cruor would be solid.

Cruor praecordialis was cruor that poured out when the skin in the region of the heart was pierced. Matthew Paris described the battlefield where the Christian defenders of the Crusader kingdom of Jerusalem were massacred by the resurgent Muslims under Saladin: *cruor praecordialis diffunditur,* precordial cruor spreads about.[17] This was the cruor released when Christ's side was pierced by a centurion while Christ was on the cross. Yet in the final sentence Grosseteste also refers to the "water together with sanguis" that emanated from Christ's side. By calling it cruor rather than sanguis Grosseteste distinguished the congealed appearance of the substance in the chalice from the fluid sanguis which also might appear mixed with water.

Grosseteste projected the vision of sacrifice that linked Christ's Passion with the Crusades and the Westminster blood relic through the substance of the cruor, which made the first two concrete through the third. Other blood relics. For instance, the relic deposited at Hales Abbey in Gloucestershire in 1267 by Prince Edward or by Edmund, Baron of Cornwall, originally from Pope Urban. When the richly outfitted cabinet that contained the *cruor Christi* was stolen in 1401 it was rated "the richest in the realm, except Canterbury."[18] The Latin word for a blood relic varied according to how it appeared and what it was intended to evoke.

The 18th century antiquary Samuel Pegge wrote a biography of Robert Grosseteste in which he provided a long footnote on blood relics long since vanished.[19] With the same investigative energy and antiquarian attention to the makeup of ancient things that he brought to his studies of Anglo-Saxon jewelry and Roman roads, Pegg gave opinions of what the blood relics were actually composed of: the relic at Hales Abbey was said to be duck's blood, or clarified honey. That was the belief.

The corpse was sanguineous in response to an outside force that stirred its cruor and sanguis to the profanity of reanimation, or to be moved with the life force that could be communicated with their application. A proto-pseudo-science developed on the utility of these materials, one use of the bodily parts of the saints. They healed and restored life through physical application. A guide to the cruor and sanguis likely to be available was provided by the ideal of Christ's own remains, a model picture of curative power realized in the actual cruor and sanguis of the saints.

That material when it must have been exhausted was again extended by reference back to Christ's body, never entirely dead, through dilution and contact.

When the sanguinous corpse was recorded as a historical event its status was negotiated among those in its vicinity who ritualized its appearance and attributes both to escape its hold and distribute its force. The death from a blow, a fall, strangulation, a forcible death, transferred to the cruor and sanguis that emerged and was contained in them.

---

[1] William of Newburgh (1856: 185-90) Book 5, Chapter 24.

[2] Caciola (2016) "Demonically possessed corpses"

[3] Saxo Grammaticus, *Gesta Danorum* 5.11.3 (11) Olrik and Raeder, eds. (1931: 135, 30)

[4] *Dum vocem defuncta in corpore quarit,*
protinus adstrictus caluit cruor, atraque fovit
vulnera...

[5] Benedict of Peterborough, *Passio Sanctae Thomae Cantuariensis*. Robertson, ed. (1876: 2, 14; 15)

[6] Herbert of Bosham, *Vita Sancti Thomae, Archiepiscopi et Martyris*. Ronertson, ed. (1877: 3, 500; 519)

[7] Benedict of Peterborough IN Robertson, ed. (1876: 2, 42-43)

[8] Benedict IN Robertson, ed, (1876: 2, 66)

[9] Benedict IN Robertson, ed. (1876: 2, 62-63)

[10] William of Canterbury, *Miracularum gloriosi Sancti Thomae* IN Robertson, ed. (1875: 1, 344)

[11] William IN Robertson, ed. (1875: 1, 188-89)

[12] Slocum (2004: 95) *lauds* in the office *Studens livor. Aqua Thome quiquies/varians colorem/in lac semel transit/quater in cruorem*

[13] Jordan (2009: 492). Jordan's article contains reproductions of Becket ampoules and stained glass windows illustrating the cures accomplished with the ampoules.

[14] Henry the VIII's Proclamation, 1538: The Unsainting of Thomas Becket. http://conclarendon.blogspot.com/2013/10/henry-viiis-proclamation-1538.html

[15] Vincent (2001: 16; 45). The procession was illustrated by Matthew Paris in the manuscript of his chronicle, Lewis (1987: Plate X). Paris's sketch of the reliquary, a cloth-covered chalice, was in the margin of his manuscript:

Paris (2012: 138)

Paris' entry on the October 13, 1247 procession in his *Historia Anglorum* Paris (1869: 29) refers to it as *sanguis Christi* carried by the king to Westminster, certified by letters from the Patriarch of Jerusalem, the commanders of the Knights Templars and Hospitallers and the bishop of the Holy Land. Paris illustrated the *vasculum sanguinis,* in which the relic, presumably the above chalice, was contained:

[16] Grosseteste (1247) IN Paris, ed.(2012: 140)
[17] Paris (1866: 441)
[18] Rous, et. al., comp. (1729: 182)
[19] Pegge (1793: 160-61n(c))

8. Death and life of a young noble

The same year he took up the position of Professor of Medicine at the newly founded
university in Wittenberg, Gregor Horst published a pamphlet on an incident that had occurred in
interior Austria (Styria) two years earlier, at the end of 1606.

The purpose of the pamphlet was not primarily to describe the incident but to propound
and address questions "on the natural conservation and cruentation of cadavers," as the
pamphlet was titled.[1] It was composed in Latin, like any work addressed to the pan-European
community of the learned to which the author belonged.

Horst was born in one of the states that made up Germany and received his early education,
learning Latin and Greek at German universities before embarking on a study voyage to Austria
and Switzerland. He was promoted to Doctor of Medicine at the University of Basel, Switzerland
in 1606. His "two books of noble exercises on the human body and the soul" were published in
Wittenberg the following year.

From that very title Horst could be known as an ally of the Paracelsans, medical theorists
and practitioners who emphasized the role of the spirit in health and illness, and less sympathetic
to the Galenists, who gauged their diagnoses and treatments according to the balance and
imbalance of bodily humors. Horst's use of the word *exercitationes*, army exercises, in the title
signaled the militancy of his approach against his rivals. His writings won him the professorship
at Wittenberg and in 1609 a professorship of anatomy and botany at the University of Giessen, as
a result of having attracted the interest of the university's founder, Landgraf Ludwig V of
Hessen-Darmstadt.

Horst's 1606 pamphlet on cadavers did not figure prominently among his many published
works; it was included in the systematic collection of writings ultimately assembled after his
death.[2] It was one marker of an interest, eventually a preoccupation, which developed in central
Europe, from the southern German states to Romania and Austria-Hungary, the Slavic states
near and within their borders and the Ottoman Empire close by.

At the very beginning of the pamphlet, before any description of the key incident, Horst
stated two "problems".

1. Is the human body able to last several weeks after death, florid in color and habit,
   without corruption, and free of incipient putrefaction, naturally, with no accompanying
   artifice?

2. Does the flow of sanguis from a human cadaver of one dead at first of murder after
   several weeks indicate the presence of the murderer?

The first problem is that of the sanctified dead who do not decay; the second one inquires into
the truth of cruentation, as many had before.

The *casus* or instance of these problems took place on December 26, 1604 at around the
ninth hour of the night. A nobleman 25 years of age standing at the upper storey window of a
house in the town of Blindmarck (Fraktur lettering)[3] in interior Austria was shot by a ball fired
from the street below. The projectile entered his left breast and exited at the left lower ribcage
(hypochondriac region). He died where he stood.

A considerable amount of sanguis poured out of the entrance and exit wounds. The young victim was dressed in new clothes and laid out for a two day quiet period, then, from December 30, as he lay in a "holy place" without being moved again, fresh sanguis percolated daily from the upper wound until it stopped on January 8, 1605. On February 13, the bleeding resumed from the lower wound for around two hours at midday as if the murder were being repeated.

The entire aspect of the body was lifelike; its color up to the time of entombment was florid and rubicund. The veins visible in the forehead were replete with sanguis. No signs of incipient putrefaction appeared for all the weeks that passed. There was no unwelcome odor like that which emanated from corpses only a few days old. The fingers of the hand were soft and mobile with no atrophy (Horst used the Greek word here) and the color was natural except that in the last week before entombment the beginnings of livor were visible in the extremities.

Horst only gives these details, not their source or any other information on the identity of the victim. He does not say he was a witness. Rather than seeking the reason for what he consistently calls a murder, or trying to identify the murderer, Horst concentrates on the remarkable preservation of the corpse fresh for weeks long after others who died at the same time were decomposing, and on the postmortem bleeding. The entombment was delayed as long as the corpse remained with no signs of decay and continued to exude sanguis.

Classical and contemporary writers about the form of the body provide Horst with a rationale for long preservation. He does not seek out comparable cases that would contribute to a common theme of bodily preservation but instead looks for the forces that shape and maintain the body during life. "Native heat" (*calor nativus*) proceeding from and residing in the heart imparts form and motion. Galen's supposition that death is the extinction of native heat is not entirely correct. Horst argues that heat is more diversified, and that after the heart stops beating will still reside in the organs and extremities, the "tempering of the body" that preserves all parts.

The young nobleman also had the thermal advantage of his flourishing youth, robust health and copious "balsam of life" (*balsamus vitae*). That phrase, for a Paracelsan like Horst, connoted the vital fluid of the body manifest as the outpouring of blood. The violent death the youth died added to the temper of his constitution. The moderation of outside temperature, neither so warm that it encouraged the start of decay, nor so cold that it initiated coagulation, was a factor in retaining the fresh state of the body.

Moving to the question of the bleeding corpse, Horst draws from his sources the conclusion that a wounded victim, while still alive, will bleed in the presence of the assailant. No question of that. Apart from the moment of wounding itself, the opponent draws out the sanguis impelled by the victim's life force.

By the same act of reasoning, however, antipathy between the murderer and the murdered does not move sanguis from the dead body of the victim. The bond created by antipathy is not sustained once the imagination has ceased to reach a spirit outside the body.

A corpse killed in revenge can continue to leak sanguis for many days, continually or at intervals, with or without the presence of the killer. The commotion of the spirit that churns up the fluids of a preserved victim of violent death can naturally perpetuate the release of sanguis for weeks at a time, though this is rare.

The challenge that the present case posed to the common belief that the presence of the killer precipitates bleeding of the victim is resolved in favor of a more general condition: the sanguis continues to boil in the heat of the fresh body uninfluenced by and unindicative of the murderer's presence.

Either the killer was in the immediate vicinity for weeks after the young nobleman's body was laid out, left the area, and then returned for a few hours weeks later, or the preservation and cruentation were natural phenomena enhanced by a few factors such as youth and the violence of the death. Horst negated the judicial value of cruentation without dismissing the principle of spirit influence on which it was based. Only while the victim was still alive could it happen. He reiterated that though preservation and cruentation were unusual, they were naturally the result of currents in the native heat.

A brief section appended to Horst's questions and answers underlined this conclusion. It was a report of the Viennese Academies of Medicine given in response to the request of the relatives of the young nobleman. The doctors of the Academies were part of the Austrian hierarchy responsive to an aristocratic family, and they had access to the remains of the victim, which Horst did not. The assessment of the Lutheran Horst, however well couched in medical reasoning it may have been, had to be addressed by Catholic experts of Habsburg medical officialdom. Religion did not figure into the report. Latin medical learning could still cross boundaries about to thicken with the religious wars of the coming century. Differences in approach between Horst and the Viennese physicians were subsumed within a common mandate.

The first article of the Viennese section of the report, attributes the preservation of the corpse and the cruentation to the victim's "well-constituted sanguineous complexion" and the youthful endowment of sanguis. The language of superior makeup used to describe the bodies of the elite extends to their sanguis quality and quantity, and adds to the force of youth Horst already observed.

Having accounted for the amount of sanguis present in the victim by his nobility, the medical faculty members then turn to the reasons for its outpouring. "Major blood vessels were transected and torn by the ball, so that the site of the wound marks the heart itself." Many of the cadavers seen in medical schools contain uncongealed sanguis for days, especially in the aorta. The area of the wound therefore was the place medical experience locates the greatest concentration of lasting fluid blood.

The sanguis appearing from the upper wound, the one closer to the heart, was absorbed by cloths wrapped and wound in that location. They showed an affinity for clear liquids and made a display of saturation by the sanguis while that which remained in the thorax was too thick to flow.

After seven weeks it was not surprising to see a thick and black flow from the wounds, impelled by the same exhalations of decay that bloat dead animals thrown into the streets. At the same time the pressure from inside prevents the sanguis from returning. The only flow is outward.

Having begun by attributing the quantity of sanguis to the victim's nobility, the medical faculty refer to the common sight of animals dead in the street to explain the thick, dark flow weeks after death. Elevated in sanguis complexion by social class, the putrefying noble still is a gross body.

The faculty do not need to state the Christian view of death as the great leveler to which all bodily life is subject. For them the more important inference from the material evidence is that these are processes of the body alone and do not indicate the presence of the murderer. As Horst wrote in his section of the report, killer present or absent the body would have continued to bleed, and this one bled more because of its nobility and the violence of the projectile.

The cold weather and open casket helped the preservation and freshness of the sanguis at the beginning. A consoling note was added in their final statement that made an allowance for spirits. "The affect of certain spirits such as most ardent love or unbridled rage dominating the body, if death intervenes the cadaver may remain a long time as alive." The young man's life after death continued his passion while alive. The affective life of the body remains the source of its own afterlife.

Horst's long *skepsis* was signed in Styria, inferior Austria, July 1605, and was followed in time by the Vienna medical faculty's report under their seal, September 1605. The dedication to a Dn. Danieli, chamberlain of the Archduchy of Austria and to Andreas Dorero, a medical doctor to the Elector of Saxony, was dated August, 1606. Horst addressed Danieli as "a witness not without sorrow and anguish of the soul to the most sad case of homicide." Horst was in Styria months after the murder and cruentation that formed the point of departure for his writing, and probably obtained his information as well as the commission to write the piece from Danieli.

Horst and the Viennese medical faculty concurred, in theory and in pathology, that the preservation and sanguis quantity were natural and there was no indication that the presence of the murderer spurred the bleeding. These are the final words of the report.

The *casus ex homicidio* was not primarily a rare opportunity for Horst and the Viennese doctors to test the validity of cruentation beliefs, to scientifically dispel the supposition that antipathy between dead victim and murderer brings out the sanguis. The specific case had to be divorced from the framework of beliefs about post-mortem sanguis and bleeding. The bleeding was natural and murderer could not have been present.

Why were Horst and the Viennese doctors asked to examine this case?

Other cases already reviewed reveal suspicions about post-mortem bleeding that persists. If it is not cruentation then it must be due to an unnatural source of the sanguis, as was suspected in William of Peterborough's leech-like case. If it is cruentation then why did it stop and start? Was it due to the continual presence of the murderer? Medical specialists of different religious and national backgrounds were called in to quiet the possible upheaval of a feud.

The identity of the murderer was not known though suspected, and the cruentation would have been a way of confirming suspicions. The victim was shot at night while standing at a window by an assassin positioned on the street below. In the turbulent Europe of the late 16th early 17th centuries religious, ethnic and dynastic rivalries fomented assassinations and localized warfare. The land was a patchwork of affiliations and impositions of faith and authority.

The Dutch Protestant leader William the Silent was killed at close range with a wheel-lock handgun by an agent of the Catholic Habsburg rulers of the Netherlands in 1584. The Protestant convert of convenience to Catholicism, Henry IV of France, was stabbed to death in his carriage by a Protestant in 1610. Both of those assassins were captured, their affiliations determined, and they were executed. The murderer of the young nobleman in 1604 wanted to remain anonymous hence the use of a firearm with a greater range than a handgun, fired from a distance out of the darkness at a figure framed in a firelit window.

The weapon of choice may have been an arquebus, but that matchlock rifle required an specialist who could rapidly follow the drill of ramming powder and ball into the muzzle, pouring powder into the pan, igniting the match and placing it on the lock, aiming and pulling the trigger while it still burned, igniting the powder and propelling the ball (with any luck). With an assistant it might have been accomplished in the dark. The prospect of detection may have dictated the use of the more portable, more easily charged and fired wheel-lock in its rifle form.

The powder in the wheel-lock's pan was ignited by a spring-driven serrated metal wheel casting sparks. No open flame or smoldering match was necessary. The number of moving parts incorporated into the mechanism made it an expensive piece of equipment, requiring frequent repairs by a watchmaker. Wheel-lock pistols and rifles were often an accoutrement of aristocrats seen holding the firearms in their portraits. The German nobility retained their prize wheel-locks after those pieces were superseded by guns with other ignition technologies. The elaborate metal scroll-work and bone inlays ornamenting the firearm made them heirlooms.[4]

A weapon that could accomplish the 1604 assassination without revealing the assassin was likely to have been the property of a wealthy noble who used it for the hunt. This in turn created an impetus to follow the clue given by the victim himself and find the responsible party among those in the vicinity while the corpse exuded sanguis. Anyone who might have been suspected for reasons known to the victim's family could be confirmed as the assassin. Immediate action against the suspected assassin would have precipitated reprisals.

The purpose of the *skepsis*, an unemotional looking around authored by Horst and his Viennese colleagues, was to undercut this current of cruentation judgment with medical reasoning substantiated by the classics and applied to the evidence at hand. It was similar to William Harvey's demonstration of the circulation of the blood later in the century.

The body and the sanguis within it were material entities formed by physical forces such as heat observable in other bodies. The present corpse differed from them only by degree. The sociopolitical context of the German states and the Archduchy of Austria at the time motivated, consumed and surrounded this study, which made a break for science by way of the classics. Another context, of this and apart from it, was beginning to reveal itself.

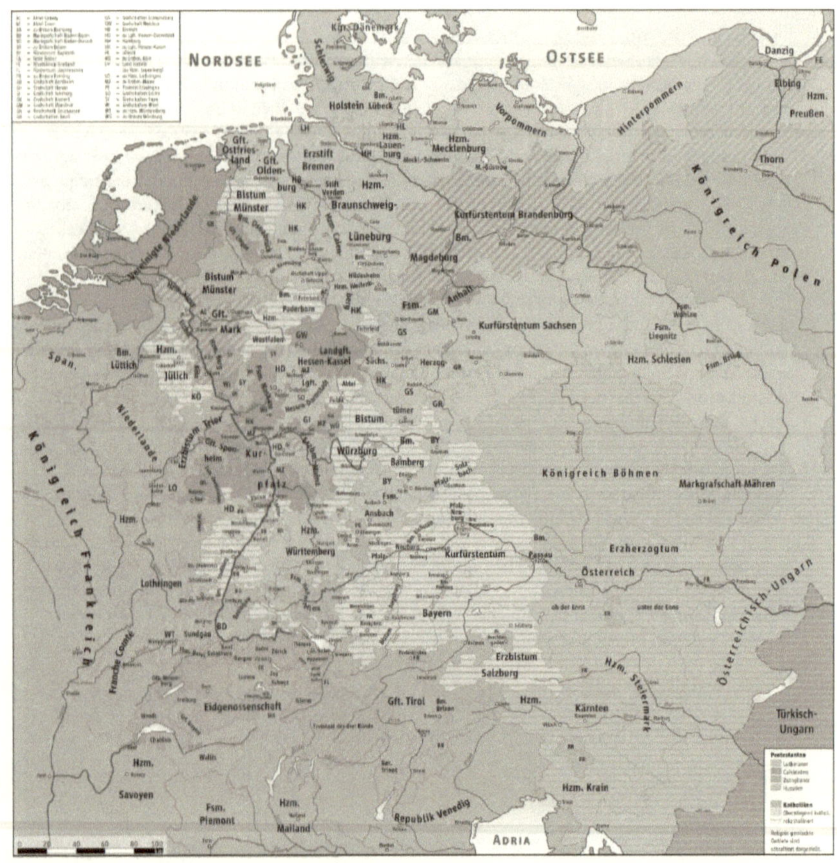

Map of Religions of the Holy Roman Empire on the Brink of the Thirty Years War (1618-48)
Plain light are Protestant areas; plain dark are Catholic. Striped areas are Protestant being
reCatholicized in the Counter-Reformation

In addition to the conflict between Catholics and Protestant denominations exacerbated by
the attempts to force a return to Catholic control in the Counter-Reformation, the early 17th
century was a period of renewed warfare between the Ottoman Empire and the Habsburg

Empire/Holy Roman Empire. The battles during the 1601-06 phase of the war were fought in Transylvania, where the Hungarian nobility resisting attempts by the Habsburgs to force them back into Catholicism obtained the support of the Ottomans, who were engaged in separate hostilities with the Habsburgs. The warfare ended by treaty in 1606 with paltry gains (and pronounced losses) on both sides, and with the technical superiority of Austrian weaponry being borne down upon the sometimes victorious Ottomans.

These battles took place a distance from the Lower Austria location of the assassination that led to Horst's report, but still within the same terrain of competing religions, ethnicities and polities. They were moments on the map and slightly off the map above, like the assassination that would bring the attention of Austrian officialdom and medical officers to cases of post-mortem bleeding.

---

[1] *Σκέψις de naturali conservatione et cruentatione cadaverum.* Skepsis on the natural conservation and cruentation of cadavers.

[2] Horst (1660: 136-48)

[3] Blindmard.

[4] Phillips (2016: 11.47)

9. Cuntius returns

Martinus Weinrichius (Martin Weinrich, 1548-1609), an instructor in the gymnasium of Breslau (Wrocław), Silesia, wanted his preface to his edition of the Florentine humanist Pico della Mirandola's dialogues on witchcraft and the havoc of demons to contain Silesian examples.

Silesia was and is an ethnic and religious borderland, a former province of the Polish kingdom heavily settled by Germans, converted to Lutheran Protestantism during the Reformation, and ruled by the Catholic Habsburgs since 1526. The province also had a Jewish population. Weinrich was a classicist teaching in one of the Lutheran Latin schools which with their libraries and small collections of artifacts became centers of humanities scholarship. Pico's Roman *lemures* (wandering ghosts before they were large-eyed prosimians) could be matched by Silesian revenants.

Weinrich did not include either of the two stories he related in his *Proemium* to Pico's dialogues in his best-known publication, *de ortu monstrorum* (*The origin of monsters*, 1595). Broadsheets with engraved news of miracles and anomalies of earth and sky were stock in trade for Silesian printers and Weinrich's Breslau-published unillustrated book was the erudite textbook of these interests. Among its many horrid births, animal hybrids, classical monsters and deformed humans there is a chapter on the returned dead, all of which earned the tome a place on the Catholic Church's *Index of Prohibited Books*.

Weinrich's Silesian lemur tales appeared three years after his death in the edition of Pico's dialogues edited by his son, Carl Weinrich, and printed in another Catholic-Protestant border city, Strassburg (Strasbourg) at some distance from the Silesian homeland.

The first of the stories concerned a shoemaker of Breslau who committed suicide in 1591, which his family initially concealed. Rumors spread, and despite the objections of his widow an inquiry was organized by residents of the town and the death was ruled due to violence administered by others or himself. With this the nighttime visitations began, the heavy spectre pressed down upon sleepers in their beds and bruised them so hard that the marks were visible.

Exhumation and reburial under the gallows only increased and expanded the haunting. Another exhumation, dismemberment and burning finished the terror. Then a maid who died after the shoemaker began her own night attacks, and was stopped only by the same exhumation-burning. No personal names were given in Weinrich's account, which was published a distance from home.

The second story, the longer one, was first set down by an unnamed *Theologus* (minister) in the Silesian town then named Pentsch. Weinrich assures his readers that there are living people who "did not hear and did not read, but saw" the happenings related.[1] Not ancient history but here and within living memory.

A well-respected and prosperous townsman named Johannes Cuntius (Johann Kuntze), a member of the town council (*senator*), after helping settle a dispute was invited to dinner by the mayor, but took leave for the present with a foreboding utterance. He ordered his horses to be brought out and with another man was about to examine a loose shoe on one of them when the horse landed them a kick. Cuntius received the worst of the blow and was brought to bed in great pain. The women having removed themselves from the room, his private parts (*pudenda*) were carefully examined and found to be without a vestige of damage though his complaints were heard "to the wonder of man."

His son at the urging of his wife approached him and to the son Cuntius declared the gravity of his sins though he did not make a confession or ask that a minister be brought to hear him. There were rumors that he told one of his sons that he had made a pact with the Devil. As his eldest son stood watch beside his bed at night a black cat opened the window and went to his bed, severely scratched his face and seemed to be trying to pull him away when it vanished. He soon breathed his last.

The commission to wash his body was given to two pauper servants. They placed the body in a water trough or bathtub, plied it, and positioned his folded hands on the sides, then lo! one hand on its own fell to the stomach area, from which it had been removed. Considering that one of the servants says, "Look! my friend, at the marvelous thing, something of the monster must be in this." But the other, more cautious, says, "Truly be quiet, you, and don't let on, lest we believe something dangerous to us, and if something of our talk gets out."

A day goes by, and then another, and rumors of this sort spread in the town, that some incubus spirit or diabolical Ephialtes [ancient Greek traitor, demon] in the shape of Cuntius violated a certain reluctant neighbor woman, pressed her down and gravely afflicted her even before the body was buried. After the funeral a spectre came to I don't know who sleeping in his upstairs and stirred him awake with these words, "I hardly can keep myself from bothering you so you can't be secure."

The voice sounded like Cuntius, so it seemed to his wife. The night watchmen said they noticed every night in Cuntius' house a tumult to be heard, things thrown and falling. The house gates were found open though they had been carefully closed and the horses stirred and dashed in the stable while the dogs howled all over town. This was only the beginning of the testimonies of Cuntius' manifestations.

Shaking and rattlings of houses with flashes of light in the windows, the appearance of unidentifiable animal tracks outside in the morning, the spectre of Cuntius himself telling the godfather of one of his sons that he had deposited a chest containing 415 florins with his eldest son and did not want the man's godson to be cheated of his inheritance. He threatened the maid who slept with his wife that if she did not cede him his proper place he would wring her neck. He forced himself on women and when one tried to exempt herself by saying how old and wrinkled she was, he only laughed and disappeared.

Cuntius was identified by people who had known him in life when he visited and assaulted them, breathing fire against a wagon driver of his acquaintance and laming him in one of his legs, setting upon the minister who wrote down these encounters while he was in bed, squeezing and exhausting him so he could scarcely move, and coming upon the minister's wife, and later his own wife in bed violently tearing at them. His own daughters had to come to his wife's rescue to prevent him from tearing out her throat. He threw a child about so violently that the child was bruised all over and soft in the bone.

He galloped through the streets of the town like a horse and made sounds like a hog eating grain. He invaded the minister's house during their evening music with a foul stench that only intensified when the minister called upon God, and sickened him severely with a poisonous bloat and pustulous eyes as he lay in his bed that night.

Incessant sounds and sights, stinks, brutalizing humans and animals, keeping the horse that kicked him in a sweat, drinking cows dry, bloodying the altar cloth in the church facing the side of the altar nearest his tomb, fouling water and cow's milk or turning it into blood, performing feats of strength lifting out pots buried in the ground, gossiping with wagon drivers and pulling numerous pranks with a sharp edge, pelting one of the woman who washed his corpse with clods of earth that left marks on a wall behind her. All of this cut into the town's commerce and demanded a solution. These interruptions of Christian life were not worthy of a Christian man.

After many deliberations of all the citizens the consensus was, if they wish to be freed of this vexation, corpses in several recent months were mandated to be dug from open graves, so that it would be clear, in which corpse the Devil would exercise his poisons and *energeia* (influence). The seniors in consultation with the minister uncovered the graves of the more recently dead and found none of the markers, and from the timing of the attacks they determined that the corpse of Cuntius should be examined.

Those buried before Cuntius and after him were already much decayed, their sutures gaping and their bones practically indistinguishable from the soil, but the corpse of Cuntius was whole and intact. His skin encircled his head and breast and the quicklime that had been thrown on the corpse before the casket was closed was gone, leaving supple, ruddy skin like that rubbed with unguents. The joints were mobile and lacking any stiffness. When a staff was placed near his hand the fingers grasped it. His eyes were sometimes closed, sometimes open. When the corpse was stood up the face turned to the north, and on another day to the south. The corpse was much exercised.

A smooth ruddy skin was found beneath the footwear, with conspicuous veins which when opened with a knife yielded a dark red sanguis, as in the living, that stained the surrounding area. The nose was not sharp as in death but rounded. Cuntius while alive was slender and of a modest stature but the corpse had a swollen face and puffed cheeks like those of the fattest pig and barely could be contained in its space. Cuntius had been in the ground from February 8 to July 20, almost half a year.

Judges were appointed and, considering the evidence of demonic activity made plain and the recent similar example of the shoemaker in the city of Breslau, decreed that the corpse be burned. A hole was made in the church wall and the corpse dragged through. The horse that had kicked Cuntius collapsed several times pulling the cart to the place of execution, though later it easily pulled a wagon and two men.

The corpse was released from its underlying soil and cloth wrappings and placed on a pyre. It lay there the whole day long, the head and the arms consumed to the elbow but from the feet to the trunk hardly at all. The executioner withdrew the intact part from the flame with hooks and proceeded to cut it into pieces, which released the purest sanguis, spiritous droplets that sprayed the executioner. Fat particles in the flame ignited brilliantly and hardly could be reduced to ashes overnight. Guards always were present. The flames were fed in the place where the pieces of trunk were set out, and something of sanguis appeared there.

The ashes were diligently collected and cast into the river. In all 620 large logs of the size used in brewing beer were used. There were no more appearances or disturbances from Cuntius. All was calm. A rock was placed in his burial place so no one else would be buried there and as a sign of what had happened. This narration of Cuntius was a little more extended than the others, but true.

Weinrich has nothing more to say of either lemur in the pages of discourse on the reality and variety of spirits that follow. He had already referred to the wandering alderman as an incubus, a sexually voracious spirit that ravishes women alone in bed at night. Cuntius is a poltergeist that wantonly throws about pottery and furniture, a fouler and drinker of cow's milk, a night flyer and a number of other named spirits that were grouped under the Christian category of demons, also categorized and subdivided. He is practically a compendium of spirits joined in one biography, or thanatography.

No one other than Cuntius is named in the account of his ravages. Though the people involved witnessed rather than merely heard about what happened after the man's death, Weinrich is satisfied to cite them only as relations or social roles-wives, sons, wagon drivers, the minister-in attesting to their encounters and representing the "most true" story on the printed page. Cuntius after death recovered his role as husband, father, businessman and community leader in a violent form that intersected with spirits and demons.

His relatives and acquaintances saw his form and heard his voice yet they were cautious in passing judgment on his corpse, and examined others for the tell-tale signs of demonic influence before opening his tomb. After he was removed and burned the corpses of the deceased relatives of one of his three wives also were unearthed and immolated by "master Generoso," not otherwise identified.

From the lethal kick and his seemingly imagined complaints to his behavior as an incubus to the washing of his corpse and the stubborn unburned, still sanguineous pieces Cuntius' posthumous life centers around the force applied to his groin. The horse's flying hoof introduced a demonic *energeia* that killed him and propelled him substance and spirit through his social and economic network newly potent. The two elderly women who wash his corpse negotiate talking about what they see in his naked body, revelation by denial of revelation. The energy resides in the deeply colored, pure sanguis that persists in the pieces of his body that retain their form in fire and under the knife.

Appended to Weinrich's edition after the main text of Pico's dialogues is a letter by Weinrich to the alchemist Andreas Libavius (cruentation specialist) on the question "Whether a *mola* can come about in virgins?" (*Utrum mola in virginibus gigni posset?*). A *mola*, literally a "millstone," also named an undifferentiated but apparently living mass forming in and sometimes ejected from the womb without the introduction of semen.[2] Weinrich also called it a "*tumor,*" a Latin word that means a swelling or growth.

With no knowledge of human zygotes, Weinrich speculated that women must have "generative properties" similar to men, and without a male contribution might coalesce something like semen. Without the complement of the other sex, it did not compose itself into the human image. An infant was made of all the elements of both sexes, a monster was made of both but was missing something from one of them and a *mola* was missing the male contribution entirely. Form depends upon the presence of vital components.

The body after death will decay unless a new force has been introduced.

A body that retains its form after death parallels the returning dead in William of Peterborough's history (one of many, he wrote) and Horst's young nobleman. All three died as the result of a violent force suddenly and unexpectedly applied to the body, a fall, a gunshot and a kick. All three remained fresh in appearance long after death in comparison with others who died at the same time or afterward, and all three bled fresh sanguis post-mortem, as cruentation or when cut. The two who had been maliciously active as physical forms after death were eliminated from society by incineration of the body; one stopped bleeding and was buried.

Sanguis is the medium for the retention of this force whether it is native heat as Horst thought or demonic influence for William of Peterborough and Weinrich. Sanguis remains a material in the corpse never entirely reduced to matter and never entirely spiritual.

Weinrich's emphasis on the verifiability of the Breslau and Pentsch traveling dead made it attractive to those who sought evidence of a spirit world and therefore the existence of God. Many tales of ghosts and demons had been written down associated with specified places and with historic persons. Weinrich offered a dated and circumstantial account that translated oft-told tales into an even more specific context. It was so credible that only the name of the village and, in the case of Cuntius, the name of the main actor need be given.

"I must confess that I am slow-witted my self," wrote the English philosopher Henry More (1614-87), "that I cannot so much as imagine what the Atheist will excogitate for a subterfuge or hiding place for so plain and evident Convictions."[3] More added this remark to the end of his abbreviated translation into English of Weinrich's Cuntius section. Abbreviated to spare the "tedious business to recite all these things at large."

More included most of Cuntius' intrusions into the lives and work of his former community, but left out the colloquy of the women washing his body and the persistence of his middle section in the incinerating fire. The attempts by the incubus (a word More never used) to "force" women and the stubbornly undecayed final body spraying the executioner with fresh blood did receive their due.

Cuntius, preceded by the Breslau shoemaker, was in More's collection of ghost, witch and beast reports (not tales) to confound the Atheist (never addressed directly) with beings and happenings not explicable by the mechanical philosophy. More took the immediate afterlife as a sign that there was more to life than its obvious substance.

More begins his *Antidote* matching atheism with enthusiasm, surprisingly, he writes, given their apparent dissimilarity. Enthusiasm was ecstatic calling upon God to enter the worshiper directly in the form of the Holy Spirit, like the tongues of flame that descended upon the Apostles and other followers of Jesus at Pentecost. In mid-17th century England the word had not yet acquired the severely pejorative meaning of an emotional religious display in public that it did after the 1688 Glorious Revolution and the following civil wars. More attributed both atheism and enthusiasm to the exercise of fancy in place of the "calm and cautious insinuations of free Reason." Atheists might claim to be applying reason to questions of the existence of God, but their approach was as fanciful as that of an enthusiast overwhelmed by what he thought was the Spirit.

Cuntius and all the other figures More introduced in his book were *energumens*. They were humans who became imbued with the Spirit of Nature and were carried away from the proceedings of reason by its force. More was interested in the physics of how this took place; he gave the individual instances as proof that there are spirits which take hold in a body. In face of this plain proof of God's existence the Atheist can only compose fancies.

More returned to Cuntius in his 1659 treatise *The Immortality of the Soul*, his effort to reconcile the mechanistic view of the universe with the spiritist view. He classifies the Silesian alderman with bodies of the dead infested by spirits that animate them ("As notorious in the History of Cuntius…").[4] He engages in a mechanistic reflection of his own on the plots of such spirits. Some people bury their dead next to the hearth to make sure they putrefy in the heat, usually without avail. The spirits are able to "replenish their Vehicle with such a Cambium, or gluish moisture, as will make it far easier to be commanded into a visible Consistence."

Cuntius and the shoemaker belong to the category of Catechanes, a term given by classical authors to the spirits of dead husbands who return to their wives as long as they can inhabit the defunct body. A law was passed allowing women afflicted in this way to have the husband's corpse exhumed and burned with a stake driven through the heart. A century later this term would be merged with "vampire".

More's positive assertion of the influence of malign spirits in the heavy depredations of the dead was contested by John Webster, physician, clergyman and opponent of the belief in witches (but not of the belief in astrology). Webster scorned the "bad Choice" More made of authors to rely upon for his arguments. If the reader thought Webster was criticizing More without cause he recommended looking at Weinrich's account of the shoemaker and Cuntius "to tell whether he can rationally believe these things to be true or possible."[5] Webster had only praise for More's gravity and standing as an author; so much the worse to find him depending upon an obscure author like Weinrich.

Webster questioned the veracity of More's source, and thus the documentation of spirit animation of the dead that it provided. And he questioned whether it could ever happen and thus the reality of spirits. More replied to Webster (not by name, he designated him a "Quack-Theologist") in the scholia to the Latin translation of his *Opera philosophica* (1678).[6]

Where Webster wondered how anyone in a "flourishing University could give credit to these stories of the Shoemaker and Cuntius" More rejoined that he spent his Providence-granted leisure in the flourishing University "cultivating my reason with the most solid arguments of those Truths which is out greatest Interest to know." The Principles he found are so demonstrably true that no Philosopher nor any "pert saucy Quack-Theologist" can enervate them. "…there is nothing in these two narrations repugnant to right reason."

The application of his principles of reason to the episodes of Cuntius makes them out to be the work of demons. The halting of the horse pulling the wagon with Cuntius' corpse is not from the great weight of the corpse but from demons obstructing the horse's travel. The milk transformed into blood is demons replacing milk with blood. The apparition of Cuntius transforming itself into a staff is the demons placing a staff in the room where Cuntius appeared. More defends Weinrich and maintains the accuracy of his reports.

Weinrich and More placed the interventions of Cuntius in spirit-based systems, and they advanced the truth of those appearances as support for a broader theism, a belief in God. The only question that arose concerned the veracity of the reports, which could only be confirmed by connecting them to a set of beliefs unquestioningly asserted. Weinrich had found a chain of causation in the force the horse's kick introduced into Cuntius' body and reverberating in his sanguis.

When More in his response to Webster explained specific apparitions in terms of demonic deceits he was moving as close as his philosophy would allow to a similarly materialist spiritualism. Cuntius and his entire environment was possessed by demons that introduced a demonic causation in place of the mechanics being impersonally articulated by Isaac Newton and other scientists.

There was another way of articulating the Cuntius narration with a world-view that affirmed it without raising the question of its veracity. Weinrich originally presented it as a Silesian history equal to Pico della Mirandola's classical examples of demonry. Lodging it firmly in the locale of its occurrence made it true for loyal residents.

Michael Joseph Fibiger, a Roman Catholic prelate at the St. Matthias beadhouse, antiquarian and historian, updated the *Silesiographia* (1613) of the chronicler Nikolaus Henel von Hennenfeld (1582-1656). Henel had composed in Latin the first regional history of Silesia. From the origins of the name and the nature of the first inhabitants Henel assembled Latin sources on places, personages and natural resources of the region. The Slavs, Poles and Bohemians, had followed the original Vandali and Germani.[7]

Fibiger's *Silesiographia Renovata* (1704) begins with the same premise, German priority, and expands Henel's framework from there.[8] Henel had composed an alphabetic list of the names of settlements in Silesia with a few notes on the size and character of the settlement. Fibiger expanded the list and the content of the entries. Pentsch was not part of either list but Fibiger did name an *opiddum*. Bendschina.[9] This "small unfortified town of the jurisdiction of Jagerndorf on the border of Moravia owes some fame to Johannes Cuntius, a man who while he lived was a Senator there, but after death as a *lemur* of particular note. The history is worth reading, head to heel described…by Martin Weinrich. Our old doctor, whose memory is still with me."

The rest of the entry is a footnote from a German chronicle recounting the 1645 capture by Swedish forces of a Hungarian count who had a pleasant country house in the vicinity of the town, and a detailed bibliographic citation of Weinrich's work.

The Swedish capture of the Hungarian was a turn in the history of Silesia and of Pentsch. Hungarians had invaded the area in the course of 15th century wars, and the Peace of Olmutz in 1478 had granted the province to the Hungarian crown, later joined to the Austrian monarchy. The count was taken prisoner as part of one of the invasions that comprised the Thirty Years War (1618-48) in which Swedish troops served as a Protestant counterpoise to the Catholic Counter Reformation being advanced by the Holy Roman Emperor. The Peace of Westphalia (1648) that ended the war closed all Protestant churches in Silesia except for three *Friedenkirche*. The Lutheran schools remained open.

Fibiger (1657-1712) was not acquainted with Weinrich (d. 1612) but was working from the extensive notes left by Henel, who was. With this sentimental statement he is evoking a memory that Henel had of the learned schoolmaster. After the devastation of the war, and the destruction of the town of Pentsch, the fame of the *lemur* Cuntius preserved in writing by Weinrich, was a collective memory that transcended the Protestant-Catholic antagonisms of the time. Pentsch was now Bendschina, "an unwalled, and except for the churches a town entirely built of wood…" as a 1702 German-language gazetteer of Silesia described it.[10]

The learned construction of the Silesian past was a Catholic-Protestant joint endeavor despite the conflicts of that past. Burial urns that contained the cremated remains of pagans (Vandali and Germani) excavated at a number of sites about Silesia were collected by antiquaries and Habsburg aristocrats for their cabinets of curiosities.[11] The rector of the Sta. Maria Magdalena Lutheran Latin school in Breslau, Christian Stieff, expanded the school's holdings of the artifacts. They were both a reminder of the accursed heathen age of the area and a pious admonition on the fleeting nature of life.

Stieff (1675-1751) served as a resource guide on the urns for the Catholic prelate Fibiger as he pieced together the new edition of Henel's *Silesiographia*. Stieff sent Fibiger a long letter that amounted to the first monograph on the burial urns, and, a dedicated researcher, made him aware of a 1544 letter on the subject, which was printed in the new edition. Stieff was a prolific baroque author of historical, rhetorical and devotional works, mostly in Latin. A German-language "Silesian" version of Defoe's *Robinson Crusoe* (1623-24) was attributed to him.

The next return of Cuntius also was in Stieff's hands. In 1737 he published in Breslau and Leipzig his *Schlesisches historisches Labyrinth (Silesian historical labyrinth)* which was a collection of 100 pieces on the "settings, locales, customs, persons and events" of the region. Stieff's university years were in Leipzig, and with this work he fashioned a new *Silesiographia* that encompassed the old topics of names and resources while intersecting a literary debate current in Leipzig. After a chapter on a celebrated rat-catching dog, there followed one titled "On the Vampires in Serbia".

The Breslau shoemaker suicide and revenant from Weinrich who comes after the Serbian vampires is not at first classified as a vampire, nor is Cuntius who is now for the first time given his German name in the chapter title, "Johann Cuntze Spectre History."[12] The spectre's history begins with Fibiger's Latin paragraph on the town of Bendschin from *Silesiographia* translated into German. Here Stieff adds a note to the received narrative: "or Pentsch, as the common people say." This is the beginning of an acknowledgment that the Latin history of Cuntius/Cuntze preserved in writing is not the only one. Stieff's primary source is still Weinrich, and he does strictly translate from Latin to German, with omissions and additions.

Cuntze remains the respected burgher who has risen to town office. Now his religious conduct also is the subject of comment: "Indeed, the devout (*Christliche*) of the place avowed that he waited diligently upon God's service, that he reverently took Communion; only that he often fell asleep during the sermon in the town's chapel." Cuntze is a Lutheran man of God, with the usual human flaws. After he is felled by the horse's hoof, the suffering Cuntze proclaims his sinfulness, and is suspected by his wife of having made a pact with Satan to know the time of his death.

The Satanic pact was not a part of Weinrich's narrative, but was in More's (Stieff does cite More's account). Stieff's Cuntze is yet more depraved. "Some people said after his death" that Cuntze had sold the life span of one of his children to an unknown person; others murmured that he had agreed with Satan to die by a horse's kick so no one would make an inquiry into any deal he might have made for a more comfortable death.

These summaries of popular opinion are the only details original with Stieff, more evidence that he is drawing from sources other than Weinrich. Like More he leaves out the colloquy of the corpse washers hinting at the physical damage of the fatal kick, and well aware of Weinrich's text, doesn't preserve the implication that Cuntze's after-death attacks on women were driven by frustrated sexual energy. Stieff retains the blood (*Blut*) marks of Cuntio's persistent life but not the force of the blood.

Similarities might well be found between the Serbian vampires as reported and the Breslau shoemaker and Bendschin Cuntze.[13] "One can be allowed the freedom of his opinion: then things that have happened might well be true, if the causes are not well researched, and as the events happened, one can register them precisely (*mathematisch*). Each one dissects them according to his own designs. It is worth considering that nowadays such Devil-tricks lightly occur no more, because proof is only perceived with care and luck. The selfsame things pass by far and wide, which are not investigated, because no right-minded scholar is at hand. Many such histories were sometimes suppressed with flesh and not painstakingly brought to paper."

The similarities between the Cuntze tale from the 1590's and the present (early 1700's) Serbian vampires is because they all are the same kind of trickery which formerly got by without being observed. The work of the Devil is in pulling off such deceits, not in the events themselves. If the activities of the returning dead are not seen for what they are at the moment, then a truth like that of Cuntze is all that remains.

Stieff ends with an approving citation of More's use of Cuntius in *Antidote for Atheism*, as an example of harmful nonsense accepted as truth. Its acceptance is hard evidence of the Devil's plots to be used against the atheists, who would reject God entirely rather than single out the deceptions.

News of "the same things being said to happen in that country [Silesia] and punishment decreed against the dead" prompted the English clergyman James Baker to reproduce More's Cuntius section in his wide-ranging history of the Inquisition.[14] The "same things" were the stories of night visits by the dead spurring panic in the town. More's account of Cuntius had an independent career in English writings and antiquarian journals in the 18th-19th centuries. It was quoted in full with or without More's own comments, as "a striking example of how far credulity may be extended."[15] It might equally well be More who was the credulous party.[16]

The question of who believed it actually happened as reported and what that meant was resolved as with many other accounts of the "supernatural," by treating it as a story. This removed the reader from the religious framework and opened the now edited text to interpretation by categorization and sociocultural analysis.

As the result of an agreement between the Austrian and Prussian monarchies in 1745, Silesia was partitioned. Most of the territory fell to the Prussian state, but the municipality of Jagerndorf, and Pentsch/Bendschin remained under Austrian rule. This did not prevent Prussian scholars from claiming the Silesian revenant among the lore of their realm.

Cuntze was picked up as a "poltergeist and vampire" by the rising Prussian state in an assemblage of *Sagen* (tales) by the Saxon state librarian and literary historian Johann George Theodor Grässe (1814-85).[17] Beginning with legends of the imperial family, Grässe's collection moves through the Prussian empire province by province. Cuntze, preceded by the Breslau shoemaker, is in the Silesia and Lower Lusatia grouping of tales. The text is taken from Stieff and credited as such at the beginning. Grässe has replaced the 18th century spelling and diction with 19th century equivalents, and cut away all of Stieff's commentary on the researcher's lessened susceptibility to such Devil-tricks as Cuntze's.

The title may be "poltergeist and vampire" but the excisions have also removed Stieff's explicit comparison between the tale of Cuntze and the Serbian vampires. This is the only piece among Grässe's two volumes in which the word "*vampyr*" is used, and that only in the title. "*Polter-geist*" does appear, as in Stieff. The events took place long ago and far away, when people believed such things.

Attached to the Cuntze story in all of the publications is a much briefer story of a young woman in the Cuntze household who died soon after he did and despite protective amulets placed in her coffin began troubling people with punishing attacks 8 days after burial. She took the form of a hen and choked another young woman, rattled doors, threw about pottery, and crushed people in their beds. She took the form of dogs, cats and goats, and guzzled down the burgermeister's rosé wine. Her months-long disruption was put to an end by burning her still fresh corpse and scattering the ashes in water.

From Weinrich to Stieff and Grässe the sequence of poltergeist disorders remains consistent with some changes in emphasis. Following are parallel portions of the sentence at the beginning of the young woman poltergeist tale that traces the source of her uncanny postmortem activities.

Weinrich
...eam ex familia illa nonihil magicae scabiei contraxisse
...she contracted from that family something of the itch for magic

Stieff
...sie möchte von dem alten Cuntze geheime Künste gelernet haben, und mit Hexen-Gift angesteckt sein
...she must have learned secret arts from old Cuntze, and was infected with witch poison

Grässe
... sie möchte von dem alten Cuntze etwas gelernet haben, und mit Hexengift angesteckt sein
...she must have learned something from old Cuntze, and was infected with witch poison

The "itch for magic" is a figurative phrase used only in this text. It is a preoccupation contagious from a family source. There is no itch in the German versions because there was no precise German equivalent of the Latin phrasing. Instead the elder Cuntze emerges as the instructor, and the concept of infection with magic is retained in the witch poison (*Hexen-Gift/Hexengift*). Grässe does not allow Stieff's "secret arts". Old Cuntze taught her something that possessed her. Her undecayed corpse contains the secret arts which are destroyed by burning and dissemination of the ashes.

The tutelary witchcraft contagion theme is confined to this annex to the Cuntze story. There are no acolytes in the main story, only victims. Blood diminishes in prominence from Weinrich onward and the vampire-bloodsucker label adopted by Stieff is a label without an actor. Grässe uses it only in the title, to the Cunze poltergeist into the current discussion. The itch for magic or witch poison is a physical thing that figures into other 17th-18th century German ghost tales. It is transmitted into and destroyed with the body but it is not associated with blood.

Before Grässe published the Cuntze story in his Prussian collection, the Austrian side of Silesia, where Pentsch/Bendschin was located, generated its own distinctive claim. The Cuntze story was a literary transmission from Latin to German then updated. Theodor Vernalaken printed a story in his *Myths and Customs of the Volk in Austria* (1859) that from its title in the index would not seem to be a Cuntze tale at all: "The Rider on a Three-Legged White Horse, and Headless."[18] Only from the heading of the text itself-"Burgermeister Kunz in Bennisch"-is there an indication of the tale's affiliations. Now Cuntze is Kunz, and Pentsch/Bendschin is known by its official Austrian name of Bennisch.

The word *volk* in the title makes it a work of the people, and the stories are not from previous written text but from their spoken traditions set down by a philologist with linguo-nationalist leanings. Theodor Vernalaken was educated in Zürich, Switzerland and filled posts in the schools bureaucracy in Vienna, and later, Graz. A correspondent of the Brothers Grimm and other German language and lore scholars, he was a peripatetic collector of tales from the villages of the Austrian empire, and pedagogue intent on exploring, recording and improving the German he heard.

As with all the others materials he collected he gives no notes on where, from whom and when he collected his Burgermeister Kunz tale. The tale itself has more earmarks of local provenance than Weinrich's more elaborate confabulation, with which it shares few features.

Burgermeister Kunz was known as a witchmaster because he rode a three-legged white horse and often rode away late at night and returned early in the morning without anyone knowing. He was friendly to traveling carters who whenever they got stuck on the hill between Bennisch and Spachendorf need only say, "If only Mr. Kunz would come." He would instantly appear in front of the stymied cart on his horse and without being seen to guide it the wagon would go forward over stick and stone even if it was stuck up to the axle. He also conducted wood-gatherers over the forested mountain.

If a carter should approach without seeking his aid by uttering his name the cart would sink to its axles and not move until the omission was made up. Kunz was seen riding at night headless like a ghost.

This state of affairs continued for some time until he died suddenly. His casket was being carried through the marketplace past a structure called "the butcher's stall". One side was the firefighting trough and on the other the magazine. As the pall bearers passed a voice sounded from the rafters of the magazine, "Who are you burying today?" When the answer came, "Burgermeister Kunz," the voice asked, "Who knows if he truly is inside the coffin?" The bearers put it down and opened the coffin. It was full of stones.

Suddenly a fearsome laugh was heard and Mr. Kunz was on the beams on his white horse. He flew down the stairs, through the building's archway in great haste and plunged into the water of the fountain, rendering it undrinkable. Mr. Kunz and his three-legged white horse were never seen again.

This story places the prominent local citizen Kunz among the features and structures of the town's topography. He has the nocturnal habits of a witchmaster, and is the demanding patron of the brotherhood of carters who transport supplies and produce among the towns, and of the firewood gatherers. He rides a horse that distinguishes him even when he is without his head. He seems to have died but actually is still alive. He makes one final appearance in the center of town before vanishing into the town's firefighting fountain, and providing a legendary explanation for the poor state of the fountain's water.

Some of the themes that appear in the Kunz tale are well-known in Teutonic mythology: the *Schimmel* or three-legged white horse, the headless horseman, the night meeting of witches. These are attached to a sequence that unites all the tales: a town leader who has business with carters and who owns a horse dies suddenly and returns from the dead, then disappears into water.

The incubus, poltergeist, *Nachtzehrer* and revenant themes of the Weinrich/Stieff tale might just as well be attached to this base. In the Weinrich/Stieff tale the claim to authenticity is supported by reference to individuals designated only through their social roles in the town, the pastor, the town councilman. In the Vernalaken tale the claim to authenticity is through evocation of local landmarks: a hill, a road to another named town, the marketplace, a building and fountain.

This section of a 1746 map drawn after the partition of Silesia between Prussia and Austria marks Bennisch in the center of the lower left quadrant, Spachendorf (the name divided) directly below it, the chief municipality of Jagerndorf in the upper left quadrant, and Troppau in the center of the lower right quadrant. The location of these towns in the Habsburg Dominions can be visualized by finding Troppau on the 50th parallel on the second map below.

IAEGERNDORF
PRINC
CARNOVIEN
Neukirch
ad Morav.
Katscher

A B East from 10 Greenwich C 15 D 20 E 25 F
NETHERLAND
SILESIA
1526-1740
1795 1809
(Third Partition)
BOHEMIA
MORAVIA
GALICIA
1772
(First Partition)
FRANCE
BAVARIA
ARCHDUCHY
OF AUSTRIA
HUNGARY
TRANSYLVANIA
COUNTY
OF TYROL
SALZBURG
CARINTHIA
Budapest
Vienna
SAVOY
CARNIOLA
VENETIA
CROATIA
BANAT OF
TEMESVAR
BANAT OF
CRAIOVA
1718-1739
GROWTH
of the
HABSBURG
DOMINIONS
Scale 1:10,000,000 (160 miles = 1 inch)
English Miles
BOSNIA
1878-1908
SERVIA
1718-1739
ADRIATIC
SEA
TUSCANY
DALMATIA
BULGARIA
Possessions of the Habsburgs in 1282
Lands acquired between 1282 & 1521
1521 & 1630
1630 & 1700
1700 & 1801
1801 & 1815
since 1815
Lands permanently incorporated are shown
in flat tints & conquests subsequent-
ly lost, in bands.

A gymnasium teacher in Troppau contributed the next version of the Kunze story. Anton Peter made a *Sage* entitled "The Witchmaster Kunze in Bennisch" part of his collection of folk literature from *Austrian* Silesia.[19] Peter lived closer geographically to the site of Kunze's activities than his predecessors, and during the summer school vacation traveled Austrian Silesia recording the words of local bearers of traditions in the manner of the Brothers Grimm and other collectors of the words of the folk.

The operative word in the title of Peter's publication was *volksthumliches,* folk-originated material, a word which had energized German collectors of language and lore since Friedrich Wilhelm Jahn's 1813 book *Deutsche Volksthum.* The communal spirit of the German people transcended political divisions, and the common history was embodied in the speech, songs, stories and histories of the folk. Peter's first folk-originated volume contained children's songs and games, folksongs and dramas. Rather than attempt to translate the *sprichworte,* the words as pronounced by the folk, Peter transcribed them in an improvised system of notation. The songs were entirely in notation, and for the parts unlikely to be transparent to educated German readers he provided an index of passages with translations.

The tales in the second folk-originated book published two years later were mostly in conventional German prose with a few spoken passages in notation. "The witchmaster Kunze" at first seems an unfamiliar figure. He lived in the town of Bennisch in the 16th century and was the subject of sinister stories. The folk said that he went to the cemetery in the midnight hours and spoke the words *"Tåpp anooch,"* 'Come out slowly,"over the graves of dead children, who were compelled to leave the grave and follow him about the grounds until midnight. An investigation into the graves found the childrens' shrouds stained at the bottom (where they had been dragged across the earth).

Kunze died and when his casket was being carried past "the butcher's stalls" in the center of town, he sat on the beams and called out, " **Waan b·gråäbt·rn** ", "who is being buried?" and when his name was uttered, he said, "**Ich bïen ju doo üon laab ju nooch.**", "I am at work from day to night." The coffin was opened and found to be full of stones.

From this moment onward he disturbed the inhabitants in numerous ways day and night. In order to gain some peace they entombed him in the wall of the Bennisch church. No mortar would stick to the wall where he was placed.

At the **Gråänz·r Hïeb·l**, a wooded hill that marked the boundary between Bennisch and Spachenburg, there still was seen the three-legged white horse Kunze rode while alive. If a carter found he could not go any farther when he came to the road over this hill all he had to do was call the horse who at once appeared and allowed itself to be harnessed. He helped as far as the chapel that stood not far from Bennisch. Then he vanished as quickly as he came.

Kunze in this variant is only a witchmaster, not a burgermeister at all. He conducts the procession of the dead children about the graveyard, a motif perhaps attached to his legend during the Thirty Years War. The scene of his appearance as his coffin is carried past the building in the center of town is repeated, but now he is horseless, and instead it is the introduction to unspecified disturbances that seem to go on until he is entombed in the church wall. His horse alone persists in the service to carters trudging over the boundary between Bennisch and Spachenburg, and vanishes when it reaches the chapel.

Both Vernalaken and Peter's versions of the Kunz/Kunze story use the Austrian name for the town. The witchmaster rides or is known to have ridden the three-legged *Schimmel*, who controls the wild portion of the route between the two towns. At the end Kunze sits on the high point in the center of town and asks a mocking question. He is not dead yet, but sooner or later is put to rest.

Neither Vernalaken nor Peter includes Weinrich's shoemaker or the girl who learned the secret arts from Cunze in the collection. There were no "folk" stories to collect about them.

In the foreward to the first volume of his *Sagenbuch des Preussisches Staats* (1868), J.T.G. Grässe extols the patriotism of the subjects of the vast Prussian state, and the diversity of the traditions they bear. This volume, and the second one that contains the version of Weinrich's Cuntius narrative, were published in Glogau, in Prussian Silesia, far from Grässe's Dresden station, but across the border from Breslau in Austrian Silesia. In 1871, when that volume was published, a Prussian Cuntze drawn from the literature faced the Austrian Kunze collected from the folk residing the pages of their respective collections.

Forty years later the thesis of the Prussian Cuntius/Cuntze and antithesis of the Austrian Kunze coalesced into synthesis. A Silesian folklore society had formed in Breslau (*Schlesisches Gesellschaft für Volkskünde*) and its members contributed both the results of collecting and studies to an annual journal. The society also sponsored the publication of a series of book-length collections of stories, songs and customs and studies of themes.

The third volume of the society's series was *Schlesische Sagen I: Spuk und Gespenstersagen* (1910), *Silesian Tales I: Ghost and Apparition Tales*, assembled by Richard Kuhnau (1858-1930). It is both a collection and a study because the texts, all of them drawn from published folk literature, are organized first by motif and second by the area of Silesia they were reported from, seven areas in all, including both Prussian and Austrian Silesia, as well as Polish and Bohemian (Czech) areas. The first section, *Teichenspuk,* is made up of cruentation/bier-right stories from four areas of Silesia.

A long section with tales from all the Silesian areas except Bohemia is devoted to *Vampirsagen.* The Austrian section contains the complete run of Cuntius/Kunze pieces, beginning with a complete translation into German of Weinrich's Latin, followed by Vernalaken and Peter's field transcriptions and the segment from Weinrich on the young girl trained in the magic arts by the witchmaster. Kuhnau references all of the sources, including Stieff and Henel, and adds Stieff's Henry More notes. Though this is a group of vampire tales that feature among them many of the themes by the twentieth century associated with vampires, Kuhnau does not add to the German translation of Weinrich any of Stieff's passages naming Cuntze a "vampire and blood-sucker."

In the introductory notes on the tale groupings Kuhnau observes, "The vampire is mainly a pattern of the Slavic peoples, however it is not foreign to the German lands, and underwent a lavish deformation (*Entstaltung*) during the witch trials of the 16th and even more during the 17th centuries."[20] Kuhnau then evokes the forms of the vampire that caught up in this turbulent deformation, the witchlike nighttime blood sucking and the still fresh, blooded corpse whose reign iis ended by decapitation and burning.

Scanning across the set of Kunze relations that he places together certainly gives a glimpse of some of these features, the night visits and the sanguineous corpse. Yet a practice of the Slavic vampire, suffocating the victim with body pressure, appears in Weinrich's Cuntius relation but not in the other stories. Stieff's affixing the blood-sucker repute to Cuntze is an artifact of his own time, when the Austrian authorities were engaged in suppressing vampire rumors among the Slavic population of their domain, as will be seen. There are no corpses or blood in the tales collected in the mid 19th century. The coffin full of stones seems a stark rejection of that image. What remains is a local legend about a Pentsch merchant named Kuntze who owned horses and governed carters with a supernatural degree of success. But that is not what came to the fore under the hand of the editor.

Kuhnau unified all the Cuntius/Kunze narratives and tales with others under the vampire rubric amid ghosts and witches. This technical joinery made a divided Silesia whole on the verge of the paroxysm of German cultural nationalism leading up to the First World War. Austria and Prussia joined forces against the western European powers and lost their monarchies and sovereignty.

Prussian Silesia became part of the restored nation of Poland after 1918; Breslau became Wrocław and Kuhnau, a village in Upper Silesia, became Kuniow. Austrian Silesia became part of the newly formed nation of Czechoslovakia; Pentsch/Bendschin became Horní Benešov and Troppau became Opava. After Germany and Austria lost another war in 1945, the German population of Silesia was forced to leave.

Cuntius/Kunze was at first a *lemur*, an incubus, a *catechanes* who after a death from a blow returned to reengage with his family and community, seeking food (like a Slavic *upir*), sex and a restoration of his authority. He is found to be a sanguineous corpse showing signs of renewed life which may be from the life he has drawn from others, though not specifically conceived as blood extracted. With changes in political authority he becomes a local spirit, a legend framed by the locale, and is classified as a vampire when the term becomes available and as his picture of the life force fades from local memory.

---

[1] Weinrich (1612: 12)

[2] Weinrich is referring to any millstone-heavy uterine growth and not specifically to molar pregnancy, generated by sperm entering an egg without a nucleus.

[3] More (1655: 227)

[4] More (1659: 173.5)

[5] Webster (1677: 292)

[6] The Latin scholia were translated into English and included in a posthumous collection of some of More's philosophical writings. More (1712: 166-70).

[7] Henel von Hennenfeld (1613: 2)

[8] Henel von Hennenfeld (1704: 1,5) *Antiquissimi Silesiae incola fuere Germani...* (The oldest inhabitants of Silesia were Germans...)

[9] Henel von Hennenfeld (1704: 2, 26)

§. 8.

BENDSCHINA.

Bendſchina Bendſchin/ Opidulum (*a*) immunitum ditionis Jägerndorffenſis in Moraviæ confinio, famam aliquam naćtum à Joanne Cuntio, viro, dum vixit, ibi Senatorio, ſed poſt mortem lemure apprimè inſigni. Hiſtoria lećtu digna, quam à capite ad calcem usque eruditè deſcripſit præmiſſam Illuſtris illius Joh, Franciſci Pici Mirandulæ Domini Concordiæque Comitis de ſtrigibus, five dæmonum ludificatione dialogis V. Cl. Martinus Weinrichius, (*b*) Dońtor olim noſter, cujus etiamnum mihi eſt memoria.

(*a*) Benſcha quoque dicitur; præter Eccleſiam lignea.

An. 1645 machte ſich der Ungriſche Graf und Obriſte Palfy überaus luſtig mit ſeiner angenehmen Geſellſchafft in einem Hof vor dem Städtlein/ ward aber vom Schwediſchen Reichwald unverſehens überfallen/ und gefangen weggeführt. F. Lucæ in Chron. Sil.

[10] *Staat von Schlesien* (1702): 753

Bendſchina iſt eine unbemaurte/ auſſer der Kirchen gantz von Holtz gebaute Stadt auff den Mähriſchen Gräntzen.

[11] Hakelberg (2012: 56-58)

[12] Stieff (1637: 363)

[13] Stieff (1637: 390-91)

[14] Baker (1736: 178-83)

[15] Letter to the editor, *The Antiquarian Repertory* 1(1780): 135-41; 2 (1808): 390-95

[16] Cuntius' account from 'The philosophical writings of Henry More (credulous) Fellow of Christ's College, Cambridge...' Ghosts, *The Recreative Review* 3 (1822): 425-48; 430.

[17] Grässe (1871: 214-23)

[18] Vernalaken (1859: 50-1)

[19] Peter (1867: 62-63)

[20] Kuhnau (1910: XXXII). Kuhnau wrote this passage before Walter Benjamin's essay on the imagination was written, but he seems to anticipate Benjamin's use of the word *Entstaltung.*

10. The village of Krinck

The village of Kringa, Croatia (photo, 2011) is in profile not unlike its appearance between 1672 and 1689, shown in the engraving below the photo, when it was known as Krinck. The remains of the bermed earth ramparts are still visible, as are the outlines of multi-storey masonry pitched roof houses called *rudera* (rubble and dilapidated houses) in the 17th century. On the outskirts of the town, graphically visible in the copperplate engraving, are the planted rows of vineyards and crops surprising to see in the stoney terrain. Johann Weikhard von Valvasor, the author of the volumes on the duchy of Carniola from which the engraving is taken, commented that there was "more wine than water" in Krinck.[1] The town, he wrote, is rich neither in dwellings nor in inhabitants.

Having pictured the scene, Valvasor opens the curtain on the drama. "In the year 1672 this place was the setting of an adventure, namely that the corpse of a man named Georg (or Giure) Grando was uncovered and with special ceremonies had its head hacked off, so that there might be peace."

In spite of Valvasor's language of small village comedy, the events leading up to Grando's 1672 decapitation are a sincerely professed narrative which he personally recovered from individuals he names. His own belief and that of the villagers are two different matters; he relates what they told him.

Sixteen years earlier Grando died and was buried with the customary Christian rites. Nothing of his occupation or manner of death is recorded. He then appeared to Father George, the monk who had conducted the funeral ceremony. When the good Father went to visit the widow with news of "the friendly buried one" (propitiatory title for the recently deceased), he was shocked to see the dead man seated behind the door when he rose to leave.

After this the buried one began his practice of going about the streets at night and rapping on the house doors, and wherever he rapped someone died. He also "gathered himself up with his widow and really slept in with her," a circumlocution for saying he raped her, which the author does state more directly later.

The wife (unlike the male characters, never named) was driven by her loathing for her deceased husband repeatedly to retreat to and stay with the *supan* or *suppan* (market director, headman), Miho Radetich, who agreed to help her. He summoned a group of courageous neighbors to his house for drink and to hear his appeal. This evil should be abolished: George or Giure Grando has already "eaten up" many neighbors and raped and slept with his wife every night.

"Whereupon they agreed to seize the restless night-goer and put an end to his handiwork." Nine of them (all named in another volume of the history) joined together and with two lanterns and a crucifix in hand opened the grave. The face of the corpse was full red and its mouth was open with laughter. The *supan* griped that nine men couldn't come to rights with a single corpse, and at the very sight ran away "like scared rabbits".

He exhorted them to return to the grave with him. They tried to drive a sharpened hawthorn stake through the chest of the corpse only to have it deflected. Playing the clergyman, the *supan* then held the crucifix in front of the corpse's face and addressed it. "Behold, thou *strigon* (as such restless dead were called in Istria). Here is Jesus Christ, who freed us from Hell and died for us! And thou, *strigon*, can have no rest!" This and all the other words from "this untimely exorcist or orator to the dead," drew sparks from the eyes of the spectre.

None of this, including the stake, penetrated the corpse. A Mehrenfels (nearby village) resident named Nicolo Nyena took a hoe and began hacking at the neck crosswise, but losing heart yielded to Stipan Milasich, who leapt to the task and detached the head, whereupon the dead man gave out a cry as if he had been alive. The grave filled with blood. The bold executors then closed the grave and went home. From that time onward the wife and other people had peace from him.

Valvasor then reassures the reader that there is no doubt about this because he heard it himself from people who were there. It is verifiable and even commonplace that when the dead are restless and seize people then the grave is opened and the body pierced with a thornwood or hawthorn stake. In a Venetian town not far from Krinck, he has it from "a steady hand," this was done, but when the authorities heard of it they judged it harshly and very low because it is the devil's work, "who deceives and blinds the people and brings them to superstition."

A citation from the Latin *Epitome delictorum* of the Cordoban jurisconsultant and demonologist, Francisco Torreblanca, gives weight to the condemnation of the belief and practice. "Apparitions and resurrections of the dead are repugnant to the nature of souls."[2]

Torreblanca in turn quotes a section of Aquinas' *Summa theologica*: "A soul separated by natural virtue cannot move any body…" It was debated among theologians whether the soul might be restored to the body before the Second Coming of Christ. The Thomist strain denied the possibility, though others considered that the body might be demonically reanimated while the soul resided in hell (Dante, for instance).

Valvasor reached into the most solemn theological precedent to affirm that the night visits, knells and rapes could not have been the work of an animated corpse as the villagers told him, but were a deception played upon them by demonic forces, to encourage superstition.

The people of Krinck were convinced that their tumbledown decapitation of Grando's corpse put his restless soul to rest. The Venetian authorities took a dimmer view of the same behavior in another Istrian town under their jurisdiction. All they saw was unearthing a corpse and driving a stake through it, an act of civic disorder and mutilating the dead contrary to the law.

In the volume of *Die Ehre von Herzogthums Crain (The Glory of the Duchy of Carniola)* devoted to manners and customs, Valvasor wrote some paragraphs on mortuary beliefs.[3] "The land and peasant folk in Istria firmly believe that there are magicians and witchmasters who suck out children's blood. They call such blood-suckers *strigon,* and just as much *vedarèz.*" He defers further discussion of this proclivity of the *strigon,* and immediately moves on to the death raps on the doors of houses also attributed to them, and then to the beset widows. He does have more to say about the widows.

"I do worry, however, that the widows, often while they are young and beautiful, quite genuinely and wakefully go to bed with right fleshly spirits. To tell the whole truth, the spirit would leave them no rest until they thrust a thornwood stake through his chest."

After this galant aside attributing the *strigon* excitements to the loneliness of widows, he relates the after midnight grave openings and corpse stakings by "the heartiest". These procedures are very common among the Istrian peasants, and though they meet with considerable disapproval and punishment from the authorities as a violation of church doctrine, yet histories abound. He then gives a summary of the Grando case with a full list of the names of the participants in the staking, and refers to the longer account under the heading of Krinck in a later volume.

Nothing Valvasor wrote in either of the Grando reports (*Berichte*) suggests that this *strigon* sucked blood from children. The town priest is the first to see Grando after death, but is no longer involved after the sighting at the wife's house. For sixteen years after Grando's death the dead man delivers warnings of deaths (or causes them) by knocking at the doors of houses. The long-used wife's complaints to the village's *supan* causes him to form a party of bold residents who turn and run at the sight of the grinning, full-blooded corpse. After several fits and starts, including the *supan*'s act as an exorcist priest, the undefeated corpse is separated from its life by decapitation and bloodletting.

Valvasor's alternate explanation for the inclusion of widows among the occupations of the invasive dead would seem to have an application to the case of Grando, though he does not make it directly. Perhaps the future widow loathed her husband, was forced by custom to receive his attentions, and perhaps complained about him while he was alive. For sixteen years after his death and burial she endured further approaches that amounted to rape. The development of attack and response is collapsed.

A drama of initial acceptance of a new nighttime companion that ended in impalement may have been more concrete than metaphoric. The resolution of whatever relations gone bad, or never good, that went on in the widow's house was aggressive action against the still fresh corpse of the husband. After that all was at peace for the wife and villagers. Anyone else coming at night would fall into a less spectral category, as Valvasor put it, "right fleshly."

The Grando case was one more example of villagers using an act of corpse uncovering and mutilation to substantiate beliefs contrary to the official line while managing the position of an adult unmarried woman in the community. Both the intact corpse and the formally unpartnered woman threatened dark rumors. Openly fixing both of them in the same action was worth antagonizing the authorities. This procedure had long been used throughout Europe to restore peace to small, enclosed communities.

The first two names of Janez Vajkard Valvasor (1641-93) are written according to his Slovenian ancestry; his last name, "master of the feud", is a title bestowed upon and adopted by urban merchants in the Holy Roman Empire. He was the twelfth child of fifteen born to parents of the Slovenian elite becoming integrated into the aristocracy of the Habsburg monarchy. After attending a Jesuit school in Ljubljana (Laibach) he made an extended grand tour of Europe, which included a time on the southern border of the Habsburg Empire as a soldier fighting the Turks.

His interests, which his wealth allowed him to cultivate, included geology, topography, language history and customs, all of which culminated in the writing and publication of the cultural physiography of Crain, or Carniola, the duchy within the Habsburg empire primarily occupied by the Slovenes. The work is formed of information that Valvasor, following a principle he states several times in the volumes, indicates whether he garnered it from direct observation or gathered it from others. His motto: I will not practice to specify for certain, what I myself have not seen and witnessed.[4]

Valvasor wrote in Latin, the international language of scholarship, and exchanged letters in that language with Thomas Gale, the secretary of the Royal Society of London, sending copperplate engraved maps of Carniola, and a paper on the hydrography of a lake in the region, which was published in their *Philosophical Transactions*.[5]

Besides his observations and conversations Valvasor amassed a library of works on his subjects of interest to serve as references for the Carniola volumes, and he set up a shop in Bogešperk, a castle he purchased, to print the engravings. The text was in German, the official language of the Habsburg Empire, and was edited and it was believed partially written by the widely read polymath Erasmus Francisci. For the survey of the towns Valvasor spoke with the "land and peasant people" in Slovene and Croat, and with Francisci's assistance set his findings down in German.

Like a cutaway of the language strata of the work, the dedications to the volumes are poems in Latin, German and Slovene, and there are passages and sample words in "Crain-Slavic language" here and there throughout *Die Ehre*. There also are Latin quotes, from the classics and more recent authors, a span of language from the local to the regional to the international.

The location of Krinck introduced another culture area: the town, as seen in the map below, is on the Istrian peninsula, the southernmost reach of Carniola (the Italian name of Crain), and close to the border with the portion of the peninsula then dominated by the Republic of Venice.

Detail of Ducatus Carnoliae map, William Hoffman, 1714 (see full map at end of text)

The Venetian authorities reacted restrictively (Valvasor learned from a reliable source) to the grave opening and corpse mutilation in a nearby town under their control. Nothing of the sort happened in Krinck, but the clampdown was a harbinger of Austrian official involvement in similar cases to come elsewhere in the empire, creating a conduit for the blending of traditions.

Following the short recital of the Grando case in Book 6 is a section marked *Anmerckungen* (Comments). It begins with an elaboration of the word *strigon* used for Grando. This Slavic word derives from Latin word *strix*, which the heathen Romans used for the night bird called the *uhu* that sucks milk or blood from nursemaids or children, and denotes the witch that does the same.

Verses from Ovid's poem *Fasti* describing the *striges* are quoted in the original Latin followed by a free German translation, and sentences from other classical and Renaissance Latin authors on the characteristics of these predatory night visitors. The Florentine philosopher and Catholic priest Marsilio Ficino added an element to their dossier when he wrote that the creatures vulgarly called *striges* "suck the blood of infants, and through the powers rejuvenate." This was the first time anyone associated renewal of life with nocturnal bloodsucking and the Krinck manifestation, but it was only by proximity. Grando, who never was accused of taking blood, only of being a sanguineous corpse, was not named or alluded to in Valvasor's Comments.

The remainder of the Comments section cites and reviews the stories of a number of reanimated corpses that wreaked havoc in Bohemia, German states and Scandinavia, and were put to rest by impalement, with beheading and burning when that was not enough. While the soul of the sinner burns in hell fire, the body inhabited by a demon is also consigned to an elemental burning.

 Saxo Grammaticus' Asmund and Aswid appear in a quotation of the "gothic" Latin and German translation. Cuntius is not among the returned in this survey, but most of them are wealthy merchants and town officials who after their lives of sinful gain have lent their corpses to satanic forces.

A particular misfortune comes when the corpse is unearthed and it is noticed that it has half-eaten the shroud, and partially pulled it from the throat. Then the coffin is as bloody as if the body had been staked. The efficacy of the driven stake is reviewed, and the final case, of a hellishly indebted Jutland tradesman and his wife, is an example of when it is not necessary.

The one comment that reaches back to the Istrian locale of the Grando story refers to the sexual dimension of his invasions. "When the Istrian peasant women defend themselves with a faithful, zealous and God-entrusting prayer, and otherwise make use of Christian practice, and forego superstitious means, the Devil might well feel that he should rape them at night in the aspect of a buried magician." When it comes to this, however, the Devil will find himself three times lacking. There are means of pinning the vehicle of this attempted attack in the grave, and otherwise preventing its rise.

The author of this Comment section, who takes an altogether more combative approach than the ethnographer of the Grando story, was likely to have been Erasmus Francisci. Rather than being merry widows welcoming fleshly spirits they can dispose of if they become too importunate, the piety of Istrian peasant women makes them the target of the Devil who is ultimately frustrated in his commandeering of the corpse for the purpose of rape.

This strain of blood and fire, the bloodsucking night birds and the versions of the pierced and incinerated corpse, permeates a long manual that Francisci published the year after Valvasor's volumes first appeared, *Der Höllische Proteus, The Hellish Proteus,* which proclaims the protean forms that Satan takes in his battle to delude and ensnare human souls. That battle is evoked from the first lines of the introduction. One long chapter in this over 1000-page book, *Der schmätzende Todte,* The smacking Dead, is dissonant with the sound of the demon-inhabited dead chewing their own flesh and garments in the grave.

The chapter contains the same excursion into the bloodthirsty *striges* as in Valvasor's book, the same quote from Ovid's *Fasti,* but this time with a comprehensive and literally trenchant rapacity. "At night they suck breasts, and likewise milk goats with their beaks and have a great appetite for human blood."[6] Grando does not appear in these pages, amid the many examples of walking corpses. Valvasor, "a very well-read and curious heart,"[7] is credited with supplying several of the devilish instances, but nothing from Istria.

Calling Grando a *strigon* and juxtaposing his story with nighttime blood feeders by the same name overcame the lack of any description of his own blood feeding and entered him into a growing literary category. The observably bleeding sanguineous corpse could be explained as a *strigon* who acquired the extra blood from victims attacked in the night. Even the historians who pledged to tell the truth they witnessed could only tell the truth of what they heard from victims and those who took part in the cemetery raid that ended the corpse's career. Valvasor didn't assert that he saw the corpse of Grando.

Valvasor's testimony as reframed by Francisci was slightly more pervasive than that surrounding Cuntius. Grando made the transition to the newly introduced category of vampire in the "conjectural thoughts" a Weimar physician named Johann Christoph Fritsche contributed to the Leipzig vampire debate of the mid-1730's. Fritsche, who had written his doctoral dissertation on the use of earthworms in medicine, began his thoughts, without at first using the word "vampire", with a sequence of cases from Bohemian, Greek and Carniolan sources.

Fritsche places Valvasor and Francisci's comments on the sexual and blood-sucking depredations of the Istrian *strigon* before the specific case of Grando, which he quotes in full.[8] The parts in separate volumes were edited and joined together on the way to Fritsche's larger subject, the blood-sucking vampires with incubus properties studied by Viennese medical authorities.

Grando was not mentioned by other Leipzig writers of this period. Fritsche's inclusion of his case among those labeled vampires confirmed Grando's eligibility for that position. This was not due to extraordinary influence of Fritsche's book, but because it expressed an emergent alignment. From this time onward whenever Grando was mentioned in print for any reason it was as a vampire. Blood-sucking repute was attached to his history though none ever was reported of him, and eventually he became a "typical" vampire,[9] and the subject of the "earliest written account" of a vampire[10].

The appearance of the corpse on opening the grave, the full-bloodedness and other signs of life and consciousness, linked Grando to other similar occasions, when members of a community had taken it upon themselves to end the scourge. If the compelling and repeated image could not be doubted, and still was present when demonic possession and blood-sucking were dismissed as superstition, how could it be explained?

The Basel physician Friedrich Fischer devoted a section of his extensive study of somnambulism to vampirism, and after reviewing the Viennese reports of the Serbian vampires he turned to Valvasor's description of the uncovering of Grando.[11]

> The reawakening of the vampire Grando allows a horrifying glance into the inner state of this man in seeming death (*Scheintod*). He awoke to the free use of muscles and limbs first in the moment, as his head, truly in a slow, clumsy manner, was hacked off. Then the laughing face was a strained, spasmodic distortion. The opening of the mouth, contrary to breathing, was an involuntary reaction to the stimulus, which the newfound urge must bring on. The tears, not a product of the vegetative process: his feeling had retained the ordinary action. These tears but prove

that the unfortunate awakened inwardly, within the paralyzed muscle
system and both saw and heard his nasty fate.

Grando according to Fischer was a victim of the dreaded premature burial, stimulated back into wakefulness at the protracted moment of decapitation. An almost cinematic suite of facial expressions ensued, conscious body reactions which the recounting villagers took to be the leers of a maleficent *strigon*.

This awakening consciousness interpretation of Grando was so alluring that Fischer ignored the also recounted fact that the corpse had been in the ground for sixteen years (1656-72) before the exhumation. The freshness of the corpse so long after burial was an explanation for the community members long afflicted by death knocks and bed intrusions. Fischer favored the shock of the awakened Grando sensing his fate, however otherwise improbable that was for someone of his medical sophistication. It was an altogether more Romantic image than the Gothic original.

The English physician Herbert Mayo, seeking out "the truths contained in popular superstitions," also edited out the sixteen years, looked directly into the face of Grando in Valvasor's account and found *Scheintod* awakening.[12]

Preserving that first shocking sight of the lifelike Grando in the grave without the preface of a long burial was fundamental to a quasi-scientific theory of Grando as vampire. The superstitious village context with its scarcely emergent sexual politics was then set aside in favor of physiology.

A compromise between science and superstition was reached in the work of Johann-Joseph von Goerres, a Roman Catholic mystic and reformer whose life (1776-1848) exactly spanned the revolutionary era.

von Goerres included a paragraph summarizing the Grando discovery in the volume on "natural mysticism" in a set that also included "divine" and "diabolical" mysticism." Like Fischer and Mayo he ignored the length of time elapsed between Grando's death and burial.[13] He surmised that the lifelike appearance was due to "vegetal life" replacing spirit and animal life in the blood of the infected corpse, making the fluid as cold as the juice of the plant.

The blood did not coagulate, continued to move in the vessels spurring the expressions and gestures of the body in the exterior air. The humidity of the tomb diluted the blood-sap and increased its volume, thus accounting for the large quantities of seemingly fresh blood moving about the body and leaking into the surrounding space. He compared the exaggerated appearance of the corpse to the underground versions of terrestrial flowers that grow to fantastic size in caves.

The vampire corpse spread its contagion to people living in its vicinity. It only seemed to suck blood from them; it actually absorbed elements from them through nervous action exercised at a distance. The wasting effect was the opposite of the vampire's underground expansion and explained the deaths of the vampire's victims without needing to document his material presence in each case.

The vampire contagion was confined to the Slavic peoples; it had been most prominently reported among them, like the plique, a hair mass they exhibited and cultivated. von Goerres both narrowed and expanded the "vampire theory" to embrace the known details about Grando and interconnect them in an underlying pattern of ethnic particularism.

These versions of Grando attest to the effort to verify the reported picture of the sanguineous corpse associated with him, and place it in the context of a vampire type referred back to Eastern Europe. Because there was no narrative of Grando as a bloodsucker, he did not figure by name or locale into the fictional invention of the vampire in the 19th century and afterward. The scrutinizing of records for instances to which the label of vampire could be attached sometimes brought Valvasor and Francisci to light. No *volkisch* investigators interviewed the Croat-speaking villagers of Kringa as they did the German speakers of former Pentsch in the Czech region.

Italian cultural and economic hegemony in 19th century Istria also found its expression in the gathering of folklore with an eye to unearthing cultural influences from Roman times onward. Historical and archaeological journals and writings found an easy connection in the *strigon* traditions of Istrian villages. A retired bureaucrat in the regional administration of Istria turned historian, Carlo de Franceschi, drew upon Valvasor for the opinion that the dead *stregoni* returned from the grave, poking (*picchiando)* their deadly jabs upon doors at night.[14] "Which is remedied by opening the grave and burying a sharp stake in the cadaver." Such a case is detailed for the village of Coddirigo in 1672, but the name of Grando is not given, and for another village in the Venetian area, which the authorities addressed harshly.

Grando lingered in German, French and English texts surveying vampire lore and with embellishment was fitted into the Dracula archetype. Hermann Hesse in 1924/25 sought to combine Valvasor's Grando narrative with other ghost and witch tales extracted from the 19th century periodical *Rheinisches Antiquarius* but he could not find a publisher.[15] Both Hesse and his periodical source place Grando in the village of Krink in the *Grafschaft Mitterburg* (Mitterburg Duchy), an attempt to absorb him into Rheinland lore by default.

Dracula, seeming to absorb Grando into a homogenized international media phenomenon, also helped Istrians to assert a regional identity apart from the Croatian nationalism growing with the independence of the Croat state at the end of the 20th century. The "strong and assertive" Istrian identity countered attempts to prove Istria always had been Croatian.[16]

The Croatian novelist Boris Perić realized Grando as a fictional character in a work entitled *Vampir* (2005), which made Grando out to be the first "Byronic" vampire and yet an Istrian *štrigon,* a sorcerer with two lives, and, as he put it in an interview, "a solid component of Istrian identity".[17] Perić incorporated into his imaginative mix some of the witch and ghost stories Hermann Hesse intended to publish. Though he denied that Grando, and vampires, are a preoccupation of his, he co-authored a study of *Fantastic beings of Istria and Carniola (Fantastična bića Istria i Kvarnea,* 2008) and more recently a survey of the vampire myth in literature and film (2015), both of which have sections on Grando. The cover illustration of *Fantastic beings* shows a shrouded figure rising from a map of the Istrian peninsula.

Croatian folklorist Evelina Rudan, presenting her doctoral dissertation, "Supernatural beings and phenomena in Istria" at Vampire Night in Kringa, said that the event could not pass without bringing up Jure Grando.[18] Rudan had collected hundreds of supernatural tales from people in Istria, and the few that concerned Grando made him out to be a vampire in the Dracula mode. The forum gave her presentation press coverage, moderated by the same journalist who interviewed Perić at the launch of his book six years earlier, took place at a theme bar in Kringa designed to attract vampire tourism to the center of the peninsula.

The cafe bar, where coffee and vampire-themed drinks are served, is named Vampire (not Vampir, as in Croatian) and is subtitled "the legend of the štrigun of Kringa." The international term Vampire and the Croatian word coexist in the public presentation. The monthly Vampire Night sessions featuring talks by authors, more likely horror novelists than scholars like Rudan, began in 2006, a year after the bar was opened.[19]

Speaking to people at these gatherings, Lajla Veselica heard alternative Jure Grando stories that sounded like village gossip about a celebrity, that Grando was a burglar who faked his death and used the vampire story as cover for his break-ins. The rumor Valvasor collected that Grando's wife was entertaining a lover and accused her deceased husband of attacks to shift attention to the grave was being repeated in Kringa.

A two year project (2003-05) by students of ethnology and cultural anthropology at the university in Zagreb to collect Istrian lore on traditional healing practices found reputed informants and healers willing to speak about štriguns and kršniks only if their full names and locations were not disclosed.[20] Kringa was not among the 21 villages they visited. There was no reference to Jure Grando or any other historic individual who returned from the grave to create havoc, but elements of the Grando story, the night knockings, were related as part of local legends.

Removal of spells and inducing the recovery of the afflicted, overcoming the animosity of a neighboring village or family were the most prized skills. Preventing the return of the dead by facing the corpse down and fixing the mouth with nails were practiced rather than opening the grave, impalement and decapitation. No after-death sexual attacks were recalled, but blood-taking and crushing pressure were among the dangers from the dead become *povampiriti,* vampirized. Outside of the Kringa sphere the definition of a štrigun and related activity was less controlled by the attachment to vampires.

Besides the publication of Perić's novel and the establishment of the Vampire Caffe in Kringa, the development of Jure Grando infrastructure was chronicled over the course of 2005 by four articles in the regional newspaper *Glas istre*.[21] One of these articles briefly described a

132

short film made by the students at the Juraj Dobrila gymnasium in Pazin, the administrative center of Istria, *Vampir moga zavičaja, Vampire of my homeland* (2005).[22]

The film begins with an upward pan to a stone church tower (title) followed by a shepherd herding sheep at the edge of buildings, a stone sculpture of the crucified Christ and a view up a cobbled, shadowed alleyway of the old part of an Istrian village. The choral performance of "O Fortuna," the incantational beginning poem of Carl Orff's *Carmina Burana,* plays intermittently throughout, amid a voiceover narration and the voices of interviewees and the actors in the performance section.

At a sunny outdoor market in Pazin a young woman approaches women shoppers asking them if they believe in witches, vampires and other supernatural beings. The first few wave her away dismissively, then others admit a belief.

A panoramic shot of cultivated fields and the village of Kringa, a cross over and entryway, a man walks a pathway with a bunch of herbs cradled in his arm while a dog barks wildly in background. The only sound is the choral performance of "O Fortuna".

In a darkened interior a young woman dressed in a colorful blouse and skirt uses a hand iron to press clothes on a stone table. A priest in a cassock enters and she receives him with a bowl of broth, confesses to him tearfully that her long deceased husband, Jure Grando, has been coming to her. The priest's consoling words are interrupted by the appearance at the door of a dark-suited man scarcely visible, and the priest quickly flees, as the wife holds up her hands in a fending gesture.

She is next seen running down an empty alley and pounding on the bolted doors of the castle, at last gaining admittance to the office of Miho Radetić, the *supan.* She pleads with him on her knees. He walks in the dark accompanied by two other men bearing torches to an open area of earth which they excavate. The lid of a coffin is uncovered and removed, and beneath it the fresh face of a young man causes them to recoil. They return with the priest, who holds a cross to the corpse, which squirms tortuously. A long staff driven into the body is pushed away and finally a hoe is raised and swung down.

The reporter Davor Šišović relates the case of Jure Grando and the film to Valvasor's account-his volumes and the print of Kringa are shown-and makes the case for Grando as the earliest known vampire. A table in the vampire museum displays a "recipe for protection from vampires" (vinegar, brandy, mustard, pepper, camphor, garlic). On the wall is a fragmented mirror designed to ward of the interlopers. The owner of the Vampire Caffe speaks and there is a shot of his delivery van leaving on a mission. The film ends with a collage of vampire drawings.

The "vampire of my homeland" links the canonical Valvasor story to the international vampire imagery with a claim of national priority for Croatia and Kringa. It represents the Croatian entry in the vampire tourism competition long centered on the Romanian Dracula sites. Tradition did not have to be invented in Kringa as it did in Romania. Jure Grando, and not Vlad Tepes, was the model of the modern literary vampire, as Boris Perić argued in his writings and interviews.

Between 2005 and this initiation of possessive Grando popularization and 2011, when Evelina Rudan reported her collecting in her dissertation and at a Vampire Night talk, the growth of the Internet and other digital communications opened ground for dissemination of beliefs about vampire beliefs, and self-authenticating visual imagery. Rudan commented that stories of *štrigoni* and similar beings like those collected by the Zagreb students had become rare, and supernatural healing powers were more likely to be associated with bioenergetics and alternative medicine more affordable for rural Istrian people than clinical medicine. Jure Grando, like Dracula, has made the transition to a popular anti-hero.

At least three other brief videos on Jure Grando have been uploaded, all of them talks on Grando's authenticity and importance, with reference to the Vampire Caffe. Tourist brochures promote Kringa as "a place you would not want to visit."[23] Domestic tourism continues to be a primary object of the promotion. A stop action animation of the story of Jure Grando using puppets premiered at animation festivals in 2015. Through online brokers it is possible to rent the Rustic Villa Jure Grando for a stay in Kringa, or the Jure Grando Presidential Suite in the Kempinski Hotel in the resort town of Savudria on the Istrian coast of the Adriatic. The tasteful Mediterranean décor of these rooms contains no vampire objects.

You can purchase a cast resin tombstone 24'x2'x18' with Jure Grando's name and dates in relief on the dark cracked and rusticated surface for $69.95 plus shipping.

Jure Grando was a picture of the life force transacted in a local figure who experienced a violent death and post-mortem return until his sanguinous corpse was obliterated. He was announced to the German-literate intelligentsia of the Austro-Hungarian empire by a Slovenian noble skeptically placing local traditions in the context of the classically educated Christian with national loyalties. Grando was eventually adjusted into the vampire model, but without the same modifications as applied to Cuntius amid shifting cultural boundaries. He was reintroduced as peculiarly Istrian spirit, while being marketed as a primary vampire.

Carniola with the Istrian peninsula William Hoffman 1714

[1] Valvasor (1689: 3, 318). Book 11: Der Marcht Krinck

[2] Torreblanca (1678: 234)

[3] Valvasor (1689: 2, 335) Book 6: Von der Crainerisch-Sclavanischen Sprache

[4] *Als der ich nichts für gewiss anzugeben gewohnt, was ich selbst nicht gesehen und erfahren.* Printed by Radics (1866: 3) at the front of his "biographical sketches" of Valvasor.

[5] Birch (1757: 452; 482-83)

[6] Francisci (1690: 263)

[7] Francisci (1690: 1008)

[8] Fritsche (1732: 9-13)

[9] Concerning Vampires, *Chambers's Journal of Popular Literature* 73(1896): 731-32

[10] Ladouceur (2013: 92) Also, in other writings, "the oldest vampire," "the first vampire". The Wikipedia statement is that Grando "may have been the first real person described as a vampire".
"The first well-described modern vampire scare" Introvigne (2001: 598).

[11] Fischer (1839: 326)

[12] Mayo (1849: 32-33)

[13] von Goerres (1861: 290-96)

[14] de Franceschi (1879: 451)

[15] Haumann (2011: 77). The Grando story was included in the published collection Hesse (1986: 84-86) with no acknowledgment of Valvasor though retaining his first person statement of sources.

[16] Bellamy (2003: 122)

[17] Šišović (2005)

[18] Jure Grando je ustvari štrigun, September 18, 2011, http://www.glasistre.hr/vijesti/arhiva/342548

[19] Lalja Veselica, Croatian 'Dracula' revived to lure tourists, *Mail and Guardian*, April 24, 2006 http://mg.co.za/article/2006-04-24-croatian-dracula-revived-to-lure-tourists

[20] Vinšćak (2005)

[21] Vampir Jure Grando postao atrakcija Kringe (Vampire Jure Grando becomes attraction in Kringa), *Glas istre*, April 29, 2005; Film o vampire is Kringe (Film about vampire from Kringa), *Glas istre*, May 22, 2005; Noćni terror vampira iz Kringe (Night terror of vampire from Kringa), *Glas istre*, September 8, 2005; Jure Grando, a ne Vlad Tepeš, model je modenog kniževnog vampire (Jure Grando, and not Vlad Tepes, is the model of the modern literary vampire), *Glas istre*, October 1, 2005.

[22] Uploaded to YouTube in 2011. https://www.youtube.com/watch?v=xvR-_F2Z674

[23] Hajrudin Mohdanović, Istarski krvavo, http://www.24sata.hr/news/istarski-krvavo-kringa-mjesto-koje-sigurno-ne-zelite-posjetiti-337265 **2013**

11. The village of Kisolova

The *Wienerisches Diarium* for Saturday, July 21, 1725 was headed with the usual inscription, that it was published by leave of his Royal Romish and Catholic Majesty (the Austro-Hungarian Emperor), and was available at the Kaiserlich Hof-Buchdruckerei in Vienna. The lead news was the report of a hunt with the participation of the Czarina in St. Petersburg, followed by a progressive sequence of royal, aristocratic and high church activities nearly up to the date of the paper. On the last two pages, right before the betrothal announcements, was the "Copy of a Writing from the Gradiska District in Hungary."

The writing was a notice submitted to a government authority by an officer, the Kaiserlich Provisor in the Gradiska District, who was not otherwise named. It was first person account in stressed bureaucratese by a man attempting to escape responsibility for events he could not control, unusual fare for this daily printed organ of the monarchy.[1]

About 10 weeks ago town of Kisolova, Rahmer District, present subject Plogojoviz by name departed by death and was buried in the Serbian manner. It was observed in the aforementioned town Kisolova within 8 days 9 persons old as well as young died after enduring disease for 24 hours. As they lay still alive upon the death-bed they often said that during the mentioned 10 weeks a distinct Peter Plogojoviz came to them in sleep and lay upon them and strangled them so they must right away give up the ghost.
Likewise then the rest of the subjects were very upset such that even more would die because the wife of the deceased Peter Plogojoviz said that her husband came to her and asked for his *oppanki*, that is, shoes. Through the town of Kisolova they passed from one house to another. With such persons (they call *vampyri*) various signs of the undecayed bodies: skin and hair, nails and beard must be seen to grow on them. So the subjects resolved to open the grave of Peter Plogojoviz and see if the mentioned signs really are found on him. To which end they then betook themselves to me for the previously stated case and with me together with the local *Poppen* or divines sought to undertake the inspection. Whether they should first forward such Factum to be approved and that such an undertaking in advance must submissively and obediently be reported to the Honorable Administration and a high body of the same over this one must hear it. They in no way wanted to take comfort in this but evermore gave this short answer for themselves: I must do what I wish alone unless I allow them to proceed with the stated examination and rightful discovery of the corpse according to their custom. Otherwise, they would forsake home and property. Waiting for a reply to a respectful resolution from Belgrade the whole town (as happened 12 times under the Turks) can go to ground from such a vile spirit, which they did not wish to await. Since such people could not be deterred from their fixed resolution neither with bribes nor with threats, with a contingent of Gradiska Poppen I went with them to the named village of Kisolova, secured the already disinterred body of Peter Plogojoviz, and found the whole truth as follows,
In the first place body and the grave did not smell the slightest of the dead vile odor. The body outside of the nose, which dropped somewhat, was entirely fresh. Hair and beard, yes, even the nails, from which the old growth had fallen away, were grown on him. The old skin, which was somewhat whitish, had peeled away, and a fresh new layer under it was done. The face, hands and feet, and entire body were obtained that could not have been perfected in his lifetime. In his

mouth was beheld not without astonishment fresh blood which according to common repute he sucked from those he killed. In sum all the indications were present which the people (as already remarked above) said he should have. Now while I as well as the Popp beheld this spectacle the people were more and more aghast and bewildered. Together in short order they sharpened a stake to stab the dead body through the heart. From not only such piercing widespread blood flowed from ears and mouth. But other wild signs (which in keeping with high respect I forego) passed by. Finally they burned the aforementioned body to ashes according to the usual custom, which then to the Most Honorable Administration please wish to present and submissively and obediently that if a mistake should have been made herein such be attached not to me but to a rabble taken out of themselves by fear.

The Provisor, a mid-rank official charged with procurement of supplies for the administration and the military, apparently could speak Serbian or had contacts with the local residents who could speak German. At his seat in Velike Gradiska, he learned that Plogojoviz had died in the town of Kisolova and been given a Serbian Orthodox burial. Over the space of 8 days a total of 9 persons died after attributing their disease to a suffocating attack by the recently departed. This had all the features of a contagion spread exclusively by one person. The identification of Plogojoviz by the stricken was substantiated from testimony given by his wife. He had asked her for his wooden shoes (*oppanki*), and it was apparent that he had walked from one death-afflicted house to another by the footprints they left in the earth of the streets.

Having established Plogojoviz as the cause of the cluster of deaths, the villagers went to the Provisor with a plan to prevent further mortality. Proof that the deceased resident was one of the *vampyri*, the first time the word was used in an official document, would be established by opening the grave and finding an undecayed corpse with growth of skin, hair, nails and beard as in life. The delegation wanted the Provisor together with Orthodox priests (*Poppen*) to accompany them to the grave, to serve as official witnesses to the validity of the connection and the need to act upon the corpse to forestall further deaths.

The Provisor urged them to wait while he sent a *factum*, a finding, to Belgrade, the capital of the Kingdom of Serbia that had been established as an administrative unit of the empire when Serbia was ceded to Austria from the Ottoman Empire with the Treaty of Passarowitz in 1718. The Kingdom was part of the broader Kingdom of Hungary joined with Austria to form the Austro-Hungarian Empire, and the village of Kisolova fell within the Gradiska district governed from the nearby town of Velike Gradiska. On this present-day map Kisiljevo, identified with Kisolova (also spelled Kisilova), is on the bow of an oxbow formed by the Danube, on the opposite shore is Rumania (Little Wallachia), also included in the Kingdom of Hungary.

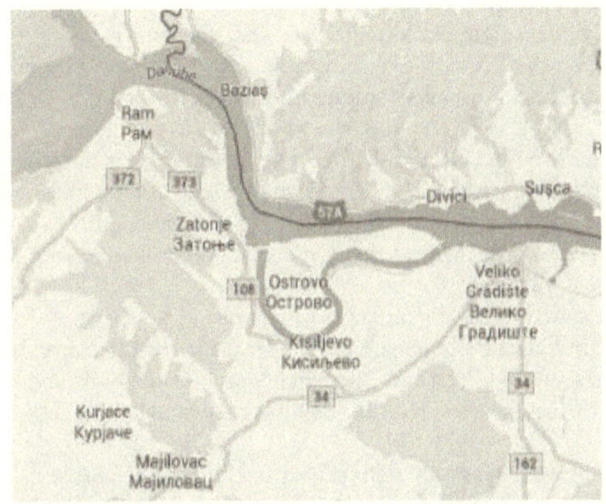

Belgrade is 109.6 kilometers due west of Kisolova on the same side of the Danube, at least two day's journey whether by land or boat at the time. The Provisor perhaps knew that the government of Carl Alexander, Prince of Würtemburg, the governor and commander-in-chief of the Habsburg Kingdom of Serbia, had already been alerted to a similar case of post-mortem lethal visitations in the town of Possega, Slavonia.

The Serbian villagers, cognizant of the slowness of the empire's reactions when it concerned their well-being, did not want to wait for a response to the Provisor's petition. While they were ruled by the Ottomans the population of Kisolova was wiped out repeatedly without an answer to their requests for help. The vampire could decimate the village if they did not act quickly. The Provisor's reason for offering to send to Belgrade was not just to observe regulations. That he tried to bribe and threaten them without avail implies that he needed time to call for armed force, not just approval of superiors, to restore order in a panic.

The villagers' urgency and refusal to wait may have been as much from fear of the imperial response as the lack of one. They in turn threatened to abandon the village if they could not act against the vampire. Depopulation of the border territories was one of the consequences of the war with the Ottomans. The threat to abandon the village was one of the few forms of leverage the villagers had against the empire, and was not to be taken lightly. The Provisor joined Orthodox priests and the residents to make the 5.3 kilometer trip to Kisolova.

The notice now makes a transition from relating what the villagers said to what actually was observed and done. The Provisor is careful to add that the body already was exhumed when they arrived to secure it. The profile of the body as seen is "the whole truth," transmitted by a literate man who has tried to still the frenzy.

The body and grave do not emit the usual odors of decay, and except for the nice detail of the sunken nose, does not look moribund. Furthermore, there has been postmortem growth of the tissues-hair and nails-that grow on the living body. Here the old tissues have fallen away to make way for new ones. A new layer of fresh skin has broken through. This is not just the growth that continues in the body for a few days after death. The generative force has been renewed and the old cast has been sloughed off. New tissues proceed by growth alone unimpeded by the accidents of the usual maturation.

Another first in a written account of postmortem life: the Provisor links the surprising presence of blood in the mouth with the vampire sucking blood from the victims who then spiral into death. This completes the transition of the life force: a vampire bleeding in the grave explains depletion of the population.

While he and the priests gaze at the corpse the villagers sharpen a stake and drive it into the body. Blood pours from the wound and other apertures. The "wild signs," which at least included a penis erection, were not specified out of "high respect" for the reader. The Provisor ends by disavowing his responsibility for mistakes and asking instead that the corpse mutilation be seen as a gauge of the fear of the common people.

The exact date of these events is not stated in the document. The deaths in the village happen during a 10 week period after the burial of Plogojoviz,[2] and the freshness of his corpse is the first evidence seen both by the villagers and the Provisor. The regeneration of the body and the emission of blood are further proof for the villagers that this man has been walking the streets and taking life from his victims.

The Provisor reports this belief. He himself sees only signs of renewed life in the corpse without connecting it to the deaths the villagers have ascribed to it. The extensive bleeding and the other signs following the staking the villagers take as further proof that it is a vampire. The Provisor does not add that the visitations stopped after the staking and burning.[3] Superstitious fear demanding relief drove the final steps.

There was no official response to the disinterment, staking and burning of the corpse other than to print the Provisor's letter in the imperial newspaper. Neither the newspaper nor any other source gives the outcome. By the late 20th century the Provisor's name is being given as "Frombald" attached to summaries of this writing in histories and critical studies.[4]

None of the reproductions of the report in the years after it first appeared attribute it to an official by that name. It may be that the name was suppressed to avoid association of an individual official with inability to control Serbian villagers. The Provisor remained an imperial official dragooned into observing a group of local people he was told were determined to eliminate a vampire from their midst.

The local people were Serbs and priests of their Orthodox faith in the party that traveled from city back to village. Their long recollection of an inability to save themselves from similar plagues under the recent Turkish rule was strong motive to take decisive action after the cause was asserted. The narrative shifted amid several boundaries in tense contiguity: the Serbian Orthodox Christian faith and local beliefs; the Serbs and the Austrians; the Serbs, Austrians and the Turks; Catholics and Protestants; the living and the dead. Substituting the Serbian Orthodox church for the Catholic Church and Serbs for Croats, the arrangement resembles the Jure Grando drama, with the difference that Valvasor was not present when Grando's grave was opened.

The *Neoacquistische Kommission* was founded by the imperial Austrian state in 1718 to address problems arising from the formerly Ottoman territories acquired by the empire through the Treaty of Passarowitz that year.[5] The commission received the Provisor's notice and, recognizing that the agitation of local residents from vampire fright and the official's demurral were two of these problems, saw to the dissemination of the report.

The publication of a "copy" in the *Wienerisches Diarium* in July, which did not contain all the information in the original, was accompanied by the appearance of copies in other centers of the empire with Slavic populations. A two page broadside, *Ensetzliche Begebenheit welche sich in dem Dorff Kisolova…(Appalling Occurrence that in the town of Kisolova…)*, with no place of publication indicated, was also printed in 1725. The publication of the Provisor's writing was motivated by the immemorial interest in beliefs about the return of the dead, but now it was beliefs about the return of the dead that drove subject populations to civic disturbances monitored by officials.

Michael Ranft obtained the copy of the report he inserted into his doctoral dissertation, which he defended on September 25, 1725, from the *Relationes Publicae Lipsiensibus*, the public records collection of the city of Leipzig.[6] The Provisor's letter did not have direct bearing on his topic, the mastication of the dead in graves, but it did provide "most recent" eyewitness evidence of signs in the corpse interpreted by the people as the work of demons, and taken as physically explicable effects of body decay by educated observers.

The appearance of the writing in regional newspapers shortly after the *Wienerisches Diarium* issue led to the first written comment on this case. "Adventurous occurrence with a reputedly returning dead person" headed the 1727 reprinting of the text in a natural science and medical periodical edited in Breslau.[7] The one line introduction gives the source as "Holstein gazettes" and dates it to August, 1725, which is probably the date of publication in the gazettes.[8] It must have come from the Vienna newspaper without acknowledgment. The new title resembles in tone the titles of other articles in this periodical, which combined weather logs with sensational yet exacting accounts of atmospheric phenomena, monster births, kidney stones and other astonishing body events.

The title alone conveys both the thrill and the skepticism that drove the circulation of this news. The author of the commentary following the replicated copy was writing over a year after the Plogojoviz grave opening, and was aware of Ranft's dissertation, among a number of other previous works cited. "This is again a story of superstition, inadvertence and vengeful excess: with no demonstrable datum available, the poor Plogojowitz is made guilty of a devilish connection and worth a sudden execution." More than one story like this has already come to the writer's attention, and the dead man is the victim rather than the perpetrator.

The 9 people dead over the course of 8 days blamed on the returned dead might be attributed to a spreading disease or food poisoning. The Provisor could not question the dead, and was left to pass on the fantasy of the crowd. The notion of being strangled or suffocated in bed at night by the dead man spread among the people with the disease. Trickery, and the vengefulness of the wife, could not be discounted.

The remarkable signs in the uncovered corpse, taken to be indicative of a vampire, were the result of natural processes that took hold after death. The absence of the smell of decay, the growth of hair and nails, the peeling away of the skin to reveal a new layer, the blood in the mouth and copiously flowing after staking and the unmentionable erection of the penis all had been observed in corpses with no reputation for leaving the grave.

Like the falling in of the nose, they all were signs of decomposition and not renewal. The author of the commentary in the *Sammlung* had textual evidence to rely upon for these revisions. The Chemnitz physician Christian Friedrich Garmann in 1670 published a tome, *de miraculis mortuorum, On the miracles of the dead*, which epitomized in books, titles and sections the classical and later precedents for one remarkable trait after another of corpses observed after time in the grave. The growth, bleeding, the erection of the penis are all well known. "The mention of the resuscitation and resurrection of the dead by many people raises the word ridiculous."[9] There has been no genuine resurrection of body and soul except for that of Christ.

Garmann attributed many of these effects in the dead, including cruentation, to the work of the Devil, but the *Sammlung* commentator could ignore this in favor of the assurances that effects were typical of corpses and not due to blood-sucking regeneration, which neither of them considers.

The terms of a coming debate are manifest in this early commentary on the Provost's notice. They all have been present in all reports of postmortem bleeding and revivification. Eyewitness testimony of has become as extensive as it will ever be. Second-hand accounts of the night-visiting corpse and the consequences of those visits will remain just that. No reliable reporter will ever see and record one of these visitations. Fiction will fill in that gap.

The appearance of the corpse, now set down by a non-community member with an official role and a connection to print dissemination, is the key. It is displayed by the villagers as evidence of the validity of pattern of death-return-death within the locale that is summarized by their word "vampire." The Provisor incorporates the word into his description but the commentator does not use it. The Provisor has seen the corpse himself, the first sighting of an alleged vampire, and offers an interpretation at odds with the one offered by the villagers. The body is growing anew after death; the surfeit of blood is either the cause or the consequence of this growth.

The commentator is committed to the view that both the deaths attributed to the vampire and the state of the corpse have a fully natural explanation. Disease and possibly trickery account for the deaths; normal putrefaction accounts for the appearance of the corpse. The commentator's chief precedent for his judgment is a medical writer who allows that all the Provisor has observed is within the realm of the ordinary for corpses, but who appeals to a demonological substrate to exposit the underlying force.

There now are four intertwined views of the same observed condition: that of the villagers' Serbian Orthodox and local beliefs; that of the official; that of the medical commentator and that of his written source, who supports that the corpse's appearance is due to material factors but retains a demonic primary cause. This is a rehearsal for the coming debate, which will take place in a flurry of publications in German drawing upon the "Serbian vampires" of which Peter Plogojoviz is the earliest publicized case.

Kisilova was peripheral to this discussion, but repeatedly generated new cases of what was instantly labeled vampirism. One of them, in 1737, was not featured in German language publications, where vampire discussions had died down, but became the center of similar discussions in French-language writings, especially those printed outside of France. Kisolova fell again under Ottoman rule together with the Serbian lands under the Treaty of Belgrade in 1739. Nonetheless, another Kisolova vampire, in 1755, galvanized the Austro-Hungarian empress to order an inquiry that led to legislation prohibiting vampire hunts.

Despite these excitements Kisolova (under its later names) did not attract folkloristic, literary and touristic interest of the Jure Grando variety.

In Serbia that process of vampire-nationalism engaged Sava Savonović, a figure of local lore in the village of Zarožte in the western mountains of the country. Sava, and the wheat mill he supposedly haunted, was unknown outside the immediate area until the Serbian author Milovan Glišić (1847-1908) published a short story, *Posle dvedeset godina*, After ninety years (1880).

A young man in love with the rich miller's daughter stayed overnight in the mill, tricked the vampire and shot him. This did not kill the vampire, but learning his name enabled the protagonist and his companions to find the grave and pierce it with a hawthorn stake. The young man married the miller's daughter. A she-moth (*leptirica*) that escaped the grave, despite being drowned in holy water, caused the deaths of children for many years afterward.

Glišić relied on folk and literary sources for his work, which occupies the space between recorded folklore and fiction asserting the values of the peasantry against snobbish urbanites. All of the elements of the story are familiar from folklore, many of them associated with vampires, but in the absence of a record of Sava Savonović lore prior to "After ninety years," inventions and introductions cannot be separated from local stories.

The author was also a playwright and a translator of Russian and French literature into Serbian. Both literatures have their own distinctive vampires, which Glišić did not imitate, but paralleled from Serbian tradition in the Serbian language. Around the same time Jure Grando was undergoing his revival in Croatian Istria, the native-factional vampire Sava Savonović was claimed to be "older" than the historic Peter Plogojović.[10]

Sava became the means for Serbs to claim a vampire of their own, one with local roots not derived from Dracula or dependent upon German texts produced by Austro-Hungarian officials.

The mill associated with the vampire, an artifact with age and mood, became a local visiting spot with a tourist infrastructure surrounding it.[11] Serbian novels and a film have perpetuated the Serbian vampire Glišić made. A 2008 article in the Serbian periodical *Politika* lamented that "Sava Savonović is still waiting to be a Serbian brand."[12] When the mill collapsed in 2012 the Zarožte village council broadcast the warning that Sava is now looking for a new home.[13]

The next publicized case in the early 18th century sequence, from a town other than Kisolova, was to attract more concerted interest from the official bodies that took note of Plogojoviz, and precipitate publication that drew in more cases, contributing to the formation of a complex around the word "vampire." That will be the subject of the next two chapters.

---

[1] Translation by the author from text printed in *Wienerisches Diarium*, July 21, 1725: unnumbered.

[2] Also written Plogojovitz, Plogojeviz, and Blagojević in various sources.

[3] Collin de Plancy (1844: 404) recounting the episode from the Provisor's writing, interjects this detail. Calmet (1746: 399-401), doing the same, does not.

[4] *Copia des vom Herrn Frombald kayserlichen Cameral Provisore zu Gradiska in Königreich Servien erlassenen Briefs anno 1725. Die im Königreich Servien damals in Schwung gegangenen sogenannten vanpiri oder Blutsauger betreffend.* Haus-,Hof und Staatsarchiv Wien, StAbt Türkei I/191, Konvolut 1725, fol. 25-26.

Hamburger (1992: 43) was the first to refer to the Provisor as Frombald, though others had made this citation.

The *Wiener Zeitung*, August 23, 1741: 760 records the death of a Mathias Frombald at the age of 62, but there are no more details.

[5] Nowasadtko (2004: 157-59)

[6] Ranft (1725: 6-7)

[7] Abenteuerliche Begebenheit mit einem vermeyntlich wieder gekommenen Todten, *Sammlung von Natur und Medecin,* Sommer Quartal 1725. Leipzig and Buditzin: David Richter, 1727: 221-25.

[8] The text was published in the Berlin *Volkische Zeitung*, August 23, 1725.

[9] Garmann (1709: 2,1202)

[10] U selu Kisiljevu razotkrivayu mysteriju prvog srpskog vampire-Pera svrgnuo Savu Savonića, *Glas javnosti* April 26, 2006.
http://arhiva.glasjavnosti.rs/arhiva/2006/04/26/srpski/R06042502.shtml

[11] Serbian vampire pulls in tourists, *The Namibian Sun*, August 17, 2010.
http://www.namibiansun.com/global-news/serbian -vampire-pulls-tourists

[12] Branko Pojević, Sava Savonović ješ čeka da postane srpski brend, *Politika* October 10, 2008

[13] Sara C. Nelson, Vampire Sava Savonović is still on the loose, Serbian village council warns (seriously), *Huffington Post,* March 12, 2012

12. Visum et Repertum

The March 12, 1732 issue of the weekly medical and natural science journal *Commercium literarium* contained excerpts of a letter from the journal's Vienna correspondent, Dr. Johann Friedrich Glaser, to its editor, Dr. Johann Christoph Goetz. Glaser's son, whom he does not name but describes as a physician in the imperial service at Paraćin in Serbia, in the Turkish border region, had written to him on February 13. On January 18, in that region, and especially in the village of Medveđa (Maduega, Mettwett) not far from Paraćin, "some sort of magical infection prevailed at that time."[1]

The dead and buried rising up from intact graves kill the living, and those killed and interred likewise rising up slaughter others, which happens in the following manner: the dead in all truth attack those sleeping at night and suck the sanguis from them, and they all die on the third day. So far no cure is found for this malady. With so many dead in a short time, it was ordered by those few who are in the highest power in those places to inquire carefully into this matter. Therefore my son as doctor and physician was assigned with the others deputed. These judges and sworn examiners questioned those gathered in various ways, clarified with production of evidence that it actually happened, admitting that they didn't know what the cause was: agitated men, trembling, fearful, anxious from loss of sleep, screaming, etc. A visit to the cemetery decreed for each and every delegate, they ordered that the graves be opened, and so ten people in their graves, like the living, they found completely free of decay, on the biers of the poor, clothes and shrouds soaked with florid sanguis, and this flowing from the nose, mouth, eyes and private parts, and finally pristine nails of the hands and feet having replaced the recent ones. From all these vampires (so they are called in these tongues) the head was removed, the corpses cremated by flame and the ashes scattered in the Morava River. Beforehand my son cut them, and found all the viscera healthy and sound, the stomach and disphragm truly full of blood. Having promptly written these things to me, he promised to add further details in the future in a broader relation to the Government and to our College of Hygiene.

This letter from Glaser senior is followed by an editorial note from Goetz.

The ancient fables often made in Hungary and Poland, those not congenial to natural history, recognize this news. Doesn't this disease suggest some orgiastic epidemic imagination, fearfulness, superstition, and likewise the fermentation of the blood beginning in cadavers of this sort and claims to itself the most and greatest putrid parts, the investigation of the singular circumstances can more deeply draw out? Feral dead of this sort are called by the loan word Vampires, and Utpertz; a chewing of shrouds and shaking of biers and graves are linked to them.

Goetz continues with citations from Garmann, Ranft, and Fabri, all of whom ascribe perturbations to the buried dead but do not credit them with nocturnal bloodsucking visits to victims who then are infected with the same urge.

The title of the Latin-language journal in which this letter appeared could be translated "Lettered Commerce": it was intended as a forum of cases and speculation among physicians and natural scientists who could bypass regional differences. Published in the cultural and printing

145

center of Nuremberg, the journal regularly contained reviews of new books published in Latin, German, Italian and French. Right before Glaser's letter was a review of Burggrave's *Lexicon medicum universalis* and immediately after, a letter by a physician describing an unusual birth. The word "vampire" is not in the lexicon. The Provisor's Kisolova report seven years earlier had been its unique use prior to this letter. In Glaser's letter it is accompanied by *"utpertz,"* one spelling of the Slavic word *"upir/upior"*.

J.F. Glaser begins his letter not with a group of Serbian villagers coming to the Austrian authorities in the administrative center panicked by their belief the dead have risen to exsanguinate and infect the living. He begins with the statement that this has happened, and with no known cure for what is apparently a contagion, the order is passed to make an inquiry. That inquiry encounters a distraught population pressured to admit what they did and did not actually see. A consequent visit to the cemetery unearths corpses emphatically bloodied and bleeding, which are termed "vampires" in the local language. They are decapitated, cremated and the ashes scattered in short order. The younger Glaser performs postmortems that make plain the lack of decomposition and the surfeit of blood. More information is promised, but there is no further letter from Glaser or his son on this subject in the *Commercium literarium*.

The report of the same incident filed in the Austrian state archives in February, 1732 is a German-language first-person narrative without a name attached.[2] The younger Glaser is likely the author. This report was reprinted several times in later studies, but not before the early 20th century.[3] It is not present or referred to in the Latin, German, French and English publications that take up the events in Medveđa in the 1730's and the subsequent centuries. Other investigators made reports on the same incident soon after 1732 while Glaser's report remained buried in the archives.

In response to notice of "a dying" in the village of Mettwett, Glaser, the "imperial plague physician" *(physicus Contumaciae Caesareae)* at Paraćin, traveled there and made a house-to-house inquiry. The borderland between the Austro-Hungarian Empire and the Ottoman lands, where the village was located, was established as a military and medical buffer zone. Approaching plague might be detected there and halted before it reached the cities. Glaser was stationed where he could quickly investigate any sign of its development.

He did not find evidence of plague, but he did find tertian and quartan fever (three and four day recurrent fever, generally malarial), *Seithenstecken* (pleurisy) and *Brustbeschwahrmussen* (pneumonia), conditions not atypical of the region during winter. The Serbian Orthodox church mandated multi-week periods of fasting over the course of the year, and the Christmas fast would have been underway during the time of Glaser's inspection. Year-round a week did not go by without a few days of fasting. The weakness due to deprivation of regular meals made the people susceptible to illness, but the *depouchen*, the heavy overindulgence in food and drink after the fasting period ended, was in Glaser's view more destructive. The religious fasting explanation of a rapid succession of deaths following illness was applied to these episodes in the following years.

In all, thirteen people died over a period of six weeks. The complaints of the dying, of the chest conditions and limb spasms, and the close succession of funerals could only have a common cause. Glaser quoted the word used by the Serbs for those who died and preyed upon the living: vampire (*Vampyr*).

There was no narrative of any one individual or group visibly coming back from the grave, pressing upon the recumbent victim and drinking blood (*Blut*). The respiratory disease, the fever, bedridden weakness in succession were signs of one after another dying and communicating the condition. They tried to stand vigil, one awake while the other slept, but that did not prevent the vampirism from being visited upon two or threhouses at a time. That no one was encountered in the process of spreading the illness, yet it still progressed, did not alter their conviction that it was carried by vampires.

In the presence of the military commander of the town of Kragobaz (Kragujevac) Glaser tried without success to reason the villagers out of their belief. He agreed to have 10 graves opened and for each burial gives the person's name, age, length of time in the ground, and crucial details of appearance. A 50-year old woman named Miliza was the focus of the villagers' fears. She had come to Mettwett from the Turkish region six years earlier. For the entire time she was neighborly with no sign of diabolical influence or practice. She did tell someone who recounted it to Glaser that she ate two sheep killed by vampires *with the intention* of becoming one after death.

Glaser wrote that it was stories like this one that formed the basis of the vampire belief among the people. He was present at Miliza's unearthing. She had been laid out seven weeks earlier on the bare earth and should have been half decomposed. Constitutionally gaunt during life, she was bloated after death. Blood was running from her half-open mouth and from her nose, suffusing her skin. Corpses of younger people, more robust in constitution who had not been ill were as decayed as expected in the same ground.

A twenty-year old woman named Stanno who had died in childbirth together with her child a month earlier also was said to have come from the Turkish lands. To escape harsh persecution by the vampires there she smeared herself with vampire blood knowing it would make her a vampire after death. Potential vampire victims smearing themselves with the blood of the bleeding dead enrolled them in a postmortem order.

The succession of others afflicted with vampirism was traced back to Miliza and Stanno. Two unbaptized children who were "taken" had to be buried away from the graveyard at their mother's house behind a fence. Two boys 15 years of age, both 5 weeks buried, had died because they overindulged at the name-day feast of the village hajduk after breaking a fast. A hajduk was a Serbian who had been recruited by the Austrian military to act as part of a militia securing the border against the Ottomans. The hajduk's wife Milosowa, thirty years old and buried three weeks, was almost entirely decayed.

In the absence of other influences, generally the younger the person at death, the briefer and more severe the illness, and the shorter the time buried the greater the likelihood of being vampirized (*sich ve(r)vampyret haben*), of being swollen, new-looking and fresh compared to others completely decayed.

The folk account of the spreading illness and death is an inexorable ability of the affected dead to absorb blood from the living, weaken and kill them and convert them into vampires who will live in the grave (not leave it) and remotely vampirize others after death. Or invite those fearing vampirization to smear themselves with their blood.

The account was brought with the vampirism itself from the Turkish area, the area under Ottoman control after the Treaty of Passarowitz. Each of the woman who absorbed vampirism there and carried it to Mettwett adopted it deliberately, for the sake of self-protection. Sheep killed by vampires, or by wolves, could transform those who consumed their flesh, and the blood of vampires likewise protects and transforms anyone who comes into contact with it. This was similar to beliefs about other contagions such as smallpox.

Glaser took his inability to dissuade the people of the village from their beliefs and expected response as an opportunity to study the physical effects that corresponded to the vampire belief. Illnesses that flourished at that time of the year in the cold, straitened environment of the village were not epidemic but collectively suffered under the circumstances. Their effects, of chest compression and sharp pain, a drained feeling and coincidental bleeding, constituted the vampire never actually observed. The cyclical fasting practices of the Orthodox Church, and the excesses after their end, amplified these effects.

Outside authorities had to be brought in to force the opening of the graves, sacrosanct under Orthodox rite, both to prove that vampirism was at the root of the serial deaths and to stop it from spreading. Glaser surveyed the corpses exposed and arrived at a plague doctor's synopsis of appearances that might with further consideration yield a non-superstitious explanation. He did not venture to propose as Goetz did fermentation of the blood as the activating principle of the inflated and bleeding corpses.

In the report Glaser petitioned to be permitted the destruction ("execution") of the vampire corpses as a means of placating the excited villagers. This had already been accomplished at the time the report was submitted, for which he, like Frombald before him, needed to save bureaucratic face. His father's letter to the *Commercium literarium* does acknowledge the fait accompli of decapitation, burning and disposal by water, which would have had the parallel practical effect of eliminating any unknown pathogen from the precincts, like the burning of plague-infected bodies.

The vampirism visitation of Medveđa did not end with Glaser's investigation. In the next weekly issue of *Commercium literarium* (March 19, 1732) appeared a section referring to the previous week's letter "on the so-called vampires."[4] An examination had been undertaken "by order of the council of war" in the village of Maduega on January 7, 1732, and a description of the result is presented. At the village the signers of the report asked questions concerning "the vampires who kill people by sucking out their sanguis." The investigators whose names are given with signatures at the end of the text are "Büttner," an army officer and "Joh. Flinkinger," a field surgeon. The name of the second was misspelled (there are several other misspellings of the name in the documents), as the other editions of the report indicate: "Flückinger" is the commonest spelling.

The investigators obtained the assistance of the hatnack, the local prefect, and the hajduk stationed there to question the villagers. "Everyone firmly asserted with one voice that around five years earlier a foot soldier of this place by the name of Arnold Paul, who died after a fall from a hay wagon, in life often declared, that while in Coussoua (Kosovo) in the part of Serbia subject to the Turks he was troubled by a vampire. He ate some earth from the grave and anointed himself with the sanguis in order to be free of the tortures he endured." This second report is the first time the name of Arnold Paul appears in the writings on Medveđa.

Twenty or thirty days after his death, the villagers said, some of them were set upon by Arnold Paul, and four persons allegedly were killed. To heal this malady the village chief (*autor*) and the hatnack, versed in cases of this sort, around forty days after his death, dug him up and found his corpse unusually whole and free of decay, florid sanguis pouring from eyes, nostrils, mouth and ears, moreover the undergarments, the linens and eyes moist with cruor, the old nails fallen away and in their place they detected new ones. From these it appeared he truly was a vampire.

By their custom they pierced his heart with a stake, and when it was done he issued a loud cry together with much sanguis out of the body itself. On that very day they cremated the body with fire, and sealed the ashes again in the grave. These same affirmed that everyone tortured and killed by this vampire also became vampires, for which reason the four persons mentioned above proceeded in the same way. To which they add that the vampire Arnold Paul not only attacked humans but also animals, despoiled them of their sanguis, and wherever humans made use of the flesh of these cattle, vampires came forth there. The report of the three investigators continues with an account of the contagion.

Within the space of three months seventeen people young and old died, who with no preceding illness passed away in two at most three days. The soldier Jouiza testifies that his daughter-in-law, Stanuicka by name, fifteen days ago went to bed safe and sound around midnight awoke with a loud and terrible cry, tremors and fear, and was overcome. The son of which soldier, Miloe by name, died nine weeks ago, his throat closed. He felt no pain in his chest, in hours he began to grow worse, then on the third day he expired. Having heard these things at midday we immediately went to the cemetery to open the suspect graves and uncover the secrets, and observed the following.

The investigators then list three of the same people (Stana, Miliza, Milloe) by name with the same gender and age that Glaser listed for them in his filed but unpublished report. All those corpses exposed showing signs of vampirism were decapitated, body with head burned to ashes, returned to their graves and reburied.

This second report on Medveđa's vampire troubles was filed in the Austrian state archives in February, 1732.[5] Unlike the Glaser report it was published independently that same year, in Nuremberg, where *Commercium literarium* was published. The text was identical with that filed in the archives. Translated into Latin for the journal, its title is the same as the archive entry. The archival and published German language reports differ from the Latin version in being signed by Flückinger and two other regimental field surgeons, with an added paragraph attesting to its authenticity and further signed by two army officers, Lt. Colonel Büttener and Fenderich (1st Lieutenant) J.H. von Lindenfels. The text of the published *Visum et Repertum* was immediately followed by a copy of the Provisor's report on Kisolova, and as the title page indicates, an appendix on the dead chewing and smacking in the grave, which had nothing to do with Medveđa.

Viſum & Repertum,
Uber die ſo genannten
VAMPIRS,
oder
Blut-Ausſauger,
So zu Medvegia in Servien, an
der Türckiſchen Granitz, den 7.
Januarii 1732. geſchehen.

Nebſt einem Anhang/
Von dem
Kauen und Schmatzen
der
Todten in Gräbern.

Nürnberg,
bey Johann Adam Schmidt.
1732.

Seen and Discovered
On the so-called
VAMPIRES,
Or
Blood-Suckers
Conducted in Medvegia in Serbia,
On the Turkish Border, the 7
Of January, 1732. Delivered.

On the
Chewing and Smacking
Of the
Dead in Graves.

Nuremberg,
by Johann Adam Schmidt.
1732.

None of the versions of Flückinger's report makes a direct reference to Glaser's. The Latin version in *Commercium literarium* only begins with an allusion to the letter "on the so-called vampires," already a stock phrase, without naming its author or source. The *Visum et Repertum*, Latin title for a German document, thereafter superseded Glaser's words and observations in all of the many commentaries and reconsiderations printed in the *Commercium literarium*, in the

German newspapers, and as separately printed treatises in Latin and German. The transition from Latin to German and from scholarly-administrative to popular discourse encircled the Latin rather than left it behind.

Once the plague doctor Glaser in the imperial service had arrived and made his assessment, that there was no plague, and conveyed his observations why it had seemed to be one, the military surgical corps, eminently well-equipped to assess the physical condition of dead bodies, moved in and took command, promoting a version of the belief associated with the Serbian word "vampires" for maximum official and public attention as they reassured the villagers whose support was needed against the Ottoman foe nearby. A comparison between the two phases of this investigation-intervention captures a blood construct being built along the social and cultural boundaries outlined earlier.

Flückinger introduced a new figure into the Medveđa outbreak, and a peremptory candidate for a primary case of vampirism in the village: Arnold Paul (Arnaut Pavle, etc.). This hajduk combined a number of the factors that affirmed his role in initiating the transmission. While he was in the Turkish zone he escaped a vampire who was troubling him by eating earth from the grave and bringing his body into contact with the vampire's blood. These procedures destined him to become a vampire himself after death, though he engaged in them in order to free himself from vampires and not to become a vampire like Glaser's Miliza and Stanno. He died after a violent accident, which reflects earlier sanguineous corpses such as that of the young Austrian noble described by Horst, Cuntius and Peter Plogojoviz.

After his death he was blamed for the affliction and deaths of others in the village. There was no account of Arnold Paul being detected taking blood from anyone of those afflicted, nor of there being specific signs of the removal of blood from their bodies. The only circumstantial accounts of the illness arriving were the sudden nighttime seizure of the daughter-in-law of the soldier Jouiza and the closure of his son's throat (diphtheria?). Arnold Paul's victims became vampires, as did people who ate the meat of cattle he attacked for their blood.

The village chief and the leader of the local militia, who narrated this to Flückinger and company six years later, knew how to act at the time. They found the sanguineous corpse in Arnold's grave, impaled and cremated it, though they reburied the ashes and did not disperse them. This apparently did not put the vampirism to rest because six years later the rash of deaths brought Glaser and then the military surgeons to their village. There is a temporal disjuncture here. The primacy of Arnold Paul rests on his story being told to the investigators, who six years after the first visitation open the graves of recent victims and witness the tell-tale signs: new growth, bloating and blood flow.

Glaser discovered endemic diseases among the villagers that coupled with religious fasts and fast-breaking debauchery could explain the deaths. The disease was a present-time transmission that stemmed from two women who had come from the Turkish area, as many did. On opening the graves Glaser observed patterns in the afflicted as opposed to the merely decayed. He recommended action, or, according to his father's letter, actually undertook action to curb the vampirism to assuage the villagers, and to halt the unknown contagion, to reassure himself as a plague doctor.

Flückinger's team took bold steps parallel to those of the village chief and hatnack years before, and parallel to Glaser's steps as his father's letter relates them. J.H. Glaser's letter may have been an attempt to claim priority for his son.

Flückinger and company arrived a little later with an overbearing authorization, summoned the support of the local military and put out his findings more forcibly. He cremated and dispersed the apparent vampires and reburied the merely decayed, eliminating all evidence that an outbreak ever took place apart from the memories of those who survived. He initiated the linkage that brought disease victims and vampires together without any evidence of blood being taken.

The Latin version of Flückinger's *Visum et Repertum* differs from the German version in minor but resonant details. As indicated in the English translation above, from the uncovered corpse of Arnold Paul recalled by the village chief and the hatnack sanguis flowed from the eyes, nose, mouth and ears, and the undergarments, linens and eyes were soaked with cruor. In German fresh blood (*frishes Blut)* flowed from the eyes, nose, mouth and ears; the shirt, linens and coffin were all bloody.[6] The Latin text distinguishes between the two species of the vital fluid by type and placement; the German leaves it at *Blut*. The two Glaser texts leave it at sanguis and Blut.

The testimony of the local officials who unearthed Arnold Paul's corpse six years before Flückinger arrived was translated into the sanguis/cruor mode for the Latin-reading audience. As Arnold Paul became the standard vampire he retained that distinction in Latin texts while his role never was preeminent in the greater number of German writings on the subject. Arnold Paul's discovery prompted the rise of sanguis- or blood-sucking vampires in Latin or German texts.

In August of 1732 a Latin dissertation "on human postmortem blood-suckers, in the vulgar tongue called vampires" was read in Leipzig. Superstition in general is condemned in the first argument, vampires are selected as a primary example of superstition and Arnold Paole (Arnold Paul) is a chief example of a vampire. With no reference to Glaser or Flückinger's writings, only a personal reference to von Kottwitz, an officer whose name was included in the reports, the academics relate the story of the soldier's death by a fall from the wagon, his reputed ingestion of soil from a vampire's grave in the Turkish zone, and the attacks and deaths attributed to him.

At the urging of the hatnack, Arnold Paul was removed from the grave, pure blood (*sanguinem sincerum)* flowing from the eyes, nostrils, mouth and ears, just so, they found that the undergarments and covering with the coffin were stained, also so much cruor, with stake through chest and heart by their solemn custom, not without a notable sigh of the deceased, at the transfixion, burst out abundantly.[7]

They have little more than this to say about Arnold Paul himself, and launch upon a set of arguments with citations of learned Latin treatises proving that the kinds of effects observed in Paul's aftermath are all natural. For instance the loud sigh made when the stake was thrust into his chest was not his reaction to the intrusion but the release of air accumulated in the vessels of the dead and not at all unusual in human remains. The final conclusion of the dissertation denied the existence of vampires and ascribed the condition of corpses with fresh blood to epidemic disease.

The Paul case is presented and interpreted strictly as a medical instance that has excited the Serbian villagers, but can readily be explained without resort to the supernatural. The beliefs are an instrument of social control. Uncovering, staking, decapitating and burning the corpses to gain the cooperation of the villagers and curtail the epidemic, ceases to be part of the presentation.

The figure of Arnold Paul is isolated and made into an example of a corpse with features taken to be those of the vampire but naturally explicable.

The fresh blood of the uncovered corpse, the sanguis against the cruor that is carried over from Flückinger's statement of observations to the dissertation, is explained away through analysis but lingers as an image. The sanguis is *sanguis sincerum*, pure and new blood, *frisches Blut, sang pur,* to project the surprise of finding it springing out of the corpse for languages without the sanguis/cruor distinction. The connection to the "blood depletion" of the alleged victims is too striking not to persist despite the lack of concrete evidence. The vampire/blood-sucker equation echoes that first sight of bright blood flowing in a corpse, a primordial blood after death. The divergence comes in whether the emphasis is on the suspect body and its condition, as in the cruentation traditions, or on the connection between the body and the surrounding community, their beliefs and contingent health.

Though there were a number of treatises with the phrase "Serbian vampires" or "Slavic vampires" in their titles in 1732 and the following years, ethnographic study of the communal roots of blood relations with the dead was curtailed by the return of the Serbian lands to Ottoman control with the Treaty of Belgrade in 1739. Episodes of "vampire panic" where Austro-Hungarian authorities were involved were more likely to bring repression, not grudging and relatively accommodating intervention and reportage.

There also was developing a history of scholars and creative writers originating in and conversant with local Slavic and Rumanian communities producing published works in international languages and their own languages. Valvasor was a precocious example of this. A signal present in the stories introduced into imperial archives and scientific literature and then lost was the protective blood-smearing ritual of enrollment in vampirism that several of the early Serbian victims made known. This was not present in accounts after these, but it is a reminder that there was a substrate of belief not consolidated into what came to be named by the Slavic word "vampire" and still there to be detected.

The strongest trend in the vampirism linkage was centered on the body of the vampire, the bodies of the vampires, a complex of collected beliefs, observations and theorizing which was spurred by the disclosure of Arnold Paul's body and its surroundings to the reading public. It also was the beginning of maintaining the life force picture in the cruor/sanguis/blood of the vampire while privileging naturalistic and scientific explanations. The atavism and fancy of life in the vital fluid hovered over the hard facts of the dead decaying in graves.

---

[1] Ex litteris D.D. Joh. Frid. Glaseri ad D. D. Goetzium, Vienna...,*Commercium literarium*, March 12, 1732: 82-84.

[2] *Bericht von der Dorffschafft Metwett an der Morava, welche sich beklagten eines Sterbens, darauf ich als Physicus Contumaciae Caesareae zu Paraskin dahin gegangen, selbiges Dorff von Haus zu Haus wohl und genau durschsuchte und examinierte den 12 Decembris 1731.* Hofkammerarchiv Wienm Hoffinanz Ungarn, Rote Nummer 654 [February 1732].fol. 1134-36r.

[3] Krauss (1908: 131-32), a German book on Slavic folklore, is the earliest reprinting of the full archival text I have been able to find.

[4] Iis, quae de Vampyris..., *Commercium literarium*, March 19, 1732: 90-92

---

⁵ *Visum et Repertum Über die sogennanten Vampyrs oder Blutaussaugers so zu Medvegya in Servien an Türkhischen Gränz den 7 Januarii 1732 geschehen Hofkammerarchiv Wien. Hoffinanz Ungarn, Rote Nummer 654 [February, 1732], fol 1138-40.*
⁶ *...sed et floridem sanguinem ex oculis, naribus, ore et auribus profundentem; quin etiam indusium, linteamen et oculos cruore madentia...* fn4: 91
...durch ihm das frisch Blut in denen Augen, Nasen, Mund und Ohren heraus geflussen; Hemd, Ubertuch und Truhe ganz blutig gewesen... Flückinger (1732: 4)
⁷ Pohl and Hertel (1732: 7)

13. The chewing and smacking by the dead in graves

The publication in early 1732 of reports of named sanguineous corpses in a Serbian village then under Austrian control was a seed crystal dropped into a supersaturated solution. The link between the corpses and the epidemic of deaths among the people of the village, and the expectation that the epidemic would be ended with the destruction of the corpses was named vampirism, using the Serbian word for such episodes.

Official documentation of the uncovered corpse, seemingly full of freshly acquired blood, passed into the public domain through publication of the reports themselves, and of a number of written commentaries on and responses to the reports. These general responses to the prospect that the physical evidence amounted to vampirism were produced primarily in Leipzig and mostly in German.

The largest city in the region of Saxony, Leipzig is on the southern edge of the German plain at the convergence of major roads and waterways. A considerable distance from Serbia to the South, it was in the late 17th early 18th century within the Saxon dukedom of the Austro-Hungarian Empire, and the large city of German speakers closest to Czech and Polish lands.

German-speaking Slavs, the Wends, lived in pockets around the city, which had a Germanized Slavic name. Annually the site of a major trade fair that drew sellers and buyers from across central Europe, Leipzig was and is a center of printing and commerce in printed matter. The University was founded in 1409; Johann Sebastian Bach was choral director for several Leipzig churches between 1723 and 1745. It was the first city in central Europe to install a system of streetlights.

The effect that Arnold Paul and his compatriots had on the Leipzig milieu can be traced through the iterations of another question about active corpses over these years. On August 16, 1679, with the indulgence of God and the superiors in the illustrious academy of Leipzig, Philip Rohr, a native of the town of Makranstadt, presented "a historico-philosophical dissertation on the mastication of the dead."[1]

Whoever has beheld the histories of the dead, the presenter begins, has encountered mention of beastly things, the twisting of their cloths, the devouring of their own flesh, sounds very like pigs eating. Rohr backs up his arguments with examples from the Latin and German literature. He dismisses the notions of corpses stimulated to working their jaws by divine virtue, by themselves, or of those impelled by an external force. They have never been known to leave the grave, and they have never been seen biting the cloth or themselves. The mastication of corpses is not due to hidden energies, nor is it the work of striga or hyenas, creatures unknown in these lands.

Having dismissed the spurious instances of corpse mastication, Rohr continues, we can come to know the true demon behind it. Satan makes the corpses act this way for theological and physical reasons that can be expounded. The Devil both produces the pig sounds and causes the corpses to make them by changes in the esophagus and the way food is swallowed. During times of plague all these effects are more frequently seen and heard. The mastication can be averted by burial in consecrated ground and by decapitating the corpse. "And so we venerate the highest Spirit with humble prayers in our provinces and especially in the "hives of the Muses" to avoid all harm, and immediately the frauds of the Demon. From the blasphemies of the Devil and from the plague, free us, Lord!"

This disturbance of the dead, for which the only evidence is what is seen in uncovered graves and heard from them, for which Rohr himself can offer no new examples, still can be studied through the scholastic process of argument and support from written texts. By the process of elimination of false causes, the demonic activity at the root of the phenomenon is exposed.

The Satanic cause is arrived at, and does not preclude examination of how the Devil brings about these sights and sounds. The gullets of the dead are discernibly modified, and the advent of the plague has a measurable effect on the frequency of these events. Steps therefore can be taken to reduce it, but in the end an appeal is made to the divine to forestall the mastication of the dead, frauds of the Demon leading Christians through fear to ascribe to him the power of resurrection.

With the power of the Demon displaced yet more, and the dread of the plague equally strong, these are the same means used by Glaser and Flückinger's team to approach the graves of the vampire (victim)s. Together with a willingness to condone the beliefs of the villagers for hygienic and political ends.

This was not the end of the subject.

M. Michael Ranft (1700-74) presented a "historico-critical dissertation on the mastication of the dead in tombs" for induction into the Leipzig Academy, on September 27, 1725.[2] The indulgence of God and the superiors was not sought; it was a public examination of the erudite, for his Masters of Liberal Arts. In his introduction Ranft allows that it alternately might be called a "historico-philosophical dissertation" and he cites the work of Rohr 46 years earlier.

The critical turn in the title, and the absence of God and the superiors from the front page, reflects a change in academic custom, and a shift in the orientation of academic discourse on this and many other subjects. Ranft also structures his dissertation as a sequence of arguments supported by evidence. Compared with Rohr's investigation by elimination in favor of the demonic cause, with side turns for physical considerations, Ranft from the start declares that there are hidden powers in nature, and "not everything must be ascribed to God or the Devil."

He gives a long list of remarkable practices and occurrences that do not come from diabolical magic, for instance cruentation of the murdered in the presence of the murderer, divination by rod (dousing), fascination by magical imagery, animal divination, Tarantism (dance compelled by a spider bite), canine rabies, and variolation (immunity to smallpox induced by introduction of matter from pustules). Medical delusions (cruentation, Tarantism) are mixed with legitimate conditions (rabies) and procedures (variolation). At the same time, Ranft adds, we dare not dismiss all influx of spirit influences in the hidden operations of nature, for the Devil can work his deceptions and frauds through concealment without being completely in control. Yet again, out of ignorance of the hidden powers of nature, the learned attributed wonders to the work of the Devil where they might have sought other explanations.

Turning to his main subject, the mastication of the dead in graves, Ranft recalls the many tales told to children by parents, of Aesop and other storytellers, which in the absence of ever having seen this actually go on, would lead to doubt. He cites the copious written evidence, giving exact citations, from general statements to instances, Schwimmer to Rohr, Luther to Francisci and the Polish Jesuit Rzaczynski, who included mastication instances with those of cruentation.

Ranft's extended exhibit was a copy of the entire text of the Provisor's report on Kisolova and Plogojoviz as printed in a Leipzig news compilation, "the most recent, that is noted by us, and the most memorable worthy example."As the most recent discovery of a sanguineous corpse reported by an official observer, whatever its circumstances, it was a stunning verification of postmortem liveliness even though there was no sheet winding or self-eating associated with it. Ranft then asserts the absence of divine or demonic influences in cases like this; it is a display of the hidden powers of nature, which then must be elucidated.

Breaking with Rohr's modest investigation of the material, and toward the most recent, best observed example of any such event, Ranft seeks to examine mastication as a natural phenomenon. That it is neither divine nor demonic is supported by the Provisor's reportage. Ranft does not engage with the villagers' beliefs that the Provisor encountered in Kisolova; he uses the word "vampire" twice in the entire text.

The five features of masticating corpses-the sounds, the cloth in mouth, the majority being female, exist not only in plague times, cause the deaths not only of those nearby-are listed and examined in sequence, with additional examples. The earth makes sounds where no one is buried. A casket was opened once and then again when sounds were heard from inside, but no signs of life or motion were found. Simple self-deception always is possible. The only observed case of the sheets being chewed was an elderly man who was not quite dead at burial. Plogojoviz didn't swallow or disturb his burial sheets. He did show blood in his mouth and flowing from his body. That will be examined later.

Ranft progresses through all five of the features of masticating corpses and with a show of evidence from the literature rejects each of them. If these are not genuine, but only the illusions of superstition and credulity, why has there been such a long history of belief in masticating corpses? Natural processes have been mistaken for the work of demons and supernatural agency. The vegetation of the cadaver, its decomposition wherever it is placed, and the same harmful operation as in the living together provide for all the appearances associated with mastication. Ranft promises to elaborate in a philosophical extension of the dissertation.

The Plogojoviz/Kisolova case must have come to Ranft's attention late in his preparation of the dissertation arguments. It is dropped into their sequence and receives only scattered attention in the following text. The promise to elaborate is fulfilled in a 1728 edition with an extended title. Ranft's name appears at the head of the title page followed by the abbreviation of his doctor of medicine (not veterinary) degree. It is no longer a dissertation, just Latin "on the mastication of the dead in graves" but now followed by German (in parentheses, and in Fraktur lettering) "or on the chewing and smacking by the dead in graves" before continuing with more Latin.

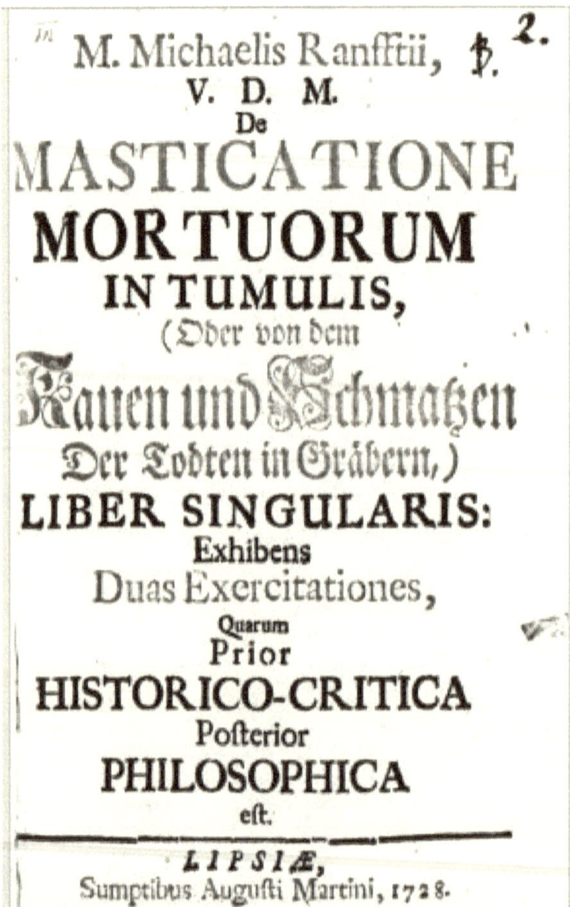

M. Michaelis Ranfftii, ♄.
V. D. M.
De
MASTICATIONE
MORTUORUM
IN TUMULIS,
(Oder von dem
Rauen und Schmatzen
Der Todten in Gräbern,)
LIBER SINGULARIS:
Exhibens
Duas Exercitationes,
Quarum
Prior
HISTORICO-CRITICA
Posterior
PHILOSOPHICA
est.

LIPSIÆ,
Sumptibus Augusti Martini, 1728.

[Latin]
Of M. Michael Ranft
Verbi Divini Minister
(Minister of the
Divine Word)
On
MASTICATION
OF THE DEAD
IN TOMBS,
[German]
(Or on the
Chewing and
Smacking
By the Dead in
Graves,)
[Latin]
Singular Book:
Displaying
Two Exercises
Of which
The prior is
Historico-Critical
The latter
Philosophical.

In Leipzig
Published by August
Martin, 1728

Books were exhibited and sold by the words and print on their front pages. The addition of the Fraktur German sound-words *kauen und schmatzen*, the phrase perhaps Ranft's own invention, was likely to attract buyers already lured by the clinical Latin "mastication of the dead" in Roman typeface above. Ranft had discredited soundmaking by the dead in his dissertation; the addition of the subterranean vocal eating effects was entirely a sales strategy perpetuated in Ranft's own work and taken up by others.

Ranft was here continuing his nascent career as a teacher and Protestant pastor, but now also as a writer to supplement his inadequate wages as teacher and pastor. In this same year (1728) the same press that published his extended dissertation also published in German his necrology of the dukes of Saxony. As he moved from post to post over the years he continued to write biographies of recent historical figures and produce a genealogical newsletter on noble families interspersed with a few theological writings. One of his final works (1773) was "the remarkable life history of the unlucky Russian Kaiser Peter the Third…brought to light by a friend of the truth."[3]

The first half of the 1728 dissertation extension reproduces the text of the historico-critical dissertation. The second half takes up the philosophical question of the incorruptibility of some corpses, of which the "Hungarian" corpse or Plogojoviz is again the primary example. He resorts to a typical late Renaissance analysis of the nature of life. The living body is composed of a "vital component" (*vivida*) and a "vegetative component" (*vegetantia*).

The specific life begins to cease in death, but not truly the universal life, in which first principles and elements essentially inhere, and the body does not relinquish its vegetative component and force, unless everything destructible is resolved into its simplicity.

Incorruptibility assures the presence of homogeneous parts. Differing temperaments and compositions make differing balances among the parts, which appear to be states of incorruptibility (not corruption).

"Our Hungarian" (Plogojoviz) remained incorruptible from many causes, adding up to the lack of the homogeneous parts of the corpse's destruction. Ranft reviews each component of the Hungarian's corpse as reported by the Provisor, giving a vegetative concordance for each, from the venom generated by his violent death to the elemental renewal of his skin, hair and nails and the erection of the penis (opium? tobacco?) inferred from the "wild signs" phrase alone. The sanguis in the mouth may well have been due to the rough handling the corpse received from the villagers who uncovered it. Cruor never is mentioned.

The "powers of the imagination" (*vires imaginationis)* of the living, especially active in a time of plague, draw the dead to the living and leave the impression of attacking incubi even unto the death of the victim. The magic of the dead operates in the living, and is sufficient for the living to see in the uncovered dead any disturbance or parts out of place, including the rearrangement of the cloths covering them and blood in the mouth, the result of mastication or vampirism. "Any perturbation of the spirit is as nourishment for the operation of magic." This alone can initiate damage to the living body and by harmful operation compass its destruction.

Ranft in his own language anticipated later discussions of such varied topics as "voodoo death" (per Walter Cannon) and the violence that can be done by sounds, visual imagery, smells and touches. The ability of objects of the imagination to damage the one doing the imagining is central to the vampire idea, and dismissive of the reality of vampires. The life force begins to make the transition to force of the imagination it always was.

The publication of Flückinger's report on Medveđa and Arnold Paul in 1732 clearly owed much to the model set by Ranft in the 1728 publication. The *Visum et Repertum* is not only that report but a compilation. It first announces vampires and blood-suckers and then an appendix on chewing and smacking by the dead. No compiler's name is given for the entire publication. The Arnold Paul report is followed by the names of the field surgeons and officials present and the Plogojoviz report carries the Provisor's signature. The appendix is the longest text in the pamphlet, relating instance after instance of its title soundings of the dead. Some examples are citations from named works, many just designated by date and location.

Though its title is from Ranft's 1728 extended dissertation, the author of the *Visum et Repertum* does not observe Ranft's academic technique of argument supported by stipulated sources. The examples of sounds heard from within graves, of the dead returned to trouble the living and of the measures taken to stop them and destroy them are all given as fearsome truths. The dead are never seen walking or flying by night, but plague, illness and death are the context and result of their doing so. Toward the end the author voices his dismay at the failure of governments to do more to contain this threat.

Ranft's dissertations and this somewhat self-contradictory compilation (reports of credulous villagers placated followed by true horrors) were key documents in the milieu that precipitated an exchange of views being sold as pamphlets, newspaper and journal articles. The authenticity the dead showing signs of life, and the real meaning of the evidence taken to be in favor was the crux of the debate. It also was a precocious employment of catch phrases, large cover, and print advertising slogans, to sell books. Tension was generated by the proximity of death, the possibility of resurrection and the threat of plague, all as real to readers as the sounds of pigs slurping believed to come from closed graves.

Ranft's own response to the debate came two years later.

M. Michael Ranft
Diaconi zu Nebra,

TRACTAT

von dem

Kauen und Schmatzen

der Todten

in Gräbern,

Worin die wahre Beschaffenheit
derer Hungarischen

VAMPYRS

und

Blut-Sauger

gezeigt,
Auch alle von dieser Materie bißher
zum Vorschein gekommene Schrifften
recensiret werden.

Leipzig, 1734.
Zu finden in Teubners Buchladen

Of M. Michael Ranft
Deacon in Nebra,
TRACTATE
on the
Chewing and Smacking
of the Dead
in Graves,
Wherein the true
Nature
of the Hungarian
VAMPIRES
and
BLOOD-SUCKERS
is shown,
Also all of these
Materials up to now
come to Attention
Writings
are Reviewed.

Leipzig, 1734
To find at Trubner's
Bookshop.

Ranft's own career and the status of the interchange he helped initiate are on display here. He occupies the post of deacon in the town of Nebra, and the book that he presents is one result of the straitened circumstances he finds himself in. For some years he will petition the presbytery to make promised repairs in his living quarters, and will continue his writing and publication in an effort to improve his condition.

He has removed "mastication of the dead in tombs" in Latin from the main title and begins with the word "*Traktat*," usually reserved for religious pronouncements and ruminations.[4] All of the title is in German. After his signature phrase, adopted by a few other writers on the subject comes in Roman capitals a title he has adopted from others, VAMPIRES joined with the Fraktur Blood-Suckers. Most frequently other authors in the vampire exchange added "so-called" to either of the terms. The vampires are Hungarian because the Serbian villages they are reported from are within the Hungarian administrative unit of the Austro-Hungarian Empire. This is a comprehensive and forward-looking review of the subject.

On opening the book the reader found an etching of a graveyard with two figures. A scroll above is lettered with the same phrase in Greek and Latin: *Nekros ou daknei/Mortuus non mordet,* the dead one doesn't bite, a quotation from Plutarch's lives of Pompey and Brutus, referring in each case to an assassination victim's inability to exact vengeance. In the context of Ranft's book its proverbial force is directed against the old mastication by the dead rumors that he dispelled.

Perched on the wooden rack where fallen gravestones were placed in cemeteries, a satyr plays a triangle with three rattling rings. The clear tone of the Trinitarian instrument mocks the supposed slurping of the dead. Below, a gowned woman, *Ewigkeit* or Eternity, sits holding ouroboros, the serpent biting its own tail, a symbol of the ever repeating cycle and in this case of the Resurrection, which will only come once for humanity, not in the occasional rise of some bodies from the grave. On the ground beside her is a fallen hourglass which has run its course. Allegorical as the picture is, Ranft could not have stated his meaning more clearly.

This etching, about which there is no written comment in the book, introduces the tractate as a whole. Ranft attempts to encircle the vampire debate that he helped initiate by bringing together a mass of critical documents in chronological order. After a fulsome dedication to "three Leipzig men learned in the ways of God," and an introduction stating his plan, the author fills the first half of the book with a German translation of the two parts of his dissertation. Articles from the Leipzig newspaper precede a full copy of the Flückinger report and von Kottwitz's January 26, 1732 letter from Belgrade.

The remainder of the tractate is composed of critical summaries of 20 books and articles on the vampirism cases in the order they were published between early 1732 and November, 1733, the date of the preface, most of them in Leipzig. They range from Putoneus (Meinig) *Besondere Nachrichten…*,which Ranft says is "nearly the first" of the "vampire or so-called blood-sucker" theme that occupied subsequent writers and the *Visum et Repertum,* to letters published in French exile journals in the Netherlands, and Latin reviews of the same books in the *Commercium literarium,* Except for a few articles in French and English periodicals, and a few more German pieces that appeared after this publication, Ranft provided an overview of the vampire debate. After this, though he was alive and writing over a gamut of historical and theological subjects when the vampire issue was revived in the mid-1750's, he wrote no more books on the supposedly returned dead. The tractate was intended to establish that his contribution was complete with his extended dissertation, which the later books could not help but confirm.

---

[1] Rohr (1679)

[2] Ranft (1725)

[3] Döring (1833: 449-53) lists a cumulative bibliography of 39 books.

[4] Ranft (1734)

14. The so-called vampires or blood-suckers

The rapidly accumulating publications in 1732 with the phrase "so-called vampires or blood-suckers," or the reverse, in their titles resembles other pamphlet-booklet wars taking place in European cities in the 17th and 18th centuries. The presence of a key phrase or a person's name was the call and response. Often there was an initiating publication containing a piece of information, a report, a claim, an attack that brought partisan outcries and participation by professional hacks for hire.

Officials of church and government, scholars and printers brought their resources to bear on what today would seem obscure religious, political and practical questions. Some of this production might be preserved because a prominent figure, a Voltaire or an Alexander Pope, took part, or because a word of long-term interest like "vampire" appeared in the ensemble.

These exchanges can resemble the media echo-chamber of today in the uptake of repeated verbiage and the attempts by individuals and groups to manage the resounding surfaces for their own gain. Ranft correctly divined the dying down of the paper vampire excitement in late 1733 and assembled at his uncomfortable station in Nebra, about 57 kilometers to the west of Leipzig, a gallery and postmortem of the exchange.

The degree to which it was an exchange and to what degree a set of independent responses to the same provocation can only be gauged from the pieces themselves, which may have referred to the previous works or been presented as first words on the subject. The 1732-33 sequence of articles reviewing books on vampires in the *Commercium literarium,* published in Nuremberg, about 280 kilometers south of Leipzig, was not the same as Ranft's chronological order. Together the two bodies of reviews provide a sense of the social networks activated by the vampire subject. Ranft's inclusion of articles from French-language journals published in a Protestant country, the Netherlands, is a measure of the extent and limitations of the network. It also traces out a trade network centered on the *Leipziger Messe,* the annual trade fair in that city where books were among the many items exhibited and distributed.

The *Dissertations sur les apparitions des anges…*(Dissertations on the apparitions of angels…,1746-51) by the French Benedictine monk Antoine Augustin Calmet (1672-1757), a prolific historian like Ranft, brought the German-Slavic vampire literature within the Roman Catholic ambit just as the matter was about to undergo a revival in the Catholic polity of the Austro-Hungarian empire with the emergence of new cases. Calmet's work is the beginning of another strain of the imagery of the after-death activity of the living, and will be explored in a later chapter.

The present is an examination of the turns and sallies of the vampire debate through the works published in the 1732-33 period with reference to the attempts by Ranft and the *Commercium literarium* writers to make an accounting. It will not be a one by one catalogue of the entries in the debate as they appeared, but a survey of the themes continuing and newly appeared.

The vampire label was a convenient catch-all for fears of the proximate foreign, and for an early modernist body that materialized in graves but could not be kept there, and had to get its blood from somewhere. Denial of the villagers' beliefs yet needing to placate them while explaining the source of that renewed life seen in the receding past required effort. The search for genuine cases preceded giving in and just imagining them on the playing field of changing polities.

Rohr and then Ranft's were the first in the line of writings that made the imagery of dead life into a subject of academic study. The word and image of the vampire was captured by Glaser and Fluckinger, but their reports' published form, the *Visum et Repertum,* was not the first time the word appeared in print. They were outdistanced, or at least rivaled by a Leipzig publication.[1]

Special Report
on the
VAMPIRES
or so-called
Blood-Suckers,
woven together the Question,
is it possible that dead People
come back to the Living through
sucking out of Blood bring Death
and therefore can despoil whole Towns
of People and Cattle?
Thoroughly researched
by
Putoneo

Leipzig, 1732
From Johann Christian Martini
in Grimma Alley

The Leipzig alley where this book was printed and sold extended from the marketplace to the Grimma Gate, becoming then a road that led to the town of Grimma and continuing east beyond that to Krakow in Poland and Kiev in the Ukraine. Shops and residences were situated along the alley, including several printshops/booksellers.

The author was Johann Christoph Meinig (?-1740), already known to the Leipzig reading public by his literary pseudonym Putoneo. His first published work was a mathematics dissertation, which he defended at Leipzig in 1710. He received a medical degree from the University of Halle in 1715, attending that school because of the presence at the University of the Pietist preacher and scholar August Hermann Francke, who had been a supporter of his family.[2] He did not write medical treatises, but did compose numerous legal *consilia*. His translation into German of a French work on hydrostatics appeared in 1724, and in 1728 he was the author of a weekly satirical newsletter with Pietist overtones, *Leipziger Socrates*.[3]

Meinig's versatility and wide range of interests stemmed from a quest to earn a living through his writing and scholarship, which veered from the abstract to the utilitarian. The son of a baker, he was able to obtain a higher education but never had the patronage to gain an academic position. In the years immediately after his *Besondere Nachricht, Special Report on the Vampires* was issued he was the author of a treatise on the sea-worms eating away at ships and piers in the Netherlands, and of a comprehensive manual on artillery, all the while continuing his legal writings.

The long title of the *Historical and Physical Description of a Type of Most-Harmful Sea-Worm* (1733) contains a language element the same as the vampire report: the sea-worms through the "ruination" (*ruinirung*) of their corruption and boring destroy ships as the vampires "ruin" (*ruiniren*) entire villages. The imagery of rotting ships and fallen villages catches the eye on the front page as the vampires do, but the pamphlets reach very different conclusions. Meinig studies the worms' ravages and has suggestions on how to forestall them; the vampires are a fraud and an illusion.

Meinig wasn't the only impecunious polymath to resort to vampires in season for a fragment of his livelihood. Ranft's 1728 augmented dissertation, which he quotes at length in the original Latin without translation into German, figures prominently among his sources, not with Ranft's wholehearted approval. The *Special Report* begins with copies of the Provisor's report on Kisolova followed by the "latest" on the same subject, the Flückinger report and the von Kottwitz letter. He provides an example of the illusion of the supernatural, a woman who deceived many by pretending to have a demon within her. Soon Meinig is prepared to make a definitive statement.

"Never has a single person been found, who can say with a basis in truth, to have seen such a vampire who sucked blood from the living and killed them as a result, nor can it even be proven that a single death of cattle is due to these vampires." The reports only depict illness and death following the demise of the key figure and the discovery of his sanguineous corpse. This is neither the work of God nor of the Devil but a simple finding and inference that might be repeated with other corpses not accused of vampirism.

Meinig looks at the cases of allegedly contagious vampirism brought from the Turkish area, for instance, by a woman who consumed the flesh of a sheep reputedly killed by vampires. Wouldn't it make more sense to conclude that she contracted something contagious from the flesh of the sheep, without any need of vampires to initiate it? Material causes can more readily explain what is attributed to vampires.

The imagination can be stimulated to a physical response. The belief that Plogojoviz came at night and suffocated people while they slept is a plague of the imagination. Meinig quotes Ranft at length in the Latin original on the proven potential of people to be stirred to bodily responses by beliefs. Likewise, the bleeding of corpses after death is not an extraordinary event that requires a supernatural explanation. The time will come when doctors seeking out the reasons for the effects actually observed in the dead will bring a "wished-for end to these superstitions and false representations."

Ranft quotes Meinig (whose actual name he deduced from a text) at length in his review in the *Tractat* later that year, the second longest of his thirty reviews of Hungarian-Serbian vampire-related publications. He offers an instance of faked demonic possession to join Meinig's example. By examining the quote from Meinig's pamphlet and a quote from Ranft's dissertation, the reader must judge if Meinig copied Ranft's work without acknowledgment. In a further comparison of texts, Ranft maintains that Meinig did not understand his meaning. Despite this, Meinig's work does demonstrate that the Hungarian corpses and so-called vampires can all be traced from "natural origins" (*aus natürlichen Ursachen begleitet werden konte*). Ranft grudgingly admits the older scholar's work into the fold without granting it priority.

The *Commercium literarium* review of Meinig's pamphlet came late in the discussion of the vampires, in the July 9, 1732 issue, printed after a set of "extemporaneous meditations" on the Serbian vampires by "Dom. Lic. Joerdens,"[4] no doubt Christian Friedrich Joerdens (the elder), a medical graduate of Leipzig University (1720) and city physician of Bayreuth. Joerdens' piece only reflects on the Plogojoviz and Paul cases, without making reference to any other writers on the subject, proceeding argument by numbered argument to question the native superstitions attached to the reputedly reviving corpses.

Joerdens wrote only in Latin, for his colleagues in the Saxon medical world, and did not feature a portentous title to draw in readers to be instructed on the superstitious delusion of vampires. That was his intention. Many of his arguments are in the form of questions. Why was the nighttime pressure on the chest due to a vampire attack and not just the imagination at work during sleep? Why were there no marks of bloodsucking on the bodies of the supposed victims?

Joerdens focusses on the matter of blood and bleeding in the corpse of Arnold Paul. "First in almost all dead we observe fluids, and especially sanguis, to be coagulated at the same time so that, as its native heat is dissipated, it allows the cruor to escape from the major veins piece by piece." This is the beginning of a motion in the body that abetted by fermentation causes the flesh to expand and sanguis to be expelled from the mouth and nostrils. Joerdens retains the material distinction between cruor and sanguis to explain the dynamics observed in the corpse attributed by the superstitious to acquisition of sanguis from victims. In conclusion, if the exacting judgment of these arguments is pondered without foregone conclusions then the "little stories redolent of superstition" (*narratiunculas superstitionem redolentes*) hardly can be found any more. Joerdens relies on reason and clearheaded experience to excise the contemptible fabrications that project vampires.

Next in this issue of the *Commercium literarium* comes the complete title and publication information with a matter of fact description in Latin of Meinig's German *Special Report*. A single sentence introduces it: "[A text] almost entirely the same in tone and argument follows the schediasma, to which we were proposing the highest toast." "Schediasma," referring to Joerdens' piece, is an impromptu, a set of thoughts spontaneously given out which, in the editor's opinion, deserves a toast. Both Joerdens and Meinig belong to the realist school of vampire interpretation. Joerdens doesn't hold up the chewing and smacking, and the rampages of the vampires, as an advertisement before he drains them of credibility within the medical club of the journal.

A close contender for the first entry in the Leipzig publishing response to the Serbian vampire reports but taking a tack different from the previous was this publication.

Acten-mäßige
und
Umständliche
RELATION
von denen
VAMPIREN
oder
Menschen-
Saugern,
Welche sich in diesem und vorigen Jahren, im
Königreich Servien hersür gethan.
Nebst einen Raisonnement darüber
und einen
Hand = Schreiben eines Officiers,
des Printz = Alexandrischen Regiments,
aus
Medvedia in Servien.
an einen berühmten Doctorem der Universität
LEIPZIG.

Gedruckt 1732. und zu finden bey Augusto Martini,
Buchhändl. auf dem alten Neumarckt an der Ecke des
Gewand-Gäßgens

Thoroughly
Documented
and
Detailed
Relation
of the
VAMPIRES
or
PEOPLE-
SUCKERS,
Which in these and
former years, in the
Kingdom of Serbia was
put forth,
Together with an Essay
thereupon
and a
Manuscript of an
Officer,
of the Prince Alexander
Regiment,
from
Medvedia in Serbia,
by a renowned Doctor
of the University

Leipzig
Printed 1732 and to be
found at the August
Martini Bookshop in
the Old Newmarket on
the Corner of the
Garment-Alley

This pamphlet begins with a preface addressed to the "curious and supportive reader" and does not launch immediately into the subject at hand. For several pages the anonymous author exercises his prerogative as a "renowned doctor of the university" by reflecting on the nature of proof and the stubbornness of implanted notions. "Then, you say, there are so many stories in the world, of witches, ghosts, kobolds and the like, which in the end are found all to be false and a fraud. Therefore? Are all histories *of metaphysical matters* (Latin in the original) of this sort?" Such sentiments come to mind, the author continues, when considering the reports of vampires or people-suckers often encountered in today's newspapers. The author has taken an approach different from Ranft, Meinig and Joerdens: so many frauds, but isn't there at least one that is true? Then the first document, dated March 5, 1732, Vienna, is presented.[5]

As heard, his Imperial Majesty has before him the recent case with the so-called vampires, as Blood-suckers are called in the Illyrian language, according to the known circumstances, specifically that an already long dead and buried person at night came to his living friends, and could suck the blood out of these very people, and after their deaths must submit again to the same blood-sucker. Also at the unearthing of such bodies, if the same after the usual practice, were pierced through the heart with a stake by the executioner, entirely fresh blood flowed out, and in place of the old scraped nails were new ones, as also fresh hair growth, were deemed to be of such curiosity and importance, that the highest authority resolved, that the most recent, like the Relation issued seven years ago from various universities, and as a whole to hand over to the famous professor at Altdorf D. Beyern, to obtain his sentiment and expert opinion on this.

The "famous professor at Altdorf" was identified much later as Johann Friedrich Ettmuller, who was in 1732 the Director of the *Kaiserlichen Leopoldina Akademie der Naturforscher*, the Imperial Leopoldina Academy of Natural Science Research at Altdorf.

This letter, which is not at all specific about the place where the vampires were found, is immediately followed by a full copy of the Flückinger report (January 7, 1732) as printed in the March 19, 1732 issue of the *Commercium literarium* and in the *Visum et Repertum*. At the end of this printing of the report are three names, von Kottwitz of the Prince Alexander Regiment, Lt. Col. Buttner and Flückinger, the field surgeon, which overlap with two of the names in the two other publications of the same report: Buttner and Flückinger (Flickinger), as well as in all the other publications of the report that include the names. von Kottwitz has been introduced in the *Acten-massige*, added to Buttner and Flückinger. The two other field surgeons and the officer von Lindenfels have been eliminated.

Following this report in the *Acten-massige,* and published for the first time anywhere, is a letter addressed to a "very learned Herr Doctor" and dated January 26, 1732 at Belgrade. The signatory of this letter is "Sigmund Alex(ander) F(riedrich) von Kottwitz, *Fähndrich* (Cadet) of the praiseworthy Prince Alexander Regiment".

von Kottwitz begins the letter stating that he takes the liberty of presenting the doctor, whom he addresses with an elaborate honorific, with a copy of the Relation (the foregoing report) from a commission appointed by the high command concerning a case in the Kingdom of Serbia. It is a matter of the vampires as they are called in the Turkish language, or people-suckers, who in a brief time ruined a village of its people and cattle resulting in almost daily complaints to the local
authorities.

The Cadet writes to inform the doctor about another village named Kucklina where the inhabitants tell of two brothers so beset by a vampire that they took turns watching over each other at night. Appearing like a dog at the door, a yell would drive it away. Finally both fell asleep at the same time and then in an instant one of them found a fleck of blood at the right ear where he was sucked. He died three days later.

In the same village the wife of a deceased and buried hajduk told the hatnack that her husband had come to her at night "and handled matters as well as he did while alive, except that the semen was all cold". She became pregnant and after 40 weeks a child was born normally proportioned in every way, except that he had no penis, but only a plain piece of flesh that after three days wrinkled up like a sausage. Overcome with wonder, the Cadet humbly asks the doctor: "Is such a thing a Sympathetic, Devilish or Astral effect of spirits?"

Before delving into Ettmuller's response to the Cadet's question it is best to consider this letter created in the context of the vampire materials it accompanied. First it is important to notice that here and only here the Flückinger report is partially fathered upon von Kottwitz, who then turns to a different Serbian village for two more vampire-related tales. This is the first time in a published writing that the word "vampire" is ascribed a Turkish origin. Unlike the other communications he does not recount an internal process of hearing from the villagers, launching an inquiry and uncovering the corpse to end the epidemic.

These are stories heard from the villagers, and they strongly resemble other vampire stories. Family members keeping vigil and the unnatural speed of the vampire attack known only from the blood mark are components of the plague. The second story repeats the sexual visitation of the dead husband, but here it extends to the wife's chilled sensation of the visit itself. The birth of a child from the attentions of the vampire-husband (not anyone else) is unusual, and the aphallic birth is unique.

Ranft exclaims after this text, "Through these reports everyone is placed in the greatest state of wonderment."[6] He does not comment specifically on von Kottwitz's Kucklina stories. E.T.A. Hoffmann, in the section of his novel *The Serapion Brothers* drawing vampire stories from Ranft, skips the vampire sex-childbirth story entirely but does repeat the question (sympathetic, devilish or astral?).[7] Only in the 21st century has it been recognized that the second part of von Kottwitz's letter and his question represent the "the terror fantasies and sexual visions of soldiers stationed on the Turkish frontier."[8] Not of the villagers but of the soldier reporting it.

The *Acten-massige* seems to be set up to give von Kottwitz the authority to pose the question answered in the vaguely labeled response at the end of the documentary section of the publication. He is the first-named author of this version of the Klückinger report on Medveđa and the sole author of the letter on Kucklina.

The answer is that the soul (*Seel*) leaves the body (*Leib*) at death and is taken up according to God's disposition as the spirit (*Geist*) rejoins the world-soul and the body rejoins the earth. The blood of a living body contains the spirit which can be sucked from the body by someone who in the final moments of life recalled contact with a vampire and thus became a soulless, spiritless body. The respondent does not quote Ranft or any other vampire commentator, but does quote the German translation of the Biblical Books of Genesis, Job and Leviticus and at the end the Book of Job once more (6:4), turning that passage to lend Biblical support to the extractability of the spirit from the body.

The effect of the *Acten-massige* to this point is to contest materialist denial of the actuality of vampire cases without ever citing any of its proponents or repeating their arguments, just by asserting an account of the act of vampirism, which would not require evidence or witnesses to blood being sucked. Here a new section of the pamphlet is introduced.

Reflexions
über
Die Acten-mäßige
und umständliche
RELATION
von denen
Vampiren oder Men-
schen-Saugern,

Wodurch die Ursachen der an denselben befundenen Unverweßlichkeit, des Wachs-thums neuer Haare, Nägel, Haut und des Barts, wie auch des aus denenselben fliessen-den frischen Geblütes, nicht weniger derer Vampiren Würckungen, in die lebendigen Menschen, nebst der Execution an deren tod-ten Cörpern, und endlich des lauten Schrey-es, so ein solcher verstorbener Vampir bey der Execution von sich gegeben hat, untersuchet, und aus der verborgenen Philosophie an das Tages-Licht gestellet worden.

Reflections
on
The Thoroughly-Documented
and detailed
RELATION
of the
Vampires or Per-
son-Suckers,

Wherein the Origins of the Incorruptibility found in them, of the growth of new Hair, Nails, Skin and Beards, also red with the fresh blood flowing out of them, not a few of the Vampire Works, on living People, in addition Execution on their dead Bodies, and finally of the loud Screams, as such a dead Vampire at its own Execution has given out, researched, and from hidden Philosophy have been brought into the light of day.

This section elaborates on the spiritualist account of vampirism developed in the answer to von Kottwitz's question, and explains each aspect of the vampiric body as outlined in the long title above in terms of soul, spirit and body mass. The incorruptibility is the result of the spirit remaining in the soulless (*entseelte*) body in the flowing liquid aspect of the spirit (*Gestalt des Geistes*) through thus receiving nutrition of the spirit (*nutriment des Geistes*). The vampire absorbs it as part of the world spirit to which all spirits belong. The body retains incorruptibility and vivacity long after death. The author refers to an "experiment" with the chemical substance tartar, which changes its crystalline appearance on exposure to air. Alchemical, rather than Biblical references predominate in these explanations.

The continued growth of nails and hair and the fresh flow of blood in the corpse have their source in spirit nutriment. How does the flow of the spirit in the vampire body gain the red color of blood? From the liver and the blood itself, which are tinted by the secret hidden within the world spirit magnetically attracted to them. Wheat grains placed in the sunlight turn bright red within a few hours by the same principle.

The process of reddening the spirit does not explain how the vampire draws the spirit into itself. During life the intention of one person can affect the spirit in others. At the moment of death a shameful intention can perpetuate ideas which persist in the dead now become vampires, drawing into themselves the spirit of others. "Vampires only had during their lives the sharp impression that they must become vampires, or they have been impregnated with such ideas by other vampires through sprinkling with the blood; so they gain this impression with their death, and they equally suck out the idea to become people-suckers, just as a mother, pregnant with a child can imprint her monstrous ideas on the child."

In the following paragraphs the author brings up the examples of Medveđa and Kisolova, cites Ranft, quotes the Provisor's letter in full, and recurs to them repeatedly for the rest of the text. There is no actual blood-sucking in these cases, but that is how the influence of the dead on the living is interpreted. The blood itself is subject to influence from afar. The imagination of the dead draws upon the life force blood of the living.

The cry of the vampire's corpse when it is transfixed with a stake is due to the continuity of the spirit embodied by the blood in the vampire that has absorbed the spirit of others. The author concludes with a story from the English hermeticist Robert Fludd.[9] Once in Paris a "worker" was engaged in treating with grades of heat a volume of blood from "poor people". The blood had been allowed to putrefy in a sealed container for two years.

Amid the instances of blood-sucking in which no blood is actually sucked this is a genuine example of genuine blood extraction from a vulnerable population. There is no further information on how the consent of the donors was gained. The story then develops into a displaced mirror of sympathy with the pauper from whom the blood was taken.[10]

As he lay in bed on a moonlit night the worker was awakened by a loud cry like the bellowing of an ox. An oval cloud condensed into the form of a human figure formed in the space between bed and window and disappeared after the cry was issued. Other people in the building and the neighbors across the street also heard the cry.

The next day the worker opened the oven which was secured with a key and found inside the retort that the blood had formed a death's head, the dun and gold colored figure of a human face in all its details. The bishop who had provided the poor people's blood told the alchemist that if any of those from whom blood had been taken died during its putrefaction there would be an apparition. A renowned chemist was more recently able to duplicate the howl and roar with an operation using a Turk's Head (alchemical vessel) in Leipzig. The enraged spirit of the Medveđa vampire (Arnold Paul) had howled and roared in the same way. God's plan is unknown, the author declares at the end.

Where Ranft and Meinig found fraud and dissembling, and sought to reduce the physical effects visible in the vampiric corpse to objective results of decay, the author of the *Acten-massige* found an alchemy of the spirit both empirical and spiritual. The dispersed sense of the world spirit is manifest in the vampire corpse which has imbibed of it by sympathy, not sympathy of feeling but of spiritual-chemical resonance. The vampire is just another corpse, or it is a precocious Romantic hero vibrating with the blood of the world.

At the end of the *Acten-Massige* the publisher affixed an announcement of two new publications by "Voigt" relevant to the foregoing text. They did indeed appear. Besides their polemics they are bent on stirring up a controversy in the publisher's marketing interest. From their appearance in libraries across Central Europe the effort was a success.

Kurtzes Bedencken
Von denen
Acten-mäßigen Relationen
Wegen derer
VAMPIREN,
Oder
Menschen-
Und
Vieh-Aussaugern,
Ingleichen
Uber das davon in Leipzig heraus-
gekommene Raisonnement
Vom
Welt-Geiste,
An gute Freunde gesandt
Von
Gottlob Heinrich Vogt,
Medic. Pract.
____
Leipzig,
Bey August Martini, Buchhändl. auf dem
alten Neumarck, 1732.

Brief Thoughts
On the
Authentic Relations
Concerning the
VAMPIRES,
Or
PEOPLE-
And
CATTLE-OUTSUCKERS,
Likewise
About the Essay on this
Coming forth in Leipzig on the
WORLD-SPIRIT,
Sent to good Friends
By
Gottlob Heinrich Vogt,
Medical Practitioner

Leipzig,
At August Martini, Bookshop on
the
old Newmarket, 1732.

"Voigt" was Gottlob Heinrich Vogt, a Leipzig physician unknown except for this pamphlet and another that quickly followed in the same year and extended the arguments of the first.[11] The *Kurzes Bedenken* title was not infrequent in brief polemic pieces, as *Acten-massige* was for documented pamphlets (about vampires, Gypsies and plagues). From the title page onward Vogt makes it clear that his focus is on the world-spirit(s) doctrine of the *Acten-massige*.

The author of the *Acten-massige* "pushes" (*schiebet*) the mistake (*Schuld*) about the World-Spirit that it has its residence in human blood throughout the world, and can form the aspect of a dog. At the beginning of the *Kurzes Bedencken* Vogt places the dog claim on page 16 of the *Acten-massige*, but as he recognizes later this is the dog that appears at the door of the vampire victim on page 17. In Vogt's interpretation the red fleck that appears at the ear of the victim is a sign of the infectious poison causing the sleep sickness and not the result of the dog's bite.

His next reference, to the incorruptibility of the body on page 28 of the *Acten-massige*, is correct in that the word is present there. Where the author attributes the long-lasting freshness of some corpses to absorbing the spirit of others, Vogt asserts that this makes all people vampires, incorruptible and possessing resources in themselves. What a World-Spirit! It holds all together with the conjoined energies that procreate, grow and multiply. It is no less than the air itself. After death the spirit abides in the body; the living being is nothing other than the spirit enclosed there.

This is critique by following the pamphlet's statements to their absurd conclusion.

Vogt also rejects the conclusions of the *Acten-massige* on a naturalistic basis. The redness of the blood imparted to the spirit from the liver might instead be due to iron content. The cry of the vampire is not a cry at all but air escaping from the bloated body when uncovered. The incorruptibility of the vampire's body must be due to a poison and not to the World-Spirit or the nature of the area where buried, otherwise everybody would be incorruptible.

The World-Spirit can't be common to all living beings. Humans have their own abilities, and animals such as hens, dogs and moles and the like are more "clever" than humans in some ways, and they alone communicate the spirit they have.

To overcome the World-Spirit idea as the central source of communicable vampirism, Vogt relies on the analogy of vampirism to madness spread by the bite of a rabid dog, which according to the beliefs of his time could be spread from one person to another in epidemic fashion.

From a named source he gives the example of a young nobleman who was bitten by a stray dog he played with unaware it was rabid. He went to bed with his bride, after a time exhibited the behavior of a rabid dog, and savaged her with his mouth. Hearing her cries, the bride's friends stabbed the groom, but she also died the next day. Vogt compares this (sexual) transfer of contagion with Arnold Paul (Arnod Paole) conveying his vampirism to his wife through intercourse.

Animals pass on infections that then spread from one person to another: the tarantula, worms in the grave, and hags who newspapers report suck the blood from wounds. Many other marvels can be found in books. May God protect us from them.

This is all there is to the World-Spirit of vampires. The talk of one overarching spirit obscures the presence of many different spirits. "Humanity from the origin has had only two parts, namely an earthly mass (*irdische Massam*) and a living breath (*lebendige Odem*)…"

"*Massam*" had come into usage with the writings of the mystic Jakob Bohme (1575-1624) with the significance of the material weight of creation. "*lebendige Odem*" was used by Martin

Luther in his 1534 translation of the Old Testament, Genesis (First Book of Moses) 2:7, for the phrase translated "breath of life" in the King James version. In the 18th century the two words were paired with or without modifiers in cosmological writings, and also descriptions of pharmaceutical preparations.[12]

Vogt's attack on the concept of the World-Spirit is in line with contemporary beliefs about human nature especially as seen through the eyes of a physician. He will continue, he indicates in the last line, in another pamphlet on the "temperaments and the very shameful teachings that follow".

The notice on the *Acten-massige* in the *Commercium literarium* is the usual epitome of the text's arguments, and concludes with an unappreciative send-off.

Ranft in his 1734 critique also takes issue with the *Acten-massige*'s tripartite division of the human creature.[13] No one would deny the first part, the soul; no orthodox theologian would accept the third part, the body (*Leib*). The body doesn't exist in simple opposition to the soul and spirit, but is one of a longer list of parts that includes understanding (*Verstand*), intellect (*Gemüthe*), reason (*Vernunft*), emotions (*Affecten*) and the like. All these many parts can be grouped into larger categories, even into a simple duality of body and soul. No one division of parts is fundamental.

Having demolished the analytic principle of the *Acten-massige*, Ranft assures the reader that the three-part division of the human creature is an easy way to make a vampire case like the "Hungarian" one seem genuine. The author of the pamphlet added to the assurance by allowing that some apparent cases of vampirism are the work of the Devil and others are just frauds. A few, however, call for clarification by the tripartite analysis. Ranft then sets about proving that its author plagiarized ideas and text from his Latin dissertation by juxtaposing quotes from his own Latin original with German text excerpts.

Ranft's rejection of the body, soul, spirit division and the vampire's connection to the world spirit would seem to put him in agreement with Vogt. The Leipzig medical practitioner's resort to a rabies-like poison as the root of the contagion and behavior of the infected is the center of his review of the *Kurzes Bedencken*. "Furthermore, we take the whole writing as an incomplete and very confused schediasm, having flowed from a hasty pen."[14]

All of the parties to this exchange accepted the reports of the Serbian vampires, Plogojoviz, Paul and the others, as fact which juxtaposes local belief with the examination of the corpse. The difference of opinion was in whether or not there was a physical and not only a spirit-based connection between vampire and victim, and what was the nature of its spread from one person for another. The apparent surplus of blood in the vampire was either derived from other people or due to a principle of increase.

The vampire cases were an opportunity to discuss issues that went beyond the mere question of a vampire's existence. Was there life in the vampire, and how was it related to life in general?

---

[1] Meinig (1732)

[2] Kevorkian (2007: 177)

[3] *Leipziger Literatur-Zeitung*, April 13, 1816, 92: 729-30.

[4] *Commercium literarium*, July 9, 1732: 219-22

[5] *Acten-massige und unständliche Relation* 1732: 7-8

[6] Ranft (1734: 178)

[7] Hoffman (1827: 227-28)
[8] Bohn (2016: 121)
[9] Fludd gives the name of the operator as La Pierre in his *Anatomia Amphitheatrum* (1623). "The Stone" may be a pseudonym for the alchemist.
[10] Craven (1902: 24-25) repeats this story from Fludd's *Anatomia Amphitheatrum* with no mention of the source of the blood from the poor.
[11] Vogt (1732a and 1732b). The title of the second is translated, *"The insidious but now widely eradicated three parts of People along with attached Sources of many Errors, namely the Doctrine of the Temperaments..."*
[12] *Microcosmische Vorspiele des neuen Himmels und der neuen Erde*, 1744: 15; Hoffman, ed. (1718: 466)
[13] Ranft (1734: 212-27)
[14] Ranft (1734: 229)

Curious
And very wondrous
RELATION,
of the new Events
in SERBIA
showing themselves
BLOOD-SUCKERS
Or
VAMPIRES
gathered from authentic Reports,
and
with Historical and Philosophical
Reflections accompanying
by
W.S.G.E.

And whatever you may choose, is of little consequence to us, provided that our ignorance does not make doubt a certainty. Joh. Clericus in Puevmat, Sect. II. C.W. on the evil Angels, and of their ministries and power, p. 83.

In the Year 1732

W.S.G.E., never identified with any certainty, placed a quote from the Swiss theologian Jean Le Clerc at the beginning of his entry in the 1732 vampire commentaries. The booklet is aimed at providing the information necessary to prevent religious doubt from becoming a certainty. It begins with the original, word for word texts of two relations that stirred the exchange of

179

pamphlets: the Provisor's 1725 letter on Plogojoviz and the 1732 Flückinger report on Arnold Paul. Only Glaser's 1731-32 letter is absent.

This author's extensive notes begin with the hierarchical descent of the news of the latest vampire reports received by Prince Carl Alexander of Württemberg, the Imperial Governor of Belgrade and Serbia, then copied and transmitted as correspondence to the newspapers.

This adventurous and previously unheard of experience awakened great wonder everywhere among us. It was no 'apple of Discord' but a fruitful release to discourses among all gatherings of people high and low. The ladies also began to chatter about it the better to prove their cleverness. No one was more on top of it than the lords of medicine who tugged at the sleeves of one another each wanting to learn what the other knew not having sufficiently studied it himself. By such prodigious oral and epistulatory disputes clever people among us wanted to comment on a new wonder work, namely that the spiritual lords could keep quiet at their pulpits for so long. They dunned us with this unusual and therefore most praiseworthy countenance like an emblem of Lot's wife pictured as a pillar of salt upon which is inscribed, Woman keeping quiet! What a wonder upon wonder! Here once more is seen a woman who can be silent. I wished myself a hundred times to be for a while under this fortunate order. I don't know why no one wanted to leave me silent. However much I excused myself, however much I repeated the old student saying, 'If thou dost not speak, thou remainest a philosopher'. So there was required here and there a monument to my ignorance, and finally people who wanted to have it over me, found the means to martyr me, together wrote what I had scattered around discussing back and forth. And I threw it into the fire, and see, it became a Calf, as in the second Book of Moses 32: 2. But not a golden one, which such an artful chemist as Moses was requires, but a fleshly one "that tastes somewhat of fat". When the people will have no other, then they must have it.

However, we want to get to the point. When I now go back over what I was questioned about, I remember that one writer is straightaway left hanging in the fact of these undecayed corpses; the other wanted to show on this occasion that he understands something of 'natural history' and warmed up the talk about pregnant women in graves. The third was clever and wanted, that one be very near the corpse of the vampires, and to ask, what to make of their blood-sucking? And the fourth remembered the eye-judgment of certain officials and, as peasants lament with the great shame of field mice found on fruit, judged, they should all the same be caught.

And so some say, when the handiwork of these leeches (*Blut-Igeln)* is put aside, out into the air, it comes time to try German blood. After these different heads I well must direct mine, and also say something.

This high Baroque introduction courses through a miniature history of the effect of the vampire reports printed in the first pages on salon society in the capital. (The booklet shows no place or press of publication but it probably is Vienna). The academic precincts of Ranft and his respondents could not contain this burst of reactions from conversationalists and letter writers, officials, doctors and most sternly, the churchmen. The author, whose coded identity probably was readily guessed by many of his readers, heroic-comically poses as a much in demand leader of opinion who, having tossed into the sacrificial fire the script of his pursuers, is finally prevailed upon to put his words into writing.

He alludes to commentators who have preceded him, rendering each viewpoint with a slant that throws into relief the seriousness with which they expected to be taken. Then with a flash of pride in his German blood he sets down his own sought-after opinions, divided into three main chapters followed by a supplement. The undecayed corpses, the (chewing and) smacking of the dead in graves, and the blood-sucking vampires are the chapter topics.

These opinions are all tossed out with the lightness that swept through the introduction, as in his first notes on the undecayed corpses.

If it is asked after history, if it already has much happened, that human bodies (of others I will in brief report nothing) after the separation of souls are undecayed for several days, weeks, years and centuries, it must be answered with a 'yes'. And thus are not understood to include such bodies as those which have not retained their outward aspect, and have crumbled so soon that they are taken up by the free air, and strongly moved around.

It's not a matter of mummies, or of corpses artificially preserved in balsam, but of corpses that of their own accord retain skin, flesh and innards, especially the blood. Besides the classically well-preserved corpses of Hector and Alexander the Great, W.S.G.E. cites the example recorded by a Württemberg pastor in 1709, of the bodies of 23 drowned men recovered from the water after 4 to 8 weeks submerged. When they were laid out a drop of blood appeared at the nose, followed by such a flood that it inundated the bier of some of them. He recalls the martyrdom and miraculous preservation of the flowing wounds and tongue of St. John Nepomuck, using that as the occasion for a homily. He also recurs to cruentation in which the blood of a murder victim rises from the body at the appearance of the murderer.

The good people of Serbia, in the barbarous borderlands of Turkey, take the undecayed corpses of the buried as the sign of fearsome vampires, plague spirits, destroying angels, blood-suckers and gruesome murderers of neighbors, brothers and even of their own children.

The Greeks consider such corpses the remains of infectious heretics or despicable criminals who died in exile, whereas the Catholics take the opposite point of view and see in them the remains of a greatly sanctified personage. Protestants look at the facts and think freely about the matter. Here his irony returns. "Some even envision a pawnbroker in an eternity of greening and flourishing souls."

A new journal that arrived on his mountain slope contains the story by a learned physician of an elderly Christian woman wracked in the dog days of summer by dropsy and other illnesses, who died at the age of 76 and was rejuvenated in the grave into the appearance of 30 year old woman. "Thus a swift death-struggle is better than a dead life."

Attributing the incorruptibility of the Serbian corpses to vampirism is just one way of looking at the phenomenon; others might see it differently, more or less favorably. W.S.G.E. sees a "strange and higher source" of incorruptibility in all cases, and counsels patience in seeking it. The same can be said of smacking in the grave.

W.S.G.E. doesn't adopt the chewing (*kauen*) of Ranft's title phrase for the sounds of the dead in graves though he is aware of Ranft's book. To the *schmatzen* sound of pigs eating he adds *batschen* (*patschen*, smack) and *kloppfen* (knock), "and other noise." The sounds alone are taken as harbingers of the plague. The condition of the cloth found in the noisy graves is due to the activity of the limbs: it is convoluted or wound around the finger, hand and arm. He does not mention finding it in the mouth. Blood might be in the throat.

Some of these dead come to relatives after death demanding food, and are called night-eaters (*Nachtfresser*). The head of such revenants must be severed with a spade, or a strap tied around the chin or a stone put in the mouth to cause them to forego seeking treats (*Nascheren*). W.S.G.E. adds lore to that presented in the Serbian vampire reports. These measures taken to immobilize the mouth of the dead are not cosmetic (to keep it from yawning open as the jaw muscles slacken) or to prevent sheet chewing in the grave, which is not among the sounds heard or sights seen in his version.

Head severing and stone placing are recalled in Rohr's 1679 *de masticatione mortuorum* and Ranft's 1725 and 1728 dissertations as methods used to prevent corpses from being overactive in the grave. For W.S.G.E. they are intended to stop them leaving the grave in search of food. That was the belief.

Archaeological examination of tombs has demonstrated that these measures actually were taken in a few burials in German, Slavic and Italian areas, and in New England in the New World.[1]

A list of citations of authors on grave sounds is followed by an equally bemused list of causes, from underground fires, wind bursting out, the sinking of the coffin, hyenas, mice, snakes and worms. Martin Luther wrote in his *Tischreden* that the sound was caused by the Devil, not influencing the dead to make it, but serving it up from the coffin himself.[2] Other examples of the unquiet dead taken to be diabolically driven include Pope Sylvester II, a master of the black arts, who long after his own death rattled and sweated in his coffin right before the death of a pope.

W.S.G.E. himself is certain that the sounds were made by living people who had been buried still alive in error. When in an effort to get to the source of the sounds the graves have been opened, the position of the corpse makes a convincing case for this conclusion. It is found inverted, sitting upright, or in contortions from its attempts to summon rescue.

In only a few known instances has rescue come. This danger is the reason corpses were lightly buried in the past and in other lands, just enough to protect from animal attack, or they were kept for a set period inside the house before entombment, as earlier laws required. Recent examples of the apparently dead come back to life: a woman plague victim who awoke to tell of heaven, a sea-captain who seized the undertaker, a "dead" woman who gave birth before she could be buried.

A Latin text with a section on the lying signs of death contains the advice that when any sound is heard from within the coffin it should be opened. "I have often said to my acquaintances that more living people are buried than anyone would believe. Physicians should have good distinctions by which the genuinely dead are distinguished from the seeming dead, especially in affectations of consciousness."

Backing away in wonder or fear blocks the source of the sounds being known, and prevents action being taken to save a precious life. "Yes indeed when the Devil launches his confusion here and there to any degree, it's no shame to go ahead with the burial and see later what happened." Later it looks as if some supernatural force was at work and there is no guilt in having buried someone alive. Often such sounds are heard coming from graves for days or even weeks, so long have the buried been able to live.

How then to make sense of the collection of "astonishing powers and intricate effects" that make up the Serbian vampire reports? Some commentators have thrown out all judgment and fall back on unreason. Michael Ranft does the opposite and relies on purely material explanations. "Our master M. Ranft has clarified the above-named, all the wondrous described experiences, through the nature of plain material, and "by the operation of body upon body" without having had need of a divine or human or English or German spirit."

W.S.G.E.'s preferred understanding of the ability of the vampire to bring death to an entire village harks back to Martin Luther's *Tischreden* and forward to psychic epidemics. Whoever believes it holds implanted objects in certain parts of the brain that are not in fact apparent to others but are before the believer as present: "people, figures, gold, a bird, an angel, 'he feels a cold hand," and so on. And without any contribution of the Devil or his works, the believer can experience impressions "which according to the laws of nature with the appearance of imagined and other things interconnected are not in fact real."

The object fixed in the imagination can provoke illness by association.

The author, evidently a medical practitioner, recalled being summoned to examine a girl who had fever, "heart-stress," and cried continually. He found that she lay in the bed of the landlord who had died a few days before and had a vision of him that led her to believe she was about to die. He ordered her to be transferred to a bed in another place, not to be left alone, and gave her some medications. She quickly recovered.

This and other cases testify to the ability of location and imaginary connections to conspire in sickening people unto death.

Can it likewise happen in Serbia? Can the wild and disgruntled inhabitants of the accounts given earlier become sick from longing, frustration, love, anger, vengefulness, implacability and other affects? In the sickness can they imagine that the beloved or wronged person came to them and embraced them from whatever effect they would? So spoke the patients, the superstitious and already preoccupied population believed it heaven-fast. The relatives grew afraid and sickened; the neighbors were scared and from fright died one after the other.

One vampire kills a person, who becomes a vampire, and so on in endless succession. Having eaten a sheep killed by a vampire, he can expect to become a vampire himself in death and avenge himself on others in his village for all the slights suffered during life. The author recalls a set of little verses on the people of the land he learned in youth from an exiled Hungarian noble:

So are the people of the earth,
Haughty in their actions,
Treacherous in disposition,
Indulgent by their blood,
Naked as monkeys,
Well dressed as parsons,
Shod like horses,
Not worth three mites!

From this it is possible to envision Arnold Paul falling from a haycart. His wife takes to thinking, from thinking arise strange terrors (*Grillen*), from strange terrors comes the deceased "courtesan", which brings a frightful conceit, the fear brings death, and death ensnares the elders, relatives, neighbors and the entire village. Or the dead intended returns to suck the blood from his bride, who also dies.

If the sickness originates in the imagination, then the cure comes from the imagination. Someone who thinks he has frogs in the body is cured when he sees frogs that have been placed in his excrement. Think you are missing your head, then a hat placed there restores it. One who thinks he is dead and will not eat or drink is placed among others lying down and wrapped in shrouds but who drink and eat, and thus he is cured.

How would it be, if we said that the vampires mentioned above in Serbia were the smart invention of a clever doctor? Who knew that if the superstitions of simple people were accommodated, the known blood-suckers were buried, a spade jabbed through the chest, and through these impressions fear was taken away from the people, then to free them from their sickness.

Imagination, however, does not account for the observed preservation of the corpses. That might be due to special properties of the earth in the Serbian part of Hungary. The narrative of the Provisor combines peasant imagination with reported physical facts that are inconsistent with each other. If the soil preserved bodies why did some decay while others of the same age did not?

The imperial Provisor accomplished the deceit of making the peasants believe that the lofty administration he reported to was not aware of the trick they pulled, showing a grave with as many as two undecayed corpses among the decayed ones. W.S.G.E. phrases this as a series of questions about what he names a "mirror-fencing solution," (*Spiegelfechterische Cur*) in which one deceives another about the degree to which he is deceiving a third party.[3]

A further complexity of the vampire condition as described by the Austrians is the role of the "Greek" (Serbian Orthodox) church beliefs of the villagers, which differ from those of the Catholic and Protestant churches. The corpse of someone who has been subject to excommunication will in Orthodox dogma remain intact and unchanging, its skin tight over a bloated body, until the ban is lifted. W.S.G.E. relates several instances of fully intact corpses turning to dust when priests ceremonially remove the excommunication.

His sources are travelers and historians who witnessed or heard of these dramatic transformations. He does use a variant of the Greek word *tympaniaios* (drum-like) for this type of corpse. The Vatican librarian Leo Allatios (1586-1669) composed an even-tempered survey *On the beliefs of the Greeks* (*de Graecorum hodie opiniationibus*, 1645) that draws upon the writings (*nomokanones*) of Greek Orthodox priests and laymen to describe the types of living dead in Greek legendry: the *vrykolakos*, a corpse in folk belief disapproved by the Church that returns to terrorize and feed upon the living, and the *tympaniaios*, the undecayed and motionless corpse strictly under the control of the Church.[4] The *vrykolakos* was, like the vampires, ascribed to the influence of the Devil and to natural causes; in either case requiring the deployment of exterminating techniques by lay people. The *tympaniaios* was the result of an ecclesiastical procedure and lay on the borderline between the saved and the damned. The only attention it could receive was the priestly ritual of ban removal.

Neither type was attested in Greek writings prior to the 16th century. In the 18th century the *vrykolakos* is named in association with vampires in Latin, German and French texts. W.S.G.E. is not the only author in the 1732-33 debate to mention the *tympaniaios;* he and other writers also compare the Serbian vampires to the Greek *brucolaccas (vrykolakos)*.

He differentiates it from the Serbian vampires but sees it as a layer of Orthodox religion serving the same purpose for the priests that the vampire does for the manipulative Austrian doctors and administrators.

Which mental disposition of the people the Devil has used as a convenient opportunity, to play a real and genuine comedy, with this invention taken from something of the Greek Church, but with its meaning, modifications and disguises listed.
Right from the example, how the learned together for the purpose hold and prove, that he made it from the histories of the writing itself of the pagans, from which it is stolen, and afterward disguised in his fashion…The Greek church now glories in the presence and powerful demonstration of Jesus Christ in these corpses of the excommunicated remaining undecayed: so this Ass-King and Lord of Darkness no less, sought before Christ to exercise his dominion and power in so extraordinary and astounding a manner over the dead.

The author does not want to be one of those who see the workings of the Devil in everything, "finds a serpent under every stone," and seeks a middle ground between denial of any supernatural influence on the dead and immersion in superstitions. It is useful to know, though the writers of the report do not say, that Arnold Paul was excommunicated from the Greek Orthodox Church and his corpse was a *tympaniaios*, from the viewpoint of the clergy, which converged with and opposed the vampire beliefs of the villagers.

More and better information has to be gathered. Here he proposes comparative inquiry into beliefs about the dead in the grave among the people under Turkish and then under Christian rule, among Muslim and various Christian denominations, and taking into account the variety of circumstances surrounding those beliefs in order to separate notions from observations.

"It should be better determined, if to these regimental gentlemen field surgeons and also learned doctors, philosophers, jurists and theologians together, the bodies were examined anew in all parts, which were given out that they were sucked [of blood], as soon as they were dead secured and verified if blood actually was withdrawn from them, and they died from a deficiency itself, or from a kind of Ephialtes? If from this, were fear and apprehension the only source of the shortage of blood?..." W.S.G.E. continues to ask a series of question on the precise status of the alleged blood-sucking victims before and after burial.

The vampire beliefs and apparently the vampires themselves were confined to the Serbian lands. "German blood was as little tasted by these dead as French blood; and Neckar wine and Saxon beer was as little tasted as their Hungarian wine." The Serbian people thought that by opening graves, driving a stake through the corpse, or hacking off the head and burning it to ashes they were freeing themselves of the plague. That was not valid medically, politically or theologically. These people fear the Devil more than God. Though the Devil acts in nature he cannot be acted against in nature.

W.S.G.E. turns to the redemptive power of Jesus from the distractions of the physical dead and the Devil's supposed influence over them. "Repent of the dead and the barren and fleeting works is better, and endlessly better, than anatomizing a thousand vampires; and with the world and its learned discourse and amazing histories there is more wonder than to awaken the vampires themselves." The vampires in the end are a metaphor for the spiritual limitations of those who would be absorbed by arguments and theorizing about the nature of the dead without being open to the wonder of the world about them.

The main text ends with a quotation recounting the conversion of the man to become Saint Augustine, from fierce pagan debater of doctrine to repentant Christian regretting how slow he was to recognize his errors. The contest W.S.G.E. has just engaged in by entering his perceptive analysis of the vampire reports is itself a diversion from the affirmation of faith to be had in turning away from the contest, but not completely. He follows the main text with a long supplement that ends with a reassertion of his middle way with a quotation from Seneca.

The summary of the booklet in *Commercium literarium* emphasizes W.S.G.E.'s theories of the natural reasons for the appearance of the vampires including the physical preservation of the corpses of the vampires because of the soil they were buried in, and his introduction of Greek Orthodox beliefs, without conveying his call for assessing the relative importance of the strains of Christian belief and local superstition in the report.[5]

"In belief and philosophy the author treads carefully, not only writes freely and gracefully, brings in with his writing various pious and useful warnings, also presents the most important if not all moments which are related to this and the rest of the conforming materials." The final denunciation of the focus on Satan and affirmation of faith in Christ is bypassed in favor of the Senecan middle way at the end of the supplement.

Michael Ranft lays down his judgment of the *Curieuse und sehr wunderbarer Relation* in the first line of his review.[6] "This is the most extensive, but truly, not the most clever writing, on these vampires that we have gotten to see." After he mentions the author's pseudonym and the work's structure as notes on the "Hungarian relations," the faint praise grows even fainter. "The author will have the view that he not only is a profound but also a witty philosopher...It only is to proclaim, that good humor has robbed him of the use of his reason, in that he has let pour out so many absurd things and false notions here and there, that it is well seen, he is far from the man whose pen is to be feared when he wants to draw it out on the field [like a sword in a duel]."

Using W.S.G.E.'s own expressions, Ranft repeatedly refers to him as a "market hawker" crying out his wares to the crowd, and, knowing he is a physician, an "empiric" and a "quacksalver," a quack who "grounds everything in experience and has no knowledge of the powers of nature, like those who ignore all the hypotheses of learned physicians and rely on their market pitches." He often turns his adversary's language against him.

Ranft makes short work of the four aspects of the Serbian vampires the author addresses in separate sections. Corpses remaining intact in soil that contributes to their preservation doesn't make it normal for all corpses. Not all the graves from which chewing and smacking sounds seem to issue are premature burials. When he comes to the question of blood-sucking Ranft ceases to address the issue directly and instead launches into a discourse on W.S.G.E.'s method of reasoning which occupies the rest of his long review.

There is a serious philosophical difference between Ranft and the object of his critical attention as Ranft explains centering on the relationship between spirit and matter, and how causality can be determined. Ranft takes issue with W.S.G.E.'s approach to his dissertations, which he insists the author did not grasp, and which the author slighted with his light remarks.

The Serbian vampires are not mentioned at all in the remaining passages, and the only use of the word "vampire" is Ranft offhandedly calling the other writer by that name.

Once more giving emphasis to loyalty to the locale Ranft ends in saying it is good that the city of Halle where W.S.G.E. practices is some distance from Leipzig/Nebra, and sets down his suspicion that the other author is closely associated with a Halle medical writer, Michael Alberti, whose vitalist principles he seems to reflect when he reflects any principles at all.

W.S.G.E.'s almost ethnological suggestions about the Serbian vampires became submerged in polemics and broader philosophical issues for Ranft, who had paved the way for such considerations with his materialist critique of the evidence provided by the Austrians.

Both W.S.G.E. and Ranft were on the cusp of imagining vampires, and they disagreed on the manner and degree of imagining them. The one was eager to explore the communal basis of vampire belief using that attested information at his disposal; the other confined himself to the resonance of the physical details and their possible causes. Neither accepted that bloodsucking actually occurred but W.S.G.E. wanted to inquire into what was considered evidence of bloodsucking. Though it figures into the title of his book, Ranft rarely mentions the subject, and not at all when discussing W.S.G.E.'s speculations.

Another writer who fell within Ranft's critical purview arrived on the scene with credentials more pleasing to his eye.

---

[1] Jenkins (2010: 6; 131-58)

[2] Forstemann, ed. (1846: 62-63)
"So wrote Pastor Georg Rorer of Wittenberg, that a woman of a certain village died and then after she was buried ate herself in the grave and as a result nearly everyone in the village died. And bidden, he would ask D. Martin what he judged of it. He spoke, "That is the deceit and wickedness of the Devil; it would not shame them if they did not believe in it, and held it for anything other than the phantom of the Devil. But because they were so superstitious, so they died all the more from it. And if it was known, people would not be thrown so fearfully into the grave, but would say, 'Go eat, Devil; you have your falsehoods! You aren't deceiving us!'..."

[3] "The writing of the imperial Provisor, its deception is to allow the lowly peasants, their most humble inquiry by the praiseworthy Administration, this lofty Administration of its own various parts, palpably to show that They must not know anything about this secret trick. It was set out to put forward such a 'mirror-fencing cure', would it take straight, that the noisy graves were reached, wherein the undecayed corpses lay, as they, a pair of them, arrived."

[4] Hartnup (2004: 182). The excommunication ban creates the *tympaniaios* which disintegrates when the priests lift the ban. W.S.G.E. cites Allatios' letters that form the basis of *"On the beliefs of the Greeks"*.

[5] *Commercium literarium,* 1732: 206-8.

[6] Ranft 1734: 229-53.

Eines Weimarischen Medici
Muthmaßliche Gedancken
Von denen
VAMPYREN,
Oder sogenannten
Blut=Saugern/
Welchen zuletzt
Das Gutachten
Der Königl. Preußischen So-
cietät derer Wissenschafften,
Von
gedachten VAMPYREN,
Mit beygefüget ist.

Leipzig,
Bey Michael Blochbergern,
1 7 3 2.

Of a Weimar Physician
Conjectural Thoughts
On the
VAMPIRES,
Or socalled
BLOOD-SUCKERS/
Which lately
THE REPORT
Of the Imperial Prussian So-
ciety of Sciences,
On
Imagined VAMPIRES,
Herewith Attached

Leipzig,
By Michael Blochbergern
1732

The Weimar physician was Johann Christoph Fritsche, who was identified as the author not by internal evidence but by common knowledge among colleagues.[1] Fritsche was already known for a doctoral dissertation defended at the University of Halle in 1698, on the medical uses of earthworms (reprinted several times in the following century), for a technical work on pyrotechnics, and, concurrent with this treatise, the first volumes of a collection of documents amounting to "theological-legal-medical and physical histories" from ancient and contemporary sources. They included arrest and trial records of people who had performed or procured abortions, by the use of drugs and other means.

The title of Fritsche's treatise on vampires includes the "vampire or so-called blood-sucker" boilerplate to attract attention. The phrase is repeated many times in the text that follows. Further down, however, under the authority of the Prussian Society of Sciences, the vampires have become imaginary. Fritsche's stand is with the materialists, who saw the body of the vampire as a set of appearances explicable in terms of physical causation, and without spiritual significance.

He begins the treatise with a diversity of narratives about the living dead, from a 1345 Bohemian murderous revenant of a woman put to rest with a stake and burning and a more recent incident in Silesia, the Greek *bucolaccas* and *tympaniaios* according to de la Croix and Allatios, *strigons* and Giure Grando according to Valvasor, and just the names of the villages of Kisolova and Medwedia where the dead allegedly returned from the grave to suck blood. Fritsche repeatedly evokes the *"Rätzen und heyducken,"* the Serbs and hajduks, the Serb Plogojovitz and the hajduk Arnold Paole.

What is a reasonable Christian to make of these stories and beliefs? Fritsche cites Old Testament verses denying that the dead return. For those who claim such returns are a miracle of God, that still doesn't prove that they actually happened. You can call anything a miracle of God. God alone has the power of life and death, so this cannot be the work of the Devil, as some say. Might a Paracelsan "middle spirit" formed of one of the elements have taken human form, abused people and sucked their blood? Their existence can be demonstrated neither from Scripture nor from the Light of Nature (observation of the world).

Still others say that the souls of the hajduks came back from eternity, reentered their bodies and practiced mischief on the living. This is at base false, and smacks of Papery (Catholicism). The Papists say that the blessed and the godless dead reenter their own or other bodies. When the souls of the faithful abide by Christ and see his Lordship, it is just a fable to say that they ever leave that state. The souls of the godless go to Hell and remain there, without returning to act as vampires and blood-suckers.

The postmortem return of the Serbs and hajduks is ascribed to astral spirits, one of the three parts of which humans are formed: body from earthly elements, spirit a particle of the world spirit and soul a flux of the Being of God. The advocates of this view force the meaning of scriptural passages, for instance 1 Thessalonians 5:23 ("…I pray God your whole spirit and soul and body be preserved blameless unto the coming of our Lord Jesus Christ"), claiming that the word "spirit" refers to the astral spirit when it actually refers to the gift of the Holy Spirit.

In Genesis 2:7 ("And the Lord God formed man of the dust of the ground, and breathed into his nostrils the breath of life; and man became a living soul.") there is no spirit joined to body and soul to make the living man. In other passages where life is restored to a dead body the soul alone is brought back.

I well know that many worldly wise ancients, such as Zoroaster, Hermes, Orpheus, Pythagoras, Plato, the Chaldaeans, Egyptians, Arabs, Gymnosophists, Stoics, some Church Fathers, such as Origen, Jerome, and so on, and in our own time Comenius and Hannemann have decreed the same world spirit; just the same, when all the wisdom they have yanked out of nature by the hairs, so to speak, is considered with reasoning eyes, it is found that they not once with the same eyes can have made it factual that such a spirit exists 'in the nature of things'.

Nor do the Aristotelian *animae*-rational, sensitive, and vegetative contribute to the understanding of the Serbian vampires, which might be understood as a tragedy of the vegetative *anima* if such a thing could be shown to be present in the body,

Unable to find a credible spirit that causes the vampire plague, Fritsche then considers the bite of a type of lizard or a tarantula. Neither is known to dwell in the houses of Serbs in Hungary, and in any event the symptoms of those suffering from a vampire attack do not match those of lizard or vampire victims. Neither spirit nor animal explains the illness and death attributed to vampires.

A small number of the learned maintain that vampires and bloodsuckers are a "fearful and crazed fantasy of the Serbs and hajduks that they have from their mothers." They speculate that the illness and death of the Serbs and hajduks is a natural disease and that the associated symptoms are from entirely natural sources. The role of God, the Devil or the world soul are in principle fictions from the fertile imagination of the community leaders.

The disease that struck the villages of Kisolova and Medwedia had the signs of an acute malignant fever that puts its victims in the grave within three days of its onslaught (half of the seven days of a fever likely to resolve). In the 1725 Kisolova relation it was recalled that a similar sickness killing all the inhabitants had occurred in the village while under the Turkish yoke. That a vampire came and caused this is a groundless tale: no one ever saw a vampire, only a dog at the door and some noises, and none of the victims bore signs of blood loss. A fleck of blood at the ear might have been from a scratch during a feverish dream, a flea bite or petechial fleck. It is quite credible that the vampire's visit was a chimera.

Fritsche rejects out of hand the contention of Johann Christian Stock, a Jena physician just at the beginning of a prolific medical career, that the Serbs and hajduks of the two villages had been set upon by an incubus.[2] From this and other sources Fritsche portrays the incubus, or *Alp*, in German, as a rampant fever in which many paroxysms precede death. The vampire, as their "superstitious delusion" maintains, came only once, and the inhabitants did not exhibit the multiple paroxysms or single sustained paroxysm they would if the incubus alone was the cause of death.

The chest pressure and feeling of strangulation were likewise not the result of the presence of an incubus but come from part physical, part moral sources. Looking back at the malignant fever that struck the village of Kisolova in 1725 brings out several of these sources.

It's well known that the days in Hungary are very hot, and not only in summer, and the wine flows freely against the cold at night. These abrupt temperature changes make the transpiration of the inhabitants irregular, leaving many impurities behind in their bodies. The air in Hungary is not the healthiest from the moisture and other impurities brought by the many rivers that flow through the country. From these waters swamps form, and out of the swamps arise diseases typical of putridity.

All the meat they eat, the heavy wine they drink, dense with sulphur, the poor air with its mixed particles, and the poor water combine in the cold of night to block the elimination of the saline-sulphur component which then concentrates in the blood. Small wonder they succumb to fever and die.

In the village of Medwedia a 60-year old woman named Miliza ate the flesh of a sheep and died after three months of illness. Seven other people became infected and subsequently died. Miliza said that the sheep had been killed by a vampire, which was the source of the illness and death that spread in the village. Miliza did not witness the vampire killing the sheep, but assumed according to superstition that it must have been killed by a vampire for her to become ill after eating it. The superstition then framed the death of Miliza and the illness and death of 7 others.

Fritsche joins Putoneus (Meinig) in proposing that an illness that killed the sheep contaminated its flesh and caused the villagers consuming it to grow ill and die. What type of disease the sheep had, mange or glanders, fatigue, lameness or plague, can't be determined from the published report. Suffice it to say that the sheep was sick and fell, the woman ate the sheep's flesh, became ill and died, infected others who also became ill and died.

It has been repeatedly shown that eating the flesh of sick animals causes sickness in humans. Those who the meat of a diseased animal that has been salted, smoked, treated with vinegar or juniper beer will not contract the illness. Josephus Lanzonus (1663-1730) recounted that in Italy the meat of calves that died in a 1713-14 pestilence was salted and smoked and did not cause illness when eaten the following winter. This and other examples make it clear that the untreated flesh conveys the disease the animal died from. Fritsche continues in a disquisition on the relationship between animal-derived food and human disease.

He also surmises that the age of Militza contributed to her susceptibility, and pictures her spreading the contagion to her neighbors. "It follows that these "nocive effluvia" which from the sick woman, came out part by "exhalation of breath," part by "pores of the body periphery" with the air pulled into the lungs, with the saliva swallowed into the stomach, and also through the sweat masses from her body, and to originate a "malignant and contagious fever" from them, and could connect one another again."

There are diseases endemic in a locality, for instance the "Hungarian disease" that might have been at the root of the villagers' mortality.

The fresh appearance of the corpses found in Kisolova and Medwedia, the absence of the smell of decay and the renewed skin is no great wonder. They would only be taken for a marvel by those who have no familiarity with natural processes in the grave "like out stupid and ignorant Serbs and hajduks." Cases of the unpreserved dead remaining natural in appearance are regularly reported. Garmann wrote of a soldier who looked better in death than he did in life.

The conditions that induce, retard, and accelerate decay, rather than miracles of preservation, decide the way the dead look when uncovered. Rather than vampiric infusions of blood that forestalled change in the corpse, several different factors natural to its physical situation govern the degree and kind of its condition. Inhibiting the free flow of air around the corpse, as by a lead casket, prevents the particles of fermentation (putrefaction) from being expelled and causes them to remain in the same mixture holding the corpse to retain the same appearance.

The humoral makeup of the corpse itself can slow putrefaction. Those dense with liquid, the remains of phlegmatics and sanguineous, decay more quickly than those of dry cholerics and melancholics. Arid diseases such as phthisis and marasmus retard decay that goes forward more rapidly in the aftermath of cachectic or hydroptic disease. The bodies of the heavy drinking-eating Romans rotted away much more quickly in the same location after a battle than the bodies of the Persians, who had a drier constitution from their diet of bread, vegetables and water.

Humidity and heat combine to speed dissolution. Cold preserves corpses.

A terrain that is high, waterless, sandy and stony, situated to the north and saline promotes resistance to decay in corpses buried there. Fritsche recalls Allatios' swollen corpses of the excommunicated, and immediately brings in de la Croix's rejoinder, that the swelling was the result of burial in a soil which had the capacity to dry out the corpses. Religion-fostered apparent wonders always have a mundane basis that do not require a supernatural agent.

The falling away of finger and toe nails of the dead is part of the process of decomposition, and has been documented by numerous learned writers. This can be observed in living people who are throwing off the malignancy of a fever. It is not possible, as the learned also claim, that the nails and hair continue to grow after death. There is no principle in the dead body to drive forward the vegetative action; the vegetative soul of the ancients doesn't exist.

Fritsche does subscribe to the notion that the mind can influence vegetative action when there is a living soul present, as in the case of a woman who saw up close a gray-haired head while pregnant and gave birth to an infant with gray hair, or the pregnant woman frightened by an eagle with large talons whose child had similar digits. "The soul of the child in the womb makes hair and nails according to the imagination of the mother." In death the soul leaves the body and hastens to eternity, and the soulless body can't grow hair or nails. Rejecting the vegetative

The body grows hair and nails out of need, the hair for protection from sun, cold and wind and as an ornament, the nails the start of our life-juices and the end of our nerves, as protection and for rightness of appearance. "What kind of need can hair and nails fulfill in a dead body, which since was laid in the lap of the earth, that after God's will it can change back to the first state of being? What need of ornament does a soulless corpse have that the hair and nails should grow there?"

In response to writers who observed, one of them evidence of nail growth in a mummy and the other of hair and nail growth in an aborted fetus of seven months, Fritsche cites others who point to the cessation of circulation in the dead body, that halts the flow of nutrients to the limbs. "So will the skin and the underlying fleshly parts, gradually withered, fall off together and disappear likewise, so that not only the hair, but also the nails on the dead body show to our eyes 'all the way to the roots'." What seems to be growth actually is exposure. Fritsche and his colleagues discredited the lore that a corpse's hair and nails grow after death in the early 18th century as the same myth is discredited by medical writers today.

The pretense of the Serbs and hajduks that the after death growth is due to vampires taking blood from living bodies is similarly groundless.

The "third phenomenon" (after lack of decay and nail-hair growth) observed in the graves of the alleged vampires Plogojovitz and Paole (Paul) is the fresh blood appearing "not without astonishment" in the mouth and other apertures, spurting out of the chest when staked, and staining the grave cloths and coffin. "This bleeding of the dead bodies now should and must be a sign and a witness that these soulless bodies must be vampires; which is fully natural when a cruentation manifests itself in certain bodies after death."

Fritsche's language here is legalistic in keeping with the traditions surrounding observed cruentation, but instead of the implied accusation of murder against someone present the blood flow witnesses the guilt of the spirit inhabiting the corpse. The Weimar doctor has translated the Serbian beliefs about vampires into the terminology of judicial procedure, which reflects the "judgment" of vampirism that led to their postmortem "execution" (staking, beheading, burning) in the Austrian official accounts. The concession made to village superstition (but not Orthodox religion) to placate the villagers and advance the rule of law has affected discourse on the subject of vampirism and cruentation.

There are many cases of corpses bleeding without a judgment of vampirism levied upon them. Apoplectics are known to bleed from nose, mouth, ears and eyes after death. Heating medicines, an all too warm regimen, deep love, and hot weather among other factors that promote putrefaction also lead the blood to flow and break out after circulation has ceased. Young people who have labored with continual, putrid or inflammatory fevers may break out with hemorrhages at the nostrils.

"If dead bodies have lain in the grave for forty days, like Arnold Paule, or seventy days, like Plogojovitz, and have really begun to putrefy, then through the decay 'fibrous solid parts of the body' have relaxed and become porous and soft, and open by tear and split to the breakthrough of bleeding…" As the decay proceeds small releases of blood become pools and the building heat adds to the strength of the flow. *"Ist also die cruentatio cadaverum bevor Rätzen und Heyducken ein ganz natürliches Werck gewesen."* "Thus the cruentation of cadavers among Serbs and hajduks has been a completely natural work." There is no supernatural force behind this flow of blood.

Fritsche finishes his thoughts on the vampires with the remark that the erection of the penis observed in Plogojovitz's corpse was not unusual in the dead, and likewise not due to wondrous influences. This he supports with a number of references to recent studies.

The text that follows without preamble is the "unprejudiced, most humble" report made by the Commission of the Imperial Prussian Academy of Sciences on the vampires in Medwedia, Serbia, a "protocol" couched in official prose. Several paragraphs in, the conclusion on the exposure of the blood, nails on hands and feet, the smells and sounds on driving the stake through the heart of the uncovered corpse of Arnold Paole is "for vampireness (*Vampyrschafft*) no succinct conclusion."

All these mentioned phenomena have their natural sources; the smell and sound are due to the air rushing into the cavity of the heart. "Moreover, it is certain that the appearance of these blood-suckers, also wherein they passed, is demonstrated with nothing, and we find no trail in history, and the present so little, as in other lands of the Gospel, apart from here and there in former times appeared stories of throwing off of grave cloths and smacking in graves found to be false with research and cast aside as shameful error and superstition."

The Commission has conducted historical research and found no record of vampires except what is proven to be false. They do not even take the time to denounce the ignorance and credulity of the villagers. The 20-year old woman Stana described in the report was called a vampire in death only showed signs in her blood vessels and organs attributable to natural sources. The woman Militza, who was full of blood and with sound inner organs, emaciated in life but fat-looking after death, was ahead of the other bodies in her decay due to her illness, her age and the time of year.

There were no living victims of the alleged vampirism at the time the Commission conducted its research, and hence no opportunity to gather their testimony. Of those who died in the plague they could find no reason why one already dead was said to have victimized another living at the time. "Finally it is especially here to remark that the previous blame of vampireness only fell upon poor people, and those without ancestors were awkward, at least did not grant us an examination, grumbled about discussion of the dead in graves and were dismissed as maleficent."

With this information the Committee retained a cautious approach, and could not find that "the same sucking out of the dead bodies happened, likewise their quality through the sucking out or the use of their blood." Thus the Committee denied that the corpses were sucked from or did the sucking. The soil of graves can't propagate the condition and the corpses did not appear to have been "executed."

With this wholesale denial that the events of the vampire report had happened or had happened and were covered up the Vice President, Doctors and Associates of the Academy with the humblest dutifulness of all offer their protocol to His Imperial Majesty in Berlin on March 11, 1732.

Fritsche's decisive if at times digressive investigations were capped with an official document that provided the missing field component. The rumored vampires were corpses uncovered going through the usual decay. Fritsche's excursions led from the medical to the judicial framework of the vampire rumors, and the Prussian Academy added an incipient sociology in inquiring into the relationships among the victims and their class position.

Commercium literarium printed a letter from Fritsche in Latin summarizing his work without further critical comment. Ranft concentrated on Fritsche's introduction of the Greek materials, from de la Tour and Allatios, for whose book he provides a reference to a version in French. He writes that Fritsche's general approach is to treat "the entire being of the vampires as a kind of sickness and he refutes as laborious all those who assign it another origin *(principio)*". Ranft signals his accord with this approach by stating with page keynotes Fritsche's demolition of the spiritual, Aristotelian *anima*, insect and the *Alp/incubus* principles of the vampires. False imaginings made the consumption of tainted sheep flesh in Kisolova into more than it was.
Ranft's reaction to Fritsche's and W.S.G.E.'s treatises sketches out the parameters of the Leipzig vampire debate. There were many other entries, and some introduced interpretations at odds with the parameters set here.

The Kisolova and Medveđa reports were cited, epitomized in some publications reproduced, with rare references to Krink and a plethora of illustrative cases drawn from medical, legal and historical literatures. They formed the raw materials of the debate, which centered on what those reports represented. The veracity of the corpse discoveries was seldom questioned; the contention was over the personal presence of a spirit in addition to the soul and body.

Body and soul alone meant that vampirism was a story based upon a mistaken understanding of body decay after death. Villager fear, ignorance and lack of a rational Christian faith were reasons given for seeing anything other than a dead body in the corpses of the vampires and their victims. These bodies were *"entseelte"* (having lost the soul) in the term used by Ranft and Fritsche but not by W.S.G.E. One dividing line in the debate is between the search for natural causes of the marks in the corpse and the possibility of a spirit presence, which gave the body marks a non-physical meaning. Those willing to consider the spirit presence were more willing to examine the beliefs of the villagers.

Both W.S.G.E. and Fritsche brought up the Greek Orthodox ecclesiastical dogma of the *tympaniaios*, the swollen corpse of the excommunicated. W.S.G.E. sought to place the dogma in relation to villagers' *vrykolakos* or vampire beliefs not condoned by the clergy. Fritsche undercut the *tympaniaios* dogma with a historian's study that interpreted the corpse swelling naturalistically. Ranft ignored W.S.G.E.'s presentation and acknowledged Fritsche's, which dispensed with a church-approved appearance of the corpse resembling the vampire.

The sanguineous corpse and postmortem bleeding were assigned to natural processes of decay, and physical evidence of blood-sucking having taken place was denied by all of the authors. The blood-sucking corpse banner at the front of the publications was just that, to attract attention with the most lurid statement. Fritsche recurred to cruentation in keeping with medical jurisprudence of the early 18th century, in order to access the thanatology of blood flow being articulated by the medical profession to the exclusion of spiritual factors. Blood remains present even in its absence.

---

[1] Fritsche disclosed his authorship in a letter to D. Goetz published in *Commercium literarium* 1732: 254-56, a summary of the pamphlet in Latin. Ranft 1734: 256n wrote that the author "ought to be" Fritsche.

[2] Stock 1732, his Latin doctoral dissertation with the dramatic title *dissertatio physica de cadaveribus sanguisugis, Physical Dissertation on Bloodsucking Cadavers*, which like the formulaic "vampire or bloodsucker" titles, belies its contents.

Vernünftige und Christliche
Gedancken
Uber die

VAMPIRS

Oder

Bluhtsaugende Todten,

So unter den Türcken und
auf den Gräntzen des Servien-
Landes den lebenden Menschen und
Viehe das Bluht auffaugen
follen,

Begleitet mit allerley theologischen,
philosophischen und historischen aus
dem Reiche der Geister hergeholten
Anmerckungen

Und entworfen
Von

Johann Christoph Harenberg,
Rect. der Stifts-Schule zu
Gandersheim.

Wolffenbüttel 1733.
Zu finden bey Johann Christoph Meißner.

Reasoned and Christian
Thoughts
On the
VAMPIRES
Or
BLOODSUCKING DEAD,
Who under the Turks and
In the borders of Serbian-
Lands would suck the Blood
from living People and Cattle,
Accompanied by all manner
of theological, philosophical
and historical notes gathered
from the Realm of the Spirits
And assembled

By
Johann Christoph Harenberg,
Rector of Abbey School in
Gandersheim.

Wolffenbüttel 1733
To be found at Johann
Christoph Meissner.

197

Harenberg (1696-1774) dated the preface of this book September 4, 1732: late enough in the publication exchange for him to review several of the earlier works with "vampires or so-called bloodsuckers" in the title. Ranft's books are not among them, which seems to have embroiled him with that fellow evangelical Protestant minister and vampire-inquirer. Harenberg's education was at Helmstedt, in eastern languages, theology and archaeology, with advanced studies at Jena and Halle. His life was apart from the Leipzig-Vienna circuit.

He spent most of his career as an educator and school administrator, at Gandersheim and ultimately in the dukedom of Braunschweig-Wolffenbüttel, where this first of his many writings was published. Most of them were theological and historical works, including those on his special interest, fossils. He wrote a "pragmatic" history of the Jesuits, the Catholic opponents of Protestant education, and an ecclesiastical history of Gandersheim, among other works.

> The appearances and operations of angels do not belong to the ordinary lice of the realm of nature; but to the extraordinary fortifications of the realm of graces. You can perceive this yourself, if you recall from the history of the foundational divine teachings and the reign of God over the pure how this stands represented in the Holy Writ. I see nothing in the history of vampires to be of especially of use to the affirmation of divine truth or the protection of believers. It also is not found in the foregoing reports, that a tortured spirit or its surroundings was seen. Or if they had seen the like, it nevertheless depended upon whether the conservation of blood in the dead bodies and the perceived choking, or murder, were to be found.

Immediately after this passage Harenberg tells of the 1708 apparition in his garden of an elderly man whom Harenberg recognized but who vanished when he approached. He later learned that this 80-year old man of his acquaintance had died around the time he saw him.

Harenberg hopes that the reader will not take him for the member of a sect whose leader teaches that the world is full of spirits. He observes how right it seems under circumstances like these to employ the common delusion of the vampire, as in the confession of a woman in the Serbian borderlands who said she had given birth to a child conceived with her dead husband who had become a vampire. Women in other countries regret that this delusion is confined to the Serbian sector. (They cannot pass off a child conceived after the husband's death as the product of his vampire incursion.)

The bloodsucker story from Medveđa (Meduegia), Arnold Paul (Parle) and others, which he will present in the second section of the book, falls into the same category of convenient delusions. The male bloodsucker is attracted to the blood of his female affines. Harenberg footnotes an etymology of the word "vampire," from the Greek word *haima*, blood, plus *piren*, attracted to an object. The Hebrew word *dham*, blood, is a parallel, the initial aspiration in either word changed into a "v". No original language is given for *piren*. Ranft disagreed with this derivation. He believed that "vampire" came from Turkish, though he did not give an etymology.

The collection of vampire stories makes up the first few sections of the book, includes Meduegia, Krink, the Greek *brucolacca (vrykolakos)* and others, but not the first one, Kisolova. Harenberg spells the name of the Austrian field surgeon Fluckinger "Flickinger" accompanied by the same list of co-investigators as in the *Commercium literarium* printing of the Medveđa

(Meduegia, Medweda) report. This is additional evidence that he was not in the same social network as Ranft and the Leipzig-centered writers of most of the other books.

Harenberg did recognize that W.S.G.E., the author of the *Curious and Very Wondrous Relation,* was a "learned and well-read man" in medicine and scripture. His contention that the blood that appeared in the corpses of the so-called vampires was the work of evil spirits who brought it from another place was a falsehood.

After the initial collection of stories, Harenberg constructs his own treatise, section by section, to disprove any assertion that blood actually was transmitted into the vampires by any means, spiritual or physical. His method is to state the beliefs and then to negate them through logic, citations scholarly and scriptural, and observations.

He reviews written lore of angels that primitive peoples fed with the blood and flesh of animal, and occasionally human, sacrifices. The spirit beliefs have to be set out in a scientific form the better to arrive at a Christian worldly-wise aid in banishing them. The Christian considerations follow the reasoned ones.

The Serbian bloodsucker beliefs can be broken down into three statements: "1) Bloodsucking happens from outside or inside; 2) The spirit of the dead remains in the corpse for a period of time, or one of the evil angels delivers the blood to him; 3) The spirit itself sucks the blood out of a living body and brings it back to the corpse as it lies in the grave."

There is nothing in the Gospel, Harenberg concludes, to suggest that the Devil has the ability to transport blood from the inside or outside of a body to another body, and there were no signs of blood having been taken away from the bodies of the victims and brought into the body of the vampire. Neither Scripture nor the nature of the materials substantiates these beliefs. No spirit could be that subtle; there were no air vents into the coffins. "Who has the power over the blood of people who are corpses, who has power over life itself, that the life of the corpse consists of circulating blood?...Hasn't fresh blood been found in corpses where no one knows of vampires?" Christ's body was preserved for 3 days from burial to resurrection. How could the Devil keep the body intact for weeks as the Serbian vampire stories assert?

Harenberg's reasoning mingles theology with examination of material circumstances to form a *reductio ad absurdum* for the impossibility of vampires. The end object, circulating blood in a corpse, is not within the power of the alleged fashioner of vampires. On the other hand, there is fresh *blood* in corpses where no vampires are known. The focus remains on blood, which is life.

If the bloodsucker is not an evil spirit passing from coffin to victim and back, then might it be the soul itself? No, the soul lacks "a subtle body" that could accomplish the deed. Then might it be an operation of God that the blood leaves one body and enters the vampire's. Why would God undertake such a negative operation that contributes not in the least to his glory? The works of God negate the order of nature and are wonderworks far more important than these vampire stories.

There are those who consider everything the wonders of God whatever its apparent nature. The world spirit, which Harenberg mentions only to denounce, is the work master of all evil, and the tempter of Christ and all believers. Such a world would require God to produce new wonders in order to support and reinforce reality, in effect to give the lie to himself, who is reality. Each soul is then considered a piece of the soul of God. "Is it not idolatry (*Abgötterey)* if a God is worshiped who is not the true and unfragmented God, but a brain-spinning (*Hirn-Gespinste),* an illusion?"

Harenberg continues through a rash of other thinkers who support his opposition to the partitioned soul of the divine, and those who are at one with this atheistical world spirit and rebirth of the soul pieces in human form, among whom he includes Baruch Spinoza. The reader might well wonder, he asks, if this ever comes back to vampires. He only hopes to take the time to illuminate the underpinnings of the "three-headed world-spirit" and leave none of the ungrounded assertions of the hermetic Christians defensible. He will put forward some of these assertions if they amount to the reasoned and Christian conclusion.

There have been instances of premature burial from which the person presumed dead has returned from the grave and lived out further years, but that can't account for all the cases of vampires discovered upon disinterment. Harenberg delayed the publication of his piece in the hope that new cases of vampirism would be uncovered, and the word he uses for this observation indicates the degree to which vampirism had become a cultural object by this time: "*Es ist nicht glaublich dass die Leibe, so vampirt haben, lebendig begraben worden,*" 'It is not credible that bodies as have vampired were buried alive.*"* The expression *vampirt haben,* to have vampired, first seen in Glaser's report, has returned.

The early 18th century scientific marvel of the air pump, which can suck the air from a room does not, contrary to one of the writers Harenberg is combatting, prove the existence of the world spirit. Nor does the hermitic process of alchemical transformation visible inside the alembic. The astral spirit of Thomasius and Tuchtfeld is just another name for the world spirit and equally unconvincing, as is the air spirit. "We leave the children to their dolls, and the fantasists to their brain-spinning and move on."

Associating hermetism and alchemy with vampirization did bridge a gap for some of his contemporaries, and offer an opportunity for imagistic advancement, as will be seen in the following chapter.

Having eliminated spirits and the partitioned soul of God as the source of vampiric appearances, Harenberg inquires into why some people think, on the basis of these appearances, that a bloodsucker is before them when a corpse is uncovered. The imagination can be induced to make objects and connections between them that do not exist. The appearance of the corpse can be assigned to physical causes only; so can the workings of the imagination. "If the surge and sucking of the blood only resides in fantasy, so we easily learn from the foregoing examples [Medveda, etc.] that the coagulation and thickening of the life-juice has brought the power of the imagination into considerable disorder."

The habit of opium use the Serbs picked up during the long period under Turkish rule caused "a thickening of the life-spirits". In addition, an old story of a plague of dead leaving their graves and taking lives through sucking the blood of the living was revived. The plague was spread by the consumption of the meat of infected cattle, through visiting the sick and carrying away infection, and polluted dust carried by the wind. All of these increased the thickening of the blood.

This disease is a form of angina, or stitch. The patients complain of constriction and pain in the breast, as if something is choking them and clogging the wind-pipe. The greater thickness and disorder of the blood especially affects the finest vessels of the head. Dense images of fantasies attach themselves to the body itself and the thoughts become mournful, anxious and confused. Memory then comes to the fore and the old tales of bloodsuckers appeal to those no longer seeking a grounded understanding of the evil. A fictitious origin (*erdichtete Uhrsache*) takes hold, confessing ignorance.

"Our romping maidens don't sleep any differently. When the incubus (*Alp*) presses them down, which is an arduous fantasy resulting from the inhibition of blood flow, they believe that a thick and heavy spirit lies on the body, and make them a lament." The old Jewish doctors put it succinctly as a *levavi* or *cardiacus* spirit inside the body that had to be expelled. Such was their judgment.

The blood that flows from the corpse thought to be a vampire has a purely physical cause; so does the fantasy of the bloodsucker taking the blood from victims. It comes down to thin running blood of the corpse and thick clogging blood of the disease victim. Contagion, opium and dust in the air make the people ill and cause them to imagine specifically the choking visit of the vampire-incubus abetted by the pressure on the brain and in the chest.

The bodily effects of the disease and the fantasies they induce originate in a blockage of blood circulation due to the consistency of the blood itself. Pathologically variable blood texture is not phrased as cruor and sanguis, but in terms of channels in the circulatory system.

Having configured this system, Harenberg immediately defaults to matters of sin and virtue. He applies his thick blood analysis directly to the nocturnal adventures of young women who, beset by thick blood, imagine the pressure of a lover. The vampirism ellipsis of sex that allowed Valvasor and others since to raise the subject without being accused of obscenity has found its way into Harenberg's discourse.

The warmth of the earth puts pressure on the standing blood to move and pour out of the dead body. It also drives the lymph into the head where it stimulates the roots to grow hair, likewise the finger and toenails. "There are workings of the body to which the soul does not contribute, otherwise beardless men at the command of their soul would sprout thick beards."

Some corpses lying near the so-called vampires have decayed for no reason other than having open sweat glands. It is to be wished that an account were made of the relationship between what the victim consumed, the time of burial and unearthing and state of preservation of each one. Then no one would need to smear himself with vampire blood, eat infected meat, consume excessive opium and become accustomed to the multiplication of vampires.

The origins of the disease would then be known and corresponding preventive measures taken to prevent its reappearance and proliferation. An additional benefit would be that fewer people in a breathless sleep (*die Athemholung einschlieffet*) would be buried between life and death, and there would be no disturbances discovered in the grave for the living to believe in vampires.

The belief that blood has been transferred from one body to another by means of evil spirits is like the belief that eclipses and obstructions of stars are the clustering of dark spirits in the sky. Or Philip Rohr's example of the hangman unearthing a corpse, finding a burial cloth bloodied, clenched in the jaws and wrapped about the neck. Rohr explained it as the work of evil spirits in the grave rather than a premature burial. Harenberg asks as Rohr and others did, was anyone ever seen actually to suck blood from someone who complained they had been attacked? Why doesn't Satan drink up spilled blood? The evil spirit explanation that covers one disturbance is not applied to another when it should be.

Women's sexual morality falls again under the author's strictures. In plague times whores blame the children they bear on the play of Satan in their bodies. Yet these hearsay accounts of miserable murder are not verified by honest research.

That the belief in vampires is mixed up with many sins, therefore also illuminates that a woman who pretends how she was pregnant by a vampire and has borne a child. Thus is recognized therefrom the fruit of an error spread everywhere, and how healing it is that the dishonesty of the common woman is discovered. Then it is not pleasing to Satan, when all kinds of shame are cloaked in the appearance of spirits and indisputable necessity, or holiness.

The common people are not easily brought to an understanding of the true nature of things that bring them fear, and priests often put that lack of understanding to use. The priests in Serbia willingly maintained a necessary error when they affirmed the corpses as vampires. "In the realm of things the state of life and the soul…can be set to rights."

The cries of those entering hell heard in the volcanic activity of Mount Aetna is one ancient example of things being used to order life and death. Harenberg recalled the churchyard in his own neighborhood where the spring snowmelt entering a crevice made a sound like the whimpering of a child. The Superintendent of the church heard it at night a distance away, and told the congregants the following Sunday that the sounds were the moans of the dead at the end of the world. They must heed this warning and repent their sins to quiet the dead. The Superintendent summoned up an experience common to local churchgoers to instill dread and encourage personal reform.

Harenberg does not evoke these instances favorably. They constitute delusion and deliberate deception for a purpose, as the vampires in the minds of the Serbs are "nothing other than absurdities and brain-webbery". He seeks to clarify "rules of practical knowledge (*Ehrfahrung*) grounded in things".

On one hand the appearances attributed to vampirism are physical traits related to disease and the body in death; on the other hand beliefs about the appearances must also be tested according to the divine order of things. Practical knowledge is grounded both in an understanding of material and of God's grace. False ideas are contrary to physics and to the divine truth. Each of Harenberg's rules mingles both.

One rule: a specific thing that is impossible or can find no place in an event is not perceived in practice. For example, it is impossible that a corpse lie in its grave and at the same time leave the grave. "It is not proper for the ordinary type of events on the surface of the earth that Satan get his fresh and flowing blood from dead bodies. He is named an impure and unclean spirit who by this designation takes more joy in foulness and waste than in incorruptibility and conservation of bodies." The incorruptible body of the vampire does not accord with the presence of unclean spirits.

Practical knowledge is not allowed that evinces a wonder contrary to divine truth and does not entail special providence over believers, or which contains things that contradict divine characteristics or exceeds the power of created spirits. Satan can't keep corpses from disintegrating because that is within the power of God alone, as in the Resurrection of Christ.

Confusion of the understanding with the experience of the senses must be avoided. The unchecked imagination can assume mastery of the senses and lead to acceptance of falsehoods as truth. "A hypochondriac and visionary hears God's voice in himself, beholds heaven and the crowned children within, takes a thousand things for truth that are contrary to reason and the word of God…" Harenberg maintains that reason and the word of God are fully compatible with each other, and always undermine crazed idiosyncratic beliefs.

He cross-examines those who claim to have had their blood sucked. Who saw the bloodsuckers and where are the holes they sucked from? Who saw the blood flowing out? It only is the product of the tainted imagination of the victims.

Finally, don't hold as practical knowledge anything that stands contrary to certain and clear truth which the light of reason and revelation make plain. This repeats what has already been said from another angle. Reason teaches that the dead don't leave the grave and that corpses in the open air quickly go foul. Yet where fantasy make it seem this way, who can resist "keeping his gold in the coffer"?

"There is a good count of living vampires in all stands against which one keep guard to the utmost. For they draw to themselves good, courage and blood (*Guht, Muht und Bluht*), either with outright violence or under the glow of rights." The vampire goes from a popular story about the dead rising to a metaphor for the rapacity of scoundrels in contemporary life. In this Harenberg anticipates the synergy of vampire fiction with vampire metaphor that is yet to develop.

I had a call to this essay not only because in part the audience entrusted to me did not want to be fobbed off with the empty words and rules of speeches and above all in the things read in newspapers, which somewhat more led them to covet my clarification, but also especially because a high personage, whose grace and command I depend upon, expressly proposed that I bring my thoughts on vampires to paper.

The emphasis in the entire discourse on the ability of unexamined appearances with an emotional context to be a work of diabolical deception that clouds reason and counters the divine order of things is a response to reportage on the vampires and suchlike in the newspapers. The treatise is addressed to a literate audience who would not be satisfied with a verbal essay or sermon on the vampires but required the firm and stable medium of print with a more reasoned approach than that of the newspapers.

The high personage who impelled his authorship may have been the abbess and duchess of Gandersheim, Elisabeth von Sachsen-Meiningen (1681-1766), who had appointed Harenberg to his teaching position at the abbey school and was the patron of the ecclesiastical history of Gandersheim he published the following year.[1] The absence of dedicatory material naming the abbess, the lack of any direct reference to her at all, suggests that her noble name was not to be associated with the common, and alien, belief in vampires even when the purpose was to contest that belief.

Ranft begins his response to Harenberg's booklet with the quotation translated above, which proclaims the author's "extraordinary call" to write it.[2] The wide-ranging and in part unheard of references oppose truth to a self-centered power of the imagination. In his preface he sets out his plan to capture the hidden workings of angels and spirits in nature with examples from scripture. The proposed etymology of the word vampire formed of Greek *haima*, blood, plus *piren*, so much Ranft ridicules as similar to deriving the word Europe from the French *oeuf rompu*, broken egg, because the surface of the world egg was broken to form the continents. Harenberg's work fittingly resembles the structure and sources of W.S.G.E.'s *Curious and very wondrous Relation*, whose author Harenberg praises, and which Ranft previously dismembered.

The section by section summation of the booklet's observations and arguments is concise and exact. At the end Ranft writes that Harenberg fulfilled the goals he set for himself in the introduction. He could have done even better with some diligence, and served the purest manner of writing by curbing the excess and repetitions. And he did make several incorrect citations of scripture.

All in all, Ranft conveys Harenberg's observations on the vampire texts without critical dismissal (apart from the etymology of "vampire"). He makes no mention of Harenberg's ghost encounter, which seems to contradict the Gandersheim pedagogue's grouping of visionaries with hypochondriacs subject to hearing and seeing what is not true and to be ripe for Ranft's disapproving notice. Harenberg published under a pseudonym (Adeisidaimone) in 1748 *Wahrhaftige Geschichte von Erschauung eines Verstorbenen in Braunschweig, Genuine History of the Appearance of a Dead Person in Braunschweig* which compiled reports of the sighting of a recently dead jurist. The appearance of the figure was genuine, Harenberg wrote, but it was a man and not a ghost, therefore a deliberate fraud. At this time Harenberg's earlier claim of having seen an apparition himself came back to haunt him.[3]

This seeing-denying paradigm gave a frame for seeing ghosts then denying that they were ghosts, the same as the blood that vampires released

---

[1] Schroeder (1973: 67)
[2] Ranft (1734: 270-79)
[3] Wübben (2007: 68n140).

Christian von Wahrmunds
heller
Spiegel,
Worin
Der Ungarische VAMPYR
bey dem
betrügerischen Laboranten/
und
Die täglich zunehmende Ungerech=
tigkeit neben der abnehmenden Gerechtig=
keit nach ihrer eigentlichen Gestalt klar
zu sehen sind.
Allen
Erfahrnen und unerfahrnen
Hermetisten/
wie auch
Gelehrten und Ungelehrten / Rei=
chen und Armen, Hohen und Niedren,
Alten und Jungen in allen Ständen zur
genaueren Beschauung in Versen
vorgestellt.

Gedruckt im Jahr Christi 1734.

Christian von Wahrmund's
Bright
MIRROR
Wherein
The Hungarian VAMPIRE
with the
Fraudulent Laboratory Workers
and
The daily growing Injustice
beside the decreasing Justice
in their actual aspect
made clear to see.
All
Experienced and Inexperienced
HERMETISTS/
Likewise
Learned and Unlearned/Rich
and Poor, High and Low,
Old and Young in all Stands
with a closer Contemplation in Verses
set out.

Printed in the Year of Christ 1734

Christian von Wahrmund is conceivably a proper name. At the head of this collection of verses it clearly is a pseudonym, "Christian the Truthmouth". This work does not contribute to the vampire debate but merges vampires with hermetism to generate an anti-alchemical nationalist

205

incantation. The translation that follows does not reproduce the meter and rhyme of the German original, alternately end-rhymed quatrains followed by 10-syllable couplets, in 15 verses.

Der mit dem fürchterlichen Blut-Sauger vergleichene böse Laborant

Was von Vampyren spricht,
Und Alkumiste prahlen,
Das ist ein Irrstern-Licht,
Ein Mublwerk sonder mahlen:
Wer von Blut-Sauger glaubt, was Jesuiten lehren,
Und Alboranten folgt, der last sich leicht be-thorn.

The evil Alchemical Laboratory Worker
Compared with the fearsome Blood-sucker.

What speaks of vampires
And alchemists boast,
That is a moving starlight,
A millwork without grinding:
Who believes in blood-suckers, what the Jesuits teach,
And the owrker follows, who lets himself easily be turned.

It is the vampireness,
Methinks, a fearful dream;
Of doctoring skill,
Power, that the dead boil over,
That the sealed blood runs from them so fresh,
And the resulting red still is on the cheeks.[1]

The false worker
Now dreams of Croesus' treasure;
He draws gold from sand
And knows full well to talk
Of his gold-tincture, which holds every harm;
His dream stands for so long, until Hantz rushes to dig.

Von Sieberg grabs away
After the dream disappears;
Then it will change the word,
One feels the deep wounds,
That the mouth of this vampire brought to the sack;
So does the pity wise, Frantz will be ridiculed.

Are vampires, Satan's poison,
From no point to divide:
The great Trismegistus
Might well both be named;
His business is deceit; sucks that blood-er, gold.
O were there no more! No, leave them in the world:

So will of light belief too,
As still more to lie,
And after the state usage,
Secret but rather cheated.
Lies of the vampire reign; rise the deed of Hermes,
Brings no golden calf, but is a silver hen.

Soon it wakes in Tyrol;
Soon it comes from other lands,
What besides the vitriol
Metals must change.
It's named too: human piss, mixed with white antimony vapor,
Betrays the great work. O most secret art!

Now goes from one thing;
Then again from many.
Soon it is so humble
That children play with it.
Now long Saturn here; it is a lion, wolf, dragon.
With these Mars and Venus make a whole.

Alone, hear, worker!
I must say something to you,
Make what is known to you,
So you can wear crowns:
Take fresh vampire blood, and cook mercury out of there,
Put the spirit of tartar here, then stands the king's house.

Does this also not go on?
Seek you soon the salt of the earth,
Calcined gold made as well,
It will become a powder,
That worn in yellow wax on silver or lead,
So have you your gold, you are of vampires free.

When you take two whiners
On warm summer days
And learn to tolerate well
The shine of the Dog Star,
The brain of some Alsophist so much burned,
That he, in spite of a hate, burns in pain and damage.

That does not arrive:

Forces through this sign ⊛,
You immediately will be lucky,
And reach your goal,
Sendivogius true and clear describes
Where Philalethes, Mynsicht and Batsdorf reside.

A nasty piece
Is revealed to you, my friend.
Luck pursues you now,
Thus mints yet ducats.
They are missing everywhere, as of the stone of wisdom,
It is believed, they swallow it down, the vampires of Germany.

Therein belongs the Jew,
And every peasant-skinner,
The goat, the brood of Nabal,
And children of Belshazzar
With them will the court by vampires be so tormented,
That is soon felt in the kitchen, soon in the cellar.

The great they honor,
The small have the sorrows;
They spare no low,
To contest the good.
So appear the vampires in morals and repute:
Of Germans there is very much, Hungarians are made up.

The 15 verses are followed by a poem of 9 quatrains of two brief rhymed lines followed by two long lines titled *Wohlgetroffene Abbildung der Ungerechtigkeit, Probable Illustration of Injustice* and a collection of 28 rhymed lines of irregular length titled *In viele Orten weggejagte Gerechtigkeit, In many Places Justice Chased away*. Neither of these poems contains the word *vampyr*, though in the end they support the picture of the vampire as a parasitic tyrant being developed throughout.

The texts are accompanied by a number of footnotes that add details and references, and are as oblique as the text. The first footnote, translated in fn1 here, cites Harenberg's treatise as the best to read on the subject of vampires. The other two footnotes that mention vampires follow Harenberg's practice of using them as a metaphor, which is the method of the entire poem.

The poem follows the steps in the great work of alchemy, the production of gold from base materials, and parallels the worker of these steps, the *laborant*, long considered a deceitful cheat, with the vampire. The vampire is a blood-sucker who deprives the innocent of both the vital fluid and the precious metal. The alchemical worker extracts value from his victims as he pretends to produce value.

Neither vampire nor alchemical worker is the subject of the poem. They both represent the extractions and misdeeds of current figures who are named incompletely and by implication (von Sieberg, Lantz, Hantz). The great age of alchemy, when rulers and the wealthy subsidized extravagant laboratory procedures in the hope of spectacular gain, had passed with the onset of warfare in the second half of the 17th century, when national fortunes and the fortunes of nations were rerouted into military costs.

The alchemists named in the poem and notes-Basil Valentine, Eirenaeus Philalethes, Sendivogius, Mynsicht-belonged to the previous century; their work had been replaced by and merged into chemistry of the 18th century. Their writings were republished, often in translations if originally in Latin or Greek, and became exclusively metaphysical in import, where before they had matched the progress of the soul to the chemical progress toward gold. In the shorter span of the early 18th century this was accompanied by rejection of vampires' ability actually to suck blood (or be anything other than a misperception of body decay after death) while leaving them open for use as metaphor.

Wahrmund sticks to a language and imagery of alchemy and hermetism that were suspect in his time, and thus all the more readily applicable to current distress and a sense of victimization by the vampires/laboratory workers. Gold, mercury, lead, silver, vitriol, lime and human piss all put in appearances, as do the planets and astrological animals. The *globus cruciger*, an orb surmounted by a cross that symbolized Christian and royal dominion, the highest state of alchemical transformation, is printed into the text.

Renowned alchemical "processes" are rehearsed: gold from sand, silver or lead disguised as gold with wax and powder.

Es heist auch: Menschen-harn, vermischt mit Spiessglass-dunst,
Verräth das grosse Werk O sehr geheime
Kunst!

It's named too: human piss, mixed with white antimony vapor,
Betrays the great work. O most secret
art!

Spiessglass was a whitish translucent mineral source of antimony found in the Spiess mountains. As with many alchemical materials its physical appearance hinted at its contents and combinations. Vaporized and mixed with human piss it yields a gold-hued condensate of great interest to the seekers after the secret art. This passage is extended by a footnote to human piss.

Many work in this material. They reap mainly wind and quark, because they do not follow nature, and fewer find fragments of philosopher's gold. And where do the mercury and salt of the magi reside? The two doves of Diana are also not to be found here.

The two doves of Diana, as noted by Philalethes and others, were either silver pieces or alkaline salts added to mercury being refined to the most subtle medicinal form. Human piss was not an ingredient in this preparation.

In 1689 the Hamburg merchant-alchemist Hennig Brand, in search of the philosopher's stone, discovered a method of generating white phosphorus ("cold fire") from quantities of putrified urine, which he tried to keep secret. This was the first chemical element artificially extracted and not occurring pure in nature. The many who worked in the material were after the same gold but only found wind and whitish curds. O most secret art!

Blood had many uses in alchemy; vampire's blood was a new ingredient introduced by Wahrmund. Amid vampireness (*Vampyrschafft*), a word used exclusively by the Imperial Prussian Society of Sciences in their report, it pours out of the dead in a nightmare of doctors' attentions. It is replaced by gold being sucked out of the body by Hermes Trismegistus, one of many names, a footnote adds, for an Egyptian priest at the root of the gold philosophy. From Trismegistus came many schools, none of them of the Art (of alchemy). Trismegistus has become a vampire in the extractions of the many fraudulent hermetic schools that bear his name.

Vampire's blood finally is the source of a form of mercury that can be added to spirit of tartar (*Weingeist dunst*) to make "the king's house". This new form of blood is incorporated into the alchemical goal of fixing mercury with tartar ending the quest in an expression, *des Königs Haus*, that is an idiom for the completion of a cheat in gambling.

The three forms of vampire blood in the poem-blood copiously flowing from the corpse, blood and gold, and blood as part of a chemical process-anticipate expanding fictional blood in imagery from the early 18th century to the present. Vampire blood is fictional, like vampires themselves, but all the more available for figuration and fakery.

Vampyr is the most frequently repeated word in the poem. In the first stanza it is associated with the light of moving stars (the planets, as opposed to fixed stars), an unreliable light for navigation, and millwork that moves without producing anything. Belief in the bloodsuckers is like the teachings of the Jesuits, misleading and sophistic. Whoever follows the workers will be turned like the first two letters of their name *Laboranten* is inverted in the first two letters, *Alboranten,* which now looks like an Arabic word in an obscure alchemical manual.

"Von Sieburg" at the beginning of the third stanza was Baron Johann Hendrik von Syburg, a pseudonym adopted by the German "adventurer" Theodor von Neuhoff (1694-1756). The verses refer elliptically to von Neuhoff's gambling while a member of the order of Teutonic Knights under the grand master Prince Frantz-Ludwig of the Palatinate and the scandal accompanying his departure.[2] Neuhoff made a round of cities in Germany during his 1721-33 years of wandering in the character of an alchemist-exorcist-astrologer.

The bag (*Beutel*) to which the bloodsucking vampire's mouth is applied is a tool of both the beggar and the thief. The footnote to "von Sieburg" in the first line of the stanza: "What signs and wonders of this swashbuckling castaway in the wanting-to-be-rich bag, of which whole countries can speak. The 'rise of Cajetani' awaits him, which should be the continuous wage of such a thieving area." von Syburg is likely to experience the "rise of Cajetani," to be hanged like the swindling alchemist Domenico Manuel Cajetani, who in 1709 was executed on a supposedly gold-actually tinsel-gallows.

The vampires are not just beliefs of villagers and peasants to be dismissed as superstition and folly but a label for all deceit and depredation. They can be an entire regime (*Vampyr-Reich*) that through a secret process promises a golden calf but delivers a silver hen. The vampires of Germany can swallow the philosopher's stone as it yields up ducats.

Here belongs the Jew. A note ruefully adds, "these stinking bloodsuckers and enterprise spoilers are as necessary to a well-ordered republic as goats are to a young orchard." This is not the last time the Jews would be cast as vampires. Also the *Bauernschinder*, the "peasant-skinners," moneylenders who exploited peasants, and who were denounced in sermons and poetry: in a note here they are a "type of vampire".

A miscellany of German slang for predatory types forms the footnote to the line "and the children of Belshazzar" above: "pestilential wild hags, embezzlers, serf dealers, tyrannical recruiters, dissolute spendthrifts and Egyptian pharaohs… O what dangerous vampires are these! Every country shall know it."

The final lines of the poem grant the German vampires pride of place over the Hungarians in morals and repute. The Hungarians are just *dichtung*, fabrication or poetry, compared with the Germans. A note to this passage reads: "Who doesn't forget the test of himself, he can herewith detect either effete courtly desires or the covetous persons themselves." Wahrmund advises that the reader assess the kind of greed that motivates his or her own tendency to metaphoric vampirism.

Another note at the end of the last poem epitomizes the entire pamphlet. "On this and the foregoing pages the Author describes such a type of vampire that already in all countries, cities and towns has done more harm than those in Serbia. Who is not in danger, in fear of being bitten by them, who names them, as happened here, ever pleased with their christening and naming. For whoever honest will still fiddle in these lying times, there are fiddle scores…"

Vampires are a global category that includes the range of thieves, frauds and exploiters poets and preachers had railed against since antiquity. They are suckers of the metaphoric life blood of the people now made known, not without pride in the native robustness of the German variety, exceeding the Hungarian or Serbian variety that gave the name to the type. Such a useful word could not be held back from spreading, first as a curiosity then in its character as a figure, figment and metaphor.

---

[1] (note in the original text) "Whoever wants something basic and focused to read on the vampires herewith it is above all best to recommend *The Reasoned and Christian Thoughts* of the Gandersheim rector J.A. Harenberg. This excellent tract came out in this year 1733 in Wolfenbüttel. Certain Bohemians learned in God and worldly wise Hermetic Star Spirits will also be set out here, thinking of Mr. [Melchior] Hippel and Mr. [Victor Christian] Tuchtfelden."

[2] Gaster (2013: 29; 63)

19. Dissemination

The publication of von Wahrmund's 1733 poem marks the time when the word "vampire" had become sufficiently well-known among the literate to serve as a metaphor without a great deal of descriptive background. It was the beginning of the universal vampire not tied to a time and place, associated only with certain features, and of certain features associated with vampires. The July 11, 1732 issue of the *Commercium literarium,* late in the journal's focus on that subject, printed an excerpt from a letter from Glaser, the imperial physician whose son had authored the first report on Medveđa at the beginning of the year, to the journal's editor, on the subject of growth of teeth in two women, aged 70 and 90, which he compared to what was seen in vampires, "that which we read concerning Vampires."[1] The vampires had become a standard of medical comparison for certain bodily prodigies.

In early 1732 the reproduction of the "Hungarian" vampire reports going on in numerous German publications extended westward, to the Netherlands and Great Britain. The front page of the March 3, 1732 issue of *Le Glaneur*[2], a twice-weekly newsletter written by the defrocked Benedictine monk turned Protestant (Walloon), Jean-Baptiste de la Varenne (1689-1745)[3], was filled with a text titled *Question physique sur une espèce de Prodige dûement attesté, Physick question on a type of prodigy duly attested.*

In a certain canton of Hungary, named in Latin *Oppida Beidonum,* beside the Tibisque, commonly the Teyffe; that is, between this river that waters the fortunate land of Tockay and Transylvania, the people known by the name of Heyduque believe that certain dead people, whom they call Vampires, suck all the blood of the living so that they waste away before the eyes, as a result the corpses, like leeches, fill with blood in such abundance that it exits by all the orifices, even by the pores. This belief has just been confirmed by several instances, seemingly beyond doubt given the quality of the witnesses who testified to them. We will report here several of the most imposing examples. About five years ago a certain Heyduque, inhabitant of Medreyga named Arnold Paule was fatally injured by a fall from a hay wagon. Thirty days after his death four persons died all of a sudden and from the manner of their death, according to local tradition, they were assaulted by a vampire…

The emphasis on blood in this brief introduction is greater than in the report that follows, and the direct transfer of blood from the body of the victim to the vampire corpse is made explicit though no mechanism is given.

There follows a version of the Medveđa report on Arnold Paul and others, not a direct translation into French of the original German *Visum et repertum* but a précis of that report with some modifications. Great importance is given to the attestation to these events by officers. The report is signed at the end by three unnamed surgeons, and by the trio of Battuer, Fleckhenger and Gurschitz. This list doesn't correspond fully with the signatories of the published versions of the report. The closest early 1732 one is Büttner, [von Kottwitz], Flückinger in Meinig and others.[4]

The events are given as a set of beliefs held by the people known as Heyduque (hajduk) after the name of the natives recruited as soldiers to protect the border. Neither Serbs nor Hungarians figure into the narrative, and the village of Medreyga (another spelling of Medveđa) is only named as the home of Arnold Paul, who is termed a Heyduque.

The bloodsucking is treated as a belief that corresponds to what actually happened, both in the preface above and in the extended description. The belief was confirmed (*attesté*) by witnesses of quality who are presumed to have seen the bloodsucking as well as the follow-up in the unearthing of the renewed, blood-soaked Paul and the subsequent destruction of his corpse, which lets out a cry when it is transfixed. This treatment of belief as phenomenal and affirmed by the officers is a crucial break from the Flückinger report, which treats the bloodsucking as a belief of the villagers humored and set to rest by the destruction of the corpse carried out under the officials' watchful eyes.

Arnold Paul's attempt to end his torments by eating the earth of the vampire's grave and smearing himself with his blood is described as a failed attempt to avoid becoming a vampire. The exact circumstances of uncovering him are not included, though the hadnack in control of the operation is an "expert in vampirism." An ephemeral neologism is introduced when the deceased Paul is found to be an "archi-vampire," a prototype of what the victims will become unless their corpses are pierced and burned like Paul's.

After 5 years his vampirism spread in a new outbreak. A total of 17 people died within the space of 3 months, with or without a three-day period of illness. Stanoika, the daughter of a hajduk suddenly fell ill saying that she had been visited at night by the vampire son of another hajduk who nearly strangled her. His exhumed body showed the signs of being a vampire and was treated accordingly.

Local leaders, doctors and surgeons considered why vampirism could revive five years after Arnold Paul's death and traced its survival to animals that were attacked by the vampires and later eaten by more recent victims, such as Stanoika, who then spread it to others. All the corpses were unearthed and disposed of, the entire action conducted as a judicial matter and attested by the officers of the garrison, the physicians, surgeons and inhabitants of the place. The written report was sent to Vienna where a military commission was appointed "to examine the truth of these deeds."

After escaping his monastery in France, and the thirty-year imprisonment that had been decreed for him, de la Varenne traveled northern Europe, including England and the German states before settling into a series of cities in the United Provinces, where he began publication of *Le Glaneur* in January, 1732. The vampire reports were breaking news in Germany at that time, and he presented his version of the Flückinger report around the same time German writers were constructing their commentaries around it. He says he was a professional translator or Latin and Italian into French, and did not claim fluency in German, but perhaps his French and Latin were sufficient to capture news of the vampires from contacts in Protestant Germany. His own version bears the marks of interpretation rather than loss of information through language difficulties.

The interpretation inclines toward a greater presence of blood than was warranted in the original reports, and especially in the strong supposition of a direct transfer of blood from victim to vampire corpse, which has the appearance of an engorged leech (*sangsue*), an image of the sanguinous corpse last seen in William of Newburgh's 12th century story of the vengeful husband (who had the aspect of a *sanguisugis*, see Chapter 8).

de la Varenne's object with this item as with others in his publication is to stir up interest in a sensational set of happenings and attract correspondents. His note after the signatures assures the reader that he will comment further on the matter in a later issue. He then enters into the *callotin* (capping) section of his periodical.

It is not a question of placing in doubt deeds certified, attested and avowed by persons worthy of faith and committed to examining the truth. It would be judging with scant favor the probity of many distinguished officers who have no interest in sustaining a popular rumor if it is not founded on definite experiences. We ask the gentlemen physicians who so naturally explained the convulsions suffered by the *Pâristes*[5] to shed some of their light on this prodigy of nature and to communicate their reflections to us, which we will convey exactly to the public.

The officers are unquestionably telling the truth about the vampires but please, physicians, tell how this is a natural event. On the subject of marvels, he relates the recent birth to a woman of three infants, two white and one black, who were named at baptism after the Three Magi, though it true that scripture contains no record of these names. This monstrous delivery is no less worthy of credence and of the attention of naturalists. de la Varenne uses cases like this to attract attention to his newsletter while promoting non-spiritual assessments of the seemingly miraculous events. In both the drive to win attention and the examination of marvels he resembled some of his German counterparts.

There were responses to the provocative article. The March 17, 1732 edition of *Le Glaneur* (22) contains an *Apendice au Vampirisme,* an update of the subject. "Some flatly denied this phenomenon; other made it one of the principle articles of their faith. Two equally blameworthy extremes, and which only proceed from a shameful ignorance of the simplest effects of nature."

There will arrive the judgments of physicians on this subject. In the meantime another example has come to notice, from the village of Stadlieb in the vicinity of Olmutz.[6] Several persons were attacked by the illness, corpses were unearthed full of blood showing all the same symptoms as among the Heyduques. Local leaders and magistrates sent formal notices to the academies and universities and their judgment was impatiently awaited.

The July 31, 1732 edition of *Le Glaneur* (41) begins with the news of Spanish conquests in Africa, of the Paris Parlement, the King of Prussia meeting the Austro-Hungarian Emperor and the passing of a danger in England. The rest of the pages were devoted to a long, unsigned letter from a correspondent who quotes the Norman maxim, "ruining oneself with pretty promises and enriching oneself not keeping any of them." de la Varenne had not delivered on his promise of several articles, including *Reflections sur les Vampires*.

The awaited article didn't come until the April 23, 1733 supplement (9) of *Le Glaneur*, and then it was titled *Courtes reflections physiques sur le vampirisme,* Brief physick reflections on vampirism. It begins with a concise definition of vampires: "corpses, as one pretends, with the morbid faculty for sucking the living and causing them to die by degrees…" Death by degrees is life by degrees for the corpse, which fattens, gains blood and renews skin, nails and hair as the body of the victim wastes away. Again there is no mechanical apparatus for the imagined sucking, and no discussion how it comes about. The only way to stop the wasting is to impale, decapitate and burn the vampire, then cast the ashes into water.

A footnote presents the objection of "a certain German doctor" to the ash in water ceremony. The fish who consume these vampire ashes cannot help but become vampires (*se Vampiriser*) and all the water of the sea cannot purify them of this dangerous evil. The River Teyffe that passes through the country enters the Danube which pours into the Black Sea and then the Mediterranean and the ocean beyond. One fish eats another up the food chain. The German doctor calculated that after 2 years, 17 months and 3 days the top predator become aquatic vampire will be in the Rhine. "…if this dangerous illness spreads in Germany, there is no reason to seek another cause."

Expositing this jocular maritime epidemiology of the infection does not prevent de la Varenne from dismissing the vampire system as a sham. It can't be explained naturally without recourse to trickery. Why do people living in Hungary, Serbia and Transylvania hold these superstitious ideas so closely that they act as they do?

After someone has died the relatives, friends and servants attempt to communicate with the dead to learn why they died while they were doing so well. Since the dead are not very good at discourse their silence is taken as a sign of their anger with the living. From that comes "the almost innate error" that the dead return to bite, pinch, suck and mistreat the living. A fantasy, you might say, but one with very real consequences.

After this primary cause, the silence of the dead and the channeling of all misfortune into their malice, the poor nutrition of the region, the diet of oats, roots and tree bark, causes a thickening of the blood, which turns to corruption. Dissection of those dead of the epidemic fever that ravages the region bring to light the raw grains eaten during famine attached to the wall of the stomach. That is the source of the phantoms that trouble these people.

The inclination of their spirit and a natural disposition in the mass of their blood to vampirism make them receptive to a contagious poisoning of the blood that sinks into the bone and becomes incurable. Like the madness the bite of a rabid dog communicates to the victim, vampirism, the deranged conviction that the blood has been sucked is passed from one to another together with the accompanying illness. Insomnia and delusions that they are visited by the dead who infected them occur amid the frenzy caused by the excessive fermentation the venom excites in the infected blood.

Here the discussion takes the materially metaphoric turn that also seems to be an innate predisposition of vampirism. "We would also be drawn to believe that the poison communicated by a rabid dog, by a vampire, by a tarantula, the same that produces extreme love, or every other violent passion, is nothing other than a Worm that nourishes itself on the purest substance of Man, a Worm that gnaws incessantly at the heart, that puts everything in the body it has entered into combustion and does not abandon its prey even in the depths of the tomb."

The thickened body, the uncoagulated blood boiling out and the growth of skin and hair are shared by all the corpses of those eaten by the Worm. The cry that is said to issue from a vampire being staked is a release of air through the windpipe. The execution of the vampire corpse can have no other effect than to cure the fantasy of those convinced they have been tormented by it. Piercing, decapitating and burning the corpse dissolves the conviction that its inhabitant can any longer affect those who watch the destruction.

Le Glaneur was the first periodical in Western Europe to present a version of the Flückinger report, though not by much. A different version appeared in the *London Journal* 8 days later, followed by other English and American periodicals. By the time de la Varenne published his promised *Courtes reflections* in April, 1733, there had been varying republications of the report in Germany, England and Italy with commentaries, some of which influenced the exiled French author.

That a thickening of blood caused by the diet grain, roots and bark, weather and predisposition was a major force in the vampire illusion was suggested by several of the German commentators. de la Varenne, like most of the others, highlighted the contribution of the superstitious background of the villagers, specifically of the Serbian villagers. He only joined a few of them in giving attention to the role of poverty in setting the stage for the vampire fantasy, and he gave it his own unique gustatory turn in citing the unmilled grain consumed during famine found still clinging to the stomach wall in autopsies as a spur to frenzy.

The rumor of plague and of contagion suffuse all vampire stories. Epidemic contagion of the disease that occasions feelings of sleepless fatigue associated with blood loss, and of the belief in bloodsuckers that cause the loss. The belief is accompanied by actual disease spread by venom that induces blood fermentation. de la Varenne added a *calottin* provision to contagion with the German doctor's supposed line of transmission of vampirism down rivers to the sea and from little fish to big fish and more humans. As German doctors do, the hydrographic theorist gave a timetable down to the day for the arrival of the infection.

From his neologism for the model vampire, *Archi-vampire*, to the tightening of the concept of equilibration, the living victim fades as the vampire grows, de la Varenne is close to making a new fiction out of the vampire belief. Classifying vampires as one instance of affliction by a worm, grouping them with tarantula-induced dance mania and extreme love, makes bloodsucking figurative while denying it any literal reality.

There was no expectation of finding an actual worm eating at the innards and activating the vampire fantasy, exciting wild dancing or piercing with the pain of love. Intestinal parasites were a common enough experience for a worm of vampirism to be expressive (What's eating you?). The image did not seem to have the popularity of night visits by the blood-thirsty deceased, but as a representation of contagion it has materialized in vampire fiction.[7]

This April, 1733 excursion to the boundaries of vampire belief and what might be made of it was the last time de la Varenne commented on the subject. *Le Glaneur* and its supplements continued to print news of France, Spain and Poland with the occasional literary excursion and romantic song, and a reminder that it did not carry "insipid" news or personal attacks. The periodical had already survived one attempt to have it suppressed by a French official who claimed he was accused of being an ecclesiastical spy. In June, 1733 it was suppressed by order of the Dutch States-General. The Netherlands ambassador to the French court petitioned the legislature on the grounds that passages printed in *Le Glaneur* were offensive to the French king and his ministers.

The following year Michael Ranft reviewed the entries on vampirism in *Le Glaneur*.[8] He felt that de la Varenne had made a thorough account of the matter and conducted himself thoughtfully. The French author warns that by evaluating it too much or too little there is the danger of making it into a laughingstock or an article of faith and nothing else. de la Varenne finds nothing supernatural in the entire vampire matter. He takes it for a plague that disorders peoples' brains, like the poisoned bite of a mad dog.

Ranft extracted the parts of de la Varenne's account that fit his own demythologizing project and left aside the confabulations of contagion and worms. Only the mad dog comparison was retained. No blood was exchanged, only displayed.

A version of the Flückinger report reached the network of British periodicals at almost exactly the same time as it appeared in *Le Glaneur*. Discussion of the date of appearance has been tied up with the question of when the word "vampire" first was printed in an English-language publication. An excerpt from the *White-Hall Evening Post* for March 9, 1732 set down in a handwritten journal appears to be the earliest, but that may be the date of the entry not of the newspaper.[9] The earliest for which there is a printed page is the March 11, 1732 edition of the *London Journal*, followed by the March 23, 1732 edition of the *Grub-street Journal* (116: 3). The same text also appeared in the *American Weekly Mercury* (Philadelphia) 650 (July 8-15, 1732).

These English language versions of the report are identical with each other in every detail, and seem to be reduced versions of the one that appeared in *Le Glaneur* a few days before. The names of the English versions are very similar to or the same as those in *Le Glaneur*: Medreyga, Heyduque/Heyduke Arnold Paul(e), Hadnagi Bar(r)iacrar, the three signatories Battuer/Batruer, Flichenger/Flickhenger, Gurschitz and their regiments, the "three other surgeons". Capt. Gurschitz as signatory is the same in French and English, but he doesn't appear in the body of the French text while he does in the English, as Capt. Goschutz,a different spelling of name but from the same regiment. The English versions share this spelling in the text with the *Visum et repertum*. The most variable recognizable word between English and French is the name of the place in Turkish Serbia where Arnold Paul ate the soil of the vampire's grave: Cossova/Caschaw (Gossowa in *Visum et repertum*, today's Kosovo).

Where the French and English versions overlap in the essentials of the Arnold Paul story, they share the numbers with each other and with the original German texts: Arnold Paul died five years ago, twenty-thirty days later persons were taken ill and four died, forty days after the death Paul's grave was opened and his body, found fresh and blooded, with new growth of nails, was staked and burned. The circumstances of Paul's death differ slightly from French to English, he was either crushed by the cart or just killed by its overturning. In the German versions he fell from the cart.

Medreyga in Hungary, Jan. 7. 1732.

Upon a current Report, that in the Village of Medreyga certain Dead Bodies (called here *Vampyres*) had killed several Persons by sucking out all their Blood, the present Enquiry was made by the Honourable Commander in Chief; and Capt. Gorfchuz of the Company of Stallater, the *Hadnagi Barjactar*, and the Senior Heyduke of the Village, were severely examined: Who unanimoufly declared, that about 5 Years ago a certain Heyduke named Arnold Paul was killed by the Over-turning of a Cart Load of Hay, who in his Life-time was often heard to fay, that he had been tormented near Calchow, and upon the Borders of Turkifh Servia, by a *Vampyre*; and that to extricate himself, he had eaten some of the Earth of the *Vampyres* Graves, and rubbed himself with their Blood.

That 20 or 30 Days after the Deceafe of the faid Arnold Paul, several Persons complained that they were tormented; and that, in fhort, he had taken away the Lyves of four Persons. In order, therefore, to put a Stop to such a Calamity, the Inhabitants of the Place, after having confulted their *Hardnagi*, caufed the Body of the faid Arnold Paul to be taken up, 40 Days after he had been dead; and found the fame to be frefh and free from all manner of Corruption; that he bled at the Nose, Mouth, and Ears, as pure and florid Blood as ever was feen; and that his Shrou and Winding Sheet were all over bloody; and laftly, his Finger and Toe Nails were fallen off, and new ones grown in their room.

As they obferved from all thefe Circumftances, that he was a *Vampyre*, they according to Cuftom drove a Stake through his Heart; at which he gave a horrid Groan, and loft a great deal of Blood. Afterwards they burnt his Body to Afhes the fame day, and chrew them into his Grave.

Thefe good Men fay farther, that all fuch as have been tormented or killed by the *Vampyres*, become *Vampyres* when they are dead; and therefore they ferved feveral other dead Bodies as they had done Arnold Paul's, for tormenting the Living.

Signed,

    Barner, *Firft Lieutenant of the Regiment of* Alexander.

    Flickhenger, *Surgeon Major to the Regiment of* Furftamburch.

    —————— *three other Surgeons.*

    Gorfchiz, *Captain at* Stallath.

Upon a current Report, that in the Village of
Medreyga certain Dead Bodies (called here *Vampyres*) had killed several persons by sucking out
all their Blood, the present Enquiry was made by
the Honourable Commander in Chief; and Capt.
Gorschutz of the Company of Stallater, the *Had
nagi* Bariacrar, and the Senior Heyduke of the
Village were severely examined: Who unani-
mously declared, that about 5 years ago a certain
Heyduke named Arnold Paul was killed by the
Overturning of a Cart Load of Hay, who in his
Life-time was often heard to say, that he had
that he had been tormented near Caschaw, and upon the
Borders of Turkish Servia, by a *Vampyre,* and
that to extricate himself, he had eaten some of
the Earth of the *Vampyres* Graves, and rubbed
himself with their Blood.

That 20 or 30 Days after the Decease of the
said Arnold Paul, several persons complained
that they were tormented; and that, in short, he
had taken away the Lives of four Persons. In
order, therefore, to put a Stop to such a Calamity, the Inhabitants of the Place, after having
consulted their *Hadnagi* , caused the Body of the
said Arnold Paul to be taken up, 40 Days after
he had been dead, and found the same to be fresh
and free from all manner of Corruption; that he
bled at the Nose, Mouth and Ears, as pure and
flord Blood as ever was seen; and that his Shroud
and Winding Sheet were all over bloody; and
lastly, his Finger and Toe Nails were taken off
and new ones grown in their room.

As they observed from all these Circumstances,
that he was a *Vampyre,* they according to Custom
drove a Stake through his Heart; at which he
gave a horrid Groan, and left a great deal of
Blood. Afterwards they burnt his Body to Ashes
the same day, and threw them into his Grave.

These good Men say further, that all such as
have been tormented or killed by the *Vampyres.*
became *Vampyres* when they are dead; and there
fore they served several other dead Bodies as they
had done Arnold Paul's, for tormenting the
Living.

Signed,
Batruer, First Lieutenant of the Regiment of Alexander,
Flickhenger, Surgeon Major to the Regiment of Furstembusch
__________three other Surgeons,
 Gurschitz, Captain a Stallath.

Extract of a letter from Vienna, *London Journal,* March 11, 1732

Both the French and English versions drew from the same source, the English cutting back significantly on the details. They both represent the same story as all the German versions, which vary among themselves, and no one of them seems to be the master source of the Western European publications.

None of the English periodicals publishing the Fluckinger report in March, 1732 included comments on the text. The vampire was another foreign curiosity to be added to the roster of exotics flashing through the pages of the journals. In May, 1732 another English periodical published the same text, this time with additions.[10]

"Non missura Cutem, nisi plena Cruoris Hirudo," "The leech doesn't leave the skin until it is full of cruor." The quote at the head of this publication of the English version of the Fluckinger report is from the *Ars Poetica* of the Roman poet Horace. The leech is the frenzied poet who persistently and drainingly fastens onto anyone who will hear his recital. That is not the significance intended by the use of the quote in the English periodical; it is rather a return to the idea of the vampire as leech, now with political extensions.

The journal was *The Craftsman,* founded in December, 1726 to expose "the innumerable frauds, prostitutions and enormities" of state-craft, and especially to contrive the removal from office of Robert Walpole, Chancellor of the Exchequer, for whom the journal used the title of abuse, "Prime-Minister." In the Fluckinger report, reproduced here from the *London Journal*'s March 11 publication, the author of the piece found an opportunity to forward the journal's mission.

The author refers to himself as d'Anvers, which was the pseudonym used by any of four regular contributors to *The Craftsman*. This piece is likely to have been the work of Nicolas Amhurst, the editor and co-publisher. In the guise of d'Anvers he makes an evening call upon a friend and there finds a company of ladies and gentlemen engaged in a discussion of prodigies. He then gives a full copy of the report on the one prodigy in particular, the Arnold Paul vampirism that occupied their attention.

A doctor "endeavor'd to ridicule such romantick stories, by treating them as the common Artifices of *News-writers* to fill up their Papers at a dead Season…" A beautiful young lady contests this opinion. She admits that such things are frequently done, but still insisted on the truth of a relation attested by "unexceptionable witnesses" and transmitted to the court at Vienna. No matter if the witnesses were surgeons and officers, the doctor cannot believe that, contrary to "all the Principles of Philosophy as well as the Laws of Nature," that a dead body "whose animal Powers are totally extinguish'd," could suck the blood of the living and perform other operations.

The young lady befuddles the doctor by reminding him that he once made everyone believe an equally absurd fact. She appeals to d'Anvers for support, and after reading the report he delivers his opinion: a dead corpse cannot perform any vital functions, yet there are vampires. Inhabitants of the "Eastern Part of the World" are in the habit of writing in allegory. The oppressive rule of the Turks and Germans causes the inhabitants to "couch all their complaints in Types, Figures and Parable." The relation of the vampires contains a "secret satire upon the Administration of these Countries."

"A Leech or a Bloodsucker who preys upon human Gore and fattens Himself on the Vitals of his Country" is a common phrase for a "ravenous Minister." The "Mystery of the Vampires" unfolds itself when it is understood that a "plundering Minister carries his Oppression beyond the Grave by anticipating the publick Revenues, and entailing a perpetuity of Taxes and Gabels upon the People, which must drain the Body politick by degrees of all its Blood and Spirits." Those whom he torments become vampires by being forced to sell and mortgage their estates which then drains their "unhappy Posterity," as vampires are said to do.

This "Arnold Paul or Paul Arnold" may have been a person in office, "a Tax-layer or Tax-gatherer," that requires further inquiry. As a Heyduke he was a "person of Consequence," yet more likely to have been a "ministerial tool…under some great Blood-sucker of State" because he killed only four people rather than thousands.

The discovery of the intact body in the grave might seem to counter the allegorical interpretation by proving that the deceased was pure of spirit. Corruption, however, is a wickedness of mind, not of body. In the allegorical reading the vampire left his wickedness behind him in the world rather than carrying it into the grave, where his corpse was found without decay. The groaning of the corpse when staked was clearly a fiction, a satirical invective against "some living Oppressor," and the staking was meant as a "mark of Ignominy" to deter others from his practices for the same reason that a stake is driven into the body of a suicide.

Continuing with the allegorical interpretation: the blood said to pour from the body of the vampire when staked "nothing can be understood by it but making Him refund the *corrupt Wage,* which He had suck'd out of the Veins of his Countrymen."

Taken according to the letter this account of the vampires is ridiculous, but in the figurative sense "nothing can be more rational, obvious and intelligible." The remainder of d'Anvers speech is taken up with naming, and implying, those who have earned the title of vampires in the past and in the present. "Give me leave to observe in this Place that private persons may be *Vampyres,* in some Degree, as well as Those in publick Employments. I look upon all *Sharpers, Usurers* and *Stockjobbers* in this Light, as well as *fraudulent Guardians, unjust Stewards,* and the *dry Nurses of great Estates.*"

The names of suspected vampires in office continues. "I leave it to be consider'd whether instead of driving a Stake through the Body of a *corrupt Treasurer,* when He is dead, it would not be more adviseable to administer a *certain Parliamentary Emetick,* which will make Him disgorge all his Ill-gotten Wealth, whilst he is alive. I look upon this as the most effectual method to destroy a *great overgrown Vampyre,* and secure our Posterity from his tormenting Oppressions, when an End is put to his natural Life, and his Carcass is rotten in the Ground."

His improvised speech settles the dispute between the doctor and the lady, and d'Anvers is urged by those present to write it out for publication in *The Craftsman.*

This expansive allegory was also printed concurrently in several other English journals (*London Journal, Gentleman's Magazine)* without the preamble of the Fluckinger report under the title *Political Vampires.* It also has been anthologized in more recent times as an example of English gothic literature.

The vampire is identified with a range of corrupt officials and private cheats. Like von Wahrmund the author delves into the nomenclature of dishonest beneficiaries of public and private funds.

Every aspect of d'Anvers' vampire corresponds to an aspect of thievery he and his hearers recognize. It all turns around the fundamental representation of blood as wealth, property, and currency stored up in the individual and collective victim and ready to be forcibly possessed by the vampire. Not just an equation between the sharpers, usurers, alchemists and vampires but an entire system of transfer of vitals from the living, working body to that of the greedy absorber.

von Wahrmund's hermetic secrets are an arcane version of the parable d'Anvers says inhabitants under close rule must use to criticize the current order. Under looser rules, d'Anvers can name names while von Wahrmund writes obliquely for the comprehension of a few. von Wahrmund uses categorical names-embezzler, etc.-for the types d'Anvers can both categorize and name personally.

Political Vampires signals the beginning of a fluid imagery of the vampire as figure of economic bloodsucking long before the fictional avatars became popular. In the year following *The Craftsman* publication the Prime Minister Robert Walpole, the unnamed but obvious object of some of its references, proposed extending the excise tax on salt to tobacco and wine. The tax was intended to curtail smuggling by imposing levies in warehouses rather than in ports. The protest against the new tax included public gatherings and the publication of pamphlets. "Placards representing the excise vampire sucking the blood of the populace were widely distributed."[11] Following this is a history of the state or corporate vampire declared and depicted to be sucking the life's blood of the people through taxation or alienation of labor that extends from the early 18th century excise tax upheaval to Karl Marx and Henry George in the 19th century.[12] The first fictional vampire in English penny dreadfuls, Varney (1845-47), was drawn both as a bloodsucker and a money leech.

Beneath and supporting the preserved records of and reflections on vampire sightings/beliefs was a growing mass of ephemera that sometimes intruded upon the printed page brandishing words and pictures. Blood as the material life force circulated through the vampire metaphors carrying their power of extraction from the human body into political, scientific and literary imagery. The rapacious human pictured as a bloodsucker, whether named a vampire or not, was a vehicle for the spread of vampire ideas once the issue of vampire reality seemed to be settle

---

[1] "*...id quoque de Vampyris scriptum legimus*" *Commercium literarium,* July 11, 1732: 211.

[2] The full title of the journal was *Le Glaneur Historique, Moral, Littéraire, Galant et Calottin, The Gleaner, Historical, Moral, Literary, Gallant and Ingenious.* In a notice at the end of *Le Glaneur* 20 (March 10, 1732) de la Varenne advises those sending him sharply satirical pieces

not to waste the copy effort. *Calottin* is not the same as *satyrique*: no venom is to be spilled and no reputations are to be lacerated.

[3] Biographical and professional details on de la Varenne are from http://dictionnaire-journalistes.gazettes18e.fr/journaliste/518-jean-baptiste-le-villain-de-la-varenne

[4] Batruer, Flickhenger,Gurschitz were listed at the end of an English version of the report in the English periodical *London Journal,* March 11, 1732 and others published around the same date. Nowhere is the list of names exactly as in *Le Glaneur.* Johann Gurschitz,a Serbian officer in Austrian service in the early 18th century, appears both in the body of the report and as a signatory in some versions.

[5] The Pâristes were votaries who exhibited convulsive behavior at the grave of the revered Jansenist deacon and theologian François de Pâris (1690-1727) in the cemetery of the church of St. Medard in Paris. de la Varenne, no friend of the Jesuits, whom he accused of mutilating Pâris' remains, also registered his contempt for these displays.

[6] de la Varenne seems to be the only source for this manifestation. If the location actually was Stadt Liebau near Olmutz (Olmouc, Czech Republic, today) then the vampire may have been the one reported by de Scherz (1704).

[7] The television series *The Strain* on the American network AMC combines vampire contagion with affliction by worms that enter the body and proliferate in the brain transforming the victim into a parasitic blood-drinking worm/vampire.

[8] Ranft (1734: 263-64; 269-70)

[9] MS2801 in the Wellcome Library, London. No copy of the newspaper itself has yet been reviewed.http://vamped.org/2015/11/22/does-ms-2801-reveal-the-first-appearance-of-vampires-in-english/

[10] *The Craftsman* 307 (May 20, 1732): 120-29.

[11] Robertson (1911: 68)

[12] George (1884 (1879): 330) "The ingenuity of statesmen has been exercised in devising schemes of taxation which drain the wages of labour and the earnings of capital as the vampire bat is said to drain the lifeblood of its victim." George balked at blaming a fictional human vampire. His idea of a tax draining blood without the knowledge of the victim was the definition of a vampire tax.

20. Consolidation

The 1732-33 publications on vampires, while rejecting the actual return of the dead to take the blood of the living, took differing, sometimes vacillating positions on whether there was any absorption of life essence by the corpse. They examined the meaning of the fresh, blooded and growing state of the corpses when unearthed, which was surprising only because of the inexperience of the observers in viewing the long buried dead.

"Some superstitious people in Hungary and specifically in the towns of Kisolova and Medwedia make a great outcry about the bloodsuckers, and go on as if certain people came back from the dead and sucked the blood out of the living so that they had to die, whereupon many books were written on the vampires."[1] Martin Gruhlich, a Freyberg preacher who set down year by year annals of theology and church history, plainly positioned the cause and effects of the vampire reports amid the lives and works of theologians and church events from 1517 to the 1730's. For a 1552 entry Gruhlich remarked that people in Freyberg made an issue of the smacking of the dead in graves as they wrote of vampires in his own time. Such talk was just a periodic paroxysm of chatter about the dead.

The following year the evangelical minister Georg Wegner, writing under the pseudonym Tharsander, reserved his own opinion of the vampires for the end of the chapter on "the vampires and smacking dead" in his critical compendium of secrets and marvels.[2] The chapter was a systematic review of vampire beliefs based on Michael Ranft's writings.

He finished by saying that the misconceptions about the dead arising and sucking blood came from poor record-keeping about sudden deaths. That only encouraged speculation about supernatural causes of natural phenomena. He praised the practice of the Greek [Orthodox] Church of making a written account of each death. "This approach is the surest and best. Because when the natural sources of an event can be given, you must abide by it, and not the spirits, or mix hidden features into the game."

Neither of these statements is in the context of a book or pamphlet entirely on vampirism. They ceased to be produced for a few decades by the end of 1734. Instead vampirism in general based on citations of the Kisolova and Medveđa reports and other established instances has become one objective in a general assault on superstition, and a study of the marvels of nature denying unearthly causes.

For the Schaumburg physician Christian Philip Berger the two most important words were *gewiss*, certain and *unbegreifflich*, inconceivable or ungrounded. His 1737 book was titled after an earlier work of "researches toward the enlightening of remarkable happenings in nature," and like his predecessor he trained his keen attention on wonders, of climate and the body: the crack in a cave pit in mountain weather, a maiden who in place of her monthly "purification" produced milk from her breasts, the cold in the heights, a pregnancy in a spleen, and "the so-called vampires or Hungarian bloodsuckers."[3]

After an initial section of thoughts on histories filled with ungrounded contents, Berger quotes in full from Ranft's copy the Provisor's report on Peter Plogojovitz and Kisolova. He focuses on this single instance. It is certain, he concludes, that the Provisor was inexperienced in physical things, and allowed himself to be so dazzled by appearances that he took for growing beard, hair and skin something that wasn't any of them. Saltpeter, which can look like anything, infiltrated the grave. The mineral caused the blood to recover its redness and flow loosely.

It is evident how easily something can be recounted through false perceptions, so the lesson can be taken from this that in truth there are such ungrounded tales to doubt, as they contribute to the buildup of uncertain opinions.

Berger took the Provisor to task for being deceived by what he found when the corpse was exposed. Departing from other writers, including Ranft himself, he did not take the Provisor's report at face value, and faulted him not only for unfamiliarity with postmortem decay but for ignorance of the material world. His contemporaries embraced this analysis, that there was nothing in the description of the vampire that could not be put down to natural causes, though not everyone accepted the finality of saltpeter.

All of the 1732-33 publications on vampires were based on the Arnold Paul case in Medveđa with few mentions of Peter Plogojovitz in Kisolova and Valvasor's Jure Grando. They were impelled by the newness of the phenomenon and the word used to name it. By late 1732 publication on the subject had petered out; even the *Commercium literarium* contained few articles on vampires. The books by Harenberg in 1733 and Ranft's final volume on the subject in 1734 had an air of closure. The remarks by Gruhlich, Wegner and Berger looked backward and then forward.

The October, 1736 edition of the *Mercure historique et politique* brought to notice a new vampire manifestation from Kisolova

MERCURE
HISTORIQUE
ET
POLITIQUE,

*Contenant l'Etat préſent de l'Europe,
ce qui ſe paſſe dans toutes les Cours,
les Intérêts des Princes, & ce
qu'il y a de plus curieux pour le*

Mois d'Octobre 1736.

Le tout accompagné de Réfléxions
Politiques ſur chaque Etat.

Par Mr. ROUSSET, *Membre de la
Société Royale des Sciences de Berlin.*

A LA HAYE,
Chez HENRI SCHEURLEER,
M. DCC. XXXVI.
Avec Privilege.

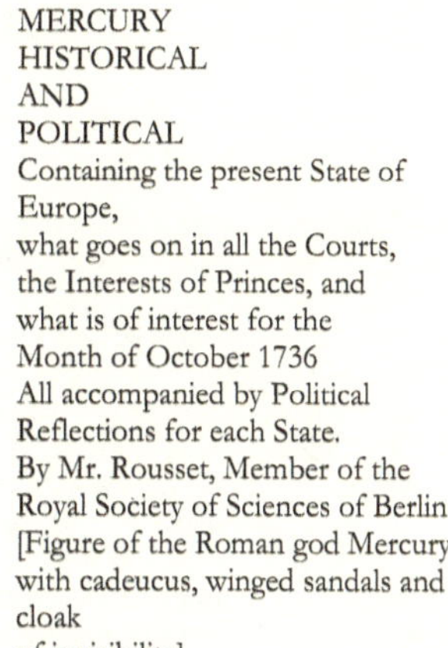

MERCURY
HISTORICAL
AND
POLITICAL
Containing the present State of
Europe,
what goes on in all the Courts,
the Interests of Princes, and
what is of interest for the
Month of October 1736
All accompanied by Political
Reflections for each State.
By Mr. Rousset, Member of the
Royal Society of Sciences of Berlin
[Figure of the Roman god Mercury
with cadeucus, winged sandals and
cloak
of invisibility]

At The Hague,
By Henri Scheurleer,
1736
By Privilege

Jean Rousset de Missy (1686-1762), the proprietor of the journal since 1724, was a French Protestant who had moved to the Netherlands, been a soldier in the army of the States-General, been baptized a Walloon, and become a naturalized citizen. He was an indefatigable researcher and writer who composed historical works on Russian royalty, and was a member of the Royal Society of Berlin and an associate of the St. Petersburg Academy. Under his editorship the *Mercure* assumed a distinct bias against the French government.

Rousset also wrote for *Le Glaneur*, and claimed to have provided the version of the Arnold Paul Medveđa vampirism appearing in that journal in 1732. He made that claim and repeated the 1732 report in the October, 1736 edition of the *Mercure*, which under the news from Hungary was headed by a "new scene of vampirism attested by two officers of the Tribunal of Belgrade, who descended on the location, and an officer of the Imperial troops at Gradisch, who was an eye-witness to the proceedings." The text is in quotes, but no other details of the source are given.[4]

At the beginning of September an aged man, 62 years old, died in the village of Kisolova, three leagues from Gradisch. Three days after having been interred he appeared at night to his son and asked him for something to eat. The son served him, he ate and disappeared. The next day the son told his neighbors what happened. That night the father did not appear but the following 1732 night he made himself visible and asked to eat. It's not known whether or not the son gave him anything, but the next morning he was found dead in his bed. The same day five or six persons suddenly fell ill in this village, and died one after the other in a few days. The officer, informed of what had happened, sent an account to the Tribunal of Belgrade, which sent to this village two of its officers with a hangman to examine this matter. The officer, from whom the present account comes, went there from Gradisch, to be witness to an event of which he had so often heard spoken. All the graves of those who had died within the last 6 weeks were opened: when they came to the one that contained the old man they found him with open eyes, skin vermillion in color, having a natural respiration though dead and immobile, from with it was concluded he was the reported vampire. The hangman drove a stake through his heart, a burning post was set up and the corpse was reduced to ashes. No mark of vampirism was found, neither in the corpse of the son nor in any of the others.

Rousset makes no reference to the 1725 vampirism in Kisolova. "Thanks to Heaven," he continues, "we are nothing less than credulous." All the illumination of physick brought to bear on the case did not reveal the causes, and fortunately the circumstances were attested judicially by people of probity. Furthermore, it is not unique: this is where he introduces the Arnold Paul report he had provided to *Le Glaneur* in 1732, signed by Battuer, Flickstenger, three surgeons and Guoschitz. After that nothing more on the subject in this or any other issue of the *Mercure historique et politique* until 1755.

This new Kisolova case resembles the other vampire cases in describing night visits of the buried dead and the death of the one visited, only here there is no rumor of plague and no claim of bloodsucking, the essential feature of vampire tales. An empirical procedure determines which of the recently buried corpses is the vampire, and most strikingly there is no mention of blood flow from the corpse only the deep red coloring, no hair of skin growth, nor is there a cry when the stake is driven into the heart. This is the only case in which the corpse is found breathing naturally. None of the other corpses unearthed shows signs of vampirism.

This open-eyed corpse has more the character of a premature burial than the previous vampire corpses. It was selected from among a group unearthed at the same time and was not identified with the man who was said to have visited his son demanding food. Rousset's explanation leaves that possibility open. All he does is return to the more "traditional" vampire type by repeating the Arnold Paul report he previously entered.

The gap in commentary was closed by the Jewish traveler Aaron Monseca, in a letter to his correspondent Isaac Onis in their home city of Constantinople. They were voices of the self-exiled French aristocrat Jean-Baptiste de Boyer, Marquis d'Argens (1704-1771) writing the 125th of his *Lettres juives*[5] in Amsterdam. The Isaac Onis Oriental persona begins his letter with a complete copy of the two reports from the *Mercure historique et politique* published the previous year. This marvel seems to push to the extreme all philosophical speculations and human reasonings, he notes by way of preface.

Monseca/d'Argens does not retain Rousset's marveling credulity in default of a physical explanation. There are two ways to destroy the belief in these pretended revenants and show the impossibility of the effects that can be made to appear in a corpse entirely without sentiment. One is to explain the vampire illusion in terms of physical causes, and the other, the wisest approach, is to deny the veracity of the report itself. "But since there are persons for whom a certificate given by the people of the place appears to be a demonstration of the reality of the most absurd tale. Rather than demonstrating how little one can rely on the forms of justice in matters uniquely the concern of philosophy, I will suppose for a time that several persons died of an illness called vampirism."

Corpses interred after several days can emit blood, and people in a violent fit of imagining vampires can believe that their blood has been sucked out and die of fear. d'Argens thus from the beginning espoused both of the main theories of the physical origins of the epidemic fanaticism that was vampirism: genuine but largely unknown postmortem events underlying a stricken imagination (*imagination frappée*). A young girl whose cries and the resulting companions would have driven away any vampire bent on sucking her blood dies just the same from the turmoil, the sadness and the languor that mark how much her imagination has been stricken.

Anyone who has been present in a village receiving plague rumors knows how quickly any affliction turns into a belief that the plague has struck. The fatal conviction is spread from person to person. In the Kisolova vampire story the son's death after the vampire father's visits is the starkest example of this. One shock of vampirism to the imagination makes the recipient fatally susceptible to further ones.

Authors are prone to exaggerate the physical effects of decay, but most of those observed in the corpses are explicable by physical causes. Terrains preserve bodies well, and the distribution of humidity in the corpse can make it swell in the parts where the vital spirits aren't needed. For the blood flow after death d'Argens evokes a chemical principle. Nitrous and sulphurous components of the soil enter the body and with heat there is fermentation. An experimental heating of one part of milk or chyle with two parts of tartar yields a type of blood, thin and very red, from the tartar dissolving and rarifying the fat. The same process might go on in the corpse where the fats mimic ample blood flow.

To be accommodating, d'Argens' surrogate Isaac goes on, one does not want to give the lie to the certification of vampires by officials. Either the vampires leave their tombs at night to suck blood or they don't. No vampires are found when someone cries out that they are attacking, so the vampires do not leave their tombs. Perhaps the soul then can gather the subtle liquid like blood in a container and carry it into the body. "It's a pleasant enough commission for the soul."

In truth it would be shameful to go on like this in an attempt to prove the truth of vampirism. Like St. Augustine, he would blush from expositing the error he is obliged to refute, and from the misfortune of those obliged to hear it.[6] He concludes with a warning about giving credit to testimony that only serves to render them more believable.

In the letter of d'Argens' enlightened and tolerant Jewish observer comes the first clear formulation of the dilemma of anyone who tries to clarify the errors of vampire beliefs from the reports of official observers who brought vampires to general attention. He doesn't attend to the discrepancies between the 1736 Kisolova report first published by Rousset and the 1732 Medveđa/Arnold Paul report joined to it. More attuned than other writers to the fear in villages where vampire beliefs and the attendant deaths are recorded, and spread like a contagion of the imagination, d'Argens balks at making it seem true by denying it.

He denies that anything seen in the vampire corpse was due to other than natural causes. As with Berger's saltpeter investiture of the corpse, d'Argens turns to a chemical principle, not for all aspects of its appearance, but only for the fluidity and mass of the blood.

He describes a formula that will yield a blood-like fluid from fats present in the corpse. This was based on an experiment in the Preface to the 1735 English translation of Pierre Pomet's history of drugs: "For example, if we boil in a Matrass one Part of Chyle or Milk, with two Parts of Oil of Tartar, *per Deliquium,* the white Liquor will become red, because the Salt of Tartar being rarified, dissolves and exalts the unctuous Part of the Milk, and reduces it to a kind of Blood."[7] This formula was not in the original French edition of Pomet; d'Argens must have read it in the English translation. It also was a technique for producing stage blood.

The Marquis' (surrogate's) view of vampires was quite influential through the publication of the *Lettres juives* in an English translation, which became the source of information for vampire instances and their meaning for the rest of the century. Even more influential, or more indicative, were d'Argens' thoughts on how the mere presentation of vampire beliefs promoted them even as they were refuted. The ease with which any expression of the vampires fleshly foundations could be taken for truth while remaining fiction was the rising subject.

Approaching truth from the side of fancy, song could suggest the fictional reality of vampires.

One of the last songs of the Dutch poet Jan van Elsland (1671-1736) was printed with musical notation in the newspaper *Historiale Courant* on the 16, 18 and 20 of October, 1736, and in the last edition of his *Gezangen, of het vrolyk Gedeschap, Songs, or the Cheerful Companionship,* two years later.[8] The *Courant,* or Stoori Crant, was published in Delft, hence the mention of that city. The song was a balladeer's delivery of a "wondrous new" happening. The following translation does not preserve the rhyme scheme of the Dutch original.

1

How new and how rare in our Stoori Crant,
A wonder upon wonder for to understand,
How a peasant, dead in the Serbian district,
From his son the next night has asked:
Because his stomach
Was just so.
Indeed was a glutton for four and sixty years,
Who after his death

(Darnn,
that's strange and rare!)
Through his coffin
 (such a ferment.)
Even the blood out of the man,
Sucked in his dead poker,
From his lust and desire.
'Twas a bloodsucking beast-corpse,
Long passed;
Because in the grave
Drew he plague
Flesh and blood,
From the earth out of many people
To an awl,
Or a flame,
Him in his bark
Was suited,
And so touched them with worm
Of here
All bound
The whole side.

2

There is an officer of the Empire (perhaps
Writes that he this miracle has seen,
in the town of Kisolova, not three miles from the city
District Gradisco that contains it well,
And decisively
Very well understood)
Yes this officer drove forward on horseback
So soon he heard
That he continues
The hangman readies himself
For this prize
For a peasant
(That one, bleeding with blood,
Now fresh and quite sound,
His breath gasping found,)
Was gleefully sawing away
Of that villain,
With his mouth
In his pit
To prevent this mope or that ninny;

Because he got,
In the dough,
An iron pin,
That stuck him.
So that he never in his box, sucked more
Or didn't gulp,
Any more drink.

3

Now brings this Fabulous and madman's story,
Here to learned Moffs often, (kind of
Power of substance, in order to show that one more of that
Of bloodsucking has heard)
Because this is
Now clear surely
Yes now the Universities in Germany,
And in Acadia--
Seek more,
With their highwise mind
More than ever,
--(Or never)
Have gathered therein,
Because these lettered men,
Hung their seal hereon,
In High German and Latin,
Like a pig,
And in French,
Like a goose
Writing each for a price and a rose garland,
--This a sight
Of this corpse
At his bloody
Firm breast,
Yes the Delft Courant,
Appears here
Hey in that
Contains so what.

4

Hear here how that this Delftian now reasons,
In this case justice then falls again;
One would do foolishly, if one this whole story

Smoothly wanted to deny entirely
But why?
It is therefore
Here so much now by a witness, all the noise
Of good decency
Breaks forth,
Here by faithfully lazy;
It sounds so forth
Thus it belongs
This case, thus spread,
Believes each (as one said)
Yes without hate or envy
But a little to there
It will set
And sure,
(All wrong).
That this bloodsucking all imagination is;
But the evil
That the act
Causes, affirms
And trusts
It's an essential case.
(That's contact)
But justice
Is now very successful.

The song is composed in the usual style of straightforward statements followed by brisk almost cryptic allusions to the subject at hand and jocular asides. The word "vampire" is not used at all, but an article in the newspaper of original publication contained a Dutch translation of a German text with basic information on the subject.[9]

The song's references are clearly to d'Argens' 125th *Lettre juive* reproducing the report of the 1736 Kisolova vampirism, but that report has no reference to bloodsucking while the song does. The man who returns from the grave to ask his son for food and then apparently causes his death was only present in that report. d'Argens' unwillingness to consign the bloodsucking entirely to the imagination because it was attested by reliable witnesses also puts in an appearance.

van Elsland set the flippancy his genre allows against the vein of seriousness in his source. The spread of vampirism through water by the fish who eat the ashes, or the worm inside the vampire of d'Argens' fancy are included in the *Historiale Courant* article but only contributed to the antic spirit of van Elsland's song.

Not as serious as the pompous German doctors sounding like pigs or the goose-squabbling French writers, van Elsland has created and in a few strokes populated a land of bloodsuckers where the meal-seeking old man is a glutton whose aperture is his penis. This song is the predecessor of all the comic vampire romps that set bumbling humanity against the undead. The still-breathing vampire corpse, another unique feature of Rousset's 1736 Kisolova story, seems to be snoring here. There is more blood than usually found in vampire comedies.

The heading of the song notes that it was set to the Harderwijk Student's March, which resembles the March of the King of Prussia, later composed by King Frederick the Great of Prussia. By 1738 the various strains and names of the bloodsucker were consolidating into a pan-European imagery not accepted as representing a reality but available for reflective metaphor and the entertainment of the literate. Including their laughter at those gullible enough to believe in it. The latest vampire news could be set to the tune of a spirited student march celebrating camaraderie and youthful rejoicing about to be co-opted by a monarch (assuming the throne in 1740) who soon was making his military moves toward political and cultural consolidation.

The 1736 Kisolova vampire story, despite its notable differences from the other vampire stories, including the 1732 Kisolova/Peter Plogojovitz story, was absorbed into the bloody mass. The two were sometimes mistaken for other stories and the names of the vampires, or at least their identities were shifted and combined in the making of a generic bloodsucker. The July, 1738 issue of a news pamphlet published in French in Amsterdam conveyed the current international state of the vampire in a few choice words.[10]

The Letters of Temeswar renew the ridiculous fable of the vampires which made so much noise four or five years ago. It's in several divisions of Hungary, situated along the Teisse and the Save, that this superstition reigns. They quite firmly believe that the dead leave their tombs during the night: that they introduce themselves into houses in a supernatural way; that they there suck the blood of sleeping persons. After which it is concluded, by a natural suite of events, that the persons sucked become in their turn vampires; so that the only remedy for this evil is to thrust a stake into the heart of the vampire and cut off his head.

The new Kisolova story, unidentified except by the administrative unit and river localities where it took place, is assimilated as is the song into the past accounts of a ridiculous superstition with a set collection of features, several of which were not part of the 1736 Kisolova story: bloodsucking, decapitation. The vampire story was becoming consolidated and standardized as the "noise of four or five years ago" receded.

One further component of the developing bloodsucker/vampire imagination was a voyage by outsiders to the areas where the attacks and discoveries took place, the beginnings of vampire tourism. "Three English gentlemen" on a grand tour of Germany from Venice to Hamburg in 1734 put up in the inn the Black Horse in Laubach (Ljubljana, Slovenia), the chief city of Carniola. This travelogue remained in manuscript form until it was published as part of the Harleian Miscellany in 1810.

The unnamed gentleman who set down their travelogue was a member of the University of Oxford and of the Royal Society, intended to provide a supplement to the published travels of other ingenious visitors to Germany which had entertained the public.

After a quantity of details about local history and custom gleaned in Laubach, the writer added, "We must not omit observing here, that our landlord seemed to pay some regard to what Baron Valvasor related of the Vampyres, said to infest some parts of this country. These Vampyres are supposed to be the bodies of deceased persons, animated by evil spirits, who come out of the graves, in the night time, suck the blood of many of the living, and thereby destroy them."[11]

The author then comments that this notion would be looked upon as "exploded and fabulous" by many people in England, but it is "countenanced" not only by Valvasor but "by many Carniolese noblemen, gentlemen, &c, as we were informed, but actually likewise embraced by some writers of good authority." A long quote translated into English from the 1733 Latin dissertation of the Essen gymnasium director Johann Friedrich Zopf then follows. It elaborates the basic definition of vampires in the section's introductory sentences.

The gentleman traveler adopts approximately the mode of discourse that Valvasor himself did in *Die Ehre* when relating the Giure Grando night visits, which he heard from local residents but did not witness himself. The traveler's own compatriots would scorn this story, but many Carniolan elite (German-speaking Slovenes) countenance it, which is not the same as accepting or believing it. The erudite Zopfius also exposits it as a belief of others, which may intersect with the explanation that the devil sometimes takes possession of a sinner's corpse to wreak havoc and encourage disbelief.

"These spectres are reported to have infested several districts of Servia, and the banat of Temewar, in the 1725." And the author continues to list those in Medvadia (Medveđa) and Cassovia (Kosovo) in 1732, Temeswar again in 1738, and those in Russia, Poland and Lithuania affirmed by Rzacynski in his 1721 natural history, and in 1693 newspaper accounts all of them agreeing with Zopf's descriptions. He groups them all together under the same set of features, with differing names, under the rubric "dead bodies, activated by spirits." The Ancient Greeks seem to have been "firmly persuaded" of the truth of this assertion.

"However it may be ridiculed," the author concludes, setting up a criterion other than observational verification, this opinion is "not altogether without foundation." Scripture is evidence that the Supreme Being has used wicked spirits as his instruments of punishment as he has plagues, wars, famines, and so on. Acceptance of the possibility of vampires under this condition is implicitly incumbent upon believing Christians. Only as an act of God are vampires possible as described in the reports.

The visit of the three gentlemen to Laubach resembles a fictional scenario of later years. The initially skeptical visitors arrive as night is falling, hear the loquacious landlord tell his tale and learn that the locals of the propertied class share this belief simply stated. The dead rise from graves and take the blood of the living leading to death. The skepticism is overcome in the fiction by an experience of witnessing or being attacked by a vampire. Lacking this, the gentleman narrator substitutes reported instances grouped under the same pattern, and a faith-based sense of its plausibility.

Others writers drew a wider arc to include a greater range of instances consolidated into the same vampire pattern. A wavering division appeared between considering them curious lore and evidence of divine displeasure, which was tentatively resolved by political mandate and fiction. Parallel with, and being joined with the Protestant vampire complex was a Roman Catholic stream that brought with it a set of beliefs indigenous to Poland.

---

[1] Gruhlich (1734: 979)

[2] Wegner (1735: 492)

[3] Berger (1737: 121-46)

[4] Rousset de Missy (1736: 405-11)

[5] d'Argens (1737: 33-40)

[6] d'Argens quotes in a footnote a passage from St. Augustine's 56th letter in which he makes this statement. The author returned to this same passage in a later philosophical work (1755: 123), and adds that philosophers sometimes make "the monstrous errors" they write about too subtle, and become the dupes of their own heated imagination.

[7] Pomet (1748: viii). The English translation of the 1695 second edition had previously appeared in 1712 and 1735, with the Preface to these included in the 1748 fourth English edition.

[8] van Elsland (1738: 263-67)

[9] Penning (1932: 3861). This author, a physician in Harderwijk, cited Ranft for further vampire information.

[10] Mois de Juillet, 1738, *Mémoires historiques pour le siècle courant.* Amsterdam: Etienne Ledet et Compagie. 1738: 65.

[11] *The Harleian Miscellany, or, a selection of scarce, curious and entertaining pamphlets and tracts, as well as in manuscript and in print found in the late Earl of Oxford's library*, vol. XI: 231. London: Robert Dutton, 1810.

21. The Roman Catholic version

The Greek layman Leo Allatios, who served as the Vatican librarian in the mid-17th century, was the first of a several natives of eastern European cultures to expound on ecclesiastical traditions and popular beliefs of their homeland. Allatios' purpose was to provide a basis for reconciliation between Eastern and Western Christianity, for healing of the Great Schism between the two branches of the religion. A few of the writers of the 1732-33 treatises on the Serbian vampires, W.S.G.E. for instance (see Chapter 15), included Allatios' *tympanus/tympaniaios* and *burcolacca/vrykolakas* among the figures comparable to the vampire.

Allatios gives several alternate spellings for the name of the revenant-*Burculaccam, Bulcolaccam, Buthrolaccam*-corresponding to a common origin and a variety of local traditions. The word is a compound of two Greek words: *burka*, fetid slime formed in putrefying water and *lakkos*, a pit.[1] This is the corpse of an excommunicated person that doesn't decay but becomes distended in all of its parts, the skin stretched tightly like a drum (*tympaniaios)* that emits a sound when beaten. The acoustic and olfactory components suggested by the meaning of the name feed the imagination.

Into a body so deformed enters a demon and brings misfortune to poor mortals. Often under the guise of this corpse having left the sepulcher, going about a city or other inhabited place, especially at night, where it takes the freedom of a temple, makes itself known and by ringing at the door addresses someone of the temple assistants in a sonorous voice. If he responds, this is what happens: the next day he meets death. If he does not respond, he is saved. Thus in that island, all citizens, if addressed by someone at night, never respond the first time, for if addressed a second time, the one who asks is not a burcolacca but someone else.

Allatios then denies, at the beginning of the next section, that anyone can actually become a *burcolacca,* but affirms that God can punish wrongdoers by leaving their corpses uncorrupted and exhibiting the signs of a *tympaniaios.* The curious lore of the potentially lethal night visitant, a death knell known in the lore of the world, and the associated customary caution answering strangers at night, is mingled with the sight of the corpse of the miscreant transformed through divine displeasure into a booming skin drum. Allatios integrates folk superstition with ecclesiastical protocols. He quotes authorities in the original Greek and provides Latin translation.

The *burcolacca* of Allatios' works is attached to vampires without the sanguineous corpse/bloodsucking component. The 1736 Kisolova food-demanding father is a sanguineous corpse called a vampire and he is not a bloodsucker, though he does draw the life force from his son. For Allatios the ambulatory return of the dead and the associated death knell, its possible spread to others as a plague, is not credible, but the demon truly may enter into the body with God's leave. That rumor of the return of the dead lingers in the vicinity of the intact, visibly transformed corpse and is rejected except as a work of God perhaps allowing demons control. As the English gentleman traveling in Slovenia will do almost a hundred years later, Allatios adjusts the bar of credibility to allow for God's will.

On the verge of the eruption of eastern European beliefs about the predatory dead into Latin and vernacular language discourse came a note, or rather a letter from Poland. In May-June,

1693 the same letter from Poland was printed in two French-language journals, *Mercure galant*, dedicated to the Dauphin and published in Paris, and the pre-Rousset *Mercure historique et politique*, published by Protestant émigrés in The Hague.[2]

You perhaps have heard spoken of a quite extraordinary thing found in Poland, and chiefly in Russia. These are dead bodies called in Latin *Striges* and in the language of the country *Upierz*, and have a certain humor that the common people and several learned assure is of blood. It is said that the Demon draws this blood from the body of a living person, or from some animals, and carries it to a dead body, because it is believed that the Demon leaves this corpse at a certain time, from noon up until midnight after which he returns and places there the blood he has gathered. With time there is such a great abundance of blood that it leaves by the mouth, by the nose, and above all by the ears of the dead person, so that the corpse swims in its grave. There is more. This corpse feels a hunger that makes it eat the linens in which it is wrapped and in effect they are found in its mouth. The Demon that leaves the corpse goes at night to trouble those who were most familiar with the person during his life, and cause them much pain in the time they sleep. He strokes them, caresses them, while representing the form of a relative or of a friend, and enfeebles them so in sucking their blood to bring it to the corpse, that on waking they do not know what they feel, and call for help. They become thin and wasted, and the Demon does not quit them at all until all those of the family die one after the other. There are two types of these spirits or demons. One goes to humans, and the other to animals that they make die in the same way by sucking blood. The ravages would be great without the remedy that is brought to it. It consists of bread made, kneaded and baked with the blood found in these sorts of corpses. They are found in their graves, soft, pliant, swollen, and ruddy, not dry and barren, sometime having gone by since they were placed in the ground. When they are found in this state, having the shape of those who appeared in the dream, the head is cut off, the heart is cut open, and a quantity of blood emerges. It is gathered and mixed with flour to be kneaded and made into this bread which is a sure remedy to protect oneself against a so terrible a vexation. After the head has been cut those whom the Spirit tormented at night are no longer troubled and go on well afterward. A short time ago a young girl made a proof of this. The pain she felt while sleeping caused her to wake up calling for help. She said that she saw the shape of her mother who had died already a long time ago. This girl declined each day becoming thin and without energy. Her mother's body was disinterred and found to be soft, pliant and ruddy. The head was cut off and the heart opened from which emerged a great abundance of blood, after which the languor she felt ceased and she recovered entirely from her sickness. Priests worthy of trust who have seen these sort of executions done, affirm the truth of everything I tell you, and that is usual in the province of Russia.

This relationship between the living victim and the corpse calls for the mediacy of a demon independent of either party, in its demonic way ferrying the blood of the living into the body of the dead. Blood is a humor connoting a hot, passionate temperament. The letter writer is not clear why the demon does this, or why this corpse is selected as the repository of the blood of a relative. The relative becomes aware of the destination of the blood because the demon takes the blood "while representing the shape to him/her" (*en lui representant la figure)* of the relative or friend. The victim feels almost a tender interruption of sleep before the sucking begins, followed by a wasting away over a period of time.

A possible remedy is made plain to the victim by the vision of the relative in the grave who is the destination of the lost blood. This link is confirmed when the grave is opened and the sanguineous corpse is exposed. In addition the grave linens are chewed and drawn up into the mouth. Decapitation and staking of the corpse halts the depredations. The staking is not to pin the corpse itself into the grave in this case, but to release the blood already seen copiously flowing from body apertures. This blood is mixed with flour to make bread which presumably safeguards from further attacks when eaten.

By making blood the currency between the living and the dead this story, this prodigy, settles the question of the *vrykolakas* and *tympaniaios*. The corpse is a *tympaniaios* inflated to overflowing drum tightness with the blood stored there. It does not leave the grave, but is serviced by a demon that helpfully identifies the destination corpse to the victim, permitting discovery and remedies. God's leave to demons to enter the bodies of the dead allows the superstition of the *vrykolakas* to be denied while retaining the corpse's draw upon a living relative and the appearance of a visit. The shape represented by the demon is all that remains of the *vrykolakas*. Trustworthy priests, Russian Orthodox or Roman Catholic, oversee the veracity of the tale.

This French letter is the first time the word *upierz* "in the language of the country" (Polish or Russian), appears in a Western European language text. Its earliest appearance in written form is in the margin of a partially Glagolitic text of the *Book of Prophets (Kniga prorokov)* dated to 1047. The form it takes in that inscription is *[o]upir*, known to be the East Slavic variant of South Slavic *vampir*.

Bruce McClelland's discussion of the 1047 inscription breaks down the word into its components: *va(m)=u*, toward+ *pir*, a feast, with the aggregate meaning "someone engaged in *pirsestvo*," a customary pagan feast with drinking and libations, often mixed with blood.[3] McClelland cautions against reading supernatural associations into the phrase inscribed in the *Book of Prophets, pop' oupir likhiy*, which seems to be a penitential note by a priest (*pop'*) castigating himself for taking part in a pagan feast.

In the 1693 *Mercure historique* letter from Poland the invasive *upir* has gone to the blood feast, drunk freely and spilled the libation at the body he inhabits. The corpse itself tries to eat its own funeral cloths. Bread is made from the corpse's blood to forestall the *upir*.

All of the local vampire stories gaining currency through publication have a feasting valence, from Giure Grando "eating up" the Krinck villagers to Arnold Paul consuming the earth of a vampire's grave in his bid to stave off attacks and the collocution of "vampire" with "bloodsucker" in many volumes of commentary with no scenes of actual bloodsucking.

The 1693 letter from Poland tells of a *timpaniaios* as a sanguineous corpse supplied by a blood feasting *upir*. The blood-feaster/deliverer and blood receiver are linked bringing together the Greek and Slavic versions in the same word. Grando, Plogojovitz and Paul were all sanguineous corpses without taking any blood. The 1736 Kisolova vampire is a father demanding food, not specifically blood, from his son, who dies as a result. In 1845-47 the penny dreadfuls that comprised the saga of *Varney, the Vampire* were subtitled, *The Banquet of Blood*. The *upir* was soon joined by the vampire at the feast.

The Jesuit Gabriel Rzaczyński, after the tractatus on monster vegetables in his Latin natural history of Poland, arrives at the instances of life and death together in the same bodily precinct.

This is the tractatus on the incorruptibility, flexibility and motion of corpses, and following that, on cruentation.[4]

Rzaczyński rehearses the arguments concerning the spontaneous bleeding of the corpse in the presence of the murderer: as the result of a spirit that does not leave the body with the departure of the soul; because a demon has entered the body; because God has willed the upwelling of sanguis; or because physical forces are at work. The heat generated by breathing in an enclosed room stimulates the sanguis to move.

After the separation of the soul from the body, all power of the daimon does not immediately cease in bodies. In the meantime a malign spirit can enter the corpses of the dead, to appear in them, wondrous to behold, persevere daily until decay, and so to seem, as if endowed with a soul. It happens in Poland, Russia, Lithuania, as numerous examples testify, and I, says Gengell, S.J. in *Eversione Atheismi*, from numerous eyewitnesses, faithfully from trustworthy witnesses, that a human corpse was found, after not so long a time incorruptible, flexible in its limbs, and moreover sometimes moving head, bones, tongue, eyes, swallowing the linens in which it was wrapped, indeed even swallowing parts of its own body. At times it was noted that a corpse of this type surged out of the burial, prowling crossroads and houses, present itself looking around at these and those, and even attacks some and tries to suffocate them. If the corpse is a man it is called *Upier*, and if a woman, *Upierzyca*, as you would say, plumed, that is, the plume- or feather-endowed corpse is light, agile and in motion.

This *upier* is a corpse reanimated by a demon after the soul has left. It is enlivened not only with the usual incorruptibility and flexibility, and chewing of linens, but moving in all its parts to the extent of leaping from the grave and openly gazing and launching the suffocating attacks for which its kind is known in some places. This is unlike the Serbian vampires previously reported or about to be reported by the Austrian officials. And so far it is completely unlike the passive, recipient corpse of the 1693 letter from Poland.

The author of the travels of the three English gentlemen thought that the name "seems to be deduced from the surprising lightness and activity of these incarnate demons."[5] Rzaczyński derived the name *upier* from the Polish word *pióro*, feather, from an association with night birds, thought to be spirits of the dead that troubled people after dark. The Polish word for "feast" that incorporates the *pir* element, *birbantka*, did not suggest itself to Rzaczyński, because the similarity of words was not great and the feather-night bird analogy was too strong. It also was supported by other tales of night birds drinking human blood (*Nacht-fresser*).

As with the *upierz* of the 1693 letter the corpse is inhabited by a demon. In the letter the corpse itself does not move; it just grows bloated with the blood brought to it by the demon who does move back and forth between victim and corpse. Though the Polish Jesuit considers the *upier* to be a form of cruentation, sanguis is not mentioned beyond imparting a ruddy glow to the active corpse. Sanguis does not enter into the description until he establishes how the evil of the demon's presence is resolved.

And the agility and motion in a corpse, it is not possible to assign another sufficient cause than that the daimon inhabits that corpse for evil ends, from an antecedent pact entered upon with an evil entity, God willing, for long-term injury by the daimon, until that evil is resolved. It is considered resolved in truth ordinarily in our Kingdom by the cutting off of that corpse's head. Whether such conduct is lawful some defend, others deny.

The demon's habitation of the corpse for evil ends is an Aristotelian sufficient cause for its spontaneous movement. He then gives one of his few examples, of a woman who died followed by two others in the village of Clepardia near Cracow, Poland in 1624. At first plague was suspected, but the *upier*-like appearance of the woman's corpse, ruddy and with chewed linens, caused the authorities to decapitate it, which released great quantities of blood. There was no evidence in this case or in any of the others Rzaczyński more vaguely alludes to, of a corpse actually emerging from the grave, seen walking about or imposing itself upon random victims. He has defaulted to cruentation in a discussion of what actually could be observed when a corpse is unearthed.

It is not impossible, he concedes, for the body to drip blood due to humidity, dry heat, the age of the person at death, or the violence of the wound, but it is very rare. He cites Horst's 1604 case of the young noblemen who hemorrhaged for days after his death, stopped and then started again days later. Then come other examples of copious cruentation with no further mention of *upier*. In the end he hedges in favor of natural causes. "In sum I offer, corpses in the cheeks, more fleshly places, are seen to redden, from serous sanguis putrescent and leaking, from moving the corpse, turning it, and so on, without any wrongdoing." The corpse bleeds simply from putrescence and handling, without a suggestion that a murderer or demon is present.

"Sometimes breads are seen to drop a juice the color of sanguis." A number of instances were recorded when this happened, the bread taken from the oven dripping in red, diners spitting out the bites they took when they saw the red in the piece remaining. The grain in the fields might also have the look of an infection with sanguis.

"Breads full of red juice, in the common opinion are bleeding (because they can't arrive at a more suitable conclusion) similar to the cruentation of corpses which are seen to appear with deaths accumulated in the cruelty of famine." (*Panes ſucco rubeo pleni, opinione vulgi cruenti (quia commodiorem locum obtinere non poterant) adjunĉti ſunt cruentationi cadaverum, quæ praelusisse videntur funeribus inclementiâ famis accumulatis.*)

In his choice of words alone the Jesuit writer has not even considered that the so-called "bleeding breads" were anything other than the result of natural forces at work. The peasants, however, equate the breads with the bleeding corpses most visible when accumulated in times of famine. He has brought together the components of the *upier* of the 1693 letter, abundant blood in the corpse and blood bread, without linking them in the same way.

Rzaczyński's introduction of the *upier* under the heading of cruentation did allow him to associate copious bleeding with an otherwise bloodless if very active creature. The absence of eyewitness evidence for the existence of the *upier* was compensated by the recounted spectacle of cruentation, and by the link common opinion made between "bleeding" bread and cruentation.

The corpse entered by the demon and become bloated and fresh was associated with the corpse bleeding in the presence of the murderer, or as the result of natural forces, and with the bleeding bread. The direct link between the demon, the victim and the swollen corpse no longer is present for the Jesuit author, and cruentation is brought in to make up for the vague memory of what the *upier* originally was.

There are no more expositions that project that original folk meaning. The following year a review of Rzaczyński's natural history contained only the two Polish words *upier/upierzyca* to represent the entire complex section on cruentation.[6] Several of the "vampire or so-called bloodsucker" publications 1728-36 made the two words part of their lists of words equated with "vampire" and other words, but no more than that.[7]

The belief that a demon might inhabit a dead body and move it out of the grave to do mischief replaced the doctrinally intolerable return of the soul of the dead person, or of a personal spirit separate from the soul. Rzaczyński's resort to cruentation allowed him to marshal more evidence than existed for belief in the *upier*, and to keep the sanguineous corpse and the *timpaniaios* in the picture.

The German writers who reacted to the "Hungarian" vampires with a categorizing disdain tried to absorb all these revenants into the same circle and lay out regional variations. The Roman Catholic writers, often clerics, like the Protestants decisively rejected that anyone but God might return a soul to the body. They were less decisive about the possibility of reanimation, and the role of any accompanying blood.

A grand synthesis of beliefs and reports of apparitions and the returned dead was essayed by the Benedictine abbot and exegete of scripture Antoine Augustin Calmet (1672-1757). Already renowned for his multi-volume "literal commentary" on the Old and New Testament, and for a Bible dictionary, Calmet turned his interpretive skills to the study of seemingly supernatural manifestations beginning with visions and appearances of the divine and the claims of sorcerers. His stated aim was to reveal false beliefs and give instruction on true beliefs.[8]

Whatever you may think of it, I will take the opportunity to propound a question, which seemed to me important for the Religion: because if the Return of Vampires is real, it matters to defend it and prove it; and if it is illusory, it is of consequence for the interests of the Religion to undeceive those who think it true, and to destroy an error which can have very destructive outcomes.

As he approached the subject of the return of the dead he stated the grounding principle of his examination: "the resurrection of the dead is the work of God alone." Lazarus was revived after he had begun to decay; other asserted resurrections were not of people who clearly were dead. The only way to separate truth from error and deception was to look at the evidence case by case, "the revenants in the body, the excommunicated, the *oupires* or vampires, the *brucolaques* and so on."

The systematic survey does cover all these categories, some of them critically, others just in passing for the sake of the story. The title marks a presence of absence: it is the only place that *oupires* appears in the entire book and another spelling, *upier*, is only in the section summarizing the 1693 *Mercure historique* article. Rzaczyński and his natural history are nowhere to be seen. *Brucolaques*, a Gallicized version of *vrykolakas* (he also uses *vroucolakas*), receive more attention because Calmet considers them a unique projection of Greek religious genius. Allatios supplies the basic description; Calmet also references de Tournefort's travel episode of the disinterring of a *brucolaque*.

Peter Plogojovitz and Arnold Paul are both in evidence (Flückinger having now mutated to Clickstenger as signatory of the report), but Valvasor and Giure Grando are not present. A paragraph mentions the "large enough volumes" published in 1732 by German physicians on this subject, and the retention of Arnold Paul and a few others by the universities long afterward. Ranft and Harenberg are called to witness. Calmet brings up cases of revenants that were unknown to Ranft and his colleagues.

The 1746 *Dissertation* is the first time anyone concerned with the returned dead presented the 1706 work of a German Catholic advocate, Karl Ferdinand von Scherz, *Magia Posthuma*, with the story of a singularly active corpse not named a vampire. Calmet added to this several instances communicated to him by personal information or letters which he quotes or epitomizes in the text.

The Austrian regimental officer, the Count of Cabreras, in 1730 told someone who spoke to Calmet that a soldier was present when the dead father of an inn host came to the table one evening, after which the host died. Commissioned to investigate, the count unearthed the corpse of the father, found it as if newly dead and decapitated it. The count told of other revenants who sucked the blood of family members at mealtimes and left them dead. Their undecayed and full blooded corpses were destroyed.

While he was the commandant of a troop stationed in Hungary (distant, exotic Hungary is a preferred venue), a relative wrote Calmet in a letter, he learned of a wasting malady that ended in death. After two soldiers of his troop died a corporal undertook a remedy practiced in that country. He mounted a youth "who had not known the work of the body, that is, a virgin" on a black horse and had him ride through the cemetery. The grave that the horse would not pass with any amount of coaxing was uncovered and the fresh corpse found within bled copiously on being cut at the neck. The grave was covered again and the afflicted soldiers returned to health. The commander refrained from beating the corporal though took the cemetery horse ride without asking the commander or another officer.

Calmet does not comment on these and other accounts of fresh sanguineous corpses at the root of local illness and death. Immediately before reproducing the 1693 *Mercure galant* letter he considers natural explanations such as fermentation for blood flow in corpses. Generally he relates the incident whether in antiquity, or a dated or vaguely situated recent time, then in another chapter offers explanations for such events that exclude supernatural causes. This way he does not directly challenge an author but does not let outlandish claims pass without question. Only apparitions and returns from the dead reported in scripture are acceptable.

There is ample evidence of people who seemed to be dead but were not, who rose from the tomb themselves or were revived after seeming to have fallen or drowned. The implications of this knowledge of entirely natural returns of the dead stirs him to indignation.[9]

All that is known, and can serve to explain how it is possible to pull out of the grave some Vampires who have spoken, cried, wailed, thrown out blood; all that because they are not yet dead. They have been made to die by decapitating them, piercing the heart, burning them, and that has been very wrong, because the pretext made of their pretended return, to disturb the living, make them die, mistreat them, it is what has never been, or proven, or stated in a manner that can authorize anyone to use such inhumanity, nor to dishonor, nor to make die ignominiously because of vague, frivolous, unproven accusations, persons innocent of the thing they are charged with. Because nothing is more poorly founded than what one says of apparitions, vexations and troubles caused by the pretended Vampires and by the Broucolaques.

This casts a different light on the many stories of graveyard discovery of the cause of illness and disturbances in the village in a corpse with an undecayed appearance. Calmet wrote that the ambiguities and confusions surrounding vampires caused him to put down his pen.[10]

But looking upon the matter under another aspect, I took up the pen, resolved to undeceive the public, if I found that what was said about it was absolutely false, making it seen that everything that is set out on this subject is uncertain, and that it is necessary to be very reserved in pronouncing on these vampires who made such a noise in the world a certain amount of time ago and who divide spirits today even in the countries that make theatre out of their pretended return and apparitions: or to show that what is said and written on this subject is not destitute of probability and is worthy of the attention of the curious and the learned, and merits being studied seriously and that the deeds that are reported are examined and that the causes, circumstances and means are sought.

This paragraph first appeared in the Preface to the 1746 edition of Calmet's *Dissertations* and was repeated in each subsequent edition up to the 1759 posthumous edition of the *Traité* reflecting continued and increased determination to take a case by case approach and not reach a global conclusion about vampires, neither succumbing to their theatre nor relegating them to complete improbability. The world would have to continue what Calmet couldn't.

Calmet's opposition to disinterment and "execution" of suspected vampires did not mean that he rejected the possibility entirely, which would mean rejecting the possibility of a divine act of resurrection that had occurred in the past. It did add drive to his examination of cases to sift out the false ones the better not to repeat the same errors.

The collection of apparitions and revenants that formed Calmet's books displeased his contemporaries. From the first page of the Prelude to his *Reflections* on Calmet's work, a brother Benedictine, Idelfonse Cathelinot, expresses his dismay that such a learned and august man would take up the question of apparitions.[11] Voltaire, sometimes a guest of Calmet at his abbey, exclaimed at the very thought of vampires under the reign of enlightened thinkers.[12] "Calmet finally became their historiographer, and treated the vampires as he treated the Old and New Testament, faithfully reporting all that had been said before him."

Voltaire remarked that for a time the vampires were like the ancient martyrs, the more of them burned, the more were found. For a period between 1730 and 1735 they were found in Wallachia and Moldavia, and even in Poland, though it is of the Roman rite. The *philosophe*, like the Benedictine historian of vampires, located them in Eastern European regions where Greek Orthodoxy was the dominant religion, areas with populations subject to contagious disease and contagious delusions, though Voltaire, at the end of the vampire article, compares the vampire resurgence with other passing frenzies, convulsions, possessions, resuscitations, and the Jesuits, who are no more. Vampires may have been a regional phenomenon, but other regions have had theirs.

In unearthing a number of vampire incidents and testing their veracity Calmet singled out the characteristics that entered the vampires into the annals of revenants, as family members returning home for a meal which may have been a ritual meal to commemorate the dead and may have included quantities of blood. Calmet himself limited the blood portion of the meal. The bloodiest of the early evidences, the 1693 letter on *upiers*, was preceded by a chapter on the natural causes of postmortem bleeding. Calmet's biographer Augustin Fangé used a word that Calmet himself never used to define the vampire, *sangsue*, blood-sucker or leech.[13]

This was also what the word vampire meant in Slavic according to the Archbishop of Trani, Giuseppe Davanzati (1665-1755).[14] That prelate's *Dissertazione soppra i Vampiri* circulated in manuscript form from the year of its composition, 1739, until 1774, when his nephew published it together with other writings. It was a response to the vampire reports, by a devout Roman Catholic churchman versed in science and mathematics.

The *Dissertazione* was inspired by Davanzati's conversation some years earlier in Rome with the Bishop of Olmutz, Cardinal Schrattembach. Members of the cardinal's Consistory came to him alarmed by the widening plague of vampires in the province of Moravia. Davanzati did not know what these vampires are.

…the said Cardinal, upset, sad and scared, told me, that they are certain people dead for a few days, already buried and interred, appear anew in the same form and in the same clothing, and deportment as when they were alive, and showed themselves to their relatives and friends by day, and by night openly entering their houses, conversing, speaking, and eating with them there, and at the time they put themselves to bed, they likewise invited them to rest with them.

These vampires, the Cardinal continued, did not appear only once, but came many times in sequence, sucking the blood of "the poor peasants" until they were wretched and emaciated. Without a remedy the victims died and themselves became vampires. The only recourse was a judicial procedure before a secular tribunal which on presentation of a charge against a particular person would deliberate and issue a decree permitting the unearthing, decapitation and removal of the heart of the proven vampire, then closing the grave again. That one ceased to return.

Without the passage of judgment and subsequent execution the vampires kept coming. The adjudged corpses were a marvel to behold, ruddy, with open eyes, letting out a terrifying cry when the chest was pierced and flooding the surrounding ground with blood.

The Cardinal asked Davanzati to assist him with all due haste in preparing the presentation he must make on this frightening matter before the Cardinals of the Holy Office and the Pope. The Archbishop agreed to prepare with deliberation a report that would avoid appearing too credulous and insufficiently reflective.

Because, I told him, many times it can happen, that such things that at first appear amazing, and almost miraculous and diabolical, well then maturely considered, resolve themselves into nothing, and at most into mere illusions and timorous panics, in keeping with which I could quickly adduce for him an infinity of examples well proven, and overwhelmed by the clamor of his people of Moravia, coldly replied to me that I should not put forward new sentiments that were more appropriate to philosophy and smacked of skepticism concerning things that seemed to depart from the natural order.

The cardinal was not deceiving himself when he said that Davanzati under the name of skepticism did not believe in such apparitions of dead people as he described.

Two years after that conversation Davanzati noticed in the Viennese newspapers a story that also named vampires, and gave details of an inquiry ordered by the imperial authorities. The happenings in Olmutz that occasioned the cardinal's mission to Rome must have been before 1730 and continued thereafter.

Davanzati in the following years became aware of other reports of the returned dead. The 1736 *Mercure historique* letter on the man who returned to demand food from his son was printed in an Italian edition of the periodical published in Venice. He became conversant with the Kisilova/Peter Plogojovitz and Medveđa/Arnold Paul vampires.

So many reports in newspapers and journals by learned authors convinced him that the returned dead could not be derisively dismissed. Known as vampires only in the German and Hungarian lands, they were recognized under many different names in different countries and continents from classical antiquity to the present. He saw the word vampire labeling the notion of others that they exist. He reviews ancient and modern (mid-18th century) philosophies that the dead return, eat and commune with the living and "sleep the dead with the living." And can be put to rest only with a bloody execution in the tomb. Here he left out the bloodsucking and plague-like spread of the affliction.

There must be an explanation for this worldwide and timeless belief. Davanzati does not acknowledge that vampires are genuine but only that some people witness them or accept that others have. He does not follow Calmet's path of reviewing numerous accounts from published texts and personal statements and evaluating them for veracity and compatibility with accepted doctrine. He sets up a model of the vampire based on what Cardinal Schrattembach related to him (without the bloodsucking, however) and tries to explain it through a range of philosophies.

The Pyrrhonist philosopher and the skeptic, who doubt all appearances, can well condemn the visions and lies related to the vampires without rejecting the testimony of so many ancient and modern authors. It is odious to call into question so much worthy of faith without a penetrating shaft of the light of reason. Davanzati did not witness the vampire attacks or the subsequent uncovering and execution of the corpses. Given his unwillingness to reject all accounts as untrue, he considers general explanations for the vampire type.

They cannot be vampires because they are a work of God, Who does not cause such disturbances in His creation. For the same reason they cannot be a work of demons because demons could bring back the dead only with the leave of God. The actual state of the corpse after death allows for some of the vampire's appearances, but they are true of all corpses and there are only a few vampires who spread like plague, which also is not sufficient to initiate the effects recounted.

"…the true and unique cause of Vampires is our corrupt and depraved fantasy."[15] They come into existence as a collective illusion spawned by fear and ignorance in the face of genuine want and conflict. There are sufficient material effects to encourage this fantasy, which grows and spreads taking the same form in many times and places. "…fantasy…can at night while we are asleep represent itself as living demons, ghosts, fantasms and people already dead as alive, making themselves converse, speak, eat, drink and in the end sleep, and disport, and make it seem as in life…" All the acts of vampires Davanzati first heard from the cardinal were the workings of fantasy.

This attribution to fantasy without a concession to other causes, drastic compared to Calmet's more concessive approach, required that he make allowance for the miracles, the apparitions of Jesus, the Virgin Mary, angels and saints, and the divine dispensations central to

Catholic belief. These could not be accomplished by mere human fantasy, Davanzati responded, but only by the work of God.

Furthermore, why does the activity of spectres, demons and witches occasion prayers, conjurations and exorcisms from the church if they are fantasy? The operations said to be instigated by demons and witches are lies, or plain natural occurrences corrupted by them.

Davanzati concluded with a defense of church dogma in face of the vampires. They "made no sense theologically" and therefore did not exist.[16] Calmet and Davanzati were not aware of each other's researches and conclusions. They both independently skirted direct confrontation with doctrine that would have allowed the existence of such creatures, in a way that suggests the uniform role of religion in their thinking. Davanzati's feint in this direction is probably what kept his dissertation in manuscript form while he was alive. They both had a hierarchy to serve.

The closest either came to encountering someone that might fit the description of a vampire, or even to anyone who claimed to have had that encounter, was personal communications through letters or conversations. They set aside the ontological question in favor of the existential one: were vampires possible, or, to put it in terms of doctrine, were they allowable? A "science of vampires" would require observation of vampires, would forever yearn for that homecoming.

---

[1] Allatios (1645: 142)

[2] *Mercure galant*, May, 1693: 62-69; *Mercure historique et politique,* June, 1693: 670-71.

[3] McClelland (2006: 187-91)

[4] Rzaczyński (1721: 364-68)

[5] *Harleian Miscellany* (1810: IX, 233)

[6] *Nova acta eruditorum, Anno 1722* 17:10-18.

[7] Ranft (1728: 15); W.S.G.E. (1732: 34); Wegner (1736: 486)

[8] Calmet (1746: vi; 253-54); Calmet (1751: 2, x)

[9] Calmet (1746: 461-62)

[10] Calmet (1759: vii-viii)

[11] Cathelinot (2008: 82)

[12] Voltaire (1836: 282-83)

[13] Fangé (1762: 382)

[14] Davanzati (1774: 2n1)

[15] Davanzati (1774: 180)

[16] da Ceglia (2011: 510)

22. Revival and suppression

Tharsander (Georg Wilhelm Wegner, 1692-1765) didn't reach the subject of "vampires and the smacking dead" until the 28th sheet in the 8th part of his monthly omnibus of "secret meanings and tales" that fall under the heading of natural magic.[1] It was preceded by sheets on astrology, portends of thunder and rain, ghosts and followed by sheets on exorcism, buried treasure and ginseng.

Natural magic was "the manipulation of nature by the application of art,"[2] as opposed to the manipulation of spirits through ritual or ceremonial magic. Though there were spirits in his natural magic, as an evangelical Protestant minister Wegner cast the actions attributed to them in terms of natural forces. He sought to draw the interest in magic and the supernatural toward explanations that excluded occult forces.

On vampires and the smacking dead he declared he need do no more than repeat everything that had already been written in the shortest form possible. That he does, ranging through the apparitions that occupied Ranft and the other discussants of the previous years. From the women's corpses who are the most boisterous smackers by the Devil's attempts to dishonor them, to Saxo Grammaticus' tale of the entombed combatants, Kisolova and Medveđa, Valvasor's strigons, the Greek Burcalaccas and the Polish Upierz, Wegner inventoried the names of the active dead. He added a few new names to the repertory: the Bohemian Stephanus Hübner who was unearthed and decapitated in 1567 for no good reason.

He also refuted old vampire fantasies by citing the qualities of materials. Blood is too thick to travel from a living person to a corpse; it must be a spirit fluid that makes the transit.

Wegner concluded that vampirism had its origins in an infectious disease that spreads among the people and brings sudden death. At the same time a fantasy spreads, or an incubus establishes itself, that leads the people to imagine they are being pressed and their blood is being drunk by the dead. They look to the teaching of the Greek Orthodox Church that all incidents of death are due to certain corpses. If natural origins instead can be given for the deaths, and held firmly, then spirits and other hidden features are taken out of play.

As the vampire name had become a category label for similar beliefs, the label itself became part of a long list of erroneous notions dispelled by natural explanations. Rather than dismissing the belief entirely Wegner provided a way to see how it appeared that way to those who did not have a non-spirit-ridden recourse. His *Schau-platz, Showcase* was an early encyclopedia of magic losing its unobservable threading. It also provided a guide to handling future outbreaks of the vampire contagion, at least the fantasy component.

Vampires for the time being were no longer the subject of their own monographs, but were one more phenomenon under the enduring heading of natural magic. They had gone from wonder to marvelous norm. Vampires and their books also became a component of chronology, as in this slightly bemused entry for 1725 in annals of the Reformation from 1517 to 1733.[3]

Some superstitious people in Hungary and namely in the towns of Kisolova and Medwedia made a great noise about the bloodsuckers, and gave out that when certain dead people come back after death and suck the blood out of the living, they must die, whereupon many books were written on vampires.

Where "superstitious" (*aberglaubisch)* is used at all in this chronology it is in reference to "Papist superstition." Here, Hungary is enough. The other entries are devoted to Protestant, Catholic and Jewish activities, especially the movements and writings of prominent figures. The inclusion of this event is a measure of the impact the vampire commotion had upon Protestant consciousness of developing history since no other events of this sort were included.

The chronology entry suggests that the vampires were a passing excitement, but then a few years later that excitement once again rose to the attention of the newspapers, as reflected in a July, 1738 news compilation published in French in Amsterdam, again the work of émigré Protestants with connections to their German coreligionists.[4]

The Letters of Temeswar renew the ridiculous fable of the Vampires, which made so much noise four or five years ago. This superstition reigns in some divisions of Hungary situated along the Teisse and the Sava. It is firmly believed that the dead leave their tombs during the night: that they supernaturally introduce themselves into houses; that they suck the blood of sleeping people, and that they then return to their tombs. After which it is concluded, as by a natural succession, that the persons who have their blood sucked become Vampires in their turn; so that the unique remedy is to drive a stake into the heart of the Vampire, and cut off the head.

The Tisza (Teisse, Theiss) River flows roughly north to south through Hungary into the Danube, and the Sava from east to west through Croatia, also a tributary of the Danube further along its course. The two rivers subtend an arc that includes Hungarian, Croatian and German populations, and which does not include the Serbian-Rumanian town of Kisolova (further down the Danube) or the Serbian town of Medveđa (to the south). The entire area was part of the Austrian Empire under the regional label of Hungary. The Banat of Temeswar was to the east of this region, with its main city Temeswar (Timişoara, Rumania today) was absorbed into the Habsburg Kingdom of Hungary later in the century. This was the imaginary geography of vampires.

It also was the real geography of warfare. The Treaty of Belgrade, which ended the 1735-39 Austro-Russo-Turkish War, ceded back to the Ottoman Empire the Kingdom of Serbia, the southern part of the Banat of Temeswar and Bosnia. The towns of Medveđa and Kisolova, which had been the site of a 1736 vampire report, returned to Turkish rule. The Sava River and the

Danube River became the northern border of Turkish lands. This was the traumatic context of the 1738 vampire report, which was printed in a journal containing news of the war.

The language of this piece, based on reportage or at least rumors in German language newsletters, resembles both the entry in Bruhlichen's chronology above and others recorded later. "Superstition" and "making a noise" are associated with the disturbances caused by the belief in vampires which to the readers of this sophisticated Western European journal is never anything other than "ridiculous". This is a recurrent outbreak in "Hungary," where history is at a standstill, at least in the villages.

The editor of an English literary journal extended the notion, concurring with a French journalist: "…vampyred Corps probably would become common, should the Prejudices, and the simple Notions of the Heydukes and the Sclavonians spread about the world."[5]

The pattern of nocturnal visits by the dead is firmly established as central to the belief. The element of feasting has been reduced to blood-taking, and there is no stated family relationship between vampires and vampirized. The plague-like succession of vampirism has been preserved. The sanguineous corpse is not mentioned, and the staking-decapitation remedy is clearly the end of the matter.

Davanzati's manuscript of the *Dissertazione* was completed and first began to circulate in 1739. His recollection of his conversation with Cardinal Schrattembach years before, the 1725 notice in the Viennese newspaper, and the 1736 Italian translation of the *Mercure historique* article on the latest Kisolova manifestation were in the background, but the continuing events in 1738 must have given him a final nudge. Calmet's most recent date for a vampire/apparition story advances from 1732 with his successive editions. For both, the vampires were a work of the imagination in "Hungary" always going on, and in danger of inducing epidemics of corpse mutilation.

Prior to becoming Pope Benedict XIV (1740), Prospero Lorenzo Lambertini (1675-1758) composed a multi-volume treatise on the beatification of saints. After his election to the Papacy Benedict prepared a new edition of the treatise (1741) that included new chapters on miracles, true and false. Judging the authenticity of miracles was crucial to assessing the sanctity of a candidate for sainthood. The ejection of demons from bodies, the incorruption of corpses, and the flow of blood from the dead entered into eligibility for sainthood.

The new edition also included a section on vampires in the chapter "on the calling back of the dead to life, or resuscitation."[6] Benedict begins that section by reviewing three episodes reported in the 1732 edition of the *Commercium literarium*, and lists the marvels: the intact corpses, the flow of blood, the growth of nails, the staking, burning, spreading the ashes in water all of them dependent upon the testimony of a few. "…the power remains in the resurrection of the dead, and their acts, which here certainly are not proven, but rather are held by men 'of a wiped nose,' they are as it were inventions of deceptive fantasy."

Benedict is always reasoning in terms of the whether the testimony of witnesses to an apparent miracle can be trusted. The *Commercium literarium* vampire corpses are a resurrection of the dead, reported "*a viris emunctae naris*", "by men who have wiped their noses" and therefore smell keenly and are clearheaded. This erudite Pope recalls the Fourth Satire of the Roman poet Horace, who was writing of another poet too occupied with what was before his wiped nose. The officials do not detect the vampire deception. He then quotes another writer in the journal at length, ends with the conclusion they all reach that the resurrection of the vampires is "mere impiety driven by imaginations, fear and terror."

The Pope joins the other writers in excluding false resurrections which would throw into doubt the exclusivity of the resurrection of Christ and the ultimate resurrection of the dead at the center of Christian doctrine. He does not linger in attributing the appearance of the corpse to natural causes; it was not a genuine miracle, that is all. He was a correspondent of Calmet, whom he mentions several times in the volumes of the treatise, though not concerning vampires, which work was not yet published. A collection of extracts from Benedict's treatise on beatification published in Venice in 1752 separated the chapters of the original books into Dissertations and labeled some sections thematically. The section on vampires in Dissertation 5 was inscribed *de vanitate vampyrorum*, on the vanity of vampires,[7] which does not connote that the undead are all wrapped up in self-regard but rather that any belief in them is a vanity, futile and sinfully vain.

All the vampire reports consisted of testimony that did not meet the standard of credibility for miraculous events. If the appearance of the corpse in the grave was not as the reports said (how could it be?) then the accounts of nocturnal visits by dead family members and the subsequent vampiric cause of plague-like deaths were equally questionable. The deaths may actually have taken place in rapid sequence from plague or stress, and contributed to the atmosphere of fear that galvanized contagious imaginings.

The corpse unearthings, stakings, decapitations and burnings certainly did take place and were the reason the reports became so widely promulgated in the first place. They both revealed and induced the sanguineous corpse that became a primary confirmation of the validity of the feature. As a pattern both of impiety and civic disorder they invited a collaboration of church and civic authorities. The officials who witnessed the earlier events went along with the mutilation, leading to its reputation as a tempering measure. By the middle of the 18th century a coalition was forming at least among Roman Catholics to take a more coercive approach.

The wars of mid-century had left most of Silesia, formerly an Austrian possession, under the rule of Prussia and its monarch Frederick II ("the Great"). The Habsburg Empire, under Maria Theresa, whose succession to the throne had precipitated the international war which included the loss of Silesia, retained that part of the coal and mineral-rich province that included Troppau and the surrounding area. In the third week of April, 1755, the newspaper *Auszug der neuesten Welt-Geschichte und schönen Wissenschaften, Abstract of the newest World Relations and fine Intelligences*, contained the following lead article under the heading *Vermischte Nachrichten, Mixed Reports.*[8]

The renowned Bloodsucker, or so-called Vampire, hasn't been heard of for a long while. Nevertheless now the following substantive report from this area can be related. Two and a half years ago there died in Hermsdorf, Troppau region, a woman who in her life was known as the Tirol Doctoress. This woman practiced cures in the land around, and could call upon all sorts of secret magic arts. It is said she asked her husband to cut off her head after her death, and not to let her be buried in the Catholic cemetery. Soon after her death it was let out that it was generally believed she was a Vampire. So then by and by many people died. It was believed that they were drained to death by the Bloodsucker. As this was going on and more people died, and therefore it was concluded that Vampires caused their death, and hence it was ordered on high that a judicial inquiry take place, which turned out to be that those suspected of being Bloodsuckers by the highest government order were disinterred in the number of forty, twenty of whom were found to be innocent and were reburied and nineteen adults including one child were found with blood, even though the corpses had lain in the earth one year, some of them two years or more. These were first decapitated, then pierced through the heart and finally burned to ashes. This execution was carried out four weeks ago by Imperial Order in the town of Hermsdorf where butchers and executioners were gathered from Troppau, Jägerndorf, Teschen and the surrounding places.

The article echoes the "vampire or so-called bloodsucker" verbiage of 23 years earlier. There were several towns named Hermsdorf in Silesia, located by reference to a larger town in the vicinity. The name changes that came with the end of the Austrian Empire in 1919 and the creation of Czechoslovakia made Troppau into Opava, but it is not clear which small town in the immediate area was known as Hermsdorf.

The circumstances at first seem unusual for a vampire story since the "wise woman" tried to forestall her own vampirization by commanding her husband to decapitate her. Refusing burial in the consecrated ground of the Catholic cemetery suggests that her exercise of the secret arts even for the sake of healing made her a pariah. She had originally come to Upper Silesia from the Tirol region to the southwest, bordering Switzerland, and thus was already a foreigner. Despite her efforts to avoid the designation, she was named a vampire.[9]

A vampire plague then followed, followed by the mass unearthing of those buried since the time the Tirolian woman died over two years earlier. Blood persisting in the veins was the determining factor. Those found "guilty" in an officially sanctioned trial were then decapitated, heart-pierced and incinerated by a gathering of executioners (*Kuechte,* cooks and *Scharfrichter,* sharp-judges) from neighboring Silesian towns. Regional cooperation was secured to forestall the spread of plague. The case of the doctoress helped gain the approval of the authorities for invasive procedures that in the minds of the people were preventive.

The author of the article and proprietor of the newspaper in which it was published was Johann Gottfried Gross (1703-68). He had begun publication of the weekly journal of politics and "miscellaneous reports" in 1741 and sustained it through the turmoil of the times. The issue for the week of March 2, 1755, for instance, was devoted to the extraordinary cold of that season. His oblique criticism of Frederick II's conduct of the First Silesian War (1740-42) won him the approving attention of Maria Theresia (1717-80), the Habsburg Empress, who granted him the title of *Hofrat* and gave him the unique role of publicist-political agent.

The diplomatic immunity bestowed with his title proved useful when he so antagonized the city authorities of Nuremberg with less than oblique criticisms that they petitioned the court in Vienna to revoke the immunity and allow his arrest. By the time the petition was granted, in 1754, Gross had moved back to Erlangen. The April account of the Hermsdorf events the previous month was Gross' response to the imperial court's rescinding of his privileged status.

He set out to embarrass the imperial authorities by stating that officials of "the highest authority" condoned a vampire hunt, provided a judicial structure for the villagers' determination who was a vampire, and allowed the unearthing and destruction of corpses. It reflected poorly on the authorities that these anti-Christian beliefs had reemerged and were being encouraged. Even the corpse of an infant was desecrated.

This much is clear from an article that appeared in the third week of May issue of the *Auszug,*

"More correct report on the Silesian vampires."[10] Gross communicated the story of the vampires "with a heavy heart." He admits "the mistake" that the execution of the vampire corpses was done under orders from the highest authorities.

…now we are convinced otherwise of the purest intentions of the highest court which has made us rather to believe, as it often happens with courts, that things were either not reported at all or not correctly. And so we now rejoice to find the circumstances entirely different. As stated below, the enlightened empress, rather than reinforce such goings-on, disapproved the same to the highest degree, punished and tried to pity.
Vienna on 23 April. After the call was spread through the report put out from Upper Silesia, so then it was made known that in the country at Hermsdorf were some so-called vampires or bloodsuckers, therefore the actual unearthing and burning of some of the bodies that had fallen under suspicion of the inhabitants there was undertaken. So her Imperial Majesty ordered for investigation of the matters a separate commission of men experienced and trained for the work, by which, after the latest investigation of all circumstances it was found that this fraud for many years here rooted communal prejudices and a rigid superstition stemmed from the corrupt imagination of these peasants. Consequently everything provided thereon was basically false and this gruesome execution distinctly and alone was carried out from the impetus of the inhabitants without foreknowledge of the proper authorities. For which infuriating initiatives Her Imperial Majesty not only sharply punished those who took part but by the means of a Circular Rescript to all local representatives, to all, whether spiritual or worldly occupations, to instruct most graciously that they refrain from such rigid and barbaric errors also cease the harshest punishment conducted in such an infuriating and superstitious manner.

Gross gives his retraction the form of a smirking panegyric to imperial justice. The original report, which attributed the executions to official command was all wrong, because "in the way of courts" the report was incomplete or erroneous. The superstitious peasants were solely to blame, and their impulsiveness was addressed by punishment and by an order to all in a position of responsibility to deter the villagers from their vampire attacks.

This cagey sycophancy seems to have been a component in restoring Gross to the good graces of Maria Theresia, since he continued in the laudatory vein. But he also moved to hedge his bets, and initiated cautious praise of Frederick II of Prussia for his skill in military strategy. At least a détente with Frederick and his interests was signaled by the appearance of the April vampire story text in the May 2, 1755 issue of the *Berlinische Privilegirte Wochentliche Relation der Merwerdigsten Sachen…, Berlin Authorized Weekly Relation of Most Noteworthy Items…*, published since 1751 by Christian Friedrich Voss.[11]

This arrival of the article, at the same time Gross published his retraction in the *Auszug*, was in a newspaper authorized and censored by Frederick the Great's Prussian government. The Hermsdorf vampire trial and executions seemed to take place under the aegis of the Austrian government, which controlled the Troppau region, that is, until the paper printed a curtailed version of Gross' retraction in the May 9, 1755 edition of the paper under Vienna news.[12]

The Berlin version of the article was followed by a page of text describing the natural history of vampires drawn from a book by the philosopher Johann Friedrich Weitenkampf. This contemporary and rival of Kant outlines the bloodsucker gothic legendry of the vampires, including the vampire's delivery of blood to the *bucolaccas,* the buried corpse, a belief the Greek Orthodox priests cultivate among the peasants to their own profit. Weitenkampf attributes the delirium-causing plague attributed to night-time bloodsuckers to a poison like that of the tarantula, which induces a madness in the victim.

The Weitenkampf addendum reinforced the article's implicit indictment of the authorities who legitimized interference with burials. News of Maria Theresia's investigation and punishment of the vampire hunters in the Berlin journal a week later did not entirely overcome this indictment. The same article also occupied space in another Berlin newspaper on the same date[13], and, in a French translation, the April issue of the *Mercure historique et politique.*[14] In the first sentence the French recension of the article drops in the phrase *"folie superstitieuse"* (superstitious madness) that is not in the German original, but was a common French wording for the belief in vampires. Another French word for the phenomenon was *"fanatisme"* (fanaticism).[15]

Gerard van Swieten (1700-72) was the *Archiatros* or chief physician to the Empress at the time of the Hermsdorf vampire inquest. He was a student of Herman Boerhaave, who promoted clinical instruction and medical botany, and throughout his life authored commentaries on the work and writings of that master physician. van Swieten was the architect of Austrian imperial health policy in both the building of institutions such as a medical botanical garden and a research laboratory.

In response to the Hermsdorf crisis he composed a paper in French, *Remarques sur le vampyrisme de Silesie en l'an 1755.*[16] According to a note in the preface to the German translation of the *Remarques,* when the newspaper reports of the vampire corpse burnings in Silesia reached Vienna on January 30, 1755 and then the Empress' ears "her mild temper was so perturbed" that she dispatched an Army doctor, Christian Vabst, and an anatomy professor, Johannes Gosser, to make an inquiry. Their "investigation and sharp inquiry"showed that the whole tumult was nothing other than a "vain fear, a superstitious frivolity, a dark and confused fantasy, simplicity and ignorance by some folk."

The sequence of events was clarified a century later by the publication of the internal Austrian government documents in a systematic collection of communications and official papers on public health.[17] In response to the news of the vampire corpse burnings Maria Theresia wrote to First Chancellor Count von Haugvitz on February 8, 1755: "It should be inquired into by van Swieten and a surgeon. If he can convince these superstitious (people) of the truth he will have performed a great service. Give him (the surgeon) service pay." The government physician who edited the document did not set down in the published version the word the Empress actually used for the "people" even after 100 years had elapsed.

The following day the Empress wrote to the Bohemian-Silesian representatives and chamber in the capital. Using the phraseology long associated with these beliefs she assured them that she was apprised of the latest incident of "vampires or so-called bloodsuckers" at Hermsdorf and had dispatched Vabst and Gosser to complete a *Visum et repertum* and give the world to know their true assessment. At least the verbiage of previous vampire excitements was repeating itself.

The question they would ask was spelled out at length: "When, and in what way and manner, since when and to what time, as well as how often these so-called vampires or bloodsuckers and by other names disturb, and in what form allow themselves to be seen, furthermore how and why do they seem believable as such to the people plagued by them as well as to other people in the place?"

A *Protocollum* issued by the Empress on March 17, 1755 begins with the results of the vote by the court investigation commission. The "ghastly process" reported by the investigators is judged "on the part of spiritual and worldly law…a corrupt imagining and criminal bias, a combination of abominable superstitions and irresponsible illegalities." The language used here leans toward a Gallicized German, *Superstitionen* (rather than *Aberglauben)*, and *Illegalitaten*, which reflect the influence of van Swieten's French language *Remarques.*

The later German translation of van Swieten's piece was affixed to the text of the *Protocollum* in the 1852 publication. Within the *Protocollum* itself Maria Theresia refers to it by another French word imported into German, as van Swieten's *Deduction.*

The primary finding that led to the court commission's condemnation is that the "unsouled" corpses were, through a quasi-legal process, held by spiritual judgment unworthy of their rest in consecrated ground and by worldly judgment to be damned to the fire. The deep-seated delusional frame of mind eliminated both sound reason and the foundations of religion.

van Swieten's deduction draws upon and confirms the field findings of Vabst and Gasser, which were not presented in a separate report. He notes that corpses in general show varying rates of decay dependent upon temperature and the illness that caused death. Of 19 corpses in Hermsdorf only a few were perceived to have undecayed and flexible parts, yet with so little basis they were judged according to the criteria of vampirism and were burned, while others were reburied.

The two Commissioners unearthed some of the buried corpses and found that parts were undecayed and had a little blood in their veins. The physical state of the corpses varied according to conditions, and the authorities burning them were not even consistent applying their own criteria. Yet the condition of the corpses was the source of tales that further instilled anxiety and consequent illness in the people.

The *indicium der Magiae Posthumae,* the index of posthumous magic (mixing German and Latin) 18 weeks earlier was used to determine that the buried corpse of a woman, Maria Saligerin, or the Richter Wenzlin, both titles indicating her role as a healer and a German Czech familial position as a judge, was the source of much grief and not worthy of burial in consecrated ground. This principle condemned many corpses, both adults and children, to removal from the church through a hole in the wall, decapitation and burning.

van Swieten in his Deduction (*Remarques)* "rightly" called these procedures sacrilegious. The Empress proposes an effort to educate the people in their error of their ways. In the final lines of the *Protocollum* she decreed that van Swieten's paper be translated into Latin, German and the "Latin languages" (Italian, Spanish) and published.

Van Swieten was a devout Roman Catholic who wanted to minimize the interference of Rome and the teachings of the Jesuits in the Habsburg domains and he cannot have favored Maria Theresia's suggestion that the Jesuit college in Troppau be at the forefront of the education effort. He also reacted against inhumane beliefs of other religions. In his *Remarques* he refuted the physical evidence for vampirism and decried it as a superstitious notion that had made its way to villages under Greek Orthodox influence. The priests profited from holding hostage allegedly excommunicated corpses showing vampire signs until a ritual cleansing was paid for and performed.

van Swieten's reference to the 1755 occurrence gives a name to the woman only known as "the Tirolian doctoress" in the newspaper articles.[18] She apparently was preceded by other women suspected of vampirism after death because they were healers in life.

Rosina Polakin died 22 December, 1754. On 19 January, 1755 she was disinterred, and revealed as one of the vampiresses worthy of burning because she wasn't decayed. The anatomists kept her body in the open air in winter for 6 weeks, up to two months without decay. To this it is to be remarked that it was an extraordinarily cold winter. In the other bodies decay had already consumed the great part; it was enough that not all were decayed. They must to the fire. What ignorance! Frightening stupidity!...

van Swieten continues with his denunciation of the readiness of the Olmutz Consistory, the administrative arm of the cardinal-bishop's rule over the city, to burn unearthed bodies with the least sign of vampirism, lack of decomposition in any part and blood in the veins. The sanguineous corpse is entirely absent from those he reviews from the Consistory's notes, giving examples from earlier in the 18th century of corpses burned because they were insufficiently decayed when inspected. "Inept surgeons" with no knowledge of the human body approved some of the burnings.

The Austrian officials called to witness exhumations of vampires in the villages that became bywords of the plague (Kisolova, Medveđa) in the 1720's to 1730's affirmed the undecayed sanguineous condition of the corpses. van Swieten called into question the validity of such observations. He interviewed the hangman.

It is true that our vampires from the year 1755 did not become bloodsuckers; it might have looked that way. The hangman, a very honest man without a mistake in his handiwork, affirmed that when the bodies cut into pieces were placed in the fire, the blood flowed out forcibly and copiously, as he noted with great calm, that this copious blood scarcely could make a spoonful. This makes for a considerable change in the history.

A level-headed professional gauged the actual volume of the blood welling from the bodies of the vampires put to the fire as a fraction of what it seemed. The "so-called bloodsucker" tag fell away with the testimony of the serene hangman.

Neither the reported lack of decay in alleged vampire corpses nor the nighttime visits by the reanimated dead was supported by any real evidence. van Swieten described a present plague brought into focus on local dead (especially woman healers) whipped up in the poor who felt unprotected from its ravages and the authorities who acted as they long had and allowed the corpse judgings, mutilations and burnings to take the form of a seemingly official procedure as an act of healing and prevention.

He gives numbers that differ from those printed in the newspaper accounts when the news reached the press two months later; the gist is the same.

Eight and twenty bodies they were, that in the period of eighteen months in the named Freudhofe, where the alleged witches were entombed, and had their resting place. All were disinterred. Nine of them got mercy. The rest, however, after they were dragged through a hole in the wall of the Freudhofe, were given over to the hangman. He brought them by sleds to a remote forest an hour away from the village, where he consumed two hundred logs of wood to burn them. The sleds, the tools, everything that served this operation, had to be burned.

Everything that had come into contact with the accused witches was contaminated and had to be destroyed as they were.

At the end van Swieten, the rationalist doctor, librarian and education reformer, declares himself so carried away by rage that he lays down his pen lest he be torn from the boundaries of proper respect for the character of the people responsible for this deed. His final footnote leans upon Benedict XIV's dissertations on vampires and the incorruptibility of corpses, Calmet's dissertations, Langlet's on the apparition of spectres and d'Argens' Jewish letters. He had already invoked de Schertz's *Magia Posthuma* as the record of this practice at the beginning of the century. He brought to bear the weight of Enlightenment thinking on vampire beliefs where words failed him.

Before she issued the March 17, 1755 *Protocollum*, Maria Theresia had set the reaction to the Hermsdorf burnings in much broader legal context. On March 1 of that year she promulgated a law under the title *Aberglaubens Abstellung, Cessation of Superstition.*[19]

We, Maria Theresia,etc. We must for a time take with displeasure that not just some of our country people go so far in their gullibility that what presents to them a dream or imagination, or is concocted by deceitful people, they hold as ghosts and witchcraft, no less for the people who expend themselves being possessed as those who bypass the beliefs, but that in these also in their gullibility is strengthened with prejudices of those taken as spiritual. So then lately in our margravate of Mahren matters went so far that by the religious various corpses under the pretext that they were occupied by the so-called magia posthuma were excavated from the Freudhofe and some of them were burned, where thereafter by the following investigation it was found to be nothing other than what was natural. But however much more superstition and deceit remain, and we are determined not in any way to allow such sinful abuses in our states, but all the more to oversee with the most appropriate punishment.

It is our dearest wish that in all matters pertaining to religion not be carried out without the concurrence of the political arm, but in general, when such a case of a ghost, witchcraft, treasure hunting or of an alleged devil possession comes about, that this is immediately reported to the political entity, therefore that the matter be investigated by them with the assistance of a reasonable physician, and it should be determined, if and how a deception is hidden there, and how the deceiver is to be punished.

You will not only be bidden to make known this our highest command where you consider it necessary, but also to acquaint the religious ordinaries with the findings, that they impart to their subordinate consistories and clergy the required pastoral instruction, and they cease their prejudices with which some could be charged, as well as they should instruct about all herein, in the forespoken cases in every event to inform the political officers, and allow the new investigation to go forward, concerning which the case by case report will be transmitted to us. Vienna 1 March 1755

The law set forth in the Empress' royal first person plural recognizes that deliberate deceit caused abuses like the corpse burnings in Mahren (Silesia). Vampirism and bloodsucking are subsumed by the categories of ghosts and witchcraft, which are invariably the result of the operation of deceptions upon the gullible. The Empress commands that the secular authorities undertake the investigation of any seeming occurrence related to "ghosts, witchcraft, treasure hunting and alleged devil possession," with the participation of a "reasonable physician" (not a quack) the outcome of which will be punishment for the deceiver.

A further step is to assure that the religious be instructed in this process and that they convey the instruction to all concerned, the final step being a review of the entire matter by the imperial authorities. The inclusion of treasure hunting (*Schatzgraben*) among the other superstitions recognizes that this too was a motive for opening graves, removing contents and disposing of the bodies.

It is not stated explicitly but the subordination of religious authorities to secular and medical officials included Roman Catholic, Protestant, Greek Orthodox and Jewish institutions and clergy, any of whom might be involved in the acts of misleading the gullible for their own profit. To underline this the imperial government circulated a notice (*Circular schreiben*) on July 11, 1755 to the clergy (*Herren Pfarrer*) not to undertake any investigation of witchcraft, treasure hunting, magic or possession but to leave it to the secular authorities.[20]

These measures were followed in January, 1756 by burial rules setting a waiting period before the corpse of a poor person was buried or dissected in order to reduce the likelihood of premature burial and accompanying frauds.[21]

The Habsburg government did what it could to prevent episodes like the Hermsdorf corpse burnings, by setting punishments for those who might profit from such activities and asserting control over the process of investigation and the treatment of corpses. The current rule of Pope Benedict XIV made it unlikely that the upper church hierarchy would try to interfere with legalized regulation of superstition when it meant secular invasion of sanctified precincts.

Cardinal Schrattembach had faced down the skeptical Davanzati over the episodes of magia posthuma the Cardinal recounted in his diocese of Olmutz (where Hermsdorf was located). Davanzati went on to write his treatise just the same and receive papal approval and notice if not publication during his lifetime. van Swieten's *Remarques* was translated into Italian by Cavaliere Giuseppe Valeriano Vannetti, a papal knight, and published in 1756.

From the book's dedication (in the absence of an introduction) it is apparent that Vannetti is in full agreement with the characterization of the vampire belief as the result of ignorance, which people of different nations with different ways of thought might renounce after study. He is of the firm opinion that it is more a matter of pride than of ignorance. He cannot account for why the foolishness, so headstrong and ignorant, can have any credit. With that he offers a reading on how much the misery there is now in some parts of Germany. "Witches and sorcerers are live stuff: have a look! Here it's about certain rascals of dead sorcerers, drunkards and boozers of the blood of the Living!"

He praises the Empress for raising a hand to clear away the fog of ignorance. Truly the most pious imperial house of Austria was not always opposed to popular beliefs. He offers in evidence the liaisons that an Emperor and an Archduke were said to have had with witches.[22] With that sly aside he commends his present translation of van Swieten's book to his literary correspondent.

Ignorance is the basis of foolish beliefs and actions, and education can dispel it across nations. Vannetti's melodrama of blood-drunk orgies and nocturnal sex with witches is visible from the critical distance he occupies. His dedication casually frames van Swieten's *Remarques* as a novella about a foreign land where credulous peasants and sanctimonious aristocrats are driven to mad deeds.

van Swieten minimizes the bloodsucking vampire, yet he did define "vampire" as the Slavic word for "bloodsucker," *sangsue* in his French, *sanguesuga* in Vannetti's Italian, and *Blutsauger* in German, all of which also mean "leech," which also have the money-sucking denotation "leech" has in English. It's not that Vannetti didn't have help from his source in subtly passing along a blood excitement. The words themselves prepare the fiction, and the false etymology of "vampire" attaches the blood identity.

The 1755 vampire upheaval in Hermsdorf was either the last or last to be caught up in the afterlife debate. Maria Theresia's imposition of secular authority on the management of the response to superstitious beliefs and practices part-condoned by the church quashed the beliefs and made it likely that they would no longer be vigorously acted upon. At least the period of villages celebrated for their vampires was over. The retraction of the report in both the Austrian and Prussian newspapers made that clear.

Maria Theresia's March 1, 1755 law and the rescript circulated afterward were an expression of the emergent Roman Catholic policy toward a problem of Slavic populations under the rule of Catholic monarchs. Pope Benedict XIV's answer to a question posed to him by the Greek rite Archbishop of the city of Leopold (Lemberg, Lwów, Lviv), then in the part of Poland ruled by the Habsburgs, was an exercise of this policy.[23]

This Archbishop headed the Ukrainian Greek Catholic Church in Galicia province, who did recognize the Pope's authority but kept the same Byzantine rite as the Greek Orthodox church. The Archbishop followed his predecessors in addressing the inquiry to both the Sorbonne and to Rome: was it an outrage to the memory of the dead to mutilate a corpse excavated and found to have an "inflamed face," identifying it as a vampire? The Sorbonne replied that it was a violation of burial, but at first Rome remained silent not wanting to compromise itself.

The Archbishop, no date given for his query but clearly after the 1755 events, put the matter more forcibly. He would not set his judgment on the matter until he heard from the Pope. Benedict replied posthaste.

It's no doubt the great liberty of Poland that gives you the right to expose yourself after your trespass. Here, I avow to you, our dead are as calm as they are silent, and we have no need of archers or a jail if we had only them to fear. The Empress Queen of Hungary [Maria Theresia], must have undeceived you on the subject of vampires, that you communally call eupires. Mr. van Swieten, her doctor, as credible as he is well-informed, teaches us that the redness of certain corpses is due to a type of earth that saturates and colors them.
You have even at Kiev a multitude of perfectly preserved bodies that join the flexibility of the limbs to illuminated faces. I have said on this subject, in my article on the canonization of saints, that the conservation of bodies is not a prodigy. It belongs to you, as Archbishop, above all to uproot these superstitions. You will discover, going to the source, that there are priests who credit them in order to engage the naturally credulous people to pay them for exorcisms and masses. You recommend that you expressly interdict those who would be guilty of such

prevarications without making distinctions, and I beg you to convince yourself that it is only the living who are at fault in this matter.

The Pope's firmly worded message to the questioning Archbishop for him to embolden himself finally to accept the religious, administrative and medical consensus that the fresh and bloody appearance of corpses is not out of the ordinary, and that labeling them dangerous vampires/eupires is the work of ruthless priests looking to profit from ignorance. The Pope is acting in his pastoral role both to admonish and guide the leader of a community where this practice has gone on. It still has come down to the blood in the corpses luminous enough to shine in the eyes of those suddenly looking upon them.

The Austrian Catholic tradition of reaction to Slavic vampire beliefs received its culminating historical treatment in *de cultibus magicis eorumque perpetuo ad ecclesiam et rempublicam habitu, On magic cults and their perpetuation in church and republic* (1767) by the Viennese imperial councilor and member of the censorship commission Constantin Ignaz von Cauz, who styled himself de Cauz on the book's title page.

The title states his main thesis: magic cults last in the church and state due to human impiety and ruthlessness. Pagan idolatry can be followed through time as it passes to Christians. His "dearest Austria" once had its bias of the magic art, and in Hungary before the present century (18th) there was deplorable slaughter of so many people. "But it is well that those sad times have passed by, because today under the reign of the most wise Domina [Empress], for whom all absurd opinions, and those unseemly to human reason, we share with the same wise eyes the judgment which she wishes disclosed to her people."[24] Especially since 1755 the Empress "for whose mind no praise is great enough" has managed the regrowth of these opinions on the occasion of the vampires.

von Cauz reviews the past depredations of the vampire beliefs, and their origins in the East and among the Greeks and Romans, their various designations in Poland and elsewhere. He names Rzaczyński (a Jesuit, like those who trained von Cauz), van Swieten, Calmet and Vannetti, but not a single one of the German or French Protestant writers. After the response to Rosina Polakin's burning the Empress decreed an investigation, then the extirpation of superstitions under pain of the most severe punishment, and education through the July 11, 1755 circular.

The intervention of the Empress halted the repetition of superstition von Cauz sees as a likely process if a superior intellect does not intervene. He ends this passage with an overview of the use of reason to forward fantasies and errors. "Thus it always is, when the masses assimilate the dear history of things to fable through the principles of reason, from the history of magic it shines through ad nauseam." The recurrence of magic cults in their many forms is a danger always present even under the guidance of reason. A thoughtful and powerful authority, not just thinkers and writers, must hold this in check.

---

[1] Wegner (1736: 458-92)

[2] Eamon (1994: 51)

[3] Bruhlichen (1734: 979)

[4] *Mémoires historiques pour le siècle courant, mois de Juillet, 1738*: 65. Amsterdam: Etienne Ledet.

[5] Droz, ed. (1746: 145)

[6] Lambertini (1741: 244-45)

[7] Lambertini (1752: 237-38)

[8] *Auszug der neuesten Welt-Geschichte* 30 (April, 1755): 233-34.

[9] The Italian physician Hercules Saxonia (1603: 805) recalled the testimony of another physician, Ursinus Leopoliensis, who in 1572 in the city of Lemberg/Lviv witnessed the unearthing and decapitation-burning of the suspiciously well-preserved remains of a local woman healer.

[10] *Ausug der neuesten Welt-Geschichte* 38: 301-2.

[11] *Berlinische Privilegirte Wochentliche Relation der Merwerdigsten Sachen aus dem Reiche der Natur, der*

Staaten, und der Wissenschaften 52 (May 2, 1755): 417-18.

[12] *Berlinische Privilegirte Wochentliche Relation* 55 (May 9, 1755): 438-399.

[13] *Berlinische Nachrichten von Staats und gelehrten Sachen,* April 3, 1755.

[14] *Mercure historique et politique,* April 1755: 469.

"Letters come from High Silesia have announced the reproduction of the superstitious madness of the vampires, or bloodsuckers, that according to the recollections of these quarters and of Poland caused so many ravages thirty years ago but haven't been heard of since. A woman known by the title of Doctoress Tiroline, having died 28 to 30 months earlier at Hermsdorf in the vicinity of Troppau, begged her husband to cut off her head as soon as she was dead and not to bury her in the cemetery of the Roman Catholics. After her decease several people died in sequence, which after some conjecture, recalled the memory of the vampires. As soon as thirty corpses were disinterred, their trial was made. Ten were found innocent. They were returned to their graves; but twenty others, among them an infant, had blood in their veins though they had been buried one to two years earlier. They were declared vampires as such and sentenced to have their heads cut off, their hearts pierced, and their bodies reduced to ashes. This execution was done, it is said, at Hermsdorf in the month of February, where were summoned for this the executioners of Troppau, Jägerndorf, Teschen, &c."

[15] *"Le fanatisme des vampires, ou des Mortes revenans de leurs tombeaux pour sucer le sang des vivans, a fait bruit dans un certain public il y a du tems..."* The fanaticism of the vampires, or Dead returning from their tombs to suck the blood of the living, made a noise in a certain public a time ago. *La clef du cabinet des princes*

de l'Europe, June, 1755: 462-63, a political newspaper, reported on the Silesian event and imperial response.

[16] van Swieten's biographer Frank Brechka located a copy of the French original, not written in van Swieten's hand, in the Austrian National Library (Brechka 1970: 132n108). The text was published in an Italian translation in 1756 (Vannetti 1787) and a German translation (van Swieten 1787) some years after the incident that prompted it.

[17] Linzbauer (1852-56: 1, 722-37)

[18] van Swieten (1768: 16)
[19] von Pöck (1777: 5, 935-36)
[20] Giftschutz (1825: 26)
[21] von Pöck (1777: 5, 1092-93)
[22] Tantarotti (1749: 301). The author includes vampires among those joining in the nighttime orgies, though not specifically with Austrian royalty.
[23] Caraccioli (1783: 190-94)
[24] de Cauz (1767: 193)

23. *I Vampiri* and *The Vampyre*

The two-act *commedia per musica, I Vampiri,* premiered at the Teatro Nuovo sopra Toledo in Naples during the 1812 season.[1] The librettist Giuseppe Palomba (1765-1825) counted it among the last of the 300 or so libretti he wrote for operas with music by various composers, and his final collaboration of the at least five operas he wrote with the composer Silvestro Palma (1754-1834).

In the *Argomento* that prefaces the published text of the libretto Palomba wrote:

From the imaginary apparition of vampires in Serbia, Moravia, and Silesia arose the idea of the present commedia. The most ignorant part of these peoples sustained [the belief] that some people dead for a few days appeared once again in the same form with an insatiable thirst for human blood and at night assailed anyone and sucked all of the blood out of him. There were not a few of them who, full of fear, abandoned their own houses to settle in another country; the magistrates of Vienna did not have little to do to restrain the others. What caused such a fanaticism can be read in the already noted Dissertation on the Vampires by Davanzati.
In this we make a play that a Lieutenant Colonel, dead in Belgrade, had ordained in his testament, that Celidea and Floridoro, his niece and nephew, children of his two sisters in Italy, remained heirs of his castle that he had on the shores of Sava [in Croatia] on the condition that they marry whom he designated in his will. The events that arose from that will be seen in the course of the drama.

Act 1
Scene 1
Field with pastoral houses, river in prospect, and part of the castle to the side. Eleonora, Silvia, Sisibuto and peasants in the act of fleeing, then sergeant Zurfariello with soldiers.

Chorus
By road and by field,
No more delay,
Flee, escape,
From these vampires;
Never, they won't have
My blood to suck.

Eleonora
Not enough my heart
They afflict with love.
They also want
To torment it with fear!

Chorus
Flee, escape,
I want to save myself.

Zurfariello
Stop cowards!
Anyone who flees
Bits and pieces
I'll make right here.

Eleonora
I flee the danger.

Silvia
I flee out of fear;
In a secure land,
We want to dwell.

Zurfariello
What is this danger?
What is this fear?

Eleonora
There are vampires…

Zurfariello
It's all a fraud…

Silvia
They eat the living…

Zurfaniello
If they fry them with garlic.

Eleonora, Silvia, Sisibuto
But you're denying
The evidence there is.

Zurfaniello
I'm out of patience
They slip past me.

Chorus
By road and by field,
No more delay,
Flee, escape,

From these vampires;
Never, they won't have
My blood to suck.

Sisibuto
Does the Lord Sergeant think
I am the first gun of the country?
And who can take the lead
Against whoever opposes our escape?
You be warned
That, as it stands now,
This will be a bloody day.
Goes with the peasants.

Zurfariello
Don't flee, I tell you,
With your baggage on the shoulders.
For I stand for good order, and now I await
The Captain with reinforcements.
Where did the story come from, that the dead
Suck the blood of the living?
Buffoons, you make jokes.
Where is this vampire? Who saw him?

Silvia
Here I am who did: I stood last night
While the moon rose
Into my field entered a vampire,
He took me by the hand, and drew me…
Oh! I almost died from fear.

Zurfariello
Eh, who would be the benefactor?

Eleonora
And I, last evening while I carried
Bread in a stack,
A vampire gave me a squeeze, I got out quickly,
If he didn't suck blood
Heaven only knows what he did to me.

Zurfariello
He went for a "meal," and didn't get any.
Hello! to your houses,

And don't believe a thing about these vampires,
There isn't anything at all, it's just apprehension.
And what? Be careful
Not to speak of these things.
Already the order has been given,
That at Gradisca will come a good attack.

He goes with the soldiers.

Silvia
See how easily the Sergeant does it!

Eleonora
In the meantime I won't be going,
Because today is awaited
The testament of the Master, who died
Down at Belgrade; he
You already know raised me up, wished me well.
I hope he left me
Something, because I have a hope
To marry the ingrate Floridoro
Who spurns me, the cruel one, while I adore him.

Silva
And you will not succeed.

Eleonora
He one time
Was mad for me.

Silvia
And this time he is mad for the beautiful cousin,
Who will be the heiress.

Eleonora
I know; but at least
Leave me a moment.

Silvia
And why do you want to graze the wind?

Eleonora
I flee…I flee, because I see others flee.

Silvia
So it goes, pity us, from bad to worse!

They leave.

Scene 2

Captain Marcantonio, then Don Asdrubale, both fleeing from opposite sides.

Marcantonio
Save me, where have I come to
Among these dead, among these dogs,
That the living, without bread,
Now eat them here!

Asdrubale
O woe is me! O lost I am!
I have no strength, I have no heart!
A corpse, I am afraid,
 that soon enough will eat me!
(But who is that one I see there!)

Marcantonio
(What a vampire face he has!)

Asdrubale
(He readies himself to eat me!)

Marcantonio
(He relishes my blood!)

Both
(But courage, don't tremble,
For extremes I am ready.)

Asdrubale
Eh? Who's there?

Marcantonio
Who goes there?

Asdrubale
Are you one of ours, or are you one of those?

Marcantonio
Do you come from there, or from here?

Asdrubale
He is standing there....

Marcantonio
He stands firm...

Asdrubale
I will cut you...

Marcantonio
I will smash you...

Asdrubale
(I know one thing for sure,
That way I will make it disappear!)

Marcantonio
(I'll hit it in the belfry
So to kill it dead.)

Asdrubale
By berlicco, by berlocco,
False death, silly death,
My flesh that now I feel,
Don't you eat in big gulps,
But go to pieces by the rapier,
And funeral arrangements.

Marcantonio
By berlicco, by berlocco,
Fake death, foolish death,
Don't go ahead with the onslaught,
Brush yourself with a toothstick,
Go suck a honey beer,
And don't touch my blood.

Both
I enchanted it, I enchanted it,
All ecstatic I gaze on it!
This changes the lord Vampire,

Not at all will he suck me.

Marcantonio
(It's right it is convalescent.
Eight have put him on the ropes.)

Asdrubale
Tremble, do you…tremble I say…and if you don't tremble
You are already on the bier.

Marcantonio
Be honest, isn't that trembling?

Asdrubale
I am Captain D. Asdrubale
Battinferno, and don't think you can swallow me,
For I am here to destroy all your peers.

Marcantonio
And I am Captain
Marcantonio Treasse,
You saw this cane,
Get down, if you don't fall into the grave,
Tonight you'll do your turn without bones.

Asdrubale
You want to order me to the grave?
For mercy please do not suck me,
Leave me my veins.

Marcantonio
It seems to me, that you're the one who's sucking me.

Asdrubale
Consider, that I'm trying to make
An advantageous marriage.

Marcantonio
And you want to catch me?

Asdrubale
No, you want to catch me.

Marcantonio
And what can I do with you?

Asdrubale
At least I can
Travel safely under your word?

Marcantonio
A thousand years they seem to me.

Asdrubale
I throw myself down before you.

Marcantonio
Throw yourself down.
They won't catch you fresh.

Asdrubale
But don't come near to me.

Marcantonio
And you will not even come close to me.

Asdrubale
Oh, not at all.

Marcantonio
And I miss.

Asdrubale
And again. *Kneeling down.*

Marcantonio
And again. (Oh what sorry wreck
you are! I'm sick, and who knows,
you are trying to kill me!)

Asdrubale
(Trying to frighten me,
A most involuntary battle!)

Marcantonio
(My legs are shaking,
The well was empty!)

Asdrubale
And again. *As above.*

Marcantonio
And again. (Now I'm heading back
to the highway, and getting myself home.) *Flees*

Asdrubale
Now I can say, in life there are resorts,
Because, thanks to the gods, even death takes flight. *Goes*

After the first two scenes introduce the setting, the panic and confusion of warfare as the population flees the vampire attack, the scene shifts to the castle where Celidea and Floridoro pledge eternal love to each other. Eleonora interrupts them to say that a vampire-destroying Captain has arrived and demands Celidea's hand in marriage. She vows to reject him and leaves. Eleonora offers herself to Floridoro but he will not have her.

Peasants enter chanting the glory of Captain Asdrubale "who has saved us from the corpses." He boasts that he met a thousand vampires and took them in hand two by two. After the peasants have left Celidea asks the Captain what he would do if a ferocious vampire entered the kitchen and devoured first the cook and then the server. He says he would destroy him, and then takes his leave.

Eleonora announces a Captain from Belgrade who has brought the uncle's will. Marcantonio enters and boasts of his deeds and otherwise puts off reading the will until Floridoro reads it aloud. The uncle has left the castle to Floridoro on the condition that he marry Eleonora and to Celidea on the condition that she marry Marcantonio. As the two lovers exclaim their dismay, and the two beneficiaries their delight, Asdrubale enters still reenacting his battle with the vampire, in whose belly he will find the cook. Their separate agitations combine into the war with the *vampiraccio*, and all five sing together: "now the battle kindles/now the hosts attack/and tambors and haughty trumpets/now I hear resound."

Zurfariello arrives for the Captain's wedding leading reinforcements. Silvia tells him of the will, of Floridoro's declaration that the will is false, and plan to gather his own supporters to prevent the wedding. Zurfariello will assemble the troops and "make fire".

Celidea and Eleonora enter just as Marcantonio, who has been rambling, utters the word for excise taxes (*acciso*), think they hear *ucciso*, killed, and take it that Marcantonio has killed Floridoro. Marcantonio then seizes on that and elaborates the claim in a long-winded oration that leads Celidea to conclude he is a liar.

Floridoro arrives to tell Celidea that he has scattered his enemies and quickly leaves to punish another who has spoken of his love of her. Asdrubale enters and reports that "Captain Vampire has sucked Floridoro." Knowing that he is lying, Celidea leads him on.

Marcantonio enters and Celidea leads him on as well. She tells him that a red hot spike will remove the vigor from a vampire, which begins an exchange of methods of vampire destruction interrupted by Asdrubale, who challenges Marcantonio. At the same time Floridoro appears behind Marcantonio holding a pistol. Celidea teases Marcantonio, accusing him of refusing her.

She sings of her constant heart seemingly to one of the two men present, but actually to the unseen Floridoro. All join in singing as they march forth to Gradisca.

Act 2 begins with Celidea declaring that she will not marry Marcantonio, whom she believes to be a vampire. Floridoro announces that he will defeat the rival Captain. Next she tells Floridoro that she will not marry Marcantonio if Floridoro doesn't marry Eleonora as provided in the will. Asdrubale and Zurfariello speak of the furious peasants and vampires they have been fighting. Eleonora tells Asdrubale that she will marry Floridoro and urges him to win Celidea for himself. Celidea then plays Asdrubale against Marcantonio. Eleonora reasserts her determination to be Floridoro's wife, but he is still undecided.

To the assembled other characters and a contingent of armed peasants Celidea says she will accept Marcantonio as her uncle's will required because he has the valor to defeat the vampires. Chorus:"To our common wishes/may his valor be propitious/and of the barbarous vampires/may Treassi be the destroyer."

Celidea encourages Marcantonio to pursue her and try to take her by force pretending that he wants to drink her blood. The people, she tells him, will then see her frightened and come to her aid. They will then reveal it is a joke, and proceed with their marriage. Marcantonio plays it according to her plan, shouting that he will drink her blood in the dining room. "Oh, my poor blood," she responds, "help me, people."

Floridoro, Asdrubale, Eleonora, and Zurfaniello rush in with a company of peasants to the cry of alarm, "blood, blood, oh, stop." To Celidea's continuing shrieks of terror, Marcantonio declares himself a tiger, a lion, a wolf, a bear who will swallow her blood slurp by slurp.

"I spoke to him of love,/As his faithful spouse;/but upon me that cruel one,/Threw himself with vile desire,/And half of my blood/The traitor sucked out." Ah, scoundrel vampire, say Floridoro and Asdrubale, and call for a spike to be heated to pierce him in the heart. Marcantonio suddenly realizes that the "beautiful schemer" will cause his heart to be torn. Floridoro says the alleged vampire is full of blood. Marcantonio appeals for help. He fears he will lose his head as the others drag him off saying his head will swing like a bell in the fields.

Scene 9
Silvia, and a courier, then all.

Silvia
Where is the mistress of this castle? Where is Captain Battinferni? Quickly, because a courier has come from Belgrade.

Celidea
She is here.

Asdrubale
Who calls?
The courier gives a sheet to Celidea and one to Asdrubale.

Celidea (reads)
The people are advised

That the measures taken
By our Magistrates have ascertained
That some agitators
Of the tranquility, to commit robberies
At night pretended to be vampires
Many were captured
And have been punished
The others will be taken, everyone
May no longer be credulous
To lend faith to such folly.

Chorus
Oh what happiness, what joy!
What pleasure for the City.

Zurfariello will march off; Asdrubale has finished his commission and will return to Belgrade. Floridoro recognizes the impossibility of marrying Celidea and gives his hand to Eleonora. Celidea confesses to Marcantonio, who sees it was all a trick, and they pledge marriage to each other. The chorus, Celidea and then all join in rejoicing that the fear has passed and the populace gladdens.

I Vampiri contains elements typical of a comic opera: young lovers each seeking the best advantage, a will that sets strange terms for an inheritance, women's wiles, boasting soldiers, ambitious servants, mistaken identities, and crowds of peasants. The opera was written in the Neapolitan dialect and performed in Naples while the kingdom of which it was the capital, comprising most of southern Italy, was under the control of a family loyal to Napoleon, who was three years away from Waterloo at the time of its premiere.

The plot was set in distant Austria or Hungary, and names of cities the Gradisca and Belgrade appear, as well as the rivers Drava, Danube and Boristene. It may be set in the exotic locale but all of the characters are Neapolitan. There is a castle, an object of desire bequeathed to the two cousins Celidea and Floridoro on the condition that they wed spouses designated by their uncle: Celidea to marry an army captain, Marcantonio, presumably a comrade of the Lieutenant Colonel uncle who recently died, and Floridoro to marry the servant girl Eleonora (and not his first cousin Celidea, in whom his interest has grown since the uncle's death).

The vampires are usually referred to with that word, a few times as *cadaveri*, corpses, and a few times, without being named, as those who suck the blood of the living, or just suck (*zuchano*). The word *schiere*, hosts, is also associated with them as are various adjectives denoting fear, panic and a wish to flee.

These are the vampires that promote mass agitation and flight when they seem to be all pervasive in small villages. They have been adapted to the patterns of witches, peasant uprisings and enemy armies. When they are heard of in the first scene of the opera it is as the impetus to get away, to a safer place, and as an opportunity for a mass choral scene since this is an opera. The opera accurately represents the panic associated with vampires, and equates it with the similarly panic-inducing advent of warfare and contagious disease.

All of this could have been taken from Davanzati's interview with Cardinal Schrattembach. In the first scene as well, the stolid sergeant Zurfariello interjects Davanzati's main rejoinder to the Cardinal's vampire attack excitement. "It's all a fraud." The sergeant's skeptical sarcasm ("fried with garlic") is met by stories from the fleeing peasants that attribute to vampire attacks what might well have been sexual assaults (of the comic opera variety). The sergeant's reassurances that the soldiers will restore order are dismissed by the vampire-driven peasants with a remark on his imperturbability. Eleonora, however, will not leave while she awaits the news of her deceased master's will. The servant's prospect of social advancement overcomes fear of vampires, which she is fully capable of manipulating.

The vampires are not just an impersonal, inhuman force like the troops that crossed territories during the Napoleonic period. They are an identity that can be imposed on any unfamiliar person. When the two captains, Marcantonio, a disabled and ill veteran bearing the uncle's will, and Asdrubale, dispatched to rein in the disturbances caused by the vampires, encounter each other fleeing in opposite directions, they take each other for vampires. They issue challenges, brag about their superiority in battle, make gestures of self-abasement and continue their flight. When they encounter each other again they do not seem to recall the first encounter.

The first mode of the vampire in the opera is a bloodsucking horde like other rapacious hordes; the second is an imposed/assumed identity. There are no genuine vampires, but being a vampire, like being a spouse, can be forced upon someone or adopted as a guise. This character of the vampire culminates in Celidea's final ruse. She persuades Marcantonio to act the vampire and menace her for her blood. He already had that reputation because of his deathly appearance and warlike demeanor.

The other characters, including Celidea's cousin and co-heir Floridoro, are about to impale him with a red-hot poker when the message arrives from the authorities in Belgrade announcing that the presumed vampires are disguised bandits who have since been suppressed. This deus ex machina abruptly changes Marcantonio from play vampire in danger of being taken seriously into Celidea's intended spouse. For the barest moment the vampire fantasy is about to have tragic consequences. Tragedy averted is comedy. "Comedy is tragedy plus time." Order is restored, marriages are scheduled according to the uncle's will after all, and the soldiers, having fulfilled their mission, return to headquarters.

I Vampiri was not consequential in the early history of Neapolitan opera; it was one more novelty set before an audience eager for comic diversions. It was not the first vampire-themed opera. The lyric opera *Il Vampiro* by A. de Gasparini premiered in Turin in 1801. Its libretto does not seem to have survived. Later vampire operas treated the vampires as genuine within the context of the opera.

These later vampire operas followed the 1819 publication of the novella *The Vampyre, A Tale* by the English physician John William Polidori. That romance spurred a string of dramas from France, to England, Germany and Poland, and the operas. All of the works deriving from or inspired by Polidori's novella feature a dying and reviving seducer/bloodsucker who is phenomenally real in the fictional world created.

No vampires actually exist in *I Vampiri*; they are acknowledged from the start as a fraud and a deception perpetrated for a purpose. This is the view of vampires promoted by Davanzati against those who would tell of vampires as if they actually existed or might exist given certain evidence, in a faraway place among peasants. The theme that vampires cannot be anything other than a villainous deceit did not survive the early 18th century.

Two continuities link the early fictional vampires and those after Polidori, besides the word itself and the general description of the revenant. Blood cleanly removed from the body of one and introduced into the body of another is one of them. The characters in *I Vampiri* cry out "blood, blood", and cry out for blood as they seize the feigned vampire Marcantonio. He previously has been said to be full of blood. Celidea exclaims that he has drained her of blood. No blood ever is seen.

The other continuity is the young and beautiful female victim(s) of the older male vampire.

Polidori begins the introduction to the 1819 edition of *The Vampyre,* "The superstition upon which the tale is based is very general in the East."[2]

Among the Arabians it appears to be common: it did not, however, extend itself to the Greeks until after the establishment of Christianity; and it has only assumed its present form since the division of the Latin and Greek churches; at which time, the idea becoming prevalent, that a Latin body could not corrupt if buried in their territory, it gradually increased, and formed the subject of many wonderful stories, still extant, of the dead rising from their graves, and feeding upon the blood of the young and beautiful.

Polidori fictionalizes the background of the tale on which his novella is based, especially in making the victims of the vampire exclusively young and beautiful. This is consistent with the young and beautiful Celidea set upon by the feigned vampire Marcantonio in the comic opera. Polidori bases his story upon a fiction about fictions; in the opera the vampire fiction-making goes on within the covering story, and vampirism itself is revealed to be a fiction in the end.

Polidori wrote further in his Introduction, after a description of vampire bloodsucking and victim death: "In the London Journal of March, 1732, there is a curious, and, of course, *credible* account of a particular case of vampirism, which is stated to have occurred at Madreyga, in Hungary." He then recounts the findings of the *official* inquiry into the case of Arnold Paul, which is what makes it credible.

In the opera officials discount, get caught up in, and ultimately discredit the image of vampires; for Polidori the affirmation of the Arnold Paul story comes from "the commander-in-chief and magistrates." The questioning of the 1732 reports by many writers since that date, and the imperial chastisement of local officials for cooperating with vampirism investigations in 1755 did not inhibit Polidori, who placed the banished realm of superstition within the precincts of the novel.

Also in Polidori's introduction are references to Calmet, Tournefort, Robert Southey's poem *Thalaba,* and a long quote from Byron's poem *The Giaour,* which having gone through many editions since its original publication date, did not have to be attributed to its author. Byron was originally assumed to be the author of *The Vampyre, a Tale.* The absence of an author's name on the title page of the publication, a practice of Byron's, and the excerpt from Byron's poem encouraged that assumption.

"The vampyre" of Polidori's novella is Lord Ruthven, an aristocrat "more remarkable for his singularities than his rank," who haunts the London social season with his deadening, unpenetrating gaze. Aubrey, the narrator, joins Ruthven on a tour of the Continent, and learns that he fosters dissipation with his skill at ruinous gambling. Aubrey prevents Ruthven from carrying out an assignation with a young woman. Later, in Greece, Aubrey arrives during a storm at a remote hut in a wood he has been warned is "a resort of the vampyres in their nocturnal orgies." He has heard "shrieks of a woman mingled with the stifled, exultant mockery of a laugh" and is seized, thrown and pinned down by "one whose strength seemed superhuman."

Saved by the arrival of men with torches, he sees the pale body of Ianthe, the Greek woman who has told him of vampires, bloodied at the throat. Lord Ruthven arrives to care for Aubrey in the delirium that follows his night terror, and they become companions again. Making their way through a dangerous defile they are set upon by bandits. Lord Ruthven is shot and dies, extracting from Aubrey an oath that he will not give out "knowledge of my crimes or death" about his aristocratic friend. Aubrey cannot find the corpse the next day, either in the hovel where he lay or on the mountain where they robbers say they brought him at his request.

Returning to England, Aubrey finds among Lord Ruthven's effects the sheath of a dagger that matches one he found in the hut where Ianthe was killed. Both dagger and sheath have drops of blood. In London he is shocked to feel the presence of Lord Ruthven who reminds him of his oath, and reaches the brink of insanity as he becomes aware that the vampire has courted and will marry his sister. Ruthven whispers to him that his sister has been dishonored. Stifling his rage, he breaks a blood vessel. "The effusion of blood produced symptoms of the near approach of death."

On his deathbed, Aubrey tells the guardians of his sister the entire story. "The guardians hastened to protect Miss Aubrey; but when they arrived; it was too late. Lord Ruthven had disappeared, and Aubrey's sister had glutted the thirst of a VAMPYRE!"

There is no longer any need to say that the story of the vampire is false. Ianthe tells Aubrey the tale of the living vampire who is "forced every year, by feeding upon the life of a lovely female to prolong his existence for the ensuing months." Aubrey considers it "idle and horrible fantasies" of the "frank, infantile" Ianthe whom he loves but cannot marry because she is "an uneducated Greek girl." Then Ianthe falls victim to the vampire, whose description corresponds to the appearance of Lord Ruthven. There is no government inquiry or proclamation that renders the vampire a fiction, and the narrator himself, bleeding internally, succumbs to the force of its truth.

The fictional/nonfictional character of the vampire is established between the Neapolitan comic opera and the Gothic English novella. Marcantonio assumes the role of the vampire and nearly has it driven into him but it always is a fiction. Lord Ruthven, a genuine vampire, moves through society in the role of a gentleman, which enables him to gain access to his prey.

Both play with blood and with young women in the marital hunt. The young women range from scheming and spirited to passive and unlettered. A solitary vampire takes shape. He is a man who travels by day and night in search of blood and money and has no family or base of acquaintances. He breaks away from social bonds to seek the blood feast without the obligations of family.

---

¹ Palomba (1812). The *Argomento,* character descriptions and proclamation from the authorities read near the end are in Italian; the dialogue and songs are in Neapolitan.
² Polidori (1819: xix)

24. The Metamorphoses of the Upior

A ballad entitled *Upiór* introduces what later became known as Part II of Adam Mickiewicz's poem-drama *Djïady* (*Forefathers Eve*). At the first publication in 1823 of the Wilno-Kowno text, the portion written in the Lithuanian cities of Vilnius and Kowno, *Upiór* led the entire poem.[1] Following are the first four verses and the final verse in the Polish original and English translation.

Serce ustało, pierś już lodowata,
Ścięły się usta i oczy zawarły;
Na świecie jeszcze, lecz już nie dla świata!
Cóż to za człowiek? - Umarły.

Heart stopped, chest already ice,
Mouth and eyes closed for good;
Still in the world but not of the world!
What kind of man is this? —A dead one.

Patrz, duch nadziei życie mu nadaje,
Gwiazda pamięci promyków użycza,
Umarły wraca na młodości kraje
Szukać lubego oblicza.

Look, the spirit of hope in life suited him,
The star of memory lends rays
The dead one returns to the country of youth
To seek remembered love.

Pierś znowu tchnęła, lecz pierś lodowata,
Usta i oczy stanęły otworem,
Na świecie znowu, ale nie dla świata;
Czymże ten człowiek? - Upiorem.

The breast breathed again, but the breast is ice,
Mouth and eyes flew open,
In the world again, but not of the world;
How goes this man? – As an upior.

Ci, którzy bliżej cmentarza mieszkali,
Wiedzą, iż upiór ten co rok się budzi,
Na dzień zaduszny mogiłę odwali
I dąży pomiędzy ludzi.

Those who lived close to the cemetery,
Know that the upior woke up every year,
On All Soul's Day rolled open the grave
And searches among people.

…

"I ścigać myśli po przeszłych obrazach
Błądzące jako pasożytne ziele,
Które śród gmachu starego po głazach
Rozpierzchłe gałązki ściele".

"And to chase thoughts through past images
Wandering like the parasitic herb,
Which over an old building on the stone wall
Surges down scattered tendrils."

The *upiór* emerges cold from the grave on *Djiady* (*Ancestors Eve*), the annual festival in Poland, Lithuania and Byelorussia when dead relatives were ritually invited to return to the family to share offerings of food set aside from the feast. The Byelorussian festival, which Mickiewicz witnessed during his youth in that region, was closest to the pagan original because the Uniate Church there had not suppressed pre-Christian rituals to the degree the Catholic Church had in Poland. The dead were called with a song sung by the family seated at the table and after the repast were ushered away with a song.[2]

The *upiór* was not a one of those who returned home at *djiady*. None of the Polish writers who touched on that subject in Mickiewicz's time make the connection between the revenant and the relict pagan feast of the dead.[3] The poet imagined the dead figure drawn by hope under the impetus of memory heaving his frozen breast, reopening eyes and mouth and going forth to search among people. The star of memory is the planet Venus that opens the gate to the afterlife when it appears in the sky.[4]

The *upiór* of this poem is not the *upiór* of Rzaczyński's natural history or the 1693 *Mercure historique* report, who enters the houses of relatives to eat their food and drink their blood. When the poem's *upiór* returns to the grave later that night his breast is bloody not with the blood of his victim but from his self-inflicted mortal wound. He is a suicide who will forever wander on that eve. An old sexton hears him cry out, lamenting the lost love that led him to the desperate deed, and his fierce shame of showing himself to others. The wanderer leaves behind a final image: his search is like the "parasitic herb" (ivy) that grows over the stones of an old building raising and putting down tendril after tendril like the hands of a climber raised and grasping, one after the other.

The poet integrated the revenant with the returning dead of *djiady* and gave tangible meaning to his living deadness. Unlike the traditional *upiór* he returned to the grave not having been fed or taken drink. His incorruptibility was that of memory and longing.

Mickiewicz was in self-imposed exile bereft of the love of his life whom he could not marry due to the difference in social class. That autobiographical detail extended to the entire Polish nation, partitioned and deprived of the means of perpetuating itself. The returning dead man is not a forefather with a family to visit. He cannot he take nourishment from the living. The people dwelling near the cemetery know that he leaves on All Souls Eve, but they offer him no place to visit. They have forgotten the custom. He can remind them with his lament, which only an old sexton hears.

This *upiór* might just be considered a ghost who passes out of the graveyard for a brief mournful haunt rather than a revenant seeking a feast and revitalizing blood. The third "Dresden" part of *Djiady* (1832) is a drama centered on the prisoner Konrad, transformed from Gustaw of the first part. Taking on the appearance of a wild bard, Konrad sings:

Pieśń ma była już w grobie, już chłodna, -
Krew poczuła - spod ziemi wygląda -
I jak upiór powstaje krwi głodna:
I krwi żąda, krwi żąda, krwi żąda.
Tak! zemsta, zemsta, zemsta na wroga,
Z Bogiem i choćby mimo Boga!

The song has already been in the grave, already cold,
Felt the blood, upon the ground it looked up
And like an upiór it arises thirsty for blood:
And demands blood, demands blood, demands blood.
Yes! Revenge, revenge, revenge, on the enemy,
With God and even in spite of God!

(chorus repeats)

I Pieśń mówi: ja pójdę wieczorem,
Naprzód braci rodaków gryźć muszę,
Komu tylko zapuszczę kły w duszę,
Ten jak ja musi zostać upiorem.
Tak! zemsta, zemsta, zemsta na wroga,
Z Bogiem i choćby mimo Boga!

And the song says: I will go in the evening,
Forward brothers, I must bite compatriots,
To whom only I sink fangs into the soul,
This is how I must rise as an upiór.
Yes! Revenge, revenge, revenge, on the enemy,
With God and even in spite of God!

Potem pójdziem, krew wroga wypijem,
Ciało jego rozrąbiem toporem:
Ręce, nogi goździami przybijem,
By nie powstał i nie był upiorem.

Z duszą jego do piekła iść musim,
Wszyscy razem na duszy usiędziem,
Póki z niej nieśmiertelność wydusim,
Póki ona czuć będzie, gryźć będziem.
Tak! zemsta, zemsta,etc. etc.

Then we'll go, we'll drink the blood of the enemy,
His body we'll cut up with an axe
Hands, feet we'll pierce with nails,
So that he won't rise up and won't be an upior.
With his soul to hell we must go,
All together on his soul we will sit,
While we make it spit out its immortality,
While it feels, we'll bite it.
Yes! revenge, revenge, etc. etc.

After Konrad finishes the song the priest Lwowicz pleads with him in the name of God to stop; he is singing "a pagan song". The Corporal also present exclaims that Konrad has a savage appearance, that this is "a satanic song".

First the song itself is like the uncovered *upiór*: lying upon the ground it senses the blood already spilt there and rises up demanding more in a warlike chant, a bloodthirsty song. The song in the second verse has become the *upiór* going out in the evening prepared to sink its fangs into the soul of the *rodaki*, the revolutionary comrades whom the song will stir, but also signified in Byelorussia the ancestors and their annual return, *djiady*. The fanged song will instill the call for blood in the returning forebears.

In the final verse the person of the song turns to the second plural, which rhymes line after line in a cascade of syllables. "We will" drink the blood of the enemy, cut him up, pin him with nails so he *doesn't* return as a bloodsucker. He is now treated as an *upiór* prevented from coming back through the methods of dismemberment and staking that were used in the well-known cases. To make sure of that the comrades will literally weigh him down in hell forcing him to spit out his immortality as they bite away at him. They use the *upiór*'s own methods of crushing and biting to subdue him eternally, as Satan is restrained in the pit of Hell.

The imagery of Konrad's song evokes Christ's Passion and Resurrection, but without the return from the grave or the ascent from Hell. Far from the cold revenant of the first poem, this *upiór* burns with the heat of an uprising and with the fall into Hell, a kaleidoscopic interchange of attributes and methods of suppression. The person of the revenant changes from "it" to "we" to "he", from song, to ancestors and compatriots, to the enemy. The dismemberment and pressing visited upon the enemy *upiór* in Hell is revenge for the same treatment administered to Poland and the Poles by its occupiers.

Between the poem *Upiór* that began the earliest published part of *Djiady* (1823) and Act I of the drama that formed the third part (1832) Mickiewicz had been arrested and imprisoned by the Russian authorities for his alleged participation in revolutionary activities while at the University of Wilno, then was exiled to Russia for four and a half years under conditions that hardly constituted a hardship.[5] He then left Russia and Poland to move between cities in Western

Europe as the Polish insurrection against the partitioning powers built up force and collapsed without the poet ever being able to join it. His encounters with refugees and exiles from the revolution spurred him to compose a new *Djiady*, which he numbered Part III, in Dresden, from March to June, 1832 before proceeding to Paris.

Mickiewicz's ambivalence about armed revolt when faced with the personal calamities of its soldiers contributed to his transformation from Romantic poet with mystical leanings into a prophet of national reemergence, a *wieszcz* who would lead his people to a new life through his art.[6] That Polish word, which has the resonance of both of Biblical prophecy and of shamanism, was also applied to Frederique Chopin during his (also brief) lifetime. Gustaw, the sad Romantic *upiór* suffering the pangs of lost love, became Konrad, the *wieszcz* rousing his followers with a pagan song to drink the blood of the enemy and hammer him down to Hell.

"…the Polish poet, by assuming a station becoming the misfortune and agony of his country, makes his claim to the inalienable rights, and to the eternal claims of Nature itself,"[7] wrote the English editor of Mickiewicz's messianic book on the Polish national pilgrimage, revealing how well he communicated the role of the *wieszcz* across languages. He consciously enacted this role for the rest of his life.

In 1840-1841 he delivered a series of lectures at the Collège de France on Slavic nations and literatures. The notes on these lectures were first published in a German translation from the French original in 1843. In the first set of lectures he identifies the dominant spiritual entities of various peoples which have spread to others: the belief in genies residing in the elements among the Persians, clairvoyance among the Germans. "To the Slavs belong above all the belief in *Upiorn, Gespenster, Vampire*, it is from them the Germans and Celts partake, and it also is remarked among the old Greeks and Romans."[8] The Greek word is a translation of the Serbian "bloodsucker," the Latin *strix* from the Slavic *strzyga* and *vampire* from *upior*. The latter word he uses for the general belief in the rest of the discussion.

The stenographer's French text of the lectures was published in 1849, and it contains a longer discussion of national spirit beliefs with different wording.[9]

Among the Slavs, the best known supernatural phenomenon is vampirism (*le vampirisme*). The idea of vampirism has arisen from the depths of the Slavic people; from there it has expanded among the Germans, among the Celts; traces of it are even found among the Romans. There are proofs that all the fables on vampirism have a common origin, that they come from the peoples of the Slavic race.

He exposits the Greek and Latin words the same as in the German text, but without using the word *upior*. That word has been replaced by *vampire* throughout. "The system of vampirism" is so well developed among the Slavs that scholars have been able to reduce it to fundamental elements.

"The vampire, according to the Slavic notion, is not a possessed person dominated by a malicious spirit, but a monstrous human." The vampire is born with a double heart and a double spirit, which remain hidden until adolescence when the destructive instinct reveals itself.

This does not come from Mickiewicz's own folk knowledge, but from the dissertation of a writer named Malianowic, who called the second soul of the vampire "the negative soul." The vampires recognize each other in everyday life, and they gather for nocturnal meetings solely to plan destruction.

The German translation of Mickiewicz's lectures uses words the poet himself used during the lectures, and relies upon *upior*, which is given as the source of *vampire*. This emphasizes the Slavic, and more specifically Polish origin of the word and of the root *upior* itself, which rises from the soul of the people. In the French transcription the predominant word is *vampire*. Associated with it, however, is a peculiar set of features that seem more like the claims of a national soul possessed by some from birth and leading its possessors to gather together in secret society meetings.

In the French translations of Part III of *Djiady,* including that by Mickiewicz and his sons Alexander and Ladislas, *upior* in the Polish original of Konrad's speech is always translated by *vampire*.[10] The prominence of that word in French Romanticism had been secured by the translations and dramatizations of Polidori's novella from the 1820's onward. But *vampire* the French word obscured the valences of *upior* the Polish word, hereditary two-souled beings not preoccupied with nightwalking and bloodsucking, or so Mickiewicz wrote.

Mickiewicz's imaginative evolution of the *upior* in the sections of *Djiady* and the phases of his life converged with and separated from the evolution of the *vampire* in the broad intercommunication across languages. The growth of mass media and the spread of cultural themes like Romanticism helped create the bridges which led to an exchange of words and themes deposited in plays, poems and novels.

Upior reached *vampire* in France, and *vampire* reached back to *upior* in Poland and Germany. Mickiewicz demonstrated in his lecture on *upior/vampire* that there is always a potential to discover meanings for a native word that differentiate it from the more widely used counterpart word and its common meanings. It is a strategy of national self-assertion opposing cultural assimilation, the work of the *wieszcz*.

Students of Mickiewicz's writings have searched in vain for the dissertation Mickiewicz cited and its author Malianowic. The Serbian scholar Kresimir Georgijević speculated in 1936 that the dissertation and its author were fabrications based on the Illyrian guzla player and bard Hyacinthe Maglanovich, concocted by Prosper Mérimée as the source of some of the songs invented for his "collection of Illyrian poetry," *La Guzla* (1827).[11]

Hyacinthe Maglanovich.

The lithograph of the 60 year-old bard playing the guzla, who Mérimée claimed was one of very few singers who composed the songs he performed, was probably drawn by Mérimée, as was everything else about Maglanovich. *La Guzla* was published in the midst of the vampire enthusiasm following the translations and dramatizations of Polidori's *The Vampyre*. Charles Nodier, who co-authored the first French dramatization of the novella, was a significant influence on Mérimée. *La Guzla* contains songs describing or alluding to vampire incidents, and an essay on the vampire.

That essay includes long quotes from Calmet's *Traité,* the 1755 Kiselova and the Arnold Paul episodes, as well as a recollection of the (fictional) Italian author-song collector's 1816 visit to a village in Dalmatia. There in the house of Vnck Plogonovich (recollection of the vampire Plogojevich?) he witnesses the aftermath of an alleged vampire attack on his host's daughter. His fake cure for vampirism, which he applies thinking that a sufferer from a superstition can be healed if she believes in the treatment, is quickly unmasked by the girl, who dies after some days just the same. "I gladly quit the village some hours later, leaving to the devil the vampires, revenants, and those who recount their stories."[12]

Some of the ballads in *La Guzla* mix Slavonic orientalia, stories of warriors, magicians, seducers and tormented lovers, with vampire details. La Belle Sophie in a "dramatic scene" spurns her poor suitor, who commits suicide. The rich Bey she marries in the last phrases of the song crushes her and drains her blood.

Constantin Yacoubovich receives at his home and agrees to bury a dying warrior, who returns from the grave to afflict his child. A holy hermit from the vicinity treats the child with earth and blood from the grave of the vampire still fresh in the body, and finally banishes him when he appears in the form of a giant. Cara-Ali seduces and abducts the wife of the poor Christian Basile, who pursues the fleeing pair and shoots Cara-Ali. The horseman has presented the wife with a Koran which will give command over the spirits of earth and water to whoever opens it to the 66th page. Basile's wife placates him by handing over the talisman. When Basile opens it the spirit of Cara-Ali rises and, claiming possession over Basile because he has abjured his faith, bites him in the neck and drains all of his blood.

The ballad entitled *Le Vampire* is a brief fragment of interest for a description of a vampire: his blood still flows after three days in the ground, his hair and nails still grow, "his mouth is bloody and smiles like that of a man having fallen asleep and tormented by a hideous love." Marie, who has betrayed family and house for his sake, is drawn to come and kiss his lips.

Jeannot is a fearful peasant who has to pass through the cemetery at night on his way back to town. He hears something gnawing and thinking that it is a *broucolaque* eating in his tomb, and goes to the gravesite to eat some of the soil for protection. A dog chewing on a sheep's bone thinks that Jeannot is trying to take the bone away from him and jumps on the interloper, biting his leg "down to the blood".

Jeannot added a bumbling peasant to complement the princes, house masters, warriors, priests and lovers who gave *La Guzla* a cast of authenticity. Presenting the book as the product of translation of songs collected from Illyrian singers, Mérimée included notes explaining unfamiliar words in the original language. Contrary to his claim that he dashed the entire production off in a matter of days, there is evidence that he conducted research into the poetry and customs of the south Slavic peoples. Some of the songs can be traced to published sources.[13]

None of the songs that refer to vampires or broucolaques has a discernible source, nor can a*ny* of them be related to song types among those supposedly providing the collection. The Serbian philologist and collector of songs and lore Vuk Stefanović Karadžić had published the first three volumes of his monumental *Narodne Srpske pjesme (Popular Serbian Songs)* by 1827, when *La Guzla* was first printed. There are no songs featuring vampires and the like. Mérimée attached Calmet-derived vampire stories to Illyrian song frameworks in the 1820's context that dictated that vampires must appear in Slavic songs for the songs to seem genuine.

Mérimée's *La Guzla* was not the first collection of fake Slavonic heroic and popular songs to appear in a Western European language, but it was the first to contain vampire songs allegedly translated from Slavonic originals. The long prose romance Le Bey-Spalatin in Charles Nodier's *Smarra* (1821) contains a reference to a creature of the night that he footnotes as a *vukodlack*, but the word itself and the details of the creature are absent from the text.[14]

The effort to translate Vuk Karadžić's Serbian folksongs into German verse absorbed *La Guzla* into a publication by the Leipzig merchant and cultural impresario Wilhelm Gerhart.

In addition to making his own translations with the help of Serbian acquaintances, Gerhart drew without acknowledgment upon the translations of Louise von Jacob (Talvi) from Karadžić's Serbian song texts into German to form *Wila: Serbische Volkslieder und Helden Märchen (Wila: Serbian Folksongs and Hero Tales)*. To the fourth volume Gerhart added a section entitled Gusle in which he rendered many of the songs in Mérimée's *La Guzla* from their French prose sentences into German decasyllabic (10-syllable per line) verse, which he believed more accurately reflected the Serbian originals.

Mérimée recalled in the *Avertissement* that prefaced the second edition of *La Guzla* that Gerhart sent him the volume of *Wila* that included the translations, and commented that Gerhart had been able to discover the metre of the original Serbian beneath the French prose.[15] The Germans do discover things, he added, sarcastically implying that the earnest Gerhart had not discovered the fakery.

The German translator requested copies of the original texts of more Serbian ballads to form the basis of another volume of translations. John Bowring, who had put a selection of Karadžić's songs into English verse, also requested the original Serbian texts of *La Guzla* soon after it was published, to make his own direct translations. These requests never were fulfilled.

Besides versifying Mérimée's prose, Gerhart changed the titles of some of the songs from proper names into descriptive general nouns. *Constantin Yacoubovich* became *Die Beschwörung* (The Incantation); *Cara-Ali le Vampire* became *Die Betrugliche Talisman* (The Deceitful Talisman); and *La Belle Sophie* became *Die Vampyrbraut* (The Bride of the Vampire). That title had the unfortunate effect of giving away the ending of the "dramatic scene". *Le Vampire* became *Der Vampyr*.

Jeannot became *Der Zaghafte* (The Timid One), and where Jeannot (Iwantsche) thought he saw a *broucolaque* the word used in Gerhart's translation was *Vampyr*. Gerhart didn't resist *broucolaque*: in the glossary at the end of the volume containing Gusle he defined *Wudkodlak* as the Illyrian word for *Vampyr*. The two-syllable *Vampyr* better fit the 10-syllable rhyme scheme he maintained in his translations. The "authentic" Slavonic prosody took precedence over the "authentic" Slavonic vocabulary.

La Guzla was first published without the name of its author, and in that form Alexander Pushkin translated several of the songs into Russian verse together with others, as *Pesne zapadnih slavian, Songs of the southern Slavs* (1834). After he learned that Mérimée had originated the work he asked his friend S.A. Sobolevsky to write to the French author and query him about the source of the songs. He printed Mérimée's reply (1735), in which the French author obliquely admitted he had invented the songs, in all subsequent editions of *Songs of the southern Slavs*. Pushkin added that Mérimée had previously been the actual author of *Le Théâtre de Clara Gazul* (1825), plays supposedly by a Spanish actress whose last name is an anagram of Guzla.

Mérimée intoned in the *Avertissement* at the head of subsequent editions of *La Guzla* (1840 and after) that Pushkin translating *La Guzla* into Russian was like translating the 18th century picaresque novel *Gil Blas* from French into Spanish. The French of *Gil Blas* was such a good imitation of Spanish and the French of *La Guzla* was such a good imitation of Slavonic, why translate them into the languages so well imitated, which would be secondary to the literary impression?

Songs of the southern Slavs was not translated into French for Mérimée to see the remark Pushkin made in the Preface, that *La Guzla* and other works by their author marked a "pitiful decline" for French literature. His acquaintance Adam Mickiewicz, an astute critic and connoisseur of fine Slavonic poetry[16], judged *La Guzla* to be genuine.

Pushkin celebrated the gathering of the "artless songs of a once half-savage" tribe that were a departure of the classical models dominating poetry at the time. In his translations Pushkin was playing a double game, improving the fake Slavonic poetry of a French trickster into a Pan-Slavic verse that reflected the savage roots of his tribe now sophisticated enough to see those roots outside the confines of the classics. That was the authenticity Mickiewicz saw in the songs. "A learned German professor," by whom Pushkin probably meant Gerhart, had written a dissertation on them.

When he came to the section on Hyacinthe Maglanovitch, which was reproduced in the original French in *Songs of the Southern Slavs,* Pushkin remarked that it was unknown whether the bard existed or not. So much for Mérimée's chief source.

Les Braves Heyduques, one of the songs Pushkin translated and versified, follows the sufferings of a family trapped by their enemies in a cave. Drink my blood, one brother says to another, and we will drink the blood of our enemies after death. From the title to the text Pushkin translated the French prose into Russian verse. Where Mérimée gave no indication that the blood drinking vow was anything other than bravado, Pushkin annotated that line to point to the Southern Slavic belief in "*upirey* (vampires)".

Constantin Yakoubovich became *Marko Yakubovich* versified in Russian with a few deletions, for instance that the dying warrior was a "Greek schismatic" and might not be eligible for burial in the village cemetery. Merimée did not annotate the word "vampire" when the holy hermit (also deleted by Pushkin) pronounced it over the teeth marks on the neck Marko's ailing son. Instead of vampire Pushkin uses *vurdalak* and provides a footnote as follows: "*vurdalaki, vudkodlaki, upiry* – dead coming out of their graves and sucking the blood of living people." When the hermit takes soil from the grave of the warrior's still fresh corpse and uses it to treat the boy, Pushkin adds a note that this is medicine for the bite of an *upir*.

The only other "vampire" song from *La Guzla* that Pushkin rendered into Russian verse was *Jeannot,* which he retitled *Vurdalak.* This is a translation of the Russian that does not reflect the metre and rhyme of the original.

Cowardly was poor Vanya:
Once late in the day
All asweat, pale from fear
Through the graveyard he walks home.

Poor Vanya barely breathing,
Stumbling, slowly makes his way
Among the graves, suddenly he hears,
Someone growling, chewing bone.

Vanya stopped, cannot take a step.
God! Thinks the poor soul,
This, in truth, is a red-lipped
Vurdalak gnawing the bones.

Alas! I am weak and small,
The upir will eat me up
Unless I eat
Grave soil, with a prayer.

What then? Instead of a vurdalak-
(Imagine Vanya's surprise!)
In the dark before him a dog
On a grave gnaws a bone.

Pushkin remade the comic drama of the poem by having Vanya, Jeannot's Russian counterpart, suddenly see the dog in place of the expected *vurdalak.* The dog doesn't attack him as it does in Mérimée's original. The fear that dominates Vanya's every step brings him haltingly across the graveyard and then directly to the grave rather than away from it. His faith in grave soil protection leaves him in real danger.

Pushkin uses the word *vurdalak* three times compared to Merimée's one use of *broucolaque.* This is consistent with his introducing this and other "Slavonic" vampire words into the songs and notes where Mérimée used only *vampire,* throughout, with a single departure for Jeannot's *broucolaque.* Pushkin claimed a peculiar Slavonic music through the words filtering into the savage simplicity of the remade lines.

Mérimée did not intend *La Guzla* to become a platform for projection of cultural nationalism for Russian, Polish and Czech poets. He was so occupied with the apparent success of his ruse that he did not notice what became of it in other languages. Mickiewicz translated one of its songs into Polish verse, a melancholy piece on a Slav stranded in Venice. His invention of

Milianowic and the ideas of vampirism he supposedly uncovered among the common folk was his appropriation of the French collection.

La Guzla also inspired Alexander Chodźko (1804-1891), a Polish poet and Orientalist on the verge of entering the Russian foreign service in Iran, to imitate the subject matter of its songs in Polish verse. The long note that accompanies the poems in this manner in his *Poezye* (1829) cites *La Guzla* without naming Mérimée, and expresses the conclusion reached by him and others of his acquaintance that Hyacinthe Maglanovich was "like a bandit lying in wait along the roads"[17].

The rest of the note is a description of the *upior* or *wilkolek* belief of "our Transdanubian brothers," the Serbs and Morlacks: "the troop of those coming back from the dead to bite the living," body not decaying, hair and nails growing, and so on, put to rest by being unearthed and pierced with a stake.

Chodźko assumes that the Polish-reading audience of his poetry, published first in St. Petersburg and then in Poznan, would be familiar with the *upior* belief. That is the title of one of his poems, subtitled "A Morlack Ballad."

There in the swamps of Morloch,
Lie supine a troop of Vlachs;
This deceiver of Marylli!
This was our destroyer!
The bullet shattered his head,
In his chest stuck an arrow;
The third month ends,
The blood not yet coagulated,
But red and warm
From the wounds it drained and drained.
Grow the beard, nails,
Eyes look upward;
Let him who lives escape,
The upior captivates with a glance.

Look, look, a pile of emaciated
Wolves, vultures, crows, ravens,
Tugging at the bodies of hajduks
That lie around the troop,
But the upior passes by,
The upior kills with a glance.
Blood on the lips and face,
Mouth laughing furiously,
With the laughter of sleeping criminals,
When dreaming of Hell.
Come Maryllo! come, regret,
Come hold with pleasure,
Country betrayed him,
Home rejected him,I kiss, embrace with pleasure!

This song is cast in the form of a ballad modeled after the "fragment," *Le Vampire* in *La Guzla*. The corpse in *Le Vampire* is that of an "accursed Venetian" who has burned the villages but lying fresh in the swamp of Stavila days after his death, continues to attract Marie who betrayed her kin and nation and now is enjoined to kiss his bloody lips.

The corpse in Chodźko's poem lies uncorrupted and bleeding for three months in the swamps of Morloch, to the north of Dalmatia. The young aristocrat Mickiewicz first encountered in 1818/19, Marylla already was engaged when she and Mickiewicz formed a bond that was sustained in his imagination and verse after her marriage in 1821. He suffered the death of exile in 1823, never to see her again. Chodźko pictured him as an alluring upior passing out of his native land, whose bloody lips Marylla, like Marie in *Le Vampire,* is enjoined to kiss.

"The first heroine of Polish Romanticism," Marylla prefigures many other young women, drawn to and attractive to the upior/vampire. This is not the *strigon* Giure Grando who returns to his wife at night expecting sexual commerce, which is one reason to unearth and obliterate him. Mérimée's *vampire* and Chodźko's *upior* lure an unmarried young woman with a passion that borders on the necrophiliac (a word not yet invented). To this Chodźko adds the overlay of Mickiewicz's lost love. The erotic upior/vampire had become a symbolic province of Romanticism verging on Decadence, shared between France and Poland as refugees from failed revolutions in partitioned Poland took up residence in Paris.

A writer on geography and customs of the Polish provinces in a collection of essays on Poland written in French by émigrés in Paris during the 1830's remarks that the Polish peasant cannot distinguish true faith from superstition. "He loves stories of witches, demons, vampires, these latter the scare of young girls, who fear for the vital blood that colors their alabaster face and animates their piercing eye."[18]

This condescendingly states a rising condition in how vampirism was perceived whoever the belief was attributed to. Attraction and fear, women and men, the proximity of blood. The outpouring of dramas, novels ad operas that followed the publication of Polidori's *The Vampyre* made vampires and upiors a matter of attraction between male vampires and female victims. The up-close vampirism transcended cultural and language boundaries, and passed through conduits like those established between France and the Polish diaspora.

Commenting on the epidemic of vampire mania that spread through Poland, Hungary, Moravia and other areas between 1700 and 1740 in a treatise on the varieties of contagious insanity, the physician L.-F. Carmeil highlighted the example of one of his patients, a woman with a vampire "monomania."[19] She was in good health and showed no symptoms during the daytime, but at night she was wracked by the belief that a vampire pressed on her chest while she tried to sleep and sucked blood from her breast. She became vigilant and agitated, stirring the bedclothes in an effort to ward off her attacker. This single individual who updated the ancient incubus in the form of a vampire for Carmeil brought into contemporary view the collective vampire madness in Eastern European countries in the past.

Most of the fictive vampirism/upiorism was not that intimate. The gender, age, class and international relations figured in the vampirism fictions and reports framed as vampirism might violate strictures against obscenity to envision the kiss of the dead, the teeth into the neck and the blood being spilled rather than just the marks left afterward as in the most popular dramatizations.

When Alexandre Dumas *père* included his own versification of *Le Vampire* from *La Guzla* in a collection of adventures in the Carpathians the young woman's name, Marie, is only mentioned, and there is no kiss of the dead in the offing.[20] The singer of the ballad is shot dead before his audience of travelers as he finishes, and tumbles into a ravine.

Le Vampire in *La Guzla* retained the features of the oldest vampire belief, of the reanimated or never deanimated corpse encountered by the living person, and added an erotic interest to the fascination of that dreaded object. In the standard fictional vampirism that configuration of the immediate afterlife was inverted, and the victim became the passive object surrendering to the attentions of the active corpse, which then becomes identified with a sexual predator whose wealth, status and power enables him or her to pursue the prey.

The vampire who moves about in society was of much greater interest, had a higher metaphoric potential, than the corpse that renews itself in the grave. That vampire might be a way for a writer to skirt censorship for obscenity by substituting a blood quest for other cravings.

Aleksey Konstantinovich Tolstoy, Josef Ignacy Kraszewski, and Paul Féval are three 19th century authors of broad scope who included vampire works in their oeuvre, by turns dramatic, psychological, political and satirical in their application of the vampire trope. They also took up the variety of words and for the Slavic authors the intersection of words in their own languages demonstrably fundamental to the vampire current yet with indigenous meanings that might not accord with the international standards of vampirism.

Tolstoy (1817-1875), for instance, a Russian aristocrat who wrote in French and Russian, completed four vampire stories, two in French remained unpublished during his lifetime, one in Russian was published in a review in 1846. At the beginning of *Upir* (1841), the earliest published, Runevsky approaches a pale young man at a ball, who tells him he has seen an *upir* among the guests.

- Упырей, - отвечал очень хладнокровно незнакомец. - Вы их, Бог знает почему, называете вампирами, но я могу вас уверить, что им настоящее русское название: упырь а так как они происхождения чисто славянского, хотя встречаются во всей Европе и даже в Азии, то и неосновательно придерживаться имени, исковерканного венгерскими монахами, которые вздумали было все переворачивать на латинский лад и из упыря сделали вампира. Вампир, вампир! - повторил он с презрением, - это все равно что если бы мы, русские, говорили вместо привидения - фантом или ревенант!

Upirs, answered the unknown man very cooly. You call them vampires, God knows why, but I can assure you that their existing Russian name: upir and suchlike are of purely Slavonic origin, although spread through all of Europe and even in Asia, and this groundlessly attached to a name warped by Hungarian monks, who had turned everything back on a Latin model and from upir made vampire. Vampire, vampire! he repeated with contempt, it's as much as if we Russians said, instead of prividenia-fantome or revenant.

The pale young man, Rybarenko. has identified a purely Russian *upir* at the gathering and insists that the word *vampire* he expects Runevsky to understand is a Latinate fabrication based on *upir*. It is like calling a *prividenia,* a Russian ghost, by the French names *fantôme* or *revenant*. Runevsky is thereby launched into an elaborate fantasy that includes the *upirs* communicating with each other using a clicking language; Rybarenko claiming he attended the funerals of people seen alive at the ball; bones visible through the skin of the alleged *upirs;* Runevsky spending a night in a seemingly haunted bedroom; Rybarenko telling a long tale of ghostly doings at a house in Italy; Runevsky taking part in a delusional duel and finally being challenged by his fiancée Dasha, -"Да что с тобой? С какой стати ты хочешь, чтобы все были упырями или вампирами?" "What's with you? On what basis do you want everyone to be upirs or vampires?"

Upirs, vampires, whatever the name and nation, remain a delusion, but one that can be calculatedly induced for a purpose. The ingredients the artist brings to making vampires and upirs seem real are the sense of secret knowledge imparted to one who merely knows the words and the seemingly special bodily characteristics of the upirs/vampires that move among us. Here the artist shows himself going about fashioning the delusion: Rybarenko, who was modeled after Tolstoy's acquaintance Nikolai Gogol, was the promoter of the Slavonic upir being reclaimed from the vampire of the Latinizing Hungarian monks.

Tolstoy had submitted *Upir* to the imperial censor and advertised his approval on the front, but only named himself Krasnorogsky, after the estate Krasnorog he inherited, and did not use his own name. He made bold to do this because his intimates in St. Petersburg society would know his identity. He did not publish any of the three other vampire stories he wrote prior to *Upir* until 1849, when his Russian language *Amena,* a tale of ancient Rome and the pagan gods, appeared in a review.

La famille d'un vourdalak came out in 1884 in a Russian translation of the French original. Tolstoy had died 9 years earlier, which was long enough to distance him from the potential scandal of this and another work, the vaudeville play *Fantasia,* performed and banned in 1851(Tsar Nicholas attended the first and only performance), and published also in 1884. *Upir* treats vampires as a fraud and it passed the censor; *La famille d'un vourdalak,* discovered in a notebook in Tolstoy's desk, does not treat them as a fraud, but as *vourdalaks,* an inevitable part of life and death in a Serbian community, and as sexual interlopers.

The novella is narrated by the aged marquis d'Urfé at a ball during the 1815 Congress of Vienna, which restored the monarchical order of Europe after the Napoleonic period. Using the fine language of courtly pretense, the marquis tells of his decision to take up a diplomatic post in Moldavia in flight from an impossible affair of the heart with a flirtatious duchess. In the course of his travels he takes up lodging with a Serbian family awaiting the return of the patriarch from an expedition to capture a bandit.

The elder Gorcha had instructed his sons before his departure that, if he didn't return in ten days, to take any figure resembling him to be a *vourdalak, a vampire,* and to pierce it with a stake. d'Urfé does witness the old man's return with the head of the bandit, but suspiciously acting unlike his old self. The elder son Georges pursues him into the forest bearing a stake and is silent upon his return. Georges urges d'Urfé, who has become enamored of his sister Sdenka, to leave with all haste.

Two years later d'Urfé, having mostly forgotten his adventure, returns to the same village, and in spite of the warning of a hermit that all the members of the family have become *vourdalaks,* insists on visiting their house. As he sleeps on Sdenka's bed, she appears, more beautiful than ever. They engage in amorous discourse, but as he playfully tries to put a cross around her neck she resists and he notices she no longer wears the reliquaries she always carried. She offers him wine, and they embrace, but as she presses against him, his own cross, a gift from the duchess, touches his chest and he sees Sdenka as a corpse. The faces of her father and brother appear at the windows.

"I applied my lips to her cold, discolored lips and then I left." She reminds him that he pledged his life and his blood to her. The smell in the room reminds him of a poorly sealed wine cellar. Excusing himself to attend to his horse, he quickly rides away, seeing the house surrounded by a crowd of the dead. Sdenka pursues him; he wrestles her off him as, vowing eternal love and obedience, she tries to bite him on the neck. He eludes the other family members, the children who are tossed at him by Georges, and awakens the next morning beside his dying horse. Since then he has been cured of amorous entanglements. Had he succumbed to his enemies he would have become a *vampire* (he does not write *vourdalak)* but as it is, he tells the ladies attending to his every word, "but far from having a thirst for your blood, I do not ask better, old as I am, than to spill it in your service".

The female vampire, infected by the vampirism plague of her family, turns upon the adventuring French nobleman and demands the life and blood that he promised her. She is transformed before his eyes from an innocent and attractive love object into an aggressive and hideous corpse who pursues him physically still uttering the words of devotion. He embraces and kisses her, then flees, forcibly detaching himself from her and her family, and presumably from his habit of adventures. In the end he gallantly surrenders his blood to national service.

The indigenous Slavic vampire's embrace of the French adventurer is like the word *vourdalak* becoming attached to *vampire,* a mingling but not a fusion. Following this story, which would not have passed the censor if submitted in Russian at the time, Tolstoy dismissed the possibility of such a union through the satire of his tale *Upior.* This Russian writer encompassed the vampire words or the upior words in Russian and French, in male and female vampires, in genuine fictive vampires and fake fictive ones, and in the contemplation of the physical state of the immediate afterlife and its avoidance. He mapped out the international world of the vampire as it veered toward and away from the erotic.

In addition to levying a fine, the court in the August, 1857 trial of Charles Baudelaire and his publisher for blasphemy and offense to public decency in *Les Fleurs du Mal* required that six of the poems be omitted from subsequent editions. One of the condemned poems was *Les metamorphoses du vampire.*

La femme cependant, de sa bouche de fraise,
En se tordant ainsi qu'un serpent sur la braise,
Et pétrissant ses seins sur le fer de son busc,
Laissait couler ces mots tout imprégnés de musc:
— «Moi, j'ai la lèvre humide, et je sais la science
De perdre au fond d'un lit l'antique conscience.
Je sèche tous les pleurs sur mes seins triomphants,
Et fais rire les vieux du rire des enfants.
Je remplace, pour qui me voit nue et sans voiles,
La lune, le soleil, le ciel et les étoiles!
Je suis, mon cher savant, si docte aux voluptés,

Lorsque j'étouffe un homme en mes bras redoutés,
Ou lorsque j'abandonne aux morsures mon buste,
Timide et libertine, et fragile et robuste,
Que sur ces matelas qui se pâment d'émoi,
Les anges impuissants se damneraient pour moi!»
Quand elle eut de mes os sucé toute la moelle,
Et que languissamment je me tournai vers elle
Pour lui rendre un baiser d'amour, je ne vis plus
Qu'une outre aux flancs gluants, toute pleine de pus!
Je fermai les deux yeux, dans ma froide épouvante,
Et quand je les rouvris à la clarté vivante,
À mes côtés, au lieu du mannequin puissant
Qui semblait avoir fait provision de sang,
Tremblaient confusément des débris de squelette,
Qui d'eux-mêmes rendaient le cri d'une girouette
Ou d'une enseigne, au bout d'une tringle de fer,
Que balance le vent pendant les nuits d'hiver.

The vampire, clearly a female but referred to with the masculine article, *le vampire*, has just addressed the poet. "When she had sucked all the marrow of my bones,/and when I languidly turned toward her/to give her a love kiss, I didn't see/other than a wineskin with slimy sides, all full of pus!" This vampire, like the ancient lamia and other demonic women in lore, absorbs the semen of the male.[21] The postcoitally weakened poet turns to her to kiss the dead lover and finds a bag full of the fluid of corruption rather than the marrow or semen of life.

"I closed the two eyes, in my cold dread./and when I reopened them to living clarity,/at my side, in the place of the living mannequin/who seemed to have laid in a provision of blood,/trembled confusedly the debris of a skeleton," The revulsion he feels chills him and he opens his eyes again on a quick change from a figure that has taken blood like the traditional vampire to the collapsed ruin of a skeleton, from soft formless to hard formed and in pieces.

"Which by themselves gave out the cry of a weathervane/or of a sign, at the end of an iron rod,/that the wind sway on winter nights./" From a woman claiming the man's seminal fluid to a soft, sticky sack of pus, to a strong mannequin holding blood, to a skeleton that makes the coldest, driest sound, the vampire has passed from wet to dry, from actively consuming to passively stirring its arid members.

The history of vampires as animated corpses seeking life fluid to preserve their mobility ends here. The disarticulated skeleton is a vampire that rocks in the immediate afterlife with no possibility of other motion. Baudelaire's attorney argued before the court that the sexual imagery was condemned by the turn to disgust and then to a memento mori at the end of the poem. The court did not buy that argument. It did not matter to them that the metamorphosing vampire in all its grave potential was cinematically before them.

The actress Theda Bara later used the same argument to justify her (for the 1920's) sexually provocative displays as a "vampire" in her films. She said the "vamping" was to demonstrate the immorality of that behavior.

Another of Baudelaire's poems in the first edition of *Les fleurs du mal* was entitled *Le Vampire*, and is addressed, not to the vampire of the title, but to the maker of the vampire: "Imbecile-from her empire/If our efforts delivered you/Your kisses would resuscitate/the corpse of your vampire!/" Corpse kisses alone were not enough to get the poem banned.

The poets Zofia Trzeszczkowska (writing as Adam M-ski) and Antoni Lange translated *Les fleurs du mal* into Polish as *Kwiaty grzechu* (*Flowers of sin*) publishing it through the Warsaw press of Hieronim Cohn in 1894. They did not include any of the banned poems published in the Brussels edition as *Les épaves*, hence *Les metamorphoses du vampire* is not present. *Le vampire* was translated with the title *Upior*. The last four lines, corresponding to those translated above, read:

Gdybyś, głupcze, pęt się zbawił,
Naszych starań wysiłkami,
Ty byś wskrzesił całusami
Wampira, który cię dławił!

If, fool, you were saved from shackles
By our best efforts,
You would be resurrected by kisses
Vampire, who gorged himself!

The *wampira*, a Polish spelling of the French word *vampire*, emerges in the final line not just a corpse but a bloodsucker who has choked on the surfeit of drink. The Polish *upior* does not drink blood, but is a revenant who speaks the words of the poem to his abuser. In the end he is a *wampira* who has expired from his own hemorrhage and might be resurrected by kisses. A shift of the words, not just the language, has remade the poem into a Polish reflection on the French *vampire*, a word originating in a Slavic language. The word has come full circle and not recognized itself.

Another poem of *Les fleurs du mal* translated in the 1894 collection was *L'héautontimoroumenos*, given the same title in the Polish translation, a Greek word meaning *The self-punisher*, taken from the title of a comedy by the Roman poet and playwright Terence.

One line of the poem reads, *Je suis le vampire de mon coeur*, I am the vampire of my heart. The Polish translation is *Upiór pierś własna ssący wrogo*, Upior breast self-sucking enemy. The subjective copula of the French is supplied at the beginning of the next line in the Polish, *Jam jest z tych wielkich opuszczonych*, [Upior breast self-sucking enemy], I am of the great abandoned ones.

The *upior* once again is qualified with a statement of an act of bloodsucking, this time without the act added to make up the total of revenant plus bloodsucker implied by the French word *vampire*. The poet-translators have recreated in Polish what the poem says in French by not treating *upior* and *vampire* as interchangeable, but using *upior* to provide a dimension of expression in Polish.

As cross-cultural contacts between Polish, Russian, Serbian, German and French writers grew in the give and take of international relations, words from the respective languages were equated with "vampire" and the attributes of that being. Yet the distinctiveness of the separate traditions was asserted. The metamorphoses of the upior/upir/vurdolak were also the metamorphoses of the vampire. The literary authority and publishing prowess of any cultural center helped guide the metamorphoses, which never would be complete as long as the elemen of cultural and artistic self-assertion w present.

---

[1] Mickiewicz (1828: 3-8)
[2] The folklorist Pavel Cheyn cited and quoted by Leger (1901: 207-9)
[3] E.g. Golembiowski (1830: 170-72)
[4] Rawski (2013)
[5] Segel (2014: 14-15)
[6] Koropeckyj (2008: ix; 121-22)
[7] Mickiewicz (1833: iv)
[8] Mickiewicz (1843: 171). Mickiewicz's French editor Germanized the Polish word *upiór* in this passage.
[9] Mickiewicz (1849: 202-04)
[10] Mickiewicz (1841: 65-66) translated by Christian Ostrowski; Mickiewicz (1882: 227) translated by Mickiewicz
and his two sons.
[11] Georgijević (1936)
[12] Mérimée (1853: 385)
[13] Jovanović (1911: 325-42)
[14] Nodier (1832: 131n1)
[15] Mérimée (1853: 316-17)
[16] He was a great poet but not a critic, according to his remote successor in the Slavonic languages and literature chair at the Collège de France, Louis Leger (1899: 238).
[17] Chodźko (1829: 246). Chodźko also was the Slavonic languages professor at the Collège de France.
[18] Slowaczynski (1836-37: 86)
[19] Carmeil (1845: 433-34)
[20] Dumas (1861: 185) First published in 1849.
[21] The bone marrow was long considered the source of semen, which it was thought to resemble. Plioreschi (1996: 321n215)

25. The new *vampire*

Charles Baudelaire found the image of the vampire as revivified corpse a trenchant representation of his own physical state, continually dying and reviving in the midst of his opium addiction, and of his emotional and financial state, as he exploited and was exploited by his mistresses. The Polish translators of his works picked up the ambiguity of the word *vampire* for him, and used the Polish word *upior* to open up that ambiguity. At the ground of the metaphor was an actual dying body both vampire and vampirized.

Baudelaire's poetry gained force by bridging in its moment the growing gap between the vampire metaphor and the vampire body. It was written during the course of a development of the vampire metaphor over the previous century. The object of the metaphor need not call up any of the physical features. Vampire fiction from the Byronic school onward took advantage of turning vampires loose in society in the form of aristocrats who if anything were more vigorous than the main of their class of society (like Byron himself). The aristocrat-vampire, Lord Ruthven and his ilk, might be a literal bloodsucker, but also was a figurative bloodsucker, an exploiter of the lower classes, especially of young women.

Paris was an arena for the development of a metaphorical vampire body that kept falling back into the old material ways and rising to prey upon, or at least entertain, the public. Lord Ruthven arrived on the Paris scene in 1820 with the dramatization of *The Vampyre*.

Taking a cue from Voltaire, early 19th century writers who contemplated vampires considered belief in the reality of vampires a fashion of brief currency during the previous century. The compiler of crime annals, P.J.A. Roussel cast vampirism as "posthumous crime" placed among misdeeds famed in the past. The vampires, observing the treatment meted out to Arnold Paul (decapitation, staking, burning), retired to their graves once and for all."…vampirism, after nine to ten years of existence, during which it had troubled a part of Europe, fell all at once into the night of forgetting."[1]

This forgetting seems to have released the strain of the vampire metaphor to be extended from the aristocracy to the bourgeoisie. There already was the English tradition of the state and taxation vampire stemming from the critiques of the early 18th century and reaching toward Marx's vampire metaphors. A brief article printed in a French arts and mores newspaper, took up the tone of pretending vampires were real archly to champion Calmet over his acquaintance Voltaire.[2]

Don Calmet believed in Vampires, and Voltaire mocked him. We others, sheep-like by nature, have adopted the opinion of the *philosophe* of Ferney without examination, because he made epic poems, tragedies and other amusements in verse and prose, and we set ourselves to repeat stupidly: there are no Vampires, what madness are the Vampires! The end is however that the *philosophe* was wrong and the Benedictine was right. You demand proofs: they're right before your eyes.
These man-tigers of all terrors, thirsty for our purest blood, weren't they Vampires of the cruelest type?
These vile speculators who fatten themselves on our substance, who drink our sweat and our tears, aren't they the Vampires of public fortune?

Don't you recognize the most hideous traits of the Vampire in these administrators, these croupiers of gaming houses, who go to gorge themselves so much on private fortunes and ruin so many honorable reputations.
In long robes, in short robes, in tragedian's footwear, in comedian's footwear, in the tent, in the mansion, at the bar, at the theater and on the street, aren't you frightened by the quantity of Vampires whose glances lull you and whose caresses impoverish you.

Vampires are real, contrary to Voltaire, but the proof is a metaphor. No longer the solitary night visitor or the bloodthirsty aristocrat, the vampire is a drainer of livelihoods in the stock-trading Bourse and at the gambling tables.[3] Beyond that the vampires are all the cheats encountered in daily life threatening to consume the small holdings of the urban middle class.

The reverberations of this threat were rendered in a lithograph by the playwright, actor and printmaker of urban life, Henry Monnier.

Vampires was included in the 1828 collection of colored lithographs entitled *Paris vivant, Living Paris*. Like most of Monnier's lithograph and comic sketch collections, *Paris vivant* is mild caricatures of people and their activities in everyday Paris: elderly citizens, a maid ready for marriage, a parvenu.

Three men crowd around a stove to warm themselves; two of them reading newspapers, the third a coachman, his destination board tucked under his arm; in the background another man is seated at a table being served coffee by a waiter; and a woman is browsing the offerings of a merchant. The men reading newspapers are *agents de change*, traders on the Bourse, or stock exchange. The café waiter is Italian, and the merchant a Jew. They are all providing everyday services. To label them vampires is to stretch the applicability of the metaphor. That contrast

301

between Paris bourgeois and bloodthirsty corpses, and the hovering suggestion that one resembles the other, makes the caricature droll.

A song published in a popular collection some years later extends the list of vampires to include the doctor, the beauty, the Jew (again), the courtier, the author, the "democrat," the notary and the courtesan.[4]

When popular attention returned to the vampire in 1844 it was in the form of vaudeville. If the lectures Adam Mickiewicz was then delivering at the Collège de France had any role in the resurfacing of vampires it was not obvious from the form it took. The title of the one-act comedy, *Le Vampire*, was the sobriquet given by others at the hotel to Fréderic d'Ossanberg, a pale-skinned man dressed all in black who walks by moonlight and does not speak but communicates his anger and amorous appeals with hand gestures.[5] He is keeping silent, it is discovered, because he is a Prussian biding his time to learn French before venturing to speak and risk appearing ridiculous. All is well at the end when one of the women he is courting turns out to be his cousin and arranged marriage partner-and she speaks German.

Le Vampire is applied to d'Ossanberg to connote his mystery-he is at first not a known member of the group of acquaintances-and for his dress, manner and appearance. There is also the rumor that he may have died and yet still walks. The aura of romantic vampirism is dissipated with his identification and integration into the marital plans of his family. The title of the play, like the title of Monnier's lithograph, advertises a potentially dreadful atmosphere subverted by comic misapprehensions.

Mysterious outward appearance and behavior are sufficient to label a person and the surrounding vaudeville *Le Vampire* without qualifiers. d'Ossanberg was an amusing character; the protagonist of Jean Bruno's 1864 novel *Madame Vampire* less so.[6]

She possessed, along with the angular features of her father, this casual, cold, cruel and petrifying glance of small white eyes bordered with scarlet that give to the physiognomy the sheen of the demoniac conceits of [E.T.A.] Hoffmann. At the convent of Oiseaux, where she had completed her education, irritated by the reasoned malice of her character, they had given her the sobriquet Mademoiselle Vampire.

Mademoiselle Vampire is so named for her predatory nature, centered in her eyes. She is not actually a blood-sucking vampire in this fiction. The name given to her behind her back enrolls her among the demons of society. E.T.A. Hoffman did not write of vampires but he did write of hungry life-sapping supernatural creatures preying upon ordinary humans.

In the final sentences of the novel, subtitled *portrait of your wife,* the author reveals that Madame Vampire is a type of woman who marries and ruins her husband before abandoning him. This is a cautionary novel *with a* [verbal] *photograph*, a true picture of the prospects awaiting the incautious suitor.

From a name given to a person for his attributes *le vampire* is extended to the typology of *Madame Vampire,* still with a substrate of vampiric traits. As sobriquet melds with metaphor, and joins the rapacious bloodsucker to the mysterious night creature, the physical traits of the vampire are never entirely lost, and often are recalled to the forms of *le vampire* in grossly concrete ways.

Rebb Schmoul is the parvenu Jewish trader named in the title of Guy de Charnacé's anti-Semitic novel, *Le Baron Vampire* (1885). "Drawn by the smell of corpses like a bird of prey, Schmoul hovers over the terrain of struggle. Oh! Rest assured, only as spectator, as an active spectator, industrious and endowed with a practical philosophy."[7] de Charnacé never depicts Rebb Schmoul being named a vampire and never refers to him as a vampire in the text. No physiognomic lists of traits suggest his sepulchral or ravening character. His hereditary rapacity sets him apart. The entire novel is the name plate of the Jewish peddler from Austria who becomes a titled millionaire married into the French aristocracy. As the above passage implies, he does not do the ground work of the vulture-vampire, but remains aloof, cold and calculating, fomenting the conflicts that make the carrion he feeds upon.

The vampire label was an accusing finger pointed at profiteers and amoral financiers. de Charnacé adapted the existing imagery of finance vampirism to epitomize the career of a wealth and status seeker of foreign Jewish origin. According to the author this ethnic background made Rebb Schmoul particularly greedy. He was part of an international Jewish conspiracy to gain the upper hand over Christians through monetary manipulations. Those adept at drawing out the substance of others who exhausted themselves in conflicts among themselves were the vampires.

Auguste Vermorel (1841-1871) was a socialist journalist who became editor of the periodical *Reforme* in 1869. His denunciations of the government and politics in the Second Empire led to his imprisonment. On his release at the fall of the Empire in 1870 he joined the fighting at the barricades defending the Paris Commune, was wounded and died the following year. In the year he took up the editorship he published an electoral pamphlet titled *Les Vampires* in which he listed several current politicians without calling any one of them a vampire. They all are.[8]

Helped by inveterate abuses and fortified by all our revolutions, they have a hand in all the activities of the nation. Our riches are employed to fund the budget of a dead policy, while our intelligence is dissipated in sterile piecework. These dead are attached to us living, like veritable vampires. Under the double form of budget making and popular excitements they draw out the substance of the people and they exhaust all our living forces. So well that we, the living, succumb while they, the dead, are more vigorous, and more flourishing than ever.

Vermorel had arrived at an application of the vampire name that suited the political moment, and was compatible with the tradition of fiscal and political vampire-naming. All the scrabbling contention of his time served those who found employment as managers of the funding of state enterprises of repression and re-ordering, just as warfare would serve the fictional Rebb Schmoul.

The vampire name always returns to the predator on the body and its life forces, however they may be abstracted, and it always returns to a visceral relation between living and dead focused by blood imagery. Those who consume livelihoods leaving the victims enervated and destitute are readily seen as dead with the aspect of vampires-attached to their victims, flourishing on their blood.

Le Stryge, engraving, 1853, Charles Méryon

Charles Méryon wrote at the bottom of the third state of his etching, which he then called *La Figie* (The Figurehead*)*:

Insatiable vampire, l'eternelle luxure,
Sur la grande cite, convoite sa pâture

Insatiable vampire, the eternal Luxuria,
Over the great city, covets her gatherings

The stone sculpture poised on a west-facing balustrade of Notre Dame Cathedral in Paris had been added by Viollet-le-Duc during the 1849-50 restoration of the cathedral. It could be viewed from a balcony adjoining, which gave the artist his impression of the chimera-part woman, bird of prey and goat-overlooking the Tour de St. Jacques and the press of surrounding buildings.

In a letter to his father that accompanied a copy of the etching Meryon denied that *La Figie* was a flight of the imagination. He compared it to the wooden figures, often of women, mounted on the prows of ships he sailed on during his career as an officer in the French navy. It was a new view of the city for Parisians, consolidated before the predatory figure.

He later named it *Le Stryge*, a Gallicized version of the Latin *strix*, the devouring night bird. Méryon also told his father that he thought of the figure as the goddess Luxuria. A photograph taken that same year by Charles Nègre reveals the changes Méryon made, not only in the perspective of the city beyond, but in the figure itself, which in the print has a long serpentine tongue and a lubricious gaze, and seems to be contemplating her next flight over her domain, while the actual figure shown in the photograph appears static.

Salt-paper print, Charles Nègre, 1853

In the photograph Nègre's fellow photographer Henri Le Secq stands beside the figure looking out over the city. Nègre did not exhibit the photograph during his lifetime. The 20th century collector of photographs, André Jammes, titled it *Le Vampire* by analogy to Meryon's print.[9]

The sculpture, intended to complement the medieval decoration of the cathedral, was updated through the medium of printmaking to become a vampire feeding upon the hedonistic energies of the city. Another realization of the vampire body from a Paris landmark, the embodiment of a metaphor, was the 1875 lithograph by Chargot of an insect-like vampire, its surface peopled by speculators, as it hovers over the Bourse and its teeming crowd largely indifferent to the monster.[10]

The substrate of vampire physicality in vampire naming, the reversion to the grave and blood in metaphors, manifested in a search for instances of genuine vampires. This apprehension was charted in Alexandre Dumas and Auguste Maquet's 1851 play *Le Vampire*, a fantasmagoria that begins with a group of voyagers who tell tales among themselves of the *epire*, the night flyer that drinks the blood of young men, and then introduces Ruthwen (back to Polidori), a genuine vampire who refuses to affirm faith in God and at the end is sealed forever in a tomb as angels fill the sky. From lore to reality to cosmology in five acts.

A less solemn banishing of the vampire took place six years later in the musical review of that year *Ohé! les p'tits agneaux!, Hey! the l'tle lambs!* When a vampire rising from the earth interrupts Le Figaro and Le Charivari in their pursuit of Jocko the monkey, they make a slighting remark about forty five year-old jokes and send him back to death.[11] The vampire would not be stil

---

[1] Voltaire (1775: 530-34); Roussel (1813: 110)

[2] *La Pandore: Journal des spectacles, des lettres, des arts, des moeurs et des modes,* May 2, 1824, 292: 3-4.

[3] An anti-gambling newspaper of the 1830's was titled *Le Vampire.*

[4] Le Vaillant (1858)

[5] My account of the comedy is based on the précis in the *Journal des Demoiselles* 12 (1844) 312-15 signed by (Madame) J.J. Fouqueau de Pussy. Yes, the name implies what it sounds like in English as well.

[6] Bruno (1864: 79). Pseudonym of Jean Vaucheret (1821-1899)

[7] de Charnacé (1885: 66). Elsewhere in the novel the author describes financiers like Rebb Schmoul as attached "to the sides of the state that he exploits and sucks to the last drop of our blood, buying deputies and ministers." (1885: 163)

[8] Vermorel (1869: 161)

[9] Charles Nègre, Le Vampire http://www.musee-orsay.fr/en/collections/works-in-focus/photography/commentaire_id/the-vampire-20869.html?cHash=81162bd2cf

[10] Harvey (2003: 118)

[11] Cogniard and Clairville (1857: 62-3)

26. Vampires and necrophiles

There had been incidents of grave openings at Paris cemeteries prior to the disturbances beginning in June, 1847, but these new intrusions were not primarily robberies. Recent burials, mostly those of young women, were unearthed, the corpses were dragged out and mutilated. As the incidents continued, attempts were made to capture the elusive profaner of burials and performer of unspeakable deeds with the corpses. An explosive booby trap was triggered during a March, 1849 attack. A seriously wounded army sergeant named François Bertrand was admitted to the Val de Grace military hospital. After being identified as the culprit by the evidence of a gravedigger who overheard soldiers talking about the activities of the sergeant told the police, Bertrand confessed to the crimes.

During his court martial before a war council the twenty five year-old Bertrand told of acting unconsciously upon his urges to savage corpses, in cemeteries near where he was stationed as his troop moved about France and back to Paris during the turbulent times of the 1848 revolution. He had tried to explain his wounds as the results of a fight with revolutionaries. The efforts of the military doctor Charles-Jacob Marchal de Calvi to have him classified as *aliéné*, insane, and not as a criminal, were unsuccessful, and he was sentenced to one year imprisonment, the maximum for profanation of graves, the only crime of which he could be convicted.

Bertrand's written confession to Marchal was published with Marchal's leave in *La lancette française* on July 14, 1849 with the cautionary note that it did not contain a full account of his cemetery deeds, which he did disclose to the military tribunal.[1] These details were included in an article by the alienist Lunier Ludger, who interviewed the hospitalized Bertrand and wrote about him for the first number of the specialty journal, *Annales médico-psychologiques.*[2] These and other articles based on Bertrand's statements proclaimed the intense interest of medical psychologists in this unique figure, an opportunity to assert professional authority where the law and morality stood aghast.

Establishing authority means naming clinical entities. *Monomanie destructive,* destructive monomania and *monomanie erotique*, erotic monomania, were the two brought into play by Calvi, Ludger and other medical commentators on Bertrand. The question whether his obsession was primarily the destruction of the corpses that led him to erotic engagements with some of them or the other way around was debated. If what he did was the result of free will then he was committing a crime and should be punished accordingly, the conclusion of the court martial. If his acts were involuntary resulting from disease of the mind then he would be committed indefinitely to an asylum, the outcome preferred by the physicians.

Claude-François Michéa, an alienist who conducted a private practice with a colleague in Paris, examined Bertrand's rare case based on the published testimony.[3]

Public opinion, by habit not having difficulty with analogies and comparisons, immediately assimilated the madness of Bertrand to that of vampirism; but, except for the violation of graves and the mutilation of corpses, these two types of mental alienation have absolutely nothing in common. Vampirism, which reigned in an epidemic fashion a century and a half ago, in the north of Europe, in Hungary, Silesia, Moravia, Bohemia, Poland, etc. was a variety of the nightmare, a nocturnal delirium, prolonged during twilight sleep and characterized by this belief, to wit, that people, dead for a more or less extended time, left their graves to come suck the blood of the

living; from there a desire for vengeance that drove these afflicted [by the nightmares] together with ignorant and superstitious persons, to disinter the corpses of the supposed vampires, burn them, pierce them through the heart, and cut off the head.
In the madness of Bertrand, the opposite is seen. It's vampirism in reverse: in the place of a deceased who troubles the sleep of the living in seeking to give them death, it's a living person who troubles the peace of the tombs, who fouls and mutilates the corpses. Besides, vampirism implies delirium in the strict sense, the disorder in intellectual faculties. With Bertrand the aberration bears exclusively on the moral or affective faculties: it's reasoning madness, monomania without delirium, which French magistrates persist in misconstruing, which they regard as a chimera. Where the doctor believes to find a new domain to explore, the lawyer takes the worst course in a desperate cause.

Michéa addresses the verbiage of the newspapers and popular rumor, naming the author of the graveyard violations a vampire before his identity was known. He then draws upon the history of vampirism to define it both pragmatically and psychologically in contradistinction to Bertrand's actions both admitted and inferred from the evidence. Vampirism was a deliriously imagined emergence of the dead that led to assaults on them; Bertrand actually opened graves and assaulted the dead not in a delirium but monomaniacally, a critical distinction.

The alienist moves on to the question of which monomania is the prior one in Betrand's case, and a brief historical survey of the four *déviations maladives de l'appétit vénérien,* sickly deviations of the venereal appetite, of which the fourth, attraction to human corpses, was the rarest. The first, *l'amour grec,* Greek love, attraction to the same sex, was the most frequent, and one which Michéa himself (according to his biography) felt and experienced, and was incarcerated for pursuing. Michéa used Bertrand's case as a basis for arguing that homosexuality should be examined scientifically, not according to religious or moral strictures.[4]

The gap in terminology-if Bertrand was not a vampire, what was he? (monomaniac being too general)-was filled the following year (1850) in a lecture by the Belgian alienist Joseph Guislain. "In the category of the destructive insane (*aliénés destructeurs*) it is necessary to place certain ones to whom I of my own accord give the name necrophiles. Medical alienists have adopted as a new form the case of Sergeant Bertrand, the unearther of corpses, of whom all the newspapers have recently spoken."[5]

The word vampire does not appear in Guislain's account, nor does he take up the monomania debate, or seem to be aware of the erotic element that so concerned his French counterparts. In a historical digression he aligns Bertrand's disinterments and mutilations with what the ancients called lycanthropy, wolf transformations or wolf-like behavior by humans. The wolf-man was one identity persistently attached to Bertrand by various writers over the following years. He was taken as a human exemplar of the behavior that inspired the werewolf legends.[6]

Neither Michéa's reasoned dismissal nor Guislain's neologism deterred writers from casting Bertrand as a vampire. The word might casually be dropped into the story, as it was in the first paragraphs of the illustrated *recueil* (broadsheet) headed by the legend *Violateur des Tombeaux,* Violator of Tombs,that appeared on Paris streets in the aftermath of Bertrand's trial.[7] The text was accompanied by lithographic illustrations that showed the civilian-dressed sergeant recoiling from revenants emerging from an open grave, and, the most enduring image, of him holding by the shoulders a fully clad young woman reclining as she raises an arm in protest.

The text, occupied with the details of Bertrand's deeds and his capture, does not match the illustration's flight of fancy, which masks the nature of those deeds. Bertrand's mutilations, dismemberments and sexual assaults, not avoided in the clinical reports, were turned to fantasy marked by the word *vampire* in popular written accounts. In Charles Monselet's novel *Monsieur de Cupidon,* Brévignon seizes a newspaper and reads:[8]

Sergeant Bertrand, this modern vampire *(ce vampire moderne)* unearthed the dead in Montparnasse Cemetery, and suspended their entrails from the branches of trees. By a kind of magnetism, he reduced the guard dogs to silence.

Monselet satirizes the news reports that gave Bertrand strange powers unsupported by his own testimony. This kind of narrative encircled Bertrand as he moved into the past and was remembered through the device of vampirism. He was not just a *vampire,* but *ce moderne vampire, un nouveau vampire,* a new vampire, *un vampire d'un nouveau genre,* a vampire of a new type.

The actual Bertrand, who declared himself cured after his stay in the hospital, served his one year sentence, was released, and rejoined the army. He is recorded on crews building roads in Algeria. He returned to France, took up residence in the Mediterranean port city of Le Havre. He married and spent the rest of his life working at odd jobs, until his death in 1878.[9] The mystery writer Michel Dansel contended that grave disturbances and corpse mutilations in cemeteries about Le Havre in 1864 and 1867 while he was living there match Bertrand's known practice, and he may not have been entirely cured after all.[10]

Under the title *"Bertrand le vampire"* the sergeant lived on in the emergent true crime genre of the 1880's. The editor and librarian Arthème Fayard, writing under the pseudonym de la Brugère, compiled the melodramatic tabloid series from the published court martial proceedings.[11] Most of the text is quotations from Bertrand and others. At the end the author asks what became of Bertrand. First there is the rumor that he died in the east of France of a *maladie de langeur,* a disease of exhaustion, which was compatible with Bertrand's own great exhaustion after performing his grave incursions and implies that he continued acting upon his ghastly mania.

Or there was a letter from a former comrade of Bertrand's who served as a Union colonel during the America Civil War. The colonel sought shelter from a storm at an isolated farm, where he was well treated. The farmer revealed himself to be Bertrand who had come to America and prospered. He was married to a German woman fully informed of his past life. "Which of these is true?" de la Brugére asks by way of conclusion. "We hope, for the sake of humanity, that it is the second."

Bertrand also was included among the thieves and murderers memorialized by the author of the *Mémoires de M. Claude,* which purported to be the memoirs of Antoine Claude (1805-1880), *chef de la police du sûreté*, the chief of the French national police during the Second Empire. The actual author of this latest installment in the chief police officer memoirs genre was a crime writer named Théodore Labourieu, who published his own volume of criminal biographies four years later.

In the chapter entitled *Le Vampire* Bertrand's name is not used.[12] Throughout the narrative the unknown despoiler of graves and visitor of shameful mutilations on the corpses is known as a "new vampire," "this monster, this vampire," "this strange vampire," or "the vampire." He is subject to "an odious and strange monomania," and must possess "the ferocity of a hyena, the prudence of a serpent," and has to be "superhuman" to move as he does.

At first suspicion falls on the cemetery guardians, but after more than one cemetery is affected and the family of a young woman whose newly buried corpse is mauled and, it seems, bitten, complains to the prefect of police, the investigation "naturally" passes to M. Claude.

Claude concludes, after questioning the cemetery concierge, the guardians and the brigadiers, (the soldiers charged with keeping watch), that if it is not one of them, then it must be someone in close contact with them. The coordination between the attacks and the period of time in the evening when the brigadiers change watch has already been noticed. Now Claude learns of an elderly cemetery guardian who was once a brigadier and has been hosting his soldier nephew for the past month, exactly the period during which the attacks have occurred.

This soldier is of a mild and gentle character, Claude learns from his uncle, and is very curious about the cemetery and its orders. The soldier has become so knowledgeable that the uncle wouldn't be surprised if he puts his hand some day on the profaner of the graves. Claude has his suspect, whom he now traces to the hut an elderly worker has built against the cemetery wall. Claude and his officers watch as the worker begins to play the violin in the evening. A soldier enters the house, and not long afterward emerges dressed in the old worker's clothing.

They follow the disguised soldier to the recent burial of a young woman. As he opens the coffin, takes her into his arms and plants a kiss on her cold lips, Claude and his men spring their trap and seize him. Public opinion, and the jury, are prepared to judge the grave profaner, the nephew of the brigadier, to be insane.

The testimony of the elderly violin player establishes that he plays the violin in the evening in the deluded belief that he could summon up the soul of his dead son buried in the cemetery. The "vampire" took advantage of this belief, came to his house when he heard the violin and was welcomed as the dead son, changed into the worker's clothes and used his access door to the cemetery. Both the uncle and the violin player are judged innocent of complicity in the grave profaner's scheme, which proves that he was fully rational. He is judged a criminal and condemned.

The environment and circumstances of Claude's tale are similar to the history of Bertrand, and the description of him as a monomaniac or just a maniac introduces the psychological assessment. The chapter is titled "The Vampire," and he is referred to as a "vampire" throughout. His actions are personalized by the introduction of the brigadier uncle and given atmosphere by the nocturnal violinist on the edge of the cemetery. The decisive detective-narrator draws together the threads that Bertrand himself previously commanded. The vampire is apprehended by the reasoning forces of law and morality, and shown to be a perversion of reason, not an unreasoning lunatic.

The Bertrand-like fiction fathered upon Claude inverts the primordial vampire story in which the dead emerge from the grave and visit the dwellings of the living. The Bertrand figure gains the unwitting cooperation of the forces of order to disturb the grave and mutilate the corpse which guarantees that it remains one.

This fiction is the fact of what the vampire has become in the late 19th century. The immediate afterlife of the corpse is induced by a living person, who scandalously verifies a vampirism that never existed. The details may vary from one version to the next, but there was a Bertrand and he did attack and embrace corpses. In keeping with the original vampire as the dead returned for the feast, the Bertrand vampire was both hungry and salacious.

The alienists and protopsychiatrists who studied Bertrand and argued for his membership in a typology promoted the new vampire while rejecting the label. Proof that this was a category of behavior which could be repeated, debated and classified comes in the form of the other vampires who followed Bertrand. Copycats or not, they fell into the same class of new vampire.

"It is recalled that this sergeant Bertrand, vampire of a new type, profaned cemetery tombs at night 20 years ago, and, to satisfy an incomprehensible passion, tore recently entombed corpses from their shrouds," read the first line of an 1869 Paris newspaper article.[13] "This maniac has just had a successor." The conservator of the *cimitière de l'Est* had found three coffins opened and the corpses extracted. The police, assisted by a physician, determined that the profaner had rejected the corpses of men he uncovered and stopped only when he found the corpse of a woman, a 67 year-old widow. "This latter carried the evident traces of a recent outrage from which death could not preserve it."

This unnamed vampire successor of Bertrand preceded others initially named after the cemeteries they haunted and, after apprehended, personal names together with the vampire-cemetery name, for instance, Henri Blot, the vampire of Saint-Ouen.[14] The vampire in each case followed the established pattern of removing corpses of young women, and mutilating them in suggestive ways related to sexual engagement. Henri Blot, who also qualified in another new category, serial killer, specialized in finding the remains of young dancers, at least one of whom he removed from the cemetery and kept for his own purposes.

Honoré Ardisson, the vampire of Muy, was listed by newspapers as "the third vampire," after Bertrand and Blot.[15] He was caught after his father searched the household granary in response to local complaints about the smells issuing from it, and found the corpse of a girl. The expressions of horror and incredulity that accompanied the journalistic willingness to disseminate gruesome details continued as components of "the new vampire." "Whatever the degree of

edginess (*nervosisme)* of our epoch-one refuses to admit that there are people-rare, very happily-
who can surrender to such monstruous inclinations."

Other grave openings were reported for which no vampire ever was found.

The published thesis of Alexis Épaulard for the degree of doctor of medicine in the Faculty
of Medicine and Pharmacy in Lyon (December 23, 1901) had the heading:[16]

VAMPIRISME

NÉCROPHILIE, NÉCROSADISME, NÉCROPHAGIE

Épaulard begins the Introduction to the thesis recalling the case of Ardisson to which public
attention was attracted just two months earlier, at the end of September, 1901. "This vampire,"
he wrote, was not isolated, and in 1849 the case of Bertrand had brought similar activities to light.
His master Lacassagne encouraged him to consider the seldom discussed sexual perversion that
leads men to profane corpses, from the point of view of psychiatry and criminal anthropology.

After a review of the significance of burial practices to early humans, and the punishments
for grave-robbing and cannibalism as violations of the sanctity of the grave, Épaulard traces the
changes in the meaning of the word *vampire* (Slavic *oupir* originally based on Turkish *ubur,*
sorcerer) from legendary animated corpses to a mass delusion leading to the identification of an
accused vampire. "By one of these changes in sense common in linguistics" the word went from
designating the blood-sucking dead to those who commit acts of vampirism, who profane
corpses.

"That is why I have encompassed under the term vampirism all profanations of the corpse,
whatever their primary reason."

For Épaulard, Bertrand and his followers were called vampires because they committed acts
of vampirism as corpse profanation. Michéa had rejected that popular identification and confined
vampirism to the delusion of crowds; Bertrand, he contended, was engaged in the opposite, a
personal affective disorder.

Épaulard ratified the new vampirism of corpse animation by attack, and the feast of the
living on the dead. Extending from this vampirism there was a row of necro- terms: Guislain's
"necrophilia" which was defined as sexually predatory vampirism, "necrosadism," combining a
historic psychiatric eponym, sadism (from the Marquis de Sade), to name destruction of the
corpse by the living for pleasure, and "necrophagy," the eating of the corpse by the living, also
for the pleasure of it.

Together they comprised the new vampirism, which paralleled perversions practiced upon
the corpse with perversions practiced upon the living. Bertrand's attacks on corpses sprang from
the same sources as the attacks of the sadistic serial killer Vacher upon children. Sometimes,
rarely, a necrosadist killed a living person to provide himself with a corpse to mutilate.
"Mutilation of the corpse is enough, for certain men, to give birth to sexual excitement and even

to satisfy it." The difference between a true sadist and a necrosadist is that the sadist seeks to induce appreciable pain in his victim, a response a necrosadist can't expect from a corpse.

A review of individual cases, historic and from the experience of analysts such as Lacassagne, Krafft-Ebing, Lombroso and Épaulard himself assimilated Bertrand, Blot, Ardisson, Jack the Ripper, Vacher and others to the vampirism master scheme. In these reviews a transition in the terminology comes to the fore.

Vampirism is only the most general sort of corpse mutilation. Bertrand was a necrophile and necrosadist, which better specify his mania than leaving it at calling him a vampire. Actual blood-sucking (as opposed to the delusion of blood-sucking) is necrophagy. "Whatever it may be, it's necrophagy that seems to be the extreme point of vampirism, whether it be sexual or not." The extreme point of vampirism is the feast imagined from the first formation of the word in Old Slavonic.

At the end of his thesis Épaulard sets out his conclusions, beginning with "One should understand by vampirism all profanation of corpses, whatever its mode and whatever its origin." Then follows a much finer parsing out into necrophilia, necrosadism and necrophagy, and related behaviors such as sadism, fetishism, masturbation and with little further resort to the vampirism generality. He warns that these actions are too numerous to propose preventive measures. "They recall, however, that we should not weaken in the struggle undertaken against the primordial causes of psychic enfeeblement in our society."

The psychic enfeeblement began in the free reign of corpse mutilation vampirism, not in loss of blood. But that strain of vampirism, delusional blood-sucking, was reasserted with the force of growing image-making at the turn of the centur

---

[1] Example remarquable de monomanie déstructive et érotique...,*La Lancette Française* 1,82 (1849): 327-28

[2] Ludger (1849). Marchal's notes on Bertrand were published by Tardieu (1878: 114-20)

[3] Michéa (1849)

[4] Bertrand himself countered Michéa's assigning erotic monomania the initiating role before destructive monomania, in a (possibly apocryphal) letter sent to Marchal and printed by a colleague after Marchal and Bertrand were dead. Tardieu (1878: 121-23)

[5] Guislain (1852: 257)

[6] Bourgault de Courdray (2006: 23-25)

[7] 1849. Bibliothèque National Français, Department of Prints and Photography, BOITE FOL-LI-300 (5)

[8] Moselet (1858: 66)

[9] Reports that he was sentenced to 20 years hard labor (Pain 1901) or that he committed suicide were discredited by the printing of facsimile birth and death certificates Feray (2014: 7).

[10] Dansel (1999)

[11] Bertrand le vampire, *Le petit roman-feuilleton* August 22, 1880: 225-29; August 29, 1880: 214-44; *l'Omnibus* May 25, 1884: 88-

[12] Claude (1881: 247-59)

[13] *Le Gaulois* April 2, 1869: 3
[14] Le Vampire, *La protection des morts* September 1-September 9, 1886: 2
[15] L.F., Un vampire, *La lanterne* October 1, 1901: 1
[16] Épaulard (1901)

27. The vamp

The new vampire was a living person who preyed upon the dead, reversing the two roles of vampirism, the living person animating the dead rather than the reanimated corpse killing the live victim by drawing out the life essence. The possibility of the original vampire's blood drinking still existed, now as necrophagy.

Not until 1936 was there an illustration of Bertrand in action; none of the contemporary newspaper reports or books depicted the sergeant at his grisly work. This woodcut illustration was one of several in a two-page spread on Bertrand in the magazine of *faits divers* entitled *Détective* that mostly featured color and black and white photographs of criminals and crime scenes. It did not go beyond the conventional mildly pornographic layout of a man, who might just as easily have been the traditional male vampire, bent eagerly over the prostrate body of a partially unclad young woman.[1]

The cemetery setting and the empty coffin leaned against the wall of the open crypt suggest the source of the young woman's body and the context of the man's approach to her. The author of the article in the magazine claimed that he included details from a dossier long hidden in the prison where Bertrand had been incarcerated.

In 1872, David Henry Friston's illustration of a scene from the serialized publication of Sheridan Le Fanu's novella, *Carmilla* had utilized this same format.[2]

The passage illustrated is from Chapter XIV of *Carmilla*. General Spielsdorf tells of standing guard, sword in hand, over his sleeping niece Bertha, who is deathly ill from the attack of what a doctor has called a vampire.

I concealed myself in the dark dressing room, which opened upon the poor patient's room, in which a candle was burning, and watched there till she was fast asleep. I stood at the door, peeping through the small crevice, my sword laid on the table beside me, as my directions prescribed, until, a little after one, I saw a large black object, very ill-defined, crawl, as it seemed to me, over the foot of the bed, and swiftly spread itself up to the poor girl's throat, where it swelled, in a moment, into a great, palpitating mass.
For a few moments I had stood petrified. I now sprang forward, with my sword in my hand. The black creature suddenly contracted towards the foot of the bed, glided over it, and, standing on the floor about a yard below the foot of the bed, with a glare of skulking ferocity and horror fixed on me, I saw Millarca. Speculating I know not what, I struck at her instantly with my sword; but I saw her standing near the door, unscathed. Horrified, I pursued, and struck again. She was gone; and my sword flew to shivers against the door.

Bertha died soon afterward. Friston's illustration shows Millarca rather than the "large black object" approaching the sleeping Bertha. The conventional scene of vampirism is repeated. The recumbent woman and the approaching man are preserved but now a woman intervenes between the two. The pattern persisted no matter who was the vampire: man, woman, wolfish black thing.
These two illustrations and the texts they correspond to form the symbolic space of the vampire as the end of the 19th century approached. Rigidity of gender and social roles was met by transformation, in Bertrand's and the other new vampires, in Le Fanu's fiction and in the relationship between the subjects and their illustrations. The shift between life and death through the ingestion and release of sanguis that was the essence of the vampire afterlife was now accompanied by gender and socioeconomic role transformations, by fluid relationships between reported reality, deep history and fiction.

Richard von Krafft-Ebing recognized "the new vampire": he referred to Bertrand in Inquiry 23 of his *Psychopathia Sexualis* from the first edition (1882) onward, as a *moderne Vampir*.[3] He had another vampire to offer.[4]

Inquiry 42. A married man presents himself with numerous cut marks on his arms. He gave the origin of these marks: when he wants to approach his young, somewhat "nervous" wife, he must first make a cut on the arm. She then sucks on the wound, whereupon a high degree of sexual excitement ensues.
This case recalls the widespread vampire stories, whose origins can be traced back to such sadistic things.
Footnote: The stories are especially well distributed in the Balkan regions. Among the modern Greeks they derive from the ancient myths of Lamias and Mormolyks-bloodsucking women. Goethe reworked this matter in his [ballad, *Bride of Corinth*. The vampirism-related verses: "suck thine heart's blood," and so on are entirely understandable in relation to the ancient sources.

The psychoanalyst groups this case with his examples of "the sadism of married women," and has no more to say about it beyond finding that ancient myths of monstrous women swallowing men's blood by night were a primordial experience, rehearsed again here, of women's sexual arousal on drinking a male's fresh blood.

The phrase "suck thine heart's blood" is from Goethe's 1797 ballad, *Bride of Corinth*. An Athenian youth comes to Corinth in the hope of claiming a bride from a friend of his father who with his family have converted to Christianity. As he lies in bed at night, given hospitality by the mother who receives him after the father and daughter have retired for the night, the intended bride comes to him, and reveals that she has died and her sister is now his intended. He pleads with her to become his bride. They exchange tokens, and she lies with him, the sounds of their mutual embrace having alerted the mother, who to her horror discovers her dead daughter with the guest. There is no response from the guest. The daughter declares that she has sucked his heart's blood and he will wither away.

Blood and semen and the life essence they both share have been absorbed by the revenant girl, who has found her revenge against the living. She is like all the other females who take away the life of men, the lamia Appolonius Rhodius banishes from preying upon his student, the dead aristocratic virgin who tries to seduce the itinerant potter in the film *Ugetsu monogatari*, the man ruined by the excesses of *Madame Vampire* in Jean Bruno's 1864 novel, and many other women threatening to drain the life from young men.

The hematophagously aroused wife of Inquiry 49 is, however, alive, all the more so for having tasted her husband's blood. This very old vampirism retains the blood feast; the death of either party is optional. As Krafft-Ebing realized, this is a vampirism of greater vintage than the male blood-suckers of recent tales and or the corpse-damaging new vampires.

During the 1890's there appeared a set of images and inscriptions, stories, paintings and prints, which made this variety of vampirism more visible. They were spread across Europe with a similarity that does not imply direct mutual inference but rather a cultural resonance.

Col. "Hippy" Rowan receives a deadly kiss on the neck from a Madonna-like young woman whom he shoots without effect before he collapses. His valet long afterward shows a photograph of the XXX mark the kiss leaves on its victims, the sign that it was bestowed by a "child of

Judas" whom the colonel had insulted for his ugliness and then fixed to a tree with his own dagger after an assassination attempt. The "Moldovian" man then committed suicide with the same dagger, and returned as the lethal woman.

The novella *A Kiss of Judas* (1893) by the American socialite of decadent leanings Julian Osgood Field was illustrated in its first publication by pen-and-ink drawings of its scenes, but none of the final kiss itself.[5] The title art comes the closest.

That was left to Aubrey Beardsley, whose coolly Japonesque print was inserted at the beginning of the magazine publication. Here a male child of Judas gains his footing after he has finished planting the kiss on the wrist of a young woman who seems to have been cradling him and who has collapsed against the trunk of a tree. The gender fluidity of the novella, and of this vampire genre, is preserved in the print.

The word "vampire" is only used once in Fields' novella, to refer to the monsters that are the children of Judas. There is no spilled or drawn blood, only venom injected.

Edvard Munch wrote an "Intermezzo" in a sketchbook dated 1890-91 that seems to be what Col. Rowan expected when the child of Judas started out for him, and reached his throat.[6]

He sat with his arm around her body. Her head was so near to him. It seemed so remarkable to have her eyes, her mouth, her breasts so near to him.
And he laid his hand between her breasts. He felt her blood stream through her veins. He listened to the beat of her heart. He buried his face in her lap. She lowered her head down on him and he felt two warm, burning lips on his neck. A shudder passed through his body, a shudder of voluptuousness. And he pressed her convulsively to him

Munch completed a number of paintings, drawings, lithographs and woodcuts picturing this conjunction of a man and a woman, of various colorings and positionings, often with the woman's read hair engulfing the man. The earliest sketch of the motif was made around 1890, though Munch claimed later to have begun crafting the design several years earlier.

Munch's critical champion Stanislaw Przybyszewski wrote an essay on the painter's work based on an exhibit held in Berlin in 1893.[7]

To the next picture Munch gives the title Love and Pain: a broken man and at his neck a biting vampire face. The background is a remarkably chaotic mixture of blue, purple, green, yellow color flecks, mixed together, floating, jaggedly juxtaposed with each other, like tiny crystalline forms. There is something frighteningly calm, passionless in this picture, a tireless resignation to fate. The man rolls and rolls there in abyssal depths, without will, powerless, and assures himself, that he can roll away like a stone. He will not get rid of the vampire, and the woman will always remain there, and will always bite with a thousand nattering tongues, with a thousand poison teeth.

Przybyszewski's interpretation of the image in the first instance replaces Munch's own name with the one that will stick, despite the painter's resistance: the Vampire. The Polish critic would do the same with another image realized around the same time (though the name change is not in the same essay), Munch's Despair, which he called The Scream. In that case he also replaced an emotion with a sensation, a characteristic of advertising. The kaleidoscopic coloring, which Munch would pursue especially in the print versions of the image, catches the critic's eye. But he mistakes Munch's intention to express erotic anguish, and reduces the woman to a toxic nattering harridan, a misogynistic caricature.

Munch did make another image in 1894, a winged female figure rising triumphantly over the recumbent body of a man while a face resembling that of Przybyszewski gazes out of the corner of the frame. He called it The Vampire or The Harpy, perhaps with the intention of informing his critic what he believed a vampire actually does: slay the man (Munch's own misogyny).

Then there is the sequence of colored crayon drawings and inscriptions headed The Tree of Knowledge.[8] "The blood roared inside him. A hellish concoction brewed from the wine-like blood of the plant-mixed together with the female vampire's poison." At the bottom of the page that includes these lines is a recumbent figure in blue crayon holding up a right hand smeared in red. Munch saw the bloody death of the male in the true vampire; Love and Pain only had red hair.

The model painting of Munch's image The Kiss, included in the same 1894 Berlin exhibit as Love and Pain, is formed of a man's and a woman's face converging. Munch might show a woman bending domineeringly over a man's neck, or the other way around (The Dance of Life, 1899-1900 "fat man biting the neck of a woman" MM T184) in the history of his couple imagery he engages with the dialectic that included vampirism as the phase prioritizing the woman's neck kiss-bite or triumphant rise.

A member of the Berlin circle that included Munch and August Strindberg, Adolf Paul, in 1927 reminisced about the time in the mid 1890's he visited the artist's studio and found him painting the image of a woman model with flaming red hair.[9]

Another time in the same room! Another model, this time not dark-haired, but one with fire-red locks, which flowed out like running blood.
"Kneel down below her," he called to me. "Lay your head in her lap."
I complied. She bent over me, drew her lips to my neck, her red hair falling down over me. Munch painted, and in a short time he had his "Vampire" ready, which he thereafter often repeated in woodcut and lithography.

Paul, an aspiring composer who had turned to writing plays, incorporated himself by an act of memory into the making of the painting later named The Vampire, at the time having been incorporated by Munch into his own experience set down in his sketchbook a few years earlier. This was a lasting episode.

Jonathan Harker, detained by Count Dracula in his castle, feigns sleep as he is approached at night by three women. One of them comes near.[10]

…The girl went on her knees and bent over me, simply gloating. There was a deliberate voluptuousness that was both thrilling and repulsive, and as she arched her neck she actually licked her lips like an animal; till I could see in the moonlight the moisture shining on the scarlet lips and on the red tongue as it lapped the sharp white teeth. Lower and lower went her head as the lips went below the range of my mouth and chin and seemed about to fasten on my throat. Then she paused, and I could hear the churning sound of her tongue as it licked her teeth and lips, and could feel the hot breath on my neck. Then the skin of my throat began to tingle as one's flesh does when the hand that is to tickle it approaches nearer-nearer. I could feel the soft, shivering touch of the lips on the super-sensitive skin of my throat, and the hard dents of two sharp teeth, just touching and pausing there.

This passage is the only one in the novel where a potential victim of a vampire is conscious as the teeth approach his or her neck. It is a more detailed and erotically heated version of the female vampire's attack that killed Col. Hippy Rowan, and was experienced-imagined by Munch and Adolf Paul. Harker is passively awaiting the penetration when it is halted for the time being by the intervention of the dominant male vampire, who later leaves him to "the sisters." Harker escapes to return to England with his account of Dracula's plans for his extensive real estate acquisitions.

Like Bertrand, Count Dracula applies himself to female victims in a passive state. He arrives in England in a manner that recalls both the lycanthropic and plague modes of vampirism. There he vampirizes the trance-walking Lucy Westenra, who in all her red-lipped beauty is staked, stuffed with garlic and decapitated by van Helsing and her former suitors.

Blood transfer in the novel, sometimes compared with animal feeding, is actually more like messy transfusion. Jonathan Harker's fiancée, Mina Murray, is given a transfusion by Dracula that threatens to enslave her to him, and is saved by salubrious transfusions from the males. She survives to become a key operative in the struggle against the Count's plans of conquest, leading to the final knife fight with the males that destroys him.

Though it at times seems possible, none of the women vampires in *Dracula* achieves the triumphant pose of the woman in the painting, *The Vampire*, by Philip Burne-Jones. The painting was first exhibited in April, 1897 at the New Gallery in London, in the gallery's spring show.[11]

The woman rising over the man, a dark mark visible on his chest corresponding to the darkness on her lips, was recognized at the time to resemble the actress Mrs. Patrick Campbell (stage name of Beatrice Stella Tanner) with whom Burne-Jones was said to be "romantically involved." The act anticipated by Harker in *Dracula* or inverted in *A Kiss of Judas* is fully consummated here. Aubrey Beardsley had drawn a full length portrait of Mrs. Campbell in 1894, the year after *The Kiss of Judas* illustration.

The Vampire was placed on exhibit a month before Bram Stoker held a dramatic reading of the dramatized *Dracula* at the Lyceum Theatre (May 18), followed by the publication of the novel (May 26). Stoker sent Philip Burne-Jones a copy of the novel, and the artist replied with a promise to reciprocate with "a photograph of my vampire, a woman this time, so as to make the balance fair."[12] The male vampire, Dracula, was reputedly modeled on the actor Henry Irving, who as Stoker's employer drained his life's blood, but refused to perform the role of Dracula during the reading. The exchange evokes the revolving gender identities of vampire and vampirized about to become fixed for a moment.

Another participant in this tangle of relationships that emerged from the late Victorian theatre world into transatlantic popular culture was Rudyard Kipling, Philip Burne-Jones' cousin. Kipling wrote a poem to accompany the description of *The Vampire* in the gallery's catalogue. What little notice painting and poem received was not favorable. In 1908, a year after Kipling was awarded the Nobel Prize in Literature, he had the poem reprinted in booklet prefaced by a photo of the painting, and with a title page illustration of a begowned and shawled woman extending her hand to a bat as she stands in a moonlit cemetery.

The poem itself contains no references to bats, graveyards, the dead, blood or vampires, but it does include several resonant phrases. The first two stanzas:

A fool there was and he made his prayer
(Even as you and I!)
To a rag and a bone and a hank of hair
(We called her the woman who did not care),

But the fool he called her his lady fair-
(Even as you and I!)

Oh the years we waste and the tears we waste
And the work of our head and hand,
Belong to the woman who did not know
(And now we know that she never could know)
And did not understand!

The poem maintains Kipling's march tempo through the ruin of a man by a heedless woman who takes him for everything without grasping the sincerity of his passion. "Got a hank o'hair and a piece o'bone / And made a walkin' talkin' Honeycomb": Jimmie Rodgers' 1957 country music anthem also catches something of another character inspired by Mrs. Patrick Campbell (and performed by her), Eliza Doolittle of George Bernard Shaw's *Pygmalion*. Honeycomb was more open to love-struck appeals than Eliza Doolittle, Mrs. Patrick Campbell or The Woman.

The Woman was also called a vampire in the play titled after the first four words of Kipling's poem (A Fool There Was), written by Porter Emerson Browne at the suggestion of the actor Robert Hilliard, who played The Husband in the play's first Broadway performances in 1909.

Hilliard warned William Fox, the film producer who purchased the rights to the play, that he should sign any actress given the role to a contract since each of the six woman who was The Woman came to think of herself as Sarah Bernhardt and became unmanageable.[13] Fox did so, and after the 1915 film version proved a success, bestowed the "Arabian" name Theda Bara on the actress in the film to replace the less exotic Theodosia Burr Goodman. First name from Theodosia, and an anagram for "death," second name an anagram for "Arab." There weren't any major Arab actresses in the U.S. at the time.

The play included a monitory recital of the poem by The Husband's best friend. Copies also were distributed with the program, and toward the end a hollow voice recited it again from offstage.[14] There was a tableau vivant of the Burne-Jones painting in the play. The instrument of personal destruction in the play, in Browne's novelization of the play and in the film was the vampire's charms to lure men from the arms of wife and family, and to a life of decadence and remorseful alcoholism.

Kipling's poem assumes that it will be understood that the vampire of the title, not even specified or named in the poem, is the woman who takes life force, reputation, family, and property away from her victims without offering anything in return. Not even a show of affection. She is the metaphor of absorptive vampirism come to life, the female version of the aristocrat or the capitalist vampire.

The poem's lines appear at the beginning of the film. When The Woman appears in the film, not the first female character seen, she is maneuvering around one of her besotted victims, the title card reads "The Vampire" and gives the actress' name. Titles similarly introduce the other characters, except that each of them has a personal name within the transactions of the film while the vampire does not. She is an archetype.

As The Vampire enters a vehicle she is approached by a derelict who demands her charity as a man she has ruined, and she has a police officer drive him off. On the deck of the ship they have boarded to cruise to Europe her most recent conquest, Parmalee, comes close to her and raises a gun, which she makes him lower with light pressure from the bloom of a rose she carries. He then places the nozzle of the pistol opposite his own temple, and she comes closer, lips parted as if to kiss.

The card delivers the renowned line, "Kiss Me, My Fool," but their lips do not meet. Parmalee's body is face down on the deck in the next scene and The Vampire is nowhere to be seen.

The two key vampiric acts-the lethal kiss and the female vampire triumphant over the fallen victim-are not seen yet. A steward washes the blood off the boards. She soon attracts her next victim, the businessman and trade envoy John Schuyler (The Husband), who is distracted from his family by the sight of her preening out of a porthole.

Before long Schuyler has given up wife and young daughter, reputation and career to become a doll-like drunk, The Vampire clenches him in a fully visible kiss while his wife swoons against the friend who has been trying to reconcile the couple. Together with other men in a state of pliant inebriation he is flung around in a brutally submissive dance.

The Vampire, in a stand-alone scene early in the film, crushes a rose blossom in her palm, which she opens on petals and globular streaks of blood. The flower then becomes a stand-in for her ability to bleed men. She scatters rose petals over the face of the fallen man ("Some Of Him Lived But Most Of Him Died") in the film's final scene. Schuyler is undead, bleeding and bled, as orthochromatic film best can provide.

The novelization, published in the same year as the play's premier, contains an introductory scene neither in the play nor the film.[15] A French aristocrat arrives at the death-bed of a young Breton woman in her hovel and is shown her infant, his own unacknowledged offspring. He tosses off the name "Rien" ("Nothing") and casually removes himself from parentage. The infant will grow up to be The Vampire, who kills her father and ensnares wealthy men. The exploitative, aristocratic blood in her veins and her humble, abandoned upbringing will make her both predatorily vampiric and vengefully vampiric. The Vampire in her full flourish enfolds the recent history of vampire traits, and lives bordered by afterlives, of her mother, her father and her victims.

Theda Bara herself extended her new name to her family and so preempted the word vampire in her stardom that a new word was invented, "vamp," to name her and what she did to men. The vamp was an acting style that women could employ and evoke female figures celebrated for their maddening allure. At the 1917 premier of the Fox film Cleopatra there was a multi-ethnic pageant of vampires.[16]

The greatest historic vampire vied with merely historic vampires at the Lyric on Monday, when Theda Bara, the super-vampire, gave a matinee of "Cleopatra" to her man-snaring sisters. Miss Bara was the cynosure of attention in a stage box, but she was too overcome-no, not at the screen presentation, but at the applause-to do more than bow her acknowledgments. Senorita Lupita Perea, famed throughout Mexico for her deadly beauty and charm, had a particularly "come hither" look in her eye. Yosan, the Chinese vampire, mingled with the throng, and Blanche Johnson announced as the most renowned Ethiopian enchantress of Harlem. Mme. Yenika Lupotosky claimed supremacy among Russian vampires.

A vamp diversity not emulated in the films of the day.

A Fool There Was became Theda Bara's signature piece so memorably that a 1914 comedy short by the same title about a man whose wife inveigles him into getting her a car was retitled *She Wanted a Car* to avoid being overshadowed by its namesake. The out of context absurdity of the vamp(ire) was conveyed in the myriad of songs on the largely comic effects of vamping, with shaking shoulders and "Theda Bara looks".[17] She was comfortable in other roles in 1919, so weary was she of going about everyday tasks among people expecting her always to be her best known film persona, an early complaint of the burdens of movie stardom.[18]

A remake of *A Fool There Was* in 1922 did not star Theda Bara, and was disadvantaged by the succession from vamp to flapper, and the constrictions of film censorship.[19] Taking advantage of her unique position, Theda Bara weakly paraded her vamp style surrounded by slapstick in *Madame Mystery* (1926), directed by Stan Laurel.

The male-female cycle of balances in the vampire shifted back to the explicitly and surgically blood-seeking, female-dominating male with the production of *Nosferatu* (1922) that attempted to avoid the closely guarded copyright of *Dracula* through changes in names, time period and locations. The main female victim of *Nosferatu* sacrifices herself to lure the male vampire into the dawn light that disintegrates him. None of this prevented Mrs. Bram Stoker from enforcing the copyright and having most copies of the film seized and destroyed. *Nosferatu* did, however, return from the dead.

The authorized *Dracula* play of 1924-27 formed the basis for the 1931 film which made the Dracula that many people who became pop culture consumers in the mid-twentieth century equate with vampires in general. A resolution of the vamp was provided by F.W. Murnau, the director of *Nosferatu*, when in 1927 he released *Sunrise*, a film with no explicit connection to vampires.

A countryman is seduced by the bright lights of the big city and an entertainer who spots him as an easy mark. He conspires to take his wife on a fatal boat trip but loses her to the waves during a storm when he turns back in a fit of remorse. He renounces the city woman and ultimately is reunited with his forgiving wife who has been rescued, and returned from the dead.

The vampire gender politics of blood and living death also took the turn of the vampire dance.

---

[1] Car (1936: 6-7)

[2] Le Fanu (1872)

[3] Krafft-Ebing (1882: 70)

[4] Krafft-Ebing (1882: 88)

[5] Field (1893). The Beardsley drawing is not present in the scanned text of the *Pall Mall Magazine*, the first printing of the story, in the form available online (Hathi Trust), and neither it nor the text drawings are with the story in Field's story collection *Aut diabolus aut nihil* (1894).

[6] Munch Museum T2771:27(19) translated into English in Heller (1984: 129)

[7] Przybyszewski (1992: 154). The first version of the essay appeared under the title Psychischer Naturalismus, Psychic Naturalism in *Neue Deutsche Rundschau* 5 (1894): 150-56.

[8] Facsimile with English translation in Tøjner (2003: 115-16) Munch Museum T2547.

[9] Paul (1927)

[10] Stoker (1897: 39)

[11] It is included in the photographic catalogue of the exhibit *Art at the New Gallery, London* (1897), among the Impressionist landscapes and late Pre-Raphaelite works.Its whereabouts today are unknown.

[12] Letter from P. Burne-Jones to Stoker, June 16, 1897. Wynne (2011: 17)

[13] Sinclair (1933: 56-57)

[14] Hilliard recorded a recital of the Kipling poem for The Victor Company on April 24, 1911.

[15] Browne (1909: 19-26)

[16] *New York Tribune* November 23, 1917: 6

[17] Golden (1996: 161-62)

[18] Bara (1919)

[19] Sherwood (1922). "the vamp gave way to the baby vamp superseded by the flapper"

28. The Vampire Dance

There were not a few published stories, dramatic pieces (plays, sketches, dances) and after 1909 films with the word vampire in their titles, from European and American publishers, on the stage and on screens during the early 20th century. A number of them were spurred on by the republication of the Kipling poem in 1908.

Dramatic Compositions Copyrighted in the United States, 1870-1916 recorded 16 compositions with the word "vampire" in the title copyrighted between 1908 and 1916,[1] including a Yiddish drama (a Yiddish translation of a Russian revolutionary drama by Nicholas Dunaew), "a legendary story told in pantomime," "a realism in 1 act," "a sensational melodrama," a first draft of Porter Emerson Browne's play-in 1 act at this stage-uncompetitively called "The Vampire," and "the vampire's fool". This does not include a number of films that were recorded briefly in newspapers and trade journals, and vampire compositions that did not use the word "vampire."

"We have had three stage revelations of Rudyard Kipling's Vampire during the last season," wearily wrote *The New York Dramatic Mirror* on August 7, 1909, "a half dozen or so of Salomes and other semi-nude dances, to say nothing of several Parisian crudities of indecency. And now comes the combination of them all: Bert French and Alice Eis are responsible for this latest of dips into the world of suggestion and vulgarity…"[2]

The Vampire Dance: a tragic pantomime, that premiered on July 25, 1909 at Keith and Proctor's theatre on Broadway was a 17-minute exposition based on the Kipling poem.[3] A wood nymph, danced with abandon by Alice Eis, lures an artist, played by Bert French (who authored the program), into the forest where she entices him into an embrace. As she is about to fix her teeth into his neck he pushes her away, but she returns and transfixes him. He tumbles down the stairs of her lair and she follows, rising over his lifeless body at the bottom, consummating the Burne-Jones painting.

In earlier performances of the dance Alice Eis was a Paris prostitute drawing in her client-victim. Her transformation into a wood nymph allowed her to skirt serious charges of obscenity under the pretense of art. The scolding reviews only helped attract audiences eager to enjoy the loose raiments fluttering over flesh-colored tights as an evocation of classical refinement.[4] A San Francisco reviewer compared Alice Eis, always the central figure in the paired dance, with the classical and exotic dancers Maud Allen, Gertrude Hoffmann and Ruth St. Denis rather than with vaudeville dancers.[5]

In 1897, the year of Burne-Jones' painting and Kipling's poem, the stage performer and prolific novelist Florence Marryat published *The Blood of the Vampire.* Harriet Brandt is the daughter of a German scientist and a voodoo priestess who settles in England after she is forced to flee Haiti to escape a slave revolt. The incomprehensible pull of her wild beauty innocently draws in followers who are drained of psychic energy and destroyed without any malicious intent on her part. There are no walking dead in the novel, and the blood of the title is Harriet's biracial heritage which Marryat merged with contemporary spiritualism to account for her fatal attractiveness.

There are no references to dancing in the novel other than an offhand introduction of the tarantella. It signals the arrival of the exotic other mingled with the European as the key element in the "vampire" woman's deadly charms.

Another element entering into the mix shortly before the first performances of the vampire dance was a French import, the Apache. This was a paired dance said to be derived from clashes between members of Paris street gangs. It was worked for presentation onstage as a *discussion* between a male and female dancer, a pimp and a prostitute. The man deftly raised and swung the woman, made to hit and punch her while she recoiled. She then slid to the floor and revived, sometimes returning to the man with blows of her own.

"It opened with a crude-exceedingly crude-exposition of the Apache dance in two," continued the *Dramatic Mirror* article commenting on the Alice Eis and Bert French Vampire Dance, "playing upon the sordid brutalities of this disgusting theme." In early September, 1909 the same theatrical newspaper reported another vampire dance had opened, this with the dancers, Smith and Donaldson, executing their moves in evening dress in a parlor setting.[6] The attempt at sophistication only led the reviewer to compare the new effort unfavorably to that of Eis and French.

The Apache required the flexibility and agility on the part of the woman that was also critical to the effect of the vampire dance. French and Eis were signed for a stint at the Coliseum Theatre in London, while another pair of vampire dancers executed their moves at the Hippodrome. A reviewer for *London Magazine* wrote a detailed description of the interchanges that formed the drama of the dance, mingled with his expressions of disapproval.[7]

Amidst wild scenery a young man picks a blood red rose. As he presses it to his lips the petals scatter, the sun goes out, and from the darkness shines a blood red light, which reveals the vampire crouched watching him, in her lair….rising she swoops and slides and glides round her prey, till maddened by her bewitchments, he seizes her in his arms. He kisses her lips and as he lifts his face the vampire flies at his throat and tries to set her teeth in it. Horror-struck the wretched man pusher her away. She falls silently to the ground, formless, boneless like a dead snake (the whole proceeding is so utterly debased that only the lower animals forms suggest themselves in comparison), but in a moment with horrible, wormlike movements, she slides near him again. Now he runs from her, fighting for life but again she allures him as a snake a bird; and as he kisses her again he falls backwards to the ground, the vampire's teeth fast-fixed in his throat. For a moment he lies half-dead, while the Thing regards him with foul triumphant eyes. Then, in a last desperate effort to escape he rolls in a final ghastly agony down, down, down the steps of her lair, stark terror staring from his eyes, his mouth crooked. The Vampire woman comes snake-fashion after him, crouches bestial, and, with a sudden savage spring, is spread across her wretched victim, her sharp teeth in his throat…It is a horrid story."

The dance can be seen as an Apache in which the woman triumphs vampirically as in the Burne-Jones painting, or as Dracula's sister actually biting Harker, though the vampire of this dance is the lethal snake rather than the bloodsucker. The theriomorphic vampire executes dance rhythms across the blood-lit stage.

The vampire dance was imitated by other dancers. Mildred Deverez and Tom Terriss (Thomas Herbert F. Lewin) were performing their version in London in early 1910, and in September of that year included it in a Manhattan theatre program that centered on a *Scrooge* (*A Christmas Carol*) dramatization and a Medusa pantomime.[8] Touring cities across the United States during 1910-11 was Harry Bulger's musical comedy with orchestra and "barefoot chorus", *The*

Flirting Princess that included Joseph C. Smith dancing the Apache with Adele Rowland and the vampire dance with Vera Michelena.[9] Charles Morgan, who performed the vampire dance at other venues with the *The Flirting Princess* troupe, claimed to have invented the dance after viewing the Burne-Jones painting in a London gallery 12 years earlier.[10]

Alice Eis and Bert French developed other dances that framed the female role in a similar way, The Red and the Black (Le Rouge et le Noir), the Dance of the Temptress, and with the vampire dance performed this repertory on tour, in the United States and Europe over the following years. Eis' scrapbook of clippings preserved a record of her appearances between January 1913 and April 1915.[11] In The Red and the Black Alice Eis is Fortune covered with jewels each of which she gives away to a gambler until only one jewel remains. The gambler loses all in his attempt to acquire that one, and ends fallen before the triumphant Fortune. The Temptress inhabits a spring, her costume composed of stylized, gem-like bubbles. She lures an adventurer, who resists her but finally succumbs when she captures him with a perfumed, poisonous flower.

The photographs that accompany the scrapbook articles show Alice Eis full length in one of the expansive gestures of her performance, or in profile with a view of her spangled headdress. They also make clear as best low resolution photos of the day could the area of skin uncovered by the light and streaming fabric. The jewels and the bubbles of her later dances were variants of the vampire garb.

She commented at times that her movements were based on the slink of tigers seen in the zoo, which emphasized the sinuous watchful predation of her attack, calling upon the audience to attend to each move and the exposures it could bring.

The vampire was the center point of a dance form criss-crossed by contrasts. In the larger history of the life force and its imagery the vampire dance was the structural opposite of the necrophiliac attacks of Bertrand and company. The very much alive woman struggled with, overcame and killed a living man, rather than a living man having his way with a dead woman. The dance was on stage and illuminated; the tomb desecration was secretive, in a graveyard, at night. Both required adroitness, and both were subject to censure from which the performers escaped. Alice Eis and Bert French were arrested several times for obscenity and were soon released to perform again; Bertrand was captured and imprisoned for only a year because his activity was a performance not unknown within the militaty. The life-death and male-female dialectic of vampirism was modeled in the dance. So was the property-poverty/power-weakness dialectic that became emphatic with the vampire metaphor of acquisition in the late nineteenth century and yet more emphatic when crossed by the male-female axis. The faintest hint of a racial dialectic also is present in the remark of one article Alice Eis collected in her scrapbook that she was a "brown girl". Little information is available on her origins. She once remarked in the midst of comparing European and American dance styles that she was from Dayton, Ohio.[12]

Another important axis of contrast seeking resolution in this performance was dance as art versus dance as vaudeville. Denounced from the first instances for vulgarity and violation of the minimum standards of the terpsichorean art, this reaction occasioned attempts to refine it into evening dress or at least away from the garish. "Vampire dance at Mechanics' Fair not a bit shocking," a San Francisco reporter wrote in 1913.[13] Other dances replaced the vampire dance in Eis and French's repertory, and the other touring shows no longer presented it by 1915. Alice Eis herself hinted that she would make the transition into opera.

The Kalem film company, producers of the film *The Vampire* (1915), asked Eis and French to recreate the vampire dance on the outdoor stage at their Fort Lee, New Jersey studio.

The dance was a component of a film with a plot resembling *A Fool There Was* also released that year. This *Vampire* contains a vamp whose scheme is countered by the dancing vampire.

Ambitious Harry leaves his farm job, and his fiancée Helen, to seek his fortune selling farm goods in the big city. His success, and his continued devotion to Helen, are spoiled by Sybil of the feathered headdress, who sidles over to him in an expensive restaurant. After his money is gone and he is fired from his job, she abandons him for other suitors. Helen comes to the city in search of Harry, and, escaping being forced into prostitution, finds employment in a dress shop. The desperate Harry spends his last cash on a gun he intends to use in a robbery. Whiling away his time before the robbery in a theatre where the vampire dance is being performed, he has a change of heart. He asks for another chance at his job, succeeds, rejects the newly reinterested Sybil and, encountering Helen, marries her.

The vampire dance has been inducted into the ranks of transformative moral apothegms, and turns the fool away from downfall at the feet of the vamp. The vampire dance is still being performed in the world of the film, which contains it as an abstraction, a hieroglyph equivalent to the lettering of the poem and the brush strokes of the painting. The film permits a further refinement in the direction of allowing the victim to bleed visibly after the bite of the vampire. This was not apparent in the dance itself or in the studio publicity shot above, but was possible in the dance as filmed, as is apparent in this still.[14]

The film preserved the vampire dance as a memory of the death and the blood shed by vampirism. The recumbent victim down to the detail of the bloodied neck recalls the Burne-Jones painting and the film *A Fool There Was*.

All of the earliest vampire films were derived from Burne-Jones/Kipling complex. The earliest known so far, the Selig-Polyscope production of *The Vampire* (1910), survives only in a still and a few frames of the final moment, of the white-gowned vampire bending over the formally dressed victim at the foot of grand carpeted stairway, an asp barely visible in her hand. The plot brought the fool to his downfall through the fascinations of the Cleopatra-like vampire despite the best efforts of his brother to buy her off.

A Danish film, *Vampyrdanserinden (The Female Vampire Dancer)*, released at the beginning of 1912, was also the first vampire dance movie. Here the vampire dancer's partner becomes debilitated and his young replacement becomes enamored of her as they rehearse the performance. She is happily engaged to a count and discourages his advances. In the culminating vampire dance at the end of the film the enticement, retreat, embrace, and bite in the neck of the fallen man meets with applause and flowers from the audience. The victim does not rise once the curtain is drawn: he is dead, having swallowed poison at the beginning of the act.

The film's story coincides with the vampire dance. The inexperienced young actor cannot separate the simulation of charm from charm itself and merges his love death with that of the character he plays. Staging the vampire dance deploys dangerous forces that are not controlled by stage presence. They have been removed from the stage into the film.

Later in 1912 the German film *Der Totentanz (The Dance of Death)* repeated this sequence of events substituting a sinuous dance of death for the vampire theme. The mandolin-playing singer's husband, an engineer, is injured in an explosion, and to pay household expenses she goes on tour with a composer who becomes infatuated with her and attempts to alienate her husband by sending him a letter falsely accusing her of infidelity. She struggles with her feelings for the composer, and when he tries to force himself on her during a rehearsal of his *Lied vom Totentanz (Song of the Dance of Death)* he had written for her she stabs him to death with the dagger she holds during her performance. She is seized by the police.

The female lead, played by Asta Nielsen, is not a vampire or pretending to be one, but is a performing artist working to support a debilitated spouse, and is caught up in the visual mesh of seductive death-dealing music (this being a silent film). The semi-nude dances that in addition to the death scene roused censure were in the middle section of the hour-long version of the film, the work not of the lead actress but of a professional dancer, Gertrud Leistikow, who contributed these movements and exposure to other films of the period.[15]

The crucial identifying feature of the vampire dance is its extractive lethality. The main female object in *Der Totentanz* is a singer who sways while she performs the smitten composer's work; the dance duties are carried by another woman who has no part in the plot. She is there to make the film itself alluring. The singer kills the composer, who has been driven to uncontrollable lust by his own song. The Burne-Jones vampire is placed under arrest. When the vampire dance is reenacted the following year in the American film *The Vampire* it serves as a morality play arrested in a didactic frame to set the wayward youth on the right path to worthy marriage.

Kalem Productions and the director Robert Vignola who made the *Vampire*, in 1914 released *The Vampire's Trail* which does include a vampire, a cabaret singer who plots with an unscrupulous reporter to stage a scandalous elopement with a man she has attracted. The singer goes to the man's house and is trapped there under quarantine placed because the infant child his wife has been occupied with has developed diphtheria. The man has the opportunity to see the vampire's indifference in a domestic context, and after his wife overhears her plotting with the lurking reporter, begs the wife's forgiveness. There is no vampire dance, no dance at all, and a little singing. The vamp's listening to ragtime records in a house where there is a sick child is the closest to the opposite of a vampire dance the screen might compass.

The distancing and dissolution of the vampire dance also was on display in the 1915 serial *Les Vampires* directed by Louis Feuillade. The title of the film refers to a black-clad criminal gang with connections to the highest levels of society and government (the Chief Inquisitor of the Vampires turns out to be the Chief Justice). At the beginning of Episode 2: The Ring That Kills, the Comte de Noirmoutier is seen at his Paris club quietly receiving a ring that will poison its wearer. He bestows this ring on the ballerina Marfa Koutiloff as a token of his esteem as she completes dressing for her role in the ballet *Le Vampire*. The count watches from his private box as she swoops in and preserves her arabesque as she bends to bite the neck of a sleeping damsel. Soon her bourée becomes erratic and she folds into an unballetic collapse on the stage as the stage hands crowd around her and the count hastily leaves his box.

The ballerina was assassinated because of her romantic connection with the reporter Philipe Guérard, forever in pursuit of the Vampires. Many adventures involving robberies, chases, disguises, explosions and poisonings ensue before Philipe and his companion Mazamette are happily married to Jane and Augustine, who also have been hunted by the Vampires.

There is no vampire dance in the film. The vampire ballet contrived for it enacts the Carmilla scenario and constrains the act of female upon female vampirism through the formal language of ballet. The ballerina cannot break her arabesque to the extent of actually reaching the victim's neck. The filmed vampire ballet, like the filmed vampire dance, ends in the "actual" death of one of the characters.

The arch-villainess Irma Vep is first encountered singing at the underworld hangout The Howling Cat. The letters of her name on the billboard outside reassort themselves into "Vampire" before Phillipe's eyes. The Vampires, the Apaches of the film, when given the chance, dance the Charleston. During the wedding celebration of Irma Vep and Venomous, the Chief

Vampire, they carouse, dancing on the table and taking target practice on a caricature of Mazamette. The profane wedding is ended by a police raid, and Phillipe's wife Jane shoots Irma Vep, who is about to shoot her. Female vampires in costume, gesture or name do not prevail.

Soon after the vampire dance debuted on New York stages in 1909 it was being offered alongside the Medusa dance and a list of others as a dance taught in dance academies. There was a lull in publicized offerings, Alice Eis herself changed male partners and took up singing, and then a slight resurgence in 1920, after the Armistice that ended the First World War. The touring Broadway musical "Take It From Me" featured Marjorie Sweet, "the vampire prima-donna"; "the after-war dance sensation of Paris, the Vampire's Nature Dance," was advertised at a few American venues. The vampire dancer's gesture of arms upraised and fingers spread out could be used to label a photograph of baseball players.[16] After 1921 the vampire dance had vanished from currency as a performance or metaphor.

During its brief career the vampire dance carried the cultural note of female vampirism before the reintroduction of the male predatory form, with *Nosferatu* in 1922

---

[1] Washington, D.C.: U.S. Government Printing Office, 1918: 2, 2458.

[2] The Vampire Dance, *New York Dramatic World* 62 (August 7, 1909): 19

[3] 

New York Times July 15, 1909: 7

[4] Erdman (2004: 120-21)

[5] Alice Eis' Vampire Dance at Mechanics' Fair, Tops Daring Dances, *San Francisco Call* 114, 98 (September 6, 1913): 6.

[6] Smith and Donaldson, *New York Dramatic Mirror* 62 (September 4, 1909): 20

[7] *London Magazine* 24(1910): 53

[8] To Produce 'Scrooge' Here, *New York Times* September 19, 1910: 7

[9] All-Star Cast at the LaSalle Theatre, *Chicago Eagle* January 29, 1910: 8

[10] Vampire Dance, *Cairo* [IL] *Bulletin* April 28, 1911: 2
[11] Scrapbook January 1913-April 1915, documenting the appearances of dancer Alice Eis and her partner Bert French, Jerome Robbins Dance Division Photograph Files, New York Public Library Digital Collection
[12] "Crude and vulgar" says Miss Eis of tango as danced here, *The Sun* [NY] June 8, 1913: 8
[13] *San Francisco Call,* October 2, 1913: 3
[14] The Vampire (Kalem), *Moving Picture World* 18,1 (1915): 51
[15] Toepfer (1997: 196)
[16] Week's High Spots Seen, *Washington Times* September 12, 1920: 10

29. Ideal vampirism

The vampire imaginary has survived dimension by dimension, from cruor to sanguis, from mortuary ritual banquet to lore about the returning dead, from lore to history, from history to literature and song, from literature and song to psychoanalysis, from psychoanalysis to drama and film, and from drama and film to all of the above. The changes through time from initial hopes and credulity to present skepticism and credulity runs into cycles mirroring inward along a corridor that leads to the future in versions of the past.

POLISH PEOPLE BELIEVE
HUMAN VAMPIRE EXISTS
Chicago Jan. 29 Wierd (sic) stories of
a vampire believed by the more ignorant in the Polish colony about the
South Chicago steel mills to have
slain and mutilated 10 year-old Walter Krupa, have thrown the community into such a panic that the managers of the big manufacturing industries
in the vicinity are finding it almost
impossible to induce men to leave
their families for work on the night
shifts in the mills.
Without crediting the vampire theory, the police think it possible that
the description may fit the real murderer and are scouring the county for
the missing man.

Stark County Democrat (Canton, OH)
February 1, 1907: 3

This was only one speculation about what happened to twelve year-old Walter Krupka when he did not return from an errand to pick up meat at the butcher's a half-block away from his home. His body was found frozen in the water of a swamp 3 miles to the south on January 24, 1907. The day of his disappearance, December 15, 1906, had been unusually warm for that time of year and the temperature fell and remained below freezing up to the day when a man attempting to cross the frozen slough on the way to his job at the International Harvester plant saw a pair of shoes protruding from the ice.

The police initially believed that Walter had wandered into the swamp water, fell and was frozen in place where he drowned. He still had the parcel of meat tucked under his arm. His father, Barclay Krupka, was of the opinion that the boy had been abducted and murdered, his body then discarded in the still fluid water that same day. Walter's mother, whose first name was not given in the article, told the police lieutenant investigating the death that Walter must have been taken by medical students who wanted to experiment on him, to cure his "simplemindedness" by drilling a hole in his head that would relieve the pressure on his brain. Walter had suffered his condition since falling down the stairs at the age of 5, and never ventured outside the immediate neighborhood.[1] After he was missing for over a day, relatives assumed that he might be visiting an aunt in a neighboring town.

The boy's father also told a reporter that his playmates told him Walter had been run over by a wagon. The driver then picked him up and carried him off at a gallop.[2] A woman who witnessed the accident told another reporter that the boy was playing by the riverbank when he was struck by a cart hauling dirt. The driver alighted, placed the unconscious boy in the cart and outdistanced her when she attempted to follow him.[3]

The police cut around the ice to remove the body, which was allowed to thaw, then examined by the coroner's physician. A jury was impaneled, but the inquest was delayed while Dr. Lecount of Rush Medical College completed his supplemental report.[4] Two women gave testimony at this first hearing that they had seen Walter wandering near the slough on the day he disappeared. A neighbor girl, Hannah Bloomencranz, told the jury that she saw Walter run over by a wagon driven by a Greek or Italian peddler who picked him up and drove off. A search for the wagon did not yield results.

"Suffocation, combined with external and internal violence" was the jury's verdict issued on February 7.[5] The jury "recommends that the boy's assailants be arrested and be held to the grand jury until discharged by the due process of law." They did not name the murderer. A severe bruise on the side of the head lent credence to the wagon or cart accident account, but the authorities refused to believe that a delivery driver would strangle an unconscious boy to death after hitting him with his vehicle.

The "external and internal violence" was not specified in the reports made public, but it was enough to put the authorities in mind of a lunatic who lured the boy away from home and who fed the children the wagon story to cover his unmentionable motive. This did not account for the adult witnesses who saw the accident and its aftermath.

The determination to investigate was just the same not geared toward finding a vehicle and its driver but toward finding an individual who would entice a child for purposes not even suggested by a detailed reading of the autopsy. "Police Will Investigate the Hungarian Colony" read the headline of an article following the coroner's jury verdict.[6]

The attention of Captain Storen was called to
conditions in the Austrian colony where Walter
Krupa's body was found, and the statement of a
physician of South Deering that incidents of his
practice indicated the presence of men in the
colony who were guilty of unnatural crimes. An
investigation of these conditions will probably be
begun by the police with the idea of fastening the
mistreatment and death of the Krupa boy on some
of the men spoken of by the South Deering physician.

There was no further news of the investigation, and no arrests or charges in the case were recorded by the newspapers. "Conditions" in the Hungarian, or Austrian colony, and specific men in that colony were the object of the investigation. The language of "fastening" the boy's mistreatment and death on "some" of the men already hints at a lack of concrete evidence beyond the alleged habits of these men known to a physician with a practice in the industrial area of South Chicago where the body was found.

The article in the Canton, Ohio newspaper that began this section was printed after the discovery of the boy's body was announced but before the verdict of the coroner's jury became known. Articles on the boy's disappearance and the coroner's jury deliberations appeared in newspapers in Chicago, Joliet (Illinois), and cities in Indiana, Wisconsin and Washington State. No other piece of writing on Walter Krupa mentioned the vampire explanation, or the difficulty inducing men to work the night shift at the factories out of fear of leaving their families unprotected. Canton had a large concentration of steel mills, and a large Polish-American settlement. The local newspaper addressed those who might recognize the backward beliefs of the more "ignorant" members of that community.

It may be that someone bilingual in English and Polish brought word from Chicago that the local newspaper deemed of interest to those aware of the local Polish community. From the dearth of information it is impossible to tell which of the Polish words that could be rendered into English as "vampire" was taken to apply to Walter Krupa's murderer.

In that same year Stanisław Wasylewski asserted that the *vampire* (*wampir*) as an undead bloodsucker was a Romantic notion that in Poland belonged in the historic-literary realm, and did not correspond to any of the Polish folk demons (*upiór, zmora, strzyga*) equated with it.[7] The *upiór* was a nocturnal revenant given to strangling its victims and did not take their blood. A survey in Poland confirmed that this character of the *upiór* was current in rural Poland.[8]

News that Walter had been strangled and transported some distance from his home must have spread in the Polish community soon after his body was discovered on January 24, and well before the jury's verdict was made public on February 7, quickly enough to be reflected in the Canton newspaper on February 1. "The description that may fit the real murderer" was not that of a vampire, but of an *upiór*, and the unnamed "conditions" in the Austrian colony that directed the investigation there following the doctor's statement may have been incidents of erotic strangulation.

Speculation can only go so far in the absence of critical documentation amid the evasive language of the coroner, the police and the newspapers that reported their findings. The immediate afterlife of Walter Krupa remained frozen. The word "vampire" was as much an evasion of awareness of certain practices labeled "unnatural crimes" as it was becoming a way to dismiss the growing visibility of unmarried women with the concurrent rise of the vamp.

This cultural bridging under duress, finding, dismissing and seeking the vampire, was finally institutionalized in novels and the movies. With the help of the First World War. An ideal vampire was made of unfinished death and copious blood.

Dr. Cohn tells the ailing world traveler Frank Braun that he has read in the Journal of Tropical Diseases of the bite of a tropical bat that induces a craving for human flesh. The symptoms are similar to Frank's. "Doesn't it seem to you, Doctor," Frank responds, "that all of Europe is afflicted with this disease, in fact almost half the world?...Tell the Germans and English, the Russians, French and Turks and all the rest of them that their war is a regrettable error, the effect of a contagious South Seas disease that creates cannibal instincts in human beings, and forces them to kill one another? If people were to realize the truth of this their war would be over tomorrow and the regiments would march in formation to the Institute of Tropical Diseases in Hamburg to be inoculated."[9]

The novel *Vampir* by Hanns Heinz Ewers was published in 1921, after the author was released from internment at Fort Oglethorpe, Georgia for activities on behalf of Germany during the War. In the novel Frank Braun also is released from an American prison camp, and proceeds to renew his relationship with Lotte Lewin. He has found himself reinvigorated each time he and Lotte are bloodied in an episode of mutual contact, though only the appearances and sensations afterward are described."Then it *was* the taste of blood," Frank exclaims to himself as he discovers the traces of the previous night's meal on his face and clothes, and on the visibly wounded Lotte. Frank Braun's faith in his ability to keep these cravings voluntarily in check once their source is understood is compromised by his own needs.

This is consensual vampirism: Lotte even insists that he partake of no one else but her. Lotte, who is Jewish, sacrifices herself to Frank's appetites otherwise likely to be quenched by savaging others. She hovers between death and life and will remain that way as Frank returns to her again and again to replenish himself, forestalling bloodthirsty warfare. The contagion of vampirism and the contagion of warfare are both scarcely kept in check as the exploitations of the world brings blood cravings.

Vampirism with its arrangements of blood and death, of life force exchange, provided a way to encompass the otherwise incomprehensible urges of urban sexual crime, diverse sexual orientations, and warfare.

This voluntary sacrifice of a female victim to bring a blood-seeking monster under control was also the denouement of the film *Nosferatu,* another fiction conceived on the model of vampirism after the First World War. The film was designed and produced by Arbin Grau (whose name is matched in the film's subtitle, *eine Symphonie des Grauens, a Symphony of Terrors)* and was directed by F.W. Murnau, both he and Grau war veterans.

The pre-release publicity printed in a German film magazine (*Buhne und Film,* 1922) included Grau's article on Vampires. In 1916 he was in the German army, billeted with other soldiers in the dwelling of an old Serbian farmer who on that dark and rainy night recalled for them the story of his father's death from a falling tree, and his burial without sacraments. A plague-like sequence of deaths was associated with sightings of the dead man. The first time the father's coffin was unearthed it was empty. The men returned the following day to find him there. A stake was driven through the heart of the agitated corpse, which was burned and the ashes scattered. The plague deaths ended.

The Serbian farmer showed the soldiers an 1884 document Grau transcribed. The vampire plague beset the town of Progatza, then in Romania, and the corpse of the man named Morovitch when exposed was found to be fresh and healthy, and to have teeth grown so long that his mouth could not close. The disposal was as the farmer stated, and the names of the officials signing the report were included.

Years later, on a trip scouting exteriors for the film, Grau encountered in Prague one of the soldiers who heard the story on that night. The man said he would travel from the ends of the earth to see the film.

The enthusiasm of the veteran, the typical (and historically late) vampire tale related by the son of the undead, and the absence of any other evidence of this incident imply promotional fabrication. The setting does introduce the war as a factor in the renewed vampire legend.

The name Count Orlok, the vampire of *Nosferatu,* recalls the Dutch word *oorlog,* war, and the Count's seaborn invasion of the town of Wisborg with his coffins of rats and native soil recalls the spread of plague with invasion and conquest. Most trenchant is the rhetorical question the land agent Knock poses to Hutter when he dispatches him to seal the Count's purchase, "And young as you are, what matters it if it costs you some pain-or a little blood?" This sounds like the charge soldiers heard when being sent off to battle by the leaders of their respective nations.

Another layer of this vampirism is contributed by the book Hutter finds at the inn where he stays on his way to Orlok's castle. It eventually allows him to make the connection between Orlok and Nosferatu, the predatory bird of night. Hutter brings the book with him to Wisborg, where his wife Ellen reads it against his instructions, and there learns how to destroy Nosferatu, who has been gazing at her from the window of his house opposite. She detains him with her beauty and blood until he disintegrates in the daylight he has not noticed until it enters the room. She sacrifices herself vamping the vampire.

By changing names and scenes, providing an independent origin story with official documentation and updating the vampirism to take account of more recent associations of the word, the filmmakers thought to avoid copyright infringement charges by the Stoker estate. They dissolved Prana Studio to vacate any claims and, as ordered by the court, destroyed most copies of the film, which survived to be boldly retitled in some copies in accordance with the corresponding characters in *Dracula.* The Stoker estate's authorization of plays and a film in keeping with the novel was in part to challenge the vision of the male vampire in the deathless *Nosferatu* film.

Absorbing the vamp into the role of *Dracula*'s Mina Harker to make Ellen in *Nosferatu* was a sign of a trend toward finding a female vampire to match the resurgent male. Life force acquisition shifts between the two genders, but gravitates toward the female.

The French-Algerian novelist, poet and painter Marcello-Fabri (Jean-Louis Faivret) in 1921 published *L'inconnu sur les villes: roman des foules modernes, The unknown upon the cities: novel of the modern crowds.* In this novel without individual characters ("*suppression des personnages*") Fabri personifies the coming war as both vamp and vampire.[10]

This fresh corpse woman (*femme vert-cadavre),* for her demoniac orgies, needs what is the most vigorous and the best in the nations. She must have youth sparkling with gilt or dense and robust in hob-nail shoes; she must have, for her bloody embraces, the powerful musculature of the farm boys and the factory lads, whom she exhausts with a single kiss, because her mouth smells of death like that of vampires.

The fresh-corpse woman dreams impossibly of dyeing herself with the purple blood of battles. This woman appears elsewhere.

Wilhelm Stekel's *Sadism and Masochism* Case 49, "ideal vampirism," is based on the notes of his colleague Dr. Graven on the psychoanalysis of the client he calls Mrs. Z, translated from Graven's English.[11] By "ideal vampirism" (*ideeler Vampyrismus)* Stekel means conformity to a thought-out pattern of vampirism: Mrs. Z never called herself a vampire, or used the word during the course of her analysis.

The thirty year-old woman, a singer and dancer, sought counsel because she had spent the previous eight months in a state of maddened nervousness, had no peace in her outbreaks of anxiety and slept poorly each night. Her soul had fallen into a deep black hole where slimy reptiles gathered in a blue light. Graven added that she outwardly seemed snake-like, with small reptilian eyes and sinuous movements. "In other words, she really seems as a vampire is imagined…In following her into this hell of a vampire, we will study and possibly free the soul trapped therein."

That hell began to form in her childhood. She was born in England of Native American and French-Italian parents, and at the age of 3 was brought to the West Indies. Her "hatred against all mankind" began when she was torn from her mother's deathbed, which set her on a path of sadism. She watched dock workers brutalize each other, and was excited by the sight of blood from the slaughter of animals.

Brought to Holland then to England for schooling she was mocked and isolated because of her dark skin, and left alone for long periods by her ship's doctor father. She had a lesbian affair with a woman of the same age, who influenced her to become a singer and dancer like her. After that ended she met a young man and became the mother of a child out of wedlock. She felt angry at herself for having betrayed her father's trust, and made hatred her weapon against the world. "From this all-consuming bond of hate awoke vampirism as the blood of hate."

She had sexual relations with women in which she imagined herself as her father, and the other woman as her. She pursued relations with elderly men, but married a man her own age who roused feelings of intense jealousy in her. Thinking of seeing him with another woman she imagined biting him, smashing his skull and tearing out his brain. The vampire nature rose in her and she could taste blood, longed to drink it, had daydreams of blood streaming down in the sunshine, would like to suck and swallow blood but wouldn't lest it cause pain. Her waking thoughts were entirely occupied with blood. She did not partake of red wine; she enjoyed blood oranges.

Her fantasies of killing her son, her husband, relatives and lovers, and keeping the corpses near her preceded the impulse to consume their flesh which she spelled out in some detail for the analyst. Chewing the fresh flesh but not swallowing it allowed her to sample the taste of blood. When she thought of tearing out the eyes of her victims it was to witness the eye sockets filling with blood.

This compulsion to consume flesh extended to sexual intercourse which became like death to her. A kiss evolved into tearing the skin and finally sucking blood at the side of the neck. Her wish to kill a girl and perform these acts with her never precipitated into a distinct method of killing. She had plans for eating her way through the body of a woman or man all the way to the heart's blood without thinking of the body as dead. "Necrophilia" and "necrophagy" were not appropriate to describe her projections.

Behind her dreams of gathering a harem of young women whom she would at first treat very well "lies the sadistic monster vampirism." Each day she would seek one out and tear her to pieces. This Graven related to her early lesbian experiences in London. She envisions herself as an extraordinarily beautiful woman surrounded by lovers. An old man and a young man come to her. She incites the young man (the father of her child) to kill the old man (her father), then kills the young man and lives for all eternity in a magnificent palace.

Toward the end of her analysis this changed. The young man brought an old doctor to the house of the ailing Mrs. Z. The doctor (her father) healed her, they married and lived together happily. She told the analyst she was sure she could make an older man happy, and that she wanted to avoid sexual intercourse out of a wish to avoid pregnancy. The birth of her illegitimate child is what drove her father to his death. She will not go to women; lesbian love brought her no joy.

"Her fantasies had troubled her to the point of insanity. A short time later she left off her parapathic ways and can restore herself and her child through reasonable employment. She is rewarded with life and awaits good fortune, when she can make the acquaintance of an available older gentleman. Thus is the monster in her, the vampire, tamed and rendered harmless. Here ends our engagement with the soul of a vampire."

"Parapathy" was Stekel's favored term for an outwardly unpleasant sensation enjoyed by a person; in other words, a neurosis.

The settled bourgeois life her often absent father tried to establish for her was fractured by the underlying vampirism stirred by her sexual revolt, having relations with women and having a child out of wedlock. Mrs. Z imagines herself a vampire and a vamp, devouring the life substance of men and women without taking direct control of murdering them. She would marry her father if that were not the utmost violation of the rules imposed on her, and is stuck in a hell of violently replaying that relationship and its destruction until it is resolved by analysis.

"The wild blood of a people of nature (*Naturvolk)"* flowed in her veins, which predisposed her to sadism, and to seek revenge against the whites who abused her as a mixed blood.

Stekel treated vampirism as lycanthropy, the fantasy of becoming a ravening wolf, as a form of psychosexual infantilism.[12] He classified it with the zooanthropy of childhood, where the infant takes the role of a bloodthirsty beast who can pursue and eat living prey without being bound by adult restrictions. Lycanthropy, like vampirism, was an epidemic condition, though in this patient it found individual expression rising from her own blood.

In Stekel's view Mrs. Z's vampirism was a reversion to the hereditary inclinations toward child-like animalism spurred by her mistreatment from the violent separation from her dying mother to the racist taunting she endured. Her sexual disorientation, promiscuity and lesbianism, were due to her attraction to and revulsion from her father.

Race as a hereditary driver of behavior, and the pathologization of sexual orientation are explanatory tools only within the cultural milieu of the analyst. They trace the cultural state of vampirism and the immediate afterlife in the early 20th century. Vampirism was appealing as a way of connecting childhood urges with the remote past of human behavior to account for the bloodthirsty turns fantasies can take. Stekel cites the case of a man given to sadistic sexual fantasies and "satyriasis" (volatile promiscuity) which he later saw fit into the pattern of vampirism, regression to infantile animal hungers.

The promiscuous use of the vampire as a metaphor for any draining and destructive activity involving literal or figurative death continued and expanded. "Vampire auto" was a phrase for a hit and run driver during the 1920's.[13] Vampire appliances drain current while turned off.[14] Stekel's Case 49 is the type of applying vampirism to fantasy reversions to a presumed animalistic bloodthirsty stage of human life. The resource is brought to bear on urban crime, warfare, racial domination and revolt against normal "bourgeois" life.

In the process vampirism has provided a context for the extension of the hunger for the life force of others into a life in itself which has become the subject of a vast literature and cinema, material culture and social and commercial forms. Vampires have merged with zombies to allow mass gatherings of the ravening dead. As seen in the death of Walter Krupa and the creation of *Nosferatu* a reach to vampires of the past, an infantilism in itself, is often a feature of this more immediate afterlife.

Death is conditionally overcome in the quest for life force of the present. The living dead do not have to return to coffins, or sleep in native earth, but they still require fresh blood, they still are contagiously infected with living death and they still are sexual beings. Lily Lewin in Ewers' novel and Stekel's Mrs. Z both prefigure this arrangement of the life force exchange copiously projected into fiction but with a tendency to realize itself in fantasy and real lives.

Dion Fortune distinguished psychic vampirism, which was a deliberate attack on the vitality of a victim, from psychic parasitism, which was unconscious and involuntary and, she believed, quite common.[15] She recounted the one case of vampirism within her personal experience, related to her in part by one of her tutorial students at an abnormal psychology clinic, and in part by the adept Z, who had dispatched the "presence" troubling a teenage client.

A young man who had returned from the battlefield allegedly to recuperate from shell shock had in fact been caught in an act of necrophilia, not unknown on the front lines, and escaped serious punishment due to his family's influence. In the absence of his attendant he was visited by his cousin, the teenage client, and had "vicious relations" with him. The ex-soldier at one time bit him on the neck and drew blood.

The adept explained to Fortune that Eastern European troops brought to the battlefield in France in death could attach themselves to living soldiers and "maintain themselves in the etheric double by vampirising the wounded". These devitalized soldiers became psychic vacuums who drew upon others to feed the vampire feeding upon them. "The earth-bound soul of a vampire sometimes attaches itself permanently to the soul of one individual if it succeeds in making a functioning vampire of him, systematically drawing its etheric nutriment from him, for, since he in his turn is re-supplying himself from others, he will not die from exhaustion as victims of vampires do in the ordinary way."

An example of this ironic triumph over death in the imagery of life force quest is a television series that premiered in January, 2017, running for 10 half-hour episodes on the streaming service Netflix. *Santa Clarita Diet*, billed as a horror-comedy, takes place in one of the large suburbs of Los Angeles, California. Sheila and Joel are real estate agents who grew up in the community, she a prom queen and he a football star, who married after high school. They are parents of a teenage daughter. In the midst of a house showing one day Sheila volcanically vomits quantities of a yellowish fluid which might include an organ.

Sheila discovers that she has no heartbeat, and that her blood is very thick. A neighbor's nerdish son explains that Sheila is both dead and undead. If she is not regularly fed fresh flesh she will decay and have to be truly killed. The bite of a bat or a monkey has been known to cause conditions like this but he is unsure how it happened to Sheila.

The libidinous Sheila attracts the aggressive attentions of a rival male agent. He accosts her in the backyard of her house, and what he assumes to be sexual biting escalates to consumption.

Joel finds her on the ground gnawing at the innards of the fallen agent, and they conspire to bury the rest of him in the desert. Sheila finds that tasting human flesh has given her an appetite which cannot be satisfied by animal meat or by cadaver parts. This is vampirism as cannibalism. Her attack on a rude driver yields a source of fresh meals she and Joel decide to refrigerate and prepare in the innocent-seeming form of smoothies and deli cuts.

They decide to kill and eat only "bad people," such as a drug dealer (who turns out not to be so bad) and a corrupt neighbor cop who becomes suspicious of their sudden devotion to lawn care and finds a human finger in their backyard. With their daughter and her boyfriend in on the plans, they succeed in acquiring enough corpses to keep Sheila fed. Some manuscript pages from an ancient Serbian book Joel finds in an antiques shop pictures a calamitous contagion with symptoms like Sheila's, and he is able to get a partial translation from the Serbian grandmother of the school principal.

Sheila's condition progresses to the loss of a toe which she painstakingly tries to repair. She bites a drug dealer in an attempt to kill him for food, and Sheila and Joel find him later having mellowed into a socially conscious folk singer, who has been infected with the same condition as Sheila.

He tries to claim Sheila as a soul mate so forcibly that the pair are obliged to kill him. They locate the only copy of the Serbian book from which the prints came in the possession of a scientist who confirms that Sheila does have a virus, and offers to prepare the cure from a formula in the book. The lack of a key ingredient, the bile of a Serbian, prevents her from completing the mixture. Joel is incarcerated in an asylum, and Sheila chained in the basement at her own insistence lest she lose control and go on the hunt for walking meals.

The series is played broadly in a declamatory way, which makes the occasional viscid upheavals of vomit, blood and body parts not to be taken other than humorously. Living death, contagion, the quest for the flesh of live humans, and the vigor, especially the sexual vigor, of the infected state, the potential for actual decay and uninhibited animalistic wildness all call back the past of the life force in its many phases, itself evoked in the search for the Serbian tome and its meaning. Sheila's hesitancy to be cured and lose her new found vitality is curtailed by the possibility of infecting her family or going on a rampage and becoming truly dead. She will carry forward the picture of the woman rising triumphant over the recumbent bleeding man, the vamp over the vampire.

This is vampirism perpetuating its elements.

---

1 Lost Boy's Body Found in Swamp, *Chicago Daily Tribune* January 25, 1907: 6.

2 Boy Killed by a Madman, *Evening Statesman* (Walla Walla, WA) February 7, 1907: 2

3 Body of Boy Found, *Wood County Reporter* (Grand Rapids, WI) January 31, 1907: 6

4 Krupa Inquest is Begun, *Lake County Times* (Hammond, IN) February 1, 1907: 3

5 Declares Boy Murdered, *Chicago Daily Eagle* February 16, 1907: 9

6 *Lake County Times* February 8, 1907: 3

7 Wasylewski (1907)

8 Fischer (1926)

9 Ewers (1934: 183)

10 Marcello-Fabri (1921: 80)

[11] Stekel (1925: 626-32)
[12] Stekel (1922: 250-54)
[13] "Vampire" auto leaves victim dead in the street, *Chicago Daily Times* January 14, 1920: 1
[14] *Consumer Reports* March, 2017
[15] Fortune (1930: 26)

30. Means of Continuation

The plague of the imagination continues to spread horizontally, to include elements such as cannibalism and serial killing, and vertically, to include blood-taking and life force absorption from unrelated traditions. Many activities-commerce, politics, fashion, religion, medicine, literature and filmmaking-invite the performance and metaphor of vampirism.

Two species of blood-taking, the result of actual and hoped-for technological developments, have recently attracted vampirism labeling: the blood of the poor and the blood of the young.

The blood of the poor had been the object of non-metaphoric extractive interest for centuries, as in the story related by the alchemist Robert Fludd (see page 173), but never systematically and to an industrial degree. Individual vampires may have preyed intrusively upon the indigent or the advantaged; corporate enterprises, perhaps directed by individual vampires, made it desirable or even necessary for the poor to offer up their blood for pay.

The maturation of the market for blood products, for instance with the development and spread of efficient blood extraction technologies, provided ripe occasion for the application of the vampirism metaphor to individuals and institutions. Often it was projected from the outside by reporters and commentators, who sometimes carried the voices of those affected.

Inmates at the Cummins Prison Farm in Arkansas referred to Dr. Austin Stough, who operated a "blood concession" there from 1963 to 1967, as "the vampire."[1] The blood concession was a plasmapheresis center where the plasma of blood donors was separated from its cellular contents, which were returned to the donors, sometimes not to the donors who gave it.

Dr. Stough became a prison physician in Oklahoma in 1937 soon after completing medical school, and established his first plasmapheresis and drug testing center there in 1962, then extended his operation to prison facilities in Arkansas and Alabama during the 1960's. He was charged with endangering the health of inmates, several of whom died as a result of faulty equipment and careless procedures, and of providing dangerously inaccurate test results to the pharmaceutical companies that contracted with him. Several of his operations were closed by state authorities, though they were ignored by federal regulators.[2]

Dr. Stough's enterprise was continued in the urban market by his son following his death in 1972. His career marked the early days of the harvesting of blood products to supply the growing demand in developed countries, and the resort to impoverished and subject populations to meet the supply. He also was among the first to bring together blood collection and the accusation of vampirism since the bloodletting excesses of the early 19th century.

The advent of Western medical procedures in Africa was the occasion for European and American writers to apply the vocabulary and the imagery of vampirism to the reaction of African people. Witnessing and experiencing these procedures encouraged the belief that their practitioners were intent upon extracting one more natural resource from African colonial subjects, the vital bodily fluid.

Luise White, in the course of fieldwork in Kenya, "heard stories of the firemen in colonial Nairobi who captured Africans and took their blood."[3] She was assured that this was true, and became interested in tracing the origin of the stories, to find the missing piece of the puzzle that would explain a flat representation of firemen as bloodsuckers. Instead she found a "maze, or a maze of mazes" that would not relieve the expectation that there was a simple origin story behind the tale of the firemen.

Firemen may have become associated with theft of blood because of their white supervisors, their dark uniform and the buckets they carried, as well as ambiguities of the word naming them. Neither firemen nor any of the other categories of employee accused of taking blood were called vampires or an equivalent name by those White interviewed. She only used the word "vampire" because of its general meaning to English readers, for the same reason she used the word "witch" for other types of magic-using assailants.

She also referred to the "vampires" as "bloodsuckers," though that was no more the alleged habit of the Kenyan, Ugandan or Zambian blood-takers than it was of the night visitors designated bloodsuckers by German and other European writers in the early 18th century. Vampires proliferate in this way, now advanced by their massive presence in media circling the world.

Rumors spread in urban Malawi in late 1968 that a series of gruesome murders in Chilobwe, a section of the commercial capital Blantyre, was the work of government agents who were "draining the victims' blood and sending it to South Africa to repay a loan."[4] This was allegedly done while the victims were asleep.

At this time the government of President Hastings Banda was one of few sustaining diplomatic and economic relations with the apartheid regime. South African mining concerns recruited workers in Malawi with government approval. Banda alleged that the murders were one more plot by dissident ministers to defame his rule and replace him. None of the reported rumors or official declarations included any mention of vampires at work. Men who were tried for the murders the following year in 1969 were acquitted for lack of evidence. In 1970 a "possible gang member" named Kawisa confessed to several of them, and was hanged for his crimes.

Subsequent eruptions of stories of blood-taking by sinister agents in Malawi only included the vampire label when reported in news sources outside Africa. A 2002 article in the New York Times began with the paragraph:[5]

Rumors that the government of that land-locked southern African country was colluding with vampires to collect human blood in exchange for food sent terrified villagers fleeing, wire services reported last week. A suspected vampire helper was stoned or beaten to death; three priests were attacked and a foreign aid encampment identified as vampire headquarters was destroyed.

The author spends the rest of the article citing incidents in earlier European history of social upheavals spurred or accompanied by acts named vampirism. Presumably the Malawian villagers were responding to the same territorial and economic anxieties that motivated Europeans of an earlier age to fear bloodsuckers.

In October, 2017 news services once again promulgated reports of mobs killing accused "vampires" or "bloodsuckers" in Malawi.[6] There was still a belief that the government had made arrangements to supply outside agents with blood, but this time the recipients of the blood were said to be international aid organizations who gave food aid in exchange for the precious fluid. Beliefs associated with "witchcraft" also resurfaced: the blood was being taken for use in rituals designed to make the purchaser wealthy.

Malawi police told reporters that they had no evidence of bloodsucking, and a Member of Parliament (perhaps unwisely) offered a large sum of money to anyone who could prove that bloodsucking had actually taken place. Health workers carrying stethoscopes and drivers with battery jumper cables in their vehicles, anything that might appear to be an extractive device, were objects of suspicion. United States Peace Corps volunteers and UN personnel were withdrawn from some parts of Malawi. In a replay of a 2002 event three Roman Catholic priests were rescued by a woman who recognized them as priests. Foreigners or even Malawians unfamiliar to the residents of a specific area and equipped with an unusual apparatus were in danger.

Politicians of the party in power accused their opponents of fomenting the rumors and encouraging the mobs in the run-up to October 17 polls, to create an atmosphere of insecurity in the country. The major difference between the 2017 vampire scare and those of earlier years was the assimilation of individual enterprise to the suspicious activities of corporate bodies. The language of vampires and bloodsuckers was adopted in the English-medium quarters of the country, but was still imposed on the reports by the foreign media eager to find "uneducated" people responding to vampire fictions as if they were real.

One reason for the 1968 rumors of Malawi blood being sent to South Africa to repay national debt may have been the opening of plasmapheresis centers in the region of Transkei and the independent country of Lesotho. It is possible that Malawian workers sold their blood for extraction of the plasma in these centers and word spread back to the home country where it became associated with bloody murders tokening involuntary extraction.

Dr. Ben G. Grobbelaar, who was medical director of the Natal Blood Transfusion Service as a well as on the Executive Council of the International Society of Blood Transfusion, had come to the conclusion that unpaid donation of blood could not meet international demand.[7] He set up centers in low income areas, paying an amount for a set quantity of blood that exceeded the workers' average daily wage. He sold the collected plasma abroad at a considerable mark-up. Grobbelaar considered himself a benefactor of those who supplied the blood, though his colleagues did not all agree.

If this extraction entered rumor in Malawi as blood-taking, occasioned violent reactions, and was translated into vampirism in news reports, it did not garner those associations in South Africa. Between the late 1960's and the late 1970's the for-profit plasmapheresis business became established in many countries, but one place it documentably had the word "vampire" attached was Managua, Nicaragua.

Pedro Ramos, an exiled Cuban doctor, set up the world's largest plasmapheresis center on the grounds of a hotel owned by Nicaraguan dictator Anastasio Somoza. The payout per liter of blood was comparable to that offered by Gobbelaar-the equivalent of five to seven dollars a liter. The sum was as good a wage in earthquake-ravaged (1972) Managua as it was in South Africa. The plasma was separated into fractions and sold at progressively greater prices to buyers in Europe and America.

The vampire label was applied in the course of a press exposé. The opposition newspaper *La Prensa*, under the editorship of Pedro Joaquín Chamorro, from September, 1977 through the end of the year, ran a series of articles based on reports about the activities of *Centro-Americano Plasmaferésis*, the corporate name of the Managua blood-purchase operation. The articles were initiated by the complaint of a woman to the police that her son had gone to "the hospital" to sell his blood and had not returned. Interviews with people waiting in line yielded quotes like the following:[8]

"The Hospital of Managua is the vampire that daily extracts blood from us by the liter," cried as he was waiting in line Mr. Manuel Portobanco, of the barrio Altagracia and one of the people who receive 70 cordobas for a half liter of blood.

Mr. Portobanco's home barrio was given to verify the source and suggest the impoverished condition of those who were selling their blood. The vampire was not a person but an institution. The entire series of articles became collectively known as "*cronicas del vampiro,*" "chronicles of the vampire." It projected an image of Somoza and Ramos, themselves vampires, preying upon the destitute poor of the city through their blood-collecting vampire.

The blood harvesting was even more direct exploitation of the populace than Somoza's diversion of foreign aid sent to lessen hardship in the aftermath of the 1972 earthquake. The articles were effective in mobilizing international opinion against Somoza and his regime. They did not get Chamorro jailed as his previous attacks on the Somoza regime did. He was assassinated in early 1977, an act that intensified revolutionary opposition and led to the destruction of the plasmapheresis center by enraged citizens.

Under pressure from Sandinista revolutionaries, Somoza resigned and left the country the following year. He was not granted entrance into the United States or other countries but was allowed to settle in Paraguay, under the rule of a dictator, Alfredo Stroessner, who himself was called a vampire in news media.[9] There Somoza was assassinated in 1980, probably by agents of Cuban dictator Fidel Castro.

The vampire rumors and identifications of the period of the global blood plasma trade, from the late 1960's to the late 1970's, were for the most part stirring in the internationalized flow of news and comment, and the broadening audience.

After the death of his patron, the Haitian dictator François Duvalier, in 1971, militia head Luckner Cambronne with the support of a Miami businessman, set up a plasmapheresis center in Port-au-Prince, and in a manner similar to the operations in American prisons, Transkei-Lesotho and Managua, offered destitute residents a premium for their blood. Duvalier's son, who had assumed power, ended the enterprise late in 1972.[10] Cambronne was the recipient of the title "vampire of the Caribbean" though it is not clear whether it was imposed by outside news sources or circulated within Haiti.[11] The plasma sent to the U.S. did serve as a source for the spread of Human ImmunoVirus (HIV) during the early 1970's.

In the midst of the blood donation crisis in China in the 1990's prompted by the presence of HIV in the blood supply, officials charged with compelling donations defended themselves against the criticism that they were "vampires."[12] The expresssion they used, *xixuegui* (吸血鬼 suck-blood-demon) was constructed from the European, probably German, bloodsucker terminology of the 19th century. Chinese lore had its life force absorbers both male and female but none specifically dedicated to taking blood until the advent of the vampire complex which was then applied to blood donations.

Blood banks were a natural subject of anxiety-dispelling vampire humor. A 2004 "report" in the English-language tabloid *Weekly World News* ("the reader should suspend disbelief for the sake of enjoyment") has vampires in Romania picketing a blood bank "for refusing to let them make withdrawals that they say are necessary to supplement the meager and increasingly infrequent meals they can get from humans."[13] The vampires accuse the blood bank of drawing from donors in excess of the amount allowed by the Vampire Preservation Act, and drying out their source of nourishment.

During its twenty-eight year history (1979-2007) as a print publication (black and white only, after other tabloids turned to color) *Weekly World News* reported on vampires a number of times. A November, 1985 article registered the association between gays and AIDS during the early years of the epidemic by declaring "Dracula was gay!" and infected with the virus, according to a spurious German study.[14] The plague of the imagination had picked up another genuine plague and become attached to the generic vampire.

By 1993 the tabloid had dropped the gay-AIDS association and in a first foray into vampires and blood banks followed the quest of a female Romanian vampire to have blood banks established exclusively for her kind.[15] A spokesperson for the blood banks stated that there simply were not enough vampires to warrant such an arrangement. Vampires, known as lone individuals since the days of Arnold Paole, have become a species. In the tabloid the Romanian identity replaced the gay before being a vampire became a social identity in itself.

The vampire novels of Anne Rice, beginning with *Interview with the Vampire* in 1976 and continuing with the series known as The Vampire Chronicles in 1985 and after, were one evidence of the emergence of an imagery of vampire society. Some of Rice's vampires resort to blood banks.

Comment on any development in medicine that relates to the management of blood is susceptible to vampirism. A *New York Times* editorial on the end of the multi-decade effort to fashion an implantable artificial heart was titled "The Dracula of medical technology."[16] The program had earned the name Dracula by sucking 240 million dollars from the budget of the National Heart, Lung and Blood Institute, which had finally found the resolve to drive a stake through its heart and end it. Not the technology itself but the cost of the effort to develop it was the figurative vampire.

Both implanted and external artificial hearts were successfully tested, and have come into use as a bridge to keep patients with severely damaged hearts alive while awaiting a donor heart for a transplant, or because there is no alternative. Andrew Jones, who carried an external artificial heart in a backpack to sustain himself before receiving a transplant, said in a 2016 interview "I was essentially living as a vampire because I did not have a pulse."[17]

Jones was attached to a non-pulsatile artificial heart, which allowed him to compare himself to Dracula, whom Jonathan Harker, in the novel, finds in his daytime sleep without a pulse. In this present-day continuity of the vampire there is a discontinuity. The novel's recumbent Dracula bears many of the characteristics carried from the first bodies given the name "vampire": there is blood trickling from him (but only from his mouth), and he is to all appearances dead "no sign of movement, no pulse, no breath, no beating of the heart" (*Dracula,* Chapter 7).

Andrew Jones is anything but devoid of movement: he has become a bodybuilder in defiance of any invalidism that his condition threatens to impose upon him. The artificial heart vampire is, like the thoughtful, sensitive vampire of recent novels and films, the opposite of the cruentating corpse that does not move at all but somehow draws blood and life force from others. Jones also calls himself the best-looking zombie you will ever see.

Naming himself a vampire after never having been called one gives Jones a chance to add a tang of notoriety to his condition. Denying being a vampire after never having been called one can also add a slightly dark flavoring to a public reputation.

"I want to publicly tell you that I'm not a vampire. On the record, I am not a vampire," Peter Thiel assured his audience at the New York Times Dealbook conference on November 1, 2018. The statement was carried by news services, including The Independent, CBC and RT, and as a video clip on YouTube, but was not given notice by the major news services. The billionaire PayPal co-founder and venture capitalist spoke at the annual conference of "newsmakers at the intersection of business and policy."

Over the previous two years there had been reports on the "vampiric" start-up Ambrosia, which was allegedly "harvesting" the blood of the young for outright transfusions into paying customers for a sizable fee.[18] One of the claims of the website Gawker that incurred Thiel's ultimately destructive wrath was the unsourced tip they had received that Thiel spent $40,000 a quarter for "infusion of blood from an 18-year-old based on research conducted at Stanford on extending the lives of mice." An episode of the television series *Silicon Valley* seemed to be evoking Thiel when a businessman arrived at a meeting accompanied by a "blood boy" ready to deliver a rejuvenating dose (Season 4, Episode 5: The Blood Boy).

Thiel himself never owned up to actually getting such elective transfusions, yet his sentiments in favor of the supposedly life-extending treatments were archly defended as "vampirism."[19] In wide-ranging 2017 interview with *New York Times* columnist Maureen Dowd, Thiel said that among life-prolonging treatments he was "intrigued" by parabiosis, the bioscience term Thiel applied to blood transfusions from 16-25 year-olds to over 35 year-olds.[20] Thiel then referred to the 2016 U.S. presidential campaign, in which he supported Donald Trump, and called "the vampire accusations" the craziest of all the crazy things in this campaign. He did not elaborate on what he meant by the "the vampire accusations" in the campaign.

Several months later Thiel told another *New York Times* interviewer, Christian Lorentzen, that he was registered to be cryonically preserved if the life-extending promise of Ambrosia and other young blood plasma firms didn't work out.[21] Lorentzen commented, "Call it vampire capitalism," evoking the Marxian name of the vampire.

Thiel apparently did not want to dissociate himself entirely from vampirism because he evoked it by denying it again at the conference in November, 2018. That is the nature of the word in the contemporary environment. It can be the main subject of fictions and dramatizations which draw upon its seemingly forgotten history, or it can hover about any news of blood work whether it is a report of the science of anti-ageing transfusions or the practices of investors and managers of any firm, especially those proposing to extract blood or other vital properties from some and sell it to others.

A critical article in the online version of *Science* magazine on young blood trials does not allude to vampires,[22] yet a report on an article in the journal *Cell Reports* on a parabiosis experiment is entitled "the vampire molecule."[23] A 2015 article on a *Nature Communications* report on experiments using young blood to speed the healing of broken bones is titled "Vampire healing" and includes a reference to vampires preferring the blood of the young.[24]

Novels and films of vampires lent a metaphor to an immunology research report, "A new vampire saga: the molecular mechanism of T-cell trogdocytosis."[25] After the technical discussion the authors summarized:

…T cells that are blood cells themselves and take up protein complexes in membrane "bites" from other cells could be fancied as little vampires that feed from their victims without killing them.

The vampires here are the blood cells themselves consuming small protein bites from cells with their membrane teeth, a saga on the screen of the microscope. One characteristic of vampires from the very beginning of the plague, that they do not immediately kill the victim they feed upon, is preserved in this strictly scientific presentation.

Any report of blood-taking, even on the cellular level, invites the plague of the imagination. To discover the mechanism of continuation requires looking at similar scenarios of blood-taking where the repute and metaphor of vampirism might have arisen.

Jesse Karmazin, the founder of the Ambrosia startup, said he was motivated to conduct the young blood transfusion trials by early 20th century Soviet experiments.[26] Alexander Bogdanov was a medical doctor and prominent Bolshevik who envisioned (in a science fiction novel and then by experiment) a "physiological collective" of blood exchanges among workers that would keep them young and free of disease.

He was founding director of the state-sponsored Moscow Institute of Blood Transfusion in 1926, and undertook a program of exchanging his own blood with that of younger men. The results were invigorating for him, until he reached the 11th pint two years later. The man whose blood entered him was infected with malaria and tuberculosis. He survived the procedure and for some time afterward. Bogdanov died, but that did not immediately discourage the experiments.

Bogdanov was aware of his donor's infections, and expected that an infusion of his own uninfected blood would help cure the man in exchange for a dose of rejuvenation. His parabiosis doctrine was premised on a blood collective, not a one-way channeling of salubrious properties to an advantaged recipient.

A cartoon in the Soviet satirical magazine *Krokodil* (March, 1925) has a bloated tuxedoed man, the numeral 1 on his hat, reclining as he sucks on a tube emerging from the neck of a mine worker head bowed with the exaction.[27] "The advances of medicine in Western Europe," the caption reads, "The latest method of blood transfusion, which uncultured communists call the Dawes Plan." The cartoon only uses the then current topic of blood transfusion as a metaphor for World War I reparations that were draining German workers. The one-directional capitalist bloodsucking in the manner of Marx's critique, had nothing to do with Bogdanov's researches, which used transfusion for blood sharing.

When the author Rose George contacted Jesse Karmazin about his young blood trials she surprised him by pointing out how much a male model, a young man seated on a park bench beside a racing bicycle, on Ambrosia's website made her think of a vampire. The man was pictured to suggest the youth that could be recovered through a young blood transfusion, but George saw him as a vampire as defined by the *Twilight* series of movies and other representations of vampiric eternal youth. For that matter Karmazin himself, in his pictures a fit Paralympian rower, according to George doesn't look "far removed from his picturesque male model vampire."

George reacted to Karmazin's transition from Bogdanov's physiological collective to young blood enterprise by naming the vampire, and Karmazin reacted by removing the cause for the name, which still reverberates. Bogdanov's original project and the images it generated were

innocent of vampires, even of Marx's vampire capitalists, but it came within range of the plague when it was remade for consumption by the wealthy.

The vampire had its origins in the appearance of blood on a corpse and the night arrival of dead kin seeking one more family meal, which was then evidenced in the unearthed corpse. It was a construction of word and image that still spreads from one imagining to another.

A recent television series features the human product of genetic manipulation who is immune to disease, but also is a "lethal bloodsucking monster who we all are very careful not to call a vampire."

---

[1] Murton (1971: 24)

[2] Rugaber (1969)

[3] White (1990: xi)

[4] Power (2000: 158); Kalinga (2012: 91)

[5] Blumenthal (2002)

[6] Malawi cracks down on "vampire" lynch mobs, October 20,2017, http://www.bb.com/news/world-africa-41692944; Luke Bisani, Four things behind Malawi vampire rumours, October 20, 2017, https://malawi24.com/2017/10/20/four-things-behind-malawi-vampire-rumours/

[7] Starr (1998: 235)

[8] Nicaragua: desde el mirador de nuestra historia: Así era mercadeada la sangre humana en Nicaragua.https://eduardoperezvalle.blogspot.com/2014/06/asi-era-mercadeada-lasangre-humana-en. June 28, 2014.

[9] And later the subject of a novel, *Stroessner Vampiro* (2017) by Roberto Peña Cid.

[10] Impoverished Haitians sell plasma for use in the U.S., *New York Times* January 8: 2. Haitians end sale of plasma to the U.S., *New York Times* November 24: 13.

[11] Pepin (2011: 201)

[12] Guan (2018: 1123)

[13] Cornescu (2004)

[14] Vampires linked to AIDS, *Weekly World News* November 26, 1985: 35.

[15] Oncea (1993)

[16] The Dracula of Medical Technology, *New York Times* May 16, 1988: A10.

[17] Myall (2016)

[18] Hay (2017); Haynes (2017)

[19] Waldman (2016)

[20] Dowd (2017)

[21] Lorentzen (2017)

[22] Kaiser (2018)

[23] The vampire molecule: science discovers why young blood helps reverse aging, CBC radio, March 2, 2018 https://www.cbc.ca/radio/quirks/march-3-2018-detecting-the-first-stars-

young-blood-rejuvenation-acoustic-tractor-beam-more-1.4557129/the-vampire-molecule-
scientists-discover-why-young-blood-helps-reverse-aging-1.4557132
[24] Handwerk (2015)
[25] Topfer, Minguet and Schamel (2011)
[26] George (2018)
[27] Krementsov (2014: 172-73)

References

Abel, John J. 1915. Experimental and chemical studies of the blood with an appeal for more extended chemical training for the biological and chemical investigator, *Science* 42, 1074: 135-46.

Allatios, Leo. 1645. de Graecorum hodie quorundam opiniationibus, 113-84 IN *de templis Graecorum recentioribus*...Colonia Aggripina: Ioducus Calcovius.

d'Argens, Jean-Baptiste de Boyer, Marquis. 1737. *Lettres juives, ou correspondence philosophique, historique et critique entre un Juif Voyageur à Paris et ses Correspondants en divers endroits, tome V.* The Hague: Pierre Paupie.

d'Argens, Jean-Baptiste de Boyer, Marquis. 1755. *La philosophie du bon sens, tome premier.* The Hague: Pierre Paupie.

Armstrong, Mary Emma. 1917. *The significance of certain colors in Roman ritual.* Menasha, Wisconsin: George Banta Publishing Co.

Andral, Gabriel and Jules Gavarret. 1840. *Recherches sur les modifications de proportions de quelques principes de sang.* Paris: Victor Masson.

Aurelius Prudentius Clementis. 1845. *Aurelii Prudentii Clementis Carmina,* ed. by T. Obbarius. Tübingen: Heinrich Laupp.

B. Aegidius Columna. 1647. *Quodlibeta, revisa, correcta et varie illustrate.* Louvain: Hieronymus Neparn.

Baker, James. 1736. *A complete history of the Inquisition in Portugal, Spain, Italy, the East- and West-Indies*...Westminster: O. Payne.

Balfour, George W. 1859. Hematophobia: A historical sketch, *Edinburgh medical journal* 4,1: 214-24.

Bara, Theda. 1919. The ex-vampire: turning to the right in the motion pictures, *Vanity Fair* October

Barker, Fordyce. 1871. Blood-letting as a therapeutic resource in obstetric medicine, *Nashville Journal of medicine and surgery* 28: 158-70.

Bartlett, Robert. 2013. *The hanged man: A story of miracle, memory and colonisation.* Princeton: Princeton University Press.

Bellamy, Alex J. 2003. *The formation of Croatian national identity: a centuries-old dream?* Manchester: Manchester University Press.

Bercovici, Jeff. 2016. Peter Thiel is very, very interested in young people's blood, *inc.com*

Berger, Christian Philipp. 1737. *Versuch einer gründlichen Erläuterung merkwurdiger Begebenheiten in der Natur.* Lemgo: Johann Henrich Meyer.

Birch, Thomas. 1757. *The history of the Royal Society of London,* v. 4. London: A. Millar.

Blumenthal, Ralph. 2002. Fear of vampires can mask a fear of something much worse, *New York Times* December 29: 4,2.

Blumer, George. 1908. Thrombosis, embolism and phlebitis, 503-45 IN *Modern medicine,* v. 4, ed. by William Osler. Philadelphia: Lea and Febiger.

Bogdanov, Alexander. 1984. *Red Star: the first Bolshevik utopia,* Charles Rougle, trans. Bloomington: Indiana University Press.

Bohn, Thomas M. 2016. *Der Vampir: ein europäischer Mythos.* Koln, Weimar, Wien: Böhlau Verlag.

Botallo, Leonardo. 1660. *de curatione per missionem sanguinis* (1577) 95-244 IN *Opera omnia medica et chirurgica*, ed. by Joannis van Horne. Lyon: Daniel and Abraham.

Bourgault de Courdray, Chantal. 2006. *The curse of the werewolf: fantasy, horror, and the beast within.* London: I.B. Tauris and Co.

Brechka, Frank T. 1970. *Gerard van Swieten and his world, 1700-1772.* The Hague: Martinua Nijhoff.

Browne, Porter Emerson. 1909. *A fool there was.* New York: The H.K. Fly Company.

Bruhlichen, Martin. 1734. *Annales theologico-ecclesiastici…*Dresden and Leipzig: Johann Christian Zimmermann.

Bruno, Jean. 1864. *Madame Vampire, histoire de ta femme, avec une photographie.* Paris: Cournel.

Burgers, A. 1842. De l'action des composés ferrugineux solubles sur la vegetation, *Annales forastières* 634-42.

Burggraeve, Adolphe-Pierre. 1845. *Anatomie de texture, ou histologie.* Ghent: C. Annout-Braeckman.

Burmann, Pieter, et al., eds. 1727. *Pub. Ovidii Nasonis Opera Omnia, v. IV: Metamorphoseon, t. II.* Amsterdam: R. & J. Westenios and G. Smith.

Burmann, Pieter, et al., eds. 1821. *Pub. Ovidii Nasonis Opera Omnia, volumen tertium: Metamorphoseon.* London: A.J. Valpy.

Bynum, Catherine Walker. 2007. *Theology and practice in Late Medieval Northern Germany.* Philadelphia: University of Pennsylvania Press.

Caciola, Nancy. 2016. *Afterlives: The return of the dead in the Middle Ages.* Ithaca: Cornell University Press.

Calmet, Augustin. 1746. *Dissertations sur les apparitions des anges, des démons et des esprits., et sur les vampires et les revenans de Hongrie, de Bohême, de Moravie, et de Silésie.* Paris: de Bure l'ainé.

Calmet, Augustin. 1749. *Dissertations sur les apparitions des anges, des démons et des esprits., et sur les vampires et les revenans de Hongrie, de Bohême, de Moravie, &c.* 2 parties. Einsidlen: Princiere Abbaïe par Jean Everhard Kälin.

Calmet, Augustin. 1751. *Traité sur les apparitions des esprits et sur les vampires ou les revenans de Hongrie, de Moravie, &c.* 2 tomes. Paris: Debure l'ainé.

Calmet, Augustin. 1759. *Traité sur les apparitions des esprits et sur les vampires ou les revenans de Hongrie, de Moravie, &c.* 2 tomes. Senones: Joseph Pariset.

Capes, W.W. 1807. Introduction, 1-71, *Registrum Thome be Cantilupe Episcopii Herefordensis.* London: Canterbury and York Society.

Car., Emmanuel. 1936. Bertrand, *Détective* 410 (September 3): 67.

Carmeil, L.-F. 1845. *De la folie considerée au point de vue historique, pathologique, philosophique et judiviaire.* Paris: J.-B. Baillière.

de Carracioli, Louis Antoine. 1787. *La vie du Pape Benoit XIV Prosper Lambertini.* Paris: Rue et Hôtel Serpente.

Cathelinot, Idelfonse. 2008. *Reflections sur le traité des apparitions de Dom Calmet,* ed. by Gilles Banderier. Grenoble: Editions Jeremie Millon.

de Cauz, Constantin Franz. 1767. *de cultibus magicis eorumque perpetuo ad ecclesiam et rempublicam habitu.* Vienna: Johann Thomas von Trattnern.

da Ceglia, Francisco Paulo. 2011. The Archbishop's vampires: Giuseppe Davanzatis's *Dissertation* and the reaction of "scientific" Italian Catholicism to the "Moravian events," *Archives internationales d'histoire des sciences* 61: 488-510.

da Ceglia, Francisco Paolo. 2015. La scienza dei vampire: Giuseppe Davanzat e i confine tra vita e morte nell'Europa dell Settecento, *Atti Acc. Rev. Agiati* 265: 79-101.

de Charnacé, Guy. 1885. *Le Baron Vampire.* Paris: Dentu.

Chodźko, Alexander. 1829. *Poezye.* St. Petersburg: Karol Kray.

Claude, Antoine. 1881. *Mémoires de M. Claude, chef de la police du sûreté sous le Second Empire, deuxième tome.* Paris: J. Rouff.

Collin de Plancy, J. 1844. *Dictionnaire infernal.* Paris: Paul Mellier.A

Cornescu, Dag. 2004. Vampires picket blood bank! *Weekly World News* 25, 40 (June 4): 24.

Craven, James Brown. 1902. *Doctor Robert Fludd (Robertus de Fluctibus), the English Rosicrucian.* Kirkwall: William Peace and Son.

Culpeper, Nicholas, M. Ruland and Abdiah Cole. 1663. *Two Treatises, the first of blood-letting and the diseases to be cured thereby and the second of cupping and scarification and the diseases to be cured thereby.* London: Peter Cole.

Curtis, Thomas, ed. 1839. *The London Encyclopedia, vol. V.* London: Thomas Tegg.

Dansel, Michel. 1999. *Le cas du sergent Bertrand: portrait d'un nécrophile consequent.* Paris: Bibliothèque de l'Homme.

Davanzati, Giuseppe. 1774. *Dissertazione sopra i vampiri.* Naples: Fratelli Raimondi.

Denis, Prosper Sylvain. 1830. Recherches sur le sang humain, *Journal de physiologie experimentale et pathologique* 9: 176-224.

Denny, Harold. 1934. Artificial heart "revives" dead man, *New York Times,* October 31

Dopfer, Elaine Pashupati, Susana Minguet and Wolfgang W.A. Schamel. 2011. A new vampire saga: the molecular mechanism of T-cell trogocytosis, *Immunity* August 4 https://doi.org/10.1016/j.immuni.2011.08.004

Döring, Heinrich. 1833. *Die gelehrten Theologen Deutschlands in Achtzehnten und Neunzehnten Jahrhunderts, Dritter Band.* Neustadt a.b. Orla: Johann Karl Gottfried Wagner.

Dowd, Maureen. 2017. Peter Thiel, Trump's tech pal, explains himself, *New York Times* January 11.

Droz, J.P.,ed. 1746. *A literary journal for January, February, March.*

Duglison, Robley. 1832. *Human physiology, v. 2.* Philadelphia: Carey & Lea.

Duglison, Robley. 1868. *Medical lexicon.* Philadelphia: Henry C. Lea.

Dumas, Alexandre. 1861. *Les mille et un fantômes.* Paris: Michel Levy Frères.

Eamon, William. 1994. *Science and the secrets of nature: books of secrets in Medieval and Early Modern Culture.* Princeton: Princeton University Press.

Épaulard, Alexis. 1901. *Vampirisme, nécrophilie, nécrosadisme, nécrophagie, thèse présentée à la Faculté de Médecine et de Pharmacie de Lyon…*Lyon: A. Storck & Cie.

Ernout, A. 1922. *Cruor, cruentus, Bulletin de la Société Linguistique de Paris* 23: 23-27.

Ewers, Hanns Heinz. 1934. *Vampire,* trans. by Fritz Sallagar. New York: John Day.

Faucher, Jean-François. 1810. *Des indications de la saignée.* Draguignan: Fabre.

Feray, Jean-Claude. 2014. Les grands procès qui ont marqué l'histoire de l'homosexualité au XIXe siècle, III. L'affaire du sergent Bertrand. *Bulletin mensuel Quintes-feuilles* 17: 1-7.

Field, John Osgood. 1893. A Kiss of Judas, *Pall Mall Magazine* 1: 339-66.

Fischer, Adam. 1927. Upiór, stryzgoń czy wieszczy? *Lud* 26: 84.

Fischer, Friedrich. 1839. *Der Somnambulismus, Erster Band: Das Schlafwandeln und die Vision.* Basel: Schweighauser.

Forstemann, Edward, ed. 1846. *D. Martin Luther's Samtliche Schriften, Band XXII: Die Colloquia oder Tischreden*. Leipzig: Gebaursche Buchhandlung.

Fourcroy, Antoine-François. 1800. *Système des connaissances chimiques, Tome IX*. Paris: Baudouin.

Fourcroy, Antoine-François. 1804. *System of chemical knowledge, vol. IX*, trans. by William Nicholson. London.

de Franceschi, Carlo. 1879. *L'Istria: note storiche*. Parenzo: Gaetano Coana.

Francisi, Erasmus. 1690. *Der höllische Proteus, oder tausend kunstige Vorsteller*. Nuremberg.

Frazer, James George. 1919. *The Golden Bough: Part IV, Adonis, Attis, Osiris, Vol. I*. London: Macmillan and Co.

Fritsche, Johann Christoph. 1732. *Eines Weimarischen Medici Muthmasslichen Gedanken von denen Vampyren, oder sogennanten Blut-Saugern…*Leipzig: Michel Blochbergern.

Fyfe, Andrew. 1801. *A system of anatomy and physiology, v.2*. Edinburgh: William Creech.

Galeano, Eduardo. 1986. *Memoria del fuego: el siglo del viento*. Siglo XXI de España.

Galeano, Eduardo. 2004. *Las venas abiertas de América Latina*. Siglo XXI de España.

Gamwell, Lynn. 2016. *Mathematics + Art: a cultural history*. Princeton: Princeton University Press.

Garmann, Johann Friedrich. 1709. *De miraculis mortuorum libri tres*. 2 v. Dresden and Leipzig: Johann Christoph Zimmermann.

Gaster, Julia. 2013. *Theodor von Neuhoff, the King of Corsica: the man behind the legend*. Newark: University of Delaware Press.

George, Henry. 1884. *Progress and Poverty: An inquiry into the causes of industrial depressions…* London: William Reeves.

George, Rose. 2018. *Nine pints: a journey through the money, medicine and mysteries of blood*. Metropolitan Books.

Georgijević, Kresimir. 1936. *Srpsko hrvaska narodna pisma u Polskoj kniževosta*. Belgrade: Slovo.

Gerard, John. 1633. *The Herbal, or general history of plants*. London: Adam Islip, Joice Norton, Richard Whitakers.

Greenfield, Douglas. 2006. Revenants and revolutionaries: body and society in Bogdanov's Martian novels, *The Slavic and Eastern European Journal* 50,4: 621-34.

Giesecke, Annette. 2014. *The mythology of plants: botanical lore from Ancient Greece and Rome*. Getty Publications.

Giftschutz, Carl. 1825. *Ein paar Worte uber das Zauber und Hexenwesen*. Vienna and Trieste: Verlag der Geistingerschen Buchhandlung.

von Goerres, Johann Joseph. 1861. *La mystique divine, naturelle et diabolique, tome 3, seconde partie: La mystique naturelle*, translated from the German by Charles Sainte-Foi. Paris: Mme. Vve. Poussielque-Rusand.

Golden, Eve. 1996. *Vamp: the rise and fall of Theda Bara*. Lanham: Vestal Press.

Golębiowski, Lukasz. 1830. *Lud polski, jego zwycaje zobobony*. Warsaw: A. Gołęzowski i Spolka.

Gorlero, Cecilia Pedrazza. 2013. L'accusa del sangue: Il valore indiziario della *cruentatio cadaveris* nelle riflessione di Paolo Zacchia (1584-1659), *Historia et ius*

Gorvett, Zaria. 2016. The macabre fate of 'beating heart corpses'. http://www.bbc.com/future/story/20161103-the-macabre-fate-of-beating-heart-corpses

Grässe, Johann Georg Theodor. 1843. *Bibliotheca magica et pneumonica*. Leipzig:Wilhelm: Engelmann.

Grässe, Johann Georg Theodor. 1871. *Sagenbuch des Preussischen Staats, Zweiter Band*. Glogau: Carl Flemming.

Greene, Robert. 1727. *The principles of the philosophy of the expansive and contractive forces.* Cambridge: Cornelius Crownfield.

Gruhlich, Martin. 1734. *Annales Theologico-Ecclesiastici.* Dresden and Leipzig: Johann Christoph Zimmermann.

Guan, Yue. 2018. When voluntary donations meet the state monopoly: understanding blood shortages in China, *The China Quarterly* 236: 1111-1130.

Guislain, Joseph.1852. *Leçons orales sur les phrénopathies…, Tome premier.*Ghent: L. Hebbelynck.

Haeser, Heinrich. 1853. *Lehrbuch der Geschichte der Medezin.* Jena: Friedrich Mauke.

Hakelberg, Dietrich. 2012. For the sake of memory: practicing archaeology in early modern Silesia, 53-80 IN *Histories of archaeological practices: Reflections on methods, strategies and social organization in past fieldwork.* Stockholm: The National Historical Museum.

Hall, Marshall. 1836. *Observations on blood-letting.* London: Sherwood, Gilbert and Piper.

Hamburger, Klaus. 1992. *Mortuus non mordet: Kommentierte Dokumente zum Vampirismus, 1689-1791.* Turia & Kant.

Handwerk, Brian. 2015. Vampire healing: young blood can mend old bone, *Smithsonian* May 19 https://www.smithsonianmag.com/science-nature/vampire-healing-young-blood-can-mend-old-broken-bones-180955336/

Hartnup, Karen. 2004. *'On the beliefs of the Greeks' Leo Allatios and popular orthodoxy.* Leiden, Boston: Brill.

Harvey, David. 2003. *Paris: capital of modernity.* New York: Routledge.

Harvey, William. 1648. *Exercitatio anatomica de cordis et sanguinis motu.* Rotterdam: Arnold Leers.

Harvey, William. 1651. *Exercitationes de generatione animalium.* Amsterdam: Ludwig Elzevir.

Haumann, Heiko. 2011. *Dracula: Leben und Legende.* Munich: C.H. Beck.

Hay, Mark. 2017. Are rich people already infusing themselves with young blood? January 5. https://tonic.vice.com/en_us/article/kbwxme/are-rich-people-already-infusing-themselves-with-young-blood

Haynes, Gavin. 2017. Ambrosia: the startup harvesting the blood of the young, *The Guardian* August 2.

Heller, Reinhold. 1984. *Munch: his life and work.* Chicago: University of Chicago Press.

Hesse, Hermann. 1986. *Spuk- und Hexengeschichte aus dem Rheinischen Antiquarius.* Frankfort: Insel.

Hewson, William. 1771. *Experimental inquiry into the properties of blood.* London: T. Caddell.

Hildegard von Bingen. 1998. *Symphonia: A critical edition of the Symphonia Armonium Revelationum Celestium,* introduction, translation and comments by Barbara Newman. Ithaca: Cornell University Press.

Hoppe Seyler, Felix. 1862. Ueber die Verhalten des Blutfarbstoffes im Spektrum des Sonnenlichtes, *Archiv für Anatomische und Pathologische Physiologie* 23: 446.

Horst, Gregor. 1608. *Σκέψις de naturali conservatione et cruentatione cadaverum.* Wittemberg: Georg Muller.

Horst, Gregor. 1660. *Institutiones medicas, et reliqua scripta. v. 1: theoretica et spectantia.* Nuremberg: Endteri.

Introvigne, Massimo. 2001. Antoine Faivre: Father of contemporary vampire studies, 595-610 IN *Esotérisme, gnoses et imaginaire: mélanges offerts à Antoine Faivre*, ed. by Richard Caron, et al. Leuven: Peeters.

Jordan, Alyce A. 2009. The "water of Thomas Becket": water as medium, metaphor and relic, 479-500 IN *The nature and function of water, baths, bathing and hygiene from Antiquity through the Renaissance,* ed. by Cynthia Kosso and Anne Scott. Leiden, Boston: Brill.

Jenkins, Mark Collins. 2010. *Vampire forensics: uncovering the origins of an enduring legend.* Washington: National Geographic.

Jovanović, Voyislav. 1911. *"La Guzla" de Prosper Mérimée: étude d'historique romantique.* Paris: Hachette.

Kaiser,Jocelyn.2016.Young blood anti-ageing trial raises questions https://www.sciencemag.org/news/2016/08/young-blood-antiaging-trial-raises-questions

Kalinga, Owen J.M. 2012. *Historical dictionary of Malawi.* Lanham: Scarecrow Press.

Kirkes, William Senhouse. 1869. *Handbook of Physiology.* London: Lindsay and Blakiston.

Koropeckyj, Roman Robert. 2008. *Adam Mickiewicz: The life of a Romantic.* Ithaca and London: Cornell University Press.

von Krafft-Ebing, Richard. 1882. *Psychopathia sexualis.* Stuttgart: Ferdinand Enke.

Krauss, Friedrich Salomo. 1908. *Slavische Volksforschungen: Abhandlungen über Glauben.* Leipzig: Wilhelm Holms.

Krementsov, Nicolai. 2014. *Revolutionary experiments: the quest for immortality in Bolshevik science and ' fiction.* New York: Oxford University Press.

Kuhnau, Richard. 1910. *Schlesische Sagen,* v. 1. Leipzig: B.G. Teubner.

Ladouceur, Liisa. 2013. *How to kill a vampire: fangs in folklore, flicks and fiction.* Toronto: ECW Press.

Lambertini, Prospero Lorenzo. 1741. *Opera omnia in tomos XVII distribute: Opera de servorum dei beatificatione…, Tomus quatuor, Pars I.* Prati: Aldina.

Lambertini, Prospero Lorenzo. 1752. *Dissertationes in omni doctrina et genere selectissimae ex quatuor eiusdem auctoris de canonizatione sanctorum libri extractae.* Venice: Joannes Baptista Albritius.

Landois, Leonard. 1893. *Traité de la physiologie humaine,* trans. by Gaston Moquin-Tandon. Paris: C. Reinwald.

La Scala, Dominico. 1696. *Phlebotomia damnata.* Padua: Fratres Sardi.

Lavasseur, F.-L. 1861. *La Dalmatie ancienne et moderne.* Paris: Dentu.

Le Canu, Louis René. 1830. De l'hematosine, ou matière colorante du sang, *Annales de chimie et de physique* 45: 5-27.

Le Canu, Louis René. 1837. *Études chimiques sur le sang humain.* Paris: de Rignoux.

Le Fanu, Sheridan. 1871-72. Carmilla, *The Dark Blue* 2: 434; 592; 701.

Leger, Louis. 1899. *Russes et Slaves: études littéraires et politiques, troisièe série.* Paris: Hachette.ç

Leger, Louis. 1901. *La mythologie slave.* Paris: Ernest Leroux.

Leibowitz, Joshua Otto. 1970. *The history of coronary heart disease.* Berkeley: University of California Press.

Le Vaillant, Ondésime. 1858. Le Vampire, 23-28 IN *Au hasard du dictionnaire, chants sur mots donnés.* Paris: Appel-Vavaseur.

Lewis, Suzanne. 1987. *The art of Matthew Paris in the Chronica Majora.* Berkeley: University of California Press.

Libavius, Andreas. 1594. *Tractatus duo physici: prior de imposturia vulnerum per unguentum, posterior de cruentatione cadaverum.* Frankfort: Ioannes Saur.

Linzbauer, Franz Xavier. 1852. *Codex sanitario-medicalis Hungariae, Tomus 1.* Buda: Typis Caesarko-Regiae Scientarum Universitatis.

Lorentzen, Christian. 2017. Why are we so obsessed with the end of the world? *New York Times* (Style Magazine) April 6.

Ludger, Lunier. 1849. Examen médico-legal d'un cas de monomania instinctif, affaire de Sergent Bertrand, *Annales medico-psychologiques* 1: 351-79.

Malone, P. Colm and Paul S. Agutter. 2008. *The aetiology of deep venous thrombosis: a critical, historical and epistemological survey.* Springer.

Manget, Johannes Jacobus. 1695. *Bibliotheca medico-practica sive rerum medicarum thesaurus.* Geneva: Johannes Antonius Chouët.

Marcello-Fabri. 1921. *L'inconnu sur les villes: roman des foules modernes.* Paris: J. Povolozky.

Maxmen, Amy. 2017. Questionable "young blood" transfusions offered in US as anti-ageing remedy, *technologyreview.com*

Mayo, Herbert. 1849. *Letters on the truths contained in popular superstitions.* Frankfort: John David Sauerlaender.

McClelland, Bruce. 2006. *Slayers and their vampires.* Ann Arbor: University of Michigan Press.

Meinig, Johann Christoph (Putoneo). 1732. *Besondere Nachricht von denen Vampyren oder so-genannten Blut-Saugern…*Leipzig: Johann Christian Martini.

Mérimée, Prosper. 1853. *Chronique du règne de Charles IX…*Paris: Charpentier.

Michéa, Claude-François. 1849. Des derivations maldives de l'appétit vénérien, *La lancette française* (14 July): 338-39.

Michelotti, Pietro Antonio. 1721. *De separatione fluidarum in corpore animalium.* Venice: Pinelli.

Michelotti, Pietro Antonio. 1731. *Tractatus univeralis morborum sanguinis ductuum.*

Mickiewicz, Adam. 1828. *Poezye Adama Mickiewicza, Tom Drugi.* Paris: Barbelat et Delarue.

Mickiewicz, Adam. 1833. *The books and the pilgrimage of the Polish nation.* London: James Ridgway.

Mickiewicz, Adam. 1841. *Oeuvres d'Adam Mickiewicz, tome premier, traduction nouvelle par* Christien Ostrowski. Paris: H.-L. Delloye.

Mickiewicz, Adam. 1843. *Vorlesungen über Slavische Literatur und Zustände, erster Theil.* Leipzig and Paris: Brockhaus and Avenarius.

Mickiewicz, Adam. 1849. *Les Slaves: cours professé au Collège de France par Adam Mickiewicz (1840-1841) tome premier.* Paris: Au Comptoir des Imprimeries Unis.

Mickiewicz, Adam. 1882. *Chefs d'oeuvres poetiques d'Adam Mickiewicz, traduits par lui-même et par ses fils.* Paris: G. Charpentier.

Micyllus, Jacobus. 1543. *Pub. Ovidii Nasonis Metamorphoses libri quindecim.* Basel: Ioan. Huqvagius.

Micyllus, Jacobus. 1582. *Pub. Ovidii Nasonis Metamorphoseon.* Leipzig.

More, Henry. 1655. *An Antidote against Atheisme.* London: J. Flesher.

More, Henry. 1987. *The immortality of the soul,* ed. by A. Jacob. Dordrecht: Martinus Nijhoff.

More, Henry. 1712. *A collection of several philosophical writings of Dr. Henry More.* London: Joseph Downing.

Murton, Tom. 1971. Prison doctors, *The Humanist,* 31,3.

Myall, Steve. 2016. Man wirhout a pulse who "lived as vampire" with fake heart but transformed himself into bodybuilder, *The Mirror,* November 23 https://www.mirror.co.uk/news/real-life-stories/man-without-pulse-who-lived-9317510

N.G. 1592. *The English phlebotomy; or, method and way of healing by letting of blood.* London: Andrew Mansell.

Nichols, Anne Bijenholm. 2014. The footprints of Christ as Arma Christi: The evidence of Morgan B.54, 113-42 IN *The Arma Christi in Medieval and Early Modern Culture,* ed. by Lisa H. Cooper and Andrea Denny-Brown. Farnham: Ashgate.

Nodier, Charles. 1832. *Oeuvres de Charles Nodier, III: Smarra, Trilby, Mélange, Hélène Gillet.* Brussels: Eugène Renduel.

Nowasadtko, Jutta. 2004. Der "Vampyrus Serviensis" und sein Habitat: Impressionen von der Österreichischen Militärgrenze, *Militär und Gesellschaft in der Frühen Neuzeit* 8,2: 151-68.

Oakley, A. and J. Ashton. 1997. Introduction to the new edition, 3-13 IN Richard Titmuss, *The gift relationship: From human blood to social policy.* London: LSE Books.

Olrik, J. and H. Raeder, eds. 1931. *Saxonis Gesta Danorum.* Copenhagen.

Oncea, Aurolia. 1993. Blood banks for us, too! *Weekly World News* November 30: 39.

Oswald, Felix L. 1879. Relation of diet to yellow fever, *New York medical journal* 30: 377-86.

Pain, Olivier. 1901. Le sergent Bertrand, *L'Intransigeant* October 1: 2

Palomba, Giuseppe. 1812. *I Vampiri, commedia per musica.* Naples: Flautina.

Paracelsus. 1563. *Medicorum et philosophorum summi , Aureoli Theophrasti Paracelsi, eremitae, liber quinque, de causis, signis et curationibus ex tartaro utilissimi,* ed. by Adam Bodenstein. Basel: Petrus Perna.

Paracelsus. 1603. *Bücher und Schriften Philippi Theophrasti Bombasti.* Frankfort: Johann Wechels Erben.

Paris, Matthew. 1866. *Matthaei Parisiensis, Monachi Sancti Albani, Historia Anglorum, v. 1,* 1067-1189, ed. by Frederick Madden. London: Longmans, Green, Reader and Dyer.

Paris, Matthew. 1869. *Matthaei Parisiensis, Monachi Sancti Albani, Historia Anglorum, v. 3:* 1246-1253, ed. by Frederick Madden. London: Longmans, Green and Co..

Paris, Matthew. 2012. *Matthaei Parisiensis Chronica Majora, v. 6: Additamenta,* ed. by Henry Richards Luard. Cambridge: Cambridge University Press.

Pasquier, Estienne. 1619. *Les lettres de Estienne Pasquier, tome second.* Paris: Laurent Sonius.

de Passe, Crispin. 1602. *Metamorphoseon Ovidianarum.* Cologne.

Paul, Adolf. 1927. Errinerungen: Edvard Munch und Berlin, *Berliner Tageblatt* 175 (April 15).

Pegge, Samuel. 1793. *The life of Robert Grosseteste, Bishop of Lincoln.* London: John Nichols.

Penning, C.J.P. 1932. Iets over vampyrs, *Nederlands tijdschrift voor geneeskunde* 76 III 32: 3861-65.

Pepin, Jacques. 2011. *The origin of AIDS.* Cambridge: Cambridge University Press.

Pereira, Jonathan. 1847. *Selecta é Prescriptis: Selections from physicians' prescriptions.* London: S. Highley.

Perić, Boris. 2005. *Vampir.* Zagreb: Naklada Ljevak.

Peter, Anton. 1867. *Volksthümliches aus Oesterreich Schlesien: Sagen und Märchen, Bräuche und Volksaberglauben.* Troppau: Self-published.

Phillips, Henry Pratap. 2016. *The history and chronology of gunpowder and gunpowder weapons.* Chennai: Notion Press.

Plioreschi, Plinio. 1996. *A history of medicine, volume 1: primitive and ancient medicine.* Omaha: Horatius Press.

von Pöck, Thomas Ignaz. 1777. *Supplementum Codiacis Austriaci oder Chronologische Sammlung allen von 20ten Oktober 1740…bis letzen December 1758, Fünfter Teil.* Vienna: Johann Thomas Edlen von Trattnern.

Pohl, Io. Christophor and Io. Gottlob Hertel. 1732. *Dissertationem de hominibus postmortem sanguisugis vulgo sic dictis vampyren.* Leipzig: Io. Christian Lagenhem.

Polidori, John William. 1819. *The Vampyre, a Tale.* London: Sherwood, Neely and Jones.

Pomet, Pierre. 1748. *A complete history of drugs, written in French by Monsieur Pomet.* London.

Power, Joey. 2000. *Political culture and nationalism in Malawi: building Kwacha.* Rochester, NY: University of Rochester Press.

Przybyszewski, Stanislaw. 1992. *Kritische und essayistische Schriften.* Paderborn: IGEL Verlag Literatur.

Radics, P.V. 1866. *Valvasor.* Graz: Ceushner & Cubensky.

Ranft, Michael. 1725. *De masticatione mortuorum in tumulis…* Leipzig: August Martini.

Ranft, Michael. 1728. *De masticatione mortuorum in tumulies (oder von dem Kauen und Schmatzen den Todten in Gräbern)…* Leipzig: Sumptibus Augusti Martinii.

Ranft, Michael. 1734. *Tractat von dem Kauen und Schmatzen der Todten in Gräbern …* Leipzig: Trübners.

Rawski, Jakub. 2013. Wapirzym w *Djïadach* Adama Mickiewicza, *Filogia polska* 5: 119-25.

de Renzi, Salvator. 1842. Sur les fièvres typhoides traitées à l'hôpital de Sainte Marie de Loreto, *Gazette médicale de Paris* 10: 522-23.

Risse, Guenther. 1979. The renaissance of bloodletting: a chapter in modern therapeutics, *International journal of the history of medicine and the allied sciences,* February.

Robertson, Charles Gordon. 1911. *England under the Hanoverians.* New York: G.P. Putnam's Sons.

Robertson, James C. 1875. *Materials for the history of Thomas Becket, v. 1.* London: Longmans.

Robertson, James C. 1876. *Materials for the history of Thomas Becket, v. 2.* London: Longmans.

Robertson, James C. 1877. *Materials for the history of Thomas Becket, v. 3.* London: Longmans.

Roche, Pierre. 1922. *Une histoire metallique de la guerre, 1914-18.* Paris: Gautherin.

Rohr, Philip. 1679. *Dissertatio historico-philosophica de masticatione mortuum.* Leipzig: Michael Vogt.

Ronca, Italo. 1994. The influence of Pantegni on William of Conches's Dragmaticon, 266-85 IN *Constantine the African and ʿalī ibn al-ʿabbas al-magūsi,* ed. by Charles F. Burnett and Danielle Jacquart. Leiden: A.A. Brill.

Rous, John, et al. comp. 1729. *Historia vitae et regni Ricardi II, Angliavitae et regni Ricardi II, Angliae regis…* Oxford.

Roussel, Pierre-Joseph-Alexis. 1813. *Annales du crime et de l'innocence, tome douzième.* Paris: Le Rouge.

Rousset de Missy, Jean. 1736. *Mercure historique et politique, Octobre.* The Hague: Henri Scheurleer.

Rugaber, Walter. 1969. Prison drug and plasma projects leave a fatal trail, *New York Times,* July 29.

Ruickbie, Leo. 2013. Evidence for the undead: medical investigation in the 18th century. 75-90 IN *The universal vampire: origins and evolution of a legend.* Madison, Teaneck: Fairleigh Dickinson University Press.

Rzaczyński, Gabriel. 1721. *Historia naturalis curiosa regni Poloniae…* Sandomir: Typis Collegii Soc. Jesu.

Salomon, Bernard. 1557. *Metamorphose figurée.* Lyon: Jan de Tournes.

Saxonia, Hercule. 1603. *Pantheum medecinae selectum,* ed. by Peter Uffenbach. Frankfurt: Paltheniana.

Schroeder, Aribert 1973. *Vampirismus: Seine Entwicklung vom Thema zum Motiv.* Akademisch Verlagsgesellschaft.

Segel, Harold B. 2014. *Polish Romantic drama: three plays in English translation.* London: Routledge.

Severino, Marco Aurelio. 1654. *Seilo-phlebotome castigata sive de venae salvatellae usu et abusu.* Hanover: Christophoros Le Blon.

Sherwood, Robert. 1922. "A Fool There Was," *Life* 80, 2075: 24.

Sinclair, Upton. 1933. *Upton Sinclair presents William Fox.* Los Angles: published by the author.

Šišović, Davor. 2005. Jure Grando možda je inspirao i Lorda Byron! *Glas istre,* October 1.

Slocum, Kay Brainerd. 2004. *Liturgies in honour of St. Thomas Becket.* Toronto: University of Toronto Press.

Slowaczynski, A. 1836-37. Geographie, statistique, 81-98 IN *La Pologne historique, littéraire, Monumentale,* ed. by Leonard Chodźko. Paris: Bureau Central.

Smith, Hugh. 1781. *Formulae medicamentorum; or, a compendium of the modern practice of physic.* London: W. Johnston.

Spreng, Johann. 1563. *Metamorphoses illustratae, Virgil Solis, illus.*

Starks-Estes, Lisa S. 2014. *Violence, trauma and virtus in Shakespeare's Roman poems and plays.* N.Y.: Palgrave-Macmillan.

Starr, Douglas. 1998. *Blood: an epic history of medicine and commerce.* New York: Alfred A. Knopf.

Stekel, Wilhelm. 1922. *Psychosexueller Infantilismus: Die seelische Kinderkrankheiten der Erwachsenen.* Berlin: Vilban & Schwartzenburg.

Stekel, Wilhelm. 1925. *Sadismus und Masochismus.* Berlin: Vilban & Schwarzenburg.

Stieff, Christian. 1737. *Schlesischen historischen labyrinth.* Breslau and Leipzig: Michael Hubert.

Stites, Richard. 1991. Bolshevik ritual building in the 1920s, 295-309 IN *Russia in the era of NEP: Explorations in Soviet society and culture,* ed. by Sheila Fitzpatrick, et al.B;oomington: Indiana University Press.

Stoker, Bram. 1897. *Dracula: a mystery story.* New York: W.P. Caldwell and Co.

van Swieten, Gerard. 1768. *Vampyrismus von Herrn Baron Gerhard van Swieten verfasset, aus dem Französischen ins Deutsche übersetzet.* Augsburg. Printed as an addendum to *Abhandlung des Daseyns der Gespenster.*

Tardieu, Ambroise. 1878. *Étude médico-légale sur les attentats aux moeurs.* 7th edition. Paris: Baillière.

Thomson, George. 1665. *Galeno-pale: or, a chymical trial of the Galenists.* London: Edward Thomas.

Thorndike, Lynn. 1941. *A history of magic and experimental science, Volume VI: The sixteenth century.* New York: Columbia University Press.

Thudicum, John. 1867. Researches intended to promote an improved chemical identification of disease, 152-294 IN *Tenth report of the medical officer of the Privy Council-Appendix.* London: George Byre and William Spottiswoode.

Thudicum, John. 1882. *A manual of chemical physiology.* N.Y.: William Wood and Co.

Thudicum, John. 1896. *The progress of medical chemistry.* London: Baillière, Tindall and Cox.

Toepfer, Karl. 1997. *Empires of ecstasy: nudity and movement in German body culture, 1910-1935.* Berkeley: University of California Press.

Tøjner, Poul Erik. 2003. *Munch in his own words.* Munich: Prestel.

Torreblanca, Francisco. 1678. *Epitome delictorum, sive de magia.* Lyon: Joannis Antonius Huguetan.

van Helmont, Johann Baptista.1707. *Opera omnia,* ed. by Michael Bernhard Valentinus. Hieronymus Christian Paul.

Valvasor, Johann Weichard, Freiherr von. 1689. *Die Ehre des Herzogthums Krain.* 4 v. Laibach (Ljubljana). Republished 1867. 4 v.Rudolfswerth: J. Krajac.

Vannetti, Giambattista. 1787. *Considerazione intorno alla pretesa magia postuma per servire alla storia de' vampiri presentata al Supremo Direttorio di Vienna dal Signore Barone Gerardo van Swieten.* Naples: Giuseppe Maria Porcelli.

Velpeau, Alfred. 1839. *Nouveaux elements de médecine operatoire, tome premier.* Paris: J.-B. Baillière.

Verna, Jo. Baptista. 1716. *Princeps medicaminum omnium phlebotomia.* Padua: Joannes Manfrè.

Vernalaken, Theodor. 1859. *Mythen und Bräuche des Volk in Osterreich.* Vienna: Wilhelm Braumuller.

Vincensini, Jean-Jacques. 2005. Entre pensée savante et raison narrative: le clerc medieval et le motif du "saignement accusateur" (ou "cruentation") 833-58 IN *Par les mots et les textes: melanges…offerts a Claude Thomasset,* ed. by Danielle Jacquart, et al. Paris: PUPS.

Vincent of Beauvais. 1591. *Speculi mairoris Vincenti Burgundi praesulis Belvacensis. Tomi quattuor quorum primo tota naturalis historia.* Venice: Dominicus Nicolinus.

Vincent, Nicolas. 2001. *The holy blood: King Henry III and the Westminster Blood Relic.* Cambridge: Cambridge University Press.

Vinšćak, Tomo. 2005. O štrigama, štrigunima i krsnicima v Istri, *Studia ethnologica Croatica* 17.1: 221-35.

Vogt, Gottlob Heinrich. 1732a. *Kurzes Bedencken von denen Acten-massigen wegen derer Vampiren…*Leipzig: August Martini.

Vogt, Gottlob Heinrich. 1732b. *Der eingeschlichene, nun aber wieder ausgemetzte dritte Theil des Menschen nebstangehängter Quelle vieler Irrthumer, nehmlich der Lehre von denen Temperamenten.* Leipzig: August Martini.

Voltaire. 1775. *Questions sur l'Encyclopédie par des amateurs, tome quatrième.* Geneva.

Voltaire. 1836. *Oeuvres complètes de Voltaire, Tome VIII: Dictionnaire philosophique II.* Paris: Furne.

Waldman, Paul. 2016. In defense of Peter Thiel's vampirism, *The Week,* August 2.

Wasylewski, Stanisław. 1907. W sprawie wampiryzmu. *Lud* 13: 291-98.

Weinrich, Martin. 1595. *De ortu monstrorum commentarius.* Breslau: Heinrich Osthus.

Weinrich, Martin. 1612. Proemium, 1-60 IN *Joh. Francisci Pici Mirandulae domini concordiaeque comitis strix sive dialogi tres de ludificatione daemonum con prefatione Martini Weinrichi.* Argentorati [Strassburg]: Paul Ledertz.

Webster, John. 1677. *The displaying of supposed witchcraft.* London.

Wegner, Georg Wilhelm. *Schau-platz vielen ungereimten Meynungen und Erzehlungen, Erster Band.* Berlin: Ambrosius Haude.

Welsh, Benjamin. 1819. *A practical treatise of the efficacy of bloodletting in the epidemic fever of Edinburgh.* Edinburgh: Boll and Bradfute.

White, Luise. 2000. *Speaking with vampires: rumor and history in colonial Africa.* Berkeley: University of California Press.

William of Newburgh. 1856. *Willelmi Parvi de Newburgh Historia Rerum Anglicarum,* v. II. London: Sumptibus Societatis.

Wübben, Yvonne. 2007. *Gespenster und Gelehrte.* Tübingen: Max Niemeyer Verlag.

Wynne, Catherine. 2011. Ellen Terry, Bram Stoker, and the Lyceum's Vampires, 17-31 IN *Ellen Terry, spheres of influence,* ed. by Catherine Cockin. London and New York: Routledge.

Ypey, Adolph. 1785. *Elementa physiologiae humani corporis.* Franeker: Dionysius Romar.

Zacchia, Paolo. 1726. *Quaestionum medico-legalium, tomus primus.* Lyon: Annison et Possuel.

Zigrosser, Carl, comp. 1970. *Medicine and the artist.* New York: Dover.